WITHDRAWN

Peacekeeping in Vietnam

Peacekeeping in Vietnam
Canada, India, Poland, and the International Commission

Ramesh Thakur

The University of Alberta Press

First published by
The University of Alberta Press
450 Athabasca Hall
Edmonton, Alberta
Canada T6G 2E8

Copyright © The University of Alberta Press 1984

ISBN 0-88864-037-4

Canadian Cataloguing in Publication Data
Thakur, Ramesh Chandra, 1948–
    Peacekeeping in Vietnam
    Bibliography: p.
    Includes index.
ISBN 0-88864-037-4

1. International Commission for Supervision and Control in Vietnam.
2. Vietnamese Conflict, 1961-1975 – Peace.   I. Title.
DS559.7.T53   959.704'31   C82-091220-4

All rights reserved.
No part of this publication may be reproduced, stored in a retrieval system, or transmitted in any form or by any means, electronic, mechanical, photocopying, recording, or otherwise, without prior permission of the copyright owner.

Typesetting by Solaris Press, Inc., Rochester, Michigan
Printed by D.W. Friesen & Sons Ltd., Altona, Manitoba, Canada

To Bernadette

Contents

List of Tables, Figures, and Map   xi
Acknowledgments   xiii
Preface   xiv

1 PEACEKEEPING AND FOREIGN POLICIES   1
   Peacekeeping   5
   National Foreign Policies   8
   Canada   8
   India   16
   Bilateral Relations   22
   Poland   23

2 THE FRENCH INDOCHINA WAR   30
   Attitudes Toward the War   30
   Canada   30
   India   33
   The Eastern Bloc   39
   The West   42
   The Geneva Conference   45
   Conclusion   53

3 THE COMMISSION IN ACTION: THE MILITARY RECORD   58
   The Field Machinery   58
   The Two Commissions   59
   The Control System: Fixed and Mobile Teams and Their Movements   63
   Preserving the Status Quo: Articles 16–20   74
   Articles 16, 17   75
   The Southern Zone   78

SEATO 78
American Military Missions 85
The Northern Zone 93
The Chinese Border 93
Subversion 97
Miscellaneous 103
The Military Provisional Demarcation Line and the Demilitarized Zone 103
Regroupment 104
The 1965 Special Reports 108
Summary 113

4 THE COMMISSION ON THE DESCENDANT: HUMAN RIGHTS 116
To Be or Not to Be Political 117
Article 15(d): Civil Administration 120
Amnesty: Reprisals, Migrations, Internees 123
Article 14(c): Reprisals and Democratics Liberties 124
Article 14(d): Freedom of Movement 130
Article 21: Prisoners of War, Civilian Internees 137
Conclusion 140

5 THE COMMISSION IN THE BACKGROUND: VIETNAMESE REUNIFICATION 141
Divorce of Authority from Responsibility 141
Legal Arguments 143
Canadian and Indian Positions 146
Political Developments 149
Elections/Reunification 151
Legal Arguments 154
Canadian Position 158
Indian Position 164
Elections and the Commission: The Hapless Referee 166
Conclusion 170

6 THE COMMISSION RECORD: A SUMMING UP 174
The Commission Voting Record: A Tabular Analysis 174
The Commission Record: A Selective Summary 184

7 THE AMERICAN INTERVENTION 189
Background 189
Canadian Response 194
The Air War 198
Canadian Response 200

Canadian Complicity? 205
The American War and India 209
Poland and the American War in Vietnam 213
A Matter of Opinion 214
Canada 214
India 216
A Point of Law 220
The Canadian Brief 220
Conclusion 223

8 NATIONAL FOREIGN POLICIES 226
Canada 226
India 234
Poland and Intra-Communist Relations 247
Hanoi-Moscow-Peking 247
Warsaw 250
Conclusion 252

9 CONCLUSIONS 255
National Foreign Policies 255
Canada 255
India 258
Poland 261
Indo-Canadian Relations 262
International Peacekeeping 270
ICSC and Geneva Defects 270
Implications 277
To End It All 282

Appendix I Geneva Conference on Indo-China 287
  A. *Agreement on the Cessation of Hostilities in Vietnam* 287
  B. *Final Declaration* 305
  C. *United States Declaration* 307
  D. *Declaration by the Government of the French Republic* 308
  E. *Declaration of Tran Van Do, Delegate of Vietnam* 309

Appendix II Chronology of ICSC Reports 310
Appendix III Chronology of Events 311
Appendix IV Glossary 325

Appendix V Abbreviations 328
Notes 331
Bibliography 355
Index 369

List of Tables Figures, and Map

Tables
1 Statistical Details of Cases under Article 14(c), 1954–55   125
2 Figures of Movement of Population in Vietnam under Article 14(d), up to 20 July 1955   131
3 ICSC Decisions, Delegation Divisions   178
4 Minority Positions on the ICSC   179
5 Decisions in Favor of North Vietnam/South Vietnam   180
6 Patterns of Voting by India/ICSC in Four Periods   181
7 U.S. Forces in South Vietnam   192
8 World Opinion on the U.S. War in Vietnam, Gallup Polls, 1966   215
9 Attitudes of Indian Parliamentarians Toward U.S. Role in Vietnam, 1968   216
10 Opinions on Indian Policy Toward Vietnam, 1969   217
11 Attitudes of Indian Parliamentarians Toward the USA, USSR, and China, 1958 and 1962   218
12 Indian Images of China, 1965–71   218
13 Indian Images of Canada, 1971–76   265
14 Canadian Images of Selected Countries, 1975   266

Figures
1 Structure of the Joint Commission in Vietnam, 1954–55   60
2 Organizational Structure of the ICSC, Vietnam   62

3   Indian Images of the Superpowers: The USSR-USA
    Differential, 1966–76   219
4   Relationship Between ICSC and International Political
    Structures, 1954   272
5   ICSC and China-India-USA-USSR Structures, 1962   274
6   ICSC and China-India-USA-USSR Structures, 1972   274

Map
Vietnam After the Geneva Agreements of 1954   64

Acknowledgments

Many people have been associated with this work at different times and to varying degrees. All, however, were constantly helpful and encouraging. Not everyone can be named. It is a pleasure to record the list of those who can, beginning with C. Pentland and A. Taylor of Queen's University, J. Eayrs and J. Holmes of Toronto, and P. K. Das and Vishal Singh of Jawaharlal Nehru University. Their professional experience and expertise I found most invaluable. Similarly, reports from the three anonymous referees of The University of Alberta Press and the Social Sciences and Humanities Research Council of Canada helped to sharpen the focus of the study, tighten its organization, and tie some loose ends. I owe a particular debt of gratitude to Douglas A. Ross for permitting me access to his restricted Ph.D. thesis. This study has profited greatly from his work.

Financial support was provided by the Shastri Indo-Canadian Institute and the Canada Council. The Shastri Institute in New Delhi also provided invaluable assistance in numerous little ways to help make our stay pleasurable and productive; P. N. Malik deserves special praise for his unfailing energy and considerable talents.

This book has been published with the help of a grant from the Canadian Federation for the Humanities, using funds provided by the Social Sciences and Humanities Research Council of Canada.

The completion of the book also owes much to the efficient typing skills of Mrs. B. Larkins, Mrs. J. Macmillan, and Mrs. J. Snow. Their cheerfulness and patience was much in demand, yet always in supply.

Preface

This book is simultaneously an essay in comparative foreign policy and a study of peacekeeping in Vietnam. The comparative approach illuminates broader ideological, geopolitical, and "geohistorical" factors that influence Canadian, Indian, and Polish foreign policies. At the same time, a textual analysis of the International Commission's own deliberations and findings demonstrates that the Commission did more valuable work than is commonly believed, and that it was not responsible for the protracted Vietnam conflict. The book thus derives general propositions about foreign policy and international peacekeeping from a detailed examination of specific historical events in international politics.

There is in the literature a surprising paucity of actual case studies of comparative foreign policy. Cohen and Harris have observed that "the standard piece of foreign-policy research deals with a single policy case, or a single institution, or a single country."[1] At the other extreme, one offering of "theoretical perspectives" on national behavior proclaims, "We should hasten to add that no empirical investigations will be presented in this book"[2] — a promise that is kept. I hope I have avoided both extremes.

Several advantages accrue from approaching the Vietnam exercise in peacekeeping from the perspective of three national foreign policies. An examination of Indian policy places the study firmly in its Asian setting; a study of Canadian involvement ensures that the important North American perspective is given equal prominence; and a discussion of Polish behavior provides the Eastern-bloc frame of reference.[3] Another benefit derives from the fact that a treatment of divergent national policies encourages a contrapuntal style that is invaluable in comparative analysis. Finally, if we accept the thesis that knowledge is socially and historically conditioned, and that political knowledge is inevitably partisan, or even if we concede the weaker claim that "empirical validity" is a relational term, then we have an epistemological justification for giving due consideration to alternative points of view.

Finally, a point about sources. I have had limited access to material not yet in the public realm, and have also engaged in "discussions," rather than structured interviews, with both Canadian and Indian officials. Naturally, I have made full use of the insights gained from this. Nevertheless, as a general rule I have preferred to cite sources—even secondary ones—that can be publicly cross-checked by others, even where a line of argument may originally have been suggested in private talks. Inevitably, on occasion it has been impossible to avoid relying entirely on "confidential sources," which, for reasons of conditions attached to gaining access to them, cannot be identified more precisely.

1 Peacekeeping and Foreign Policies

The conflicts in Indochina have occupied the attention of much of international politics since the Second World War. Vietnam has been at the heart of the conflict, from the sustained fighting begun in December 1946 between the French and Vietminh, to the Chinese invasion in 1979. In the event, Vietnam acquired and retains for many a symbolic importance that exceeds the strategic value of the country. As a result, Vietnam has been the subject of several studies in our times; yet a need remains for an analysis of the Vietnam experience as an exercise in international peacekeeping. Possibly because interest in peacekeeping has tended to be concentrated on United Nations exercises, the International Commission for Supervision and Control (ICSC) in Vietnam has escaped serious study.

This work is intended to fill the lacuna partially. The achievements and shortcomings of the ICSC will be revealed by subjecting its workings to a close scrutiny. In the process, the Commission will be broken down into its constituent elements: the delegations of Canada, India, and Poland. This procedure allows us both to understand the workings of the Commission as a whole, and to comment upon the coincidence of the delegations' voting patterns with the foreign policies of their respective countries. The study is thus simultaneously an examination of ICSC behavior in Vietnam, and of Canadian, Indian, and Polish behavior in the ICSC.

The theme of the study is a detailed exploration of the relationship between international peacekeeping in the ICSC from its inception in 1954 to its termination in 1973; the foreign policies of the three countries represented on the Commission; and wider international politics. The argument is that because of the above interrelationships, peacekeeping is successful where it is limited to narrow, precisely defined tasks of overseeing a military disengagement upon the cessation of hostilities, but fails when extended to embrace political tasks of conflict resolution, and is not viable against the self-defined vital interests of a superpower.

Therefore, what follows is first and foremost an examination of the ICSC as an exercise in international peacekeeping. The intricate workings of the Commission's field machinery thus receive intensive scrutiny. This study will determine just what purpose the ICSC was meant to serve; how well, if at all, it did serve the major purpose; the factors contributing to its successes and failures; and the relationship between the performance of the Commission and the renewal of hostilities on an ever more destructive scale in the mid-1960s. Second, I believe the present work breaks new ground in explicitly placing an attempt at international peacekeeping in the context of national foreign policies. The ICSC in Vietnam is peculiarly suited to this by virtue of its structure—three national delegations—and its independence of any international guiding authority. Since the approaches of the national delegations in the ICSC reflected principles derived from broader foreign policy objectives, the latter in turn require at least preliminary mention and elucidation. Moreover, because the Vietnam war involved major powers in their capacity as international actors, national delegations in the ICSC dealt with them in ways parallel to the dealings between home governments and the major powers. It will be necessary, therefore, to complement the preliminary statement of national foreign policies by elaborating on the relations between the countries concerned and the major powers.

The linkage between international peacekeeping and national behavior is provided by a further hypothesis: for Canada, India, and Poland there was a one-to-one correspondence between their respective foreign policies and ICSC delegations. A few examples, involving each of the three delegations at different times, demonstrate this. As a general rule, the Canadian and Indian Commissioners had greater power of discretion than their Polish colleague. Canadian Commissioner Sherwood Lett's letter of instructions (24 August 1954) indicated general lines of policy. He was informed that despite extremely close relations, India and Canada pursued radically different policies in many important respects. Lett was to understand and respect Indian policy, even if he did not approve of it. The Poles, he was told, would act in the interests of the USSR, China, and the Vietminh. In the case of differences in the Commission, Lett was to woo Indian support rather than Polish. He was cautioned also against giving the impression that he was attempting to protect French interests or further American policy.[1]

An example of direct policy control exercised by New Delhi over its delegation, on a specific decision, is found in the Pentagon Papers. In May 1956, the United States decided to send an additional 350 military men to South Vietnam in the guise of a Temporary Equipment Recovery Mission (TERM). The Pentagon study disclosed that the decision to dispatch TERM was made in Washington "when it was learned informally that the Indian Government would instruct its representative on the ICC to interpose no objection."[2] Similarly, the Indian chairman of the ICSC submitted the 1962 special report to his government for clearance prior to publication.[3]

As for the Poles, they understood in 1954 that they and the Canadians had been named as representatives of conflicting interests of the cold-war antagonists, and could not be absolutely neutral and objective. Nevertheless, the USSR did not wish to see increased American involvement in the region, and also felt a sense of international obligation for having alternately chaired the Geneva Conference with Britain. Therefore, the Polish delegation was instructed "to behave as if we were neutral," because of "the historical need . . . for peaceful coexistence."[4]

International politics also played an important role. First, although Indochina has been the scene of continual conflict since the Second World War, there has not been just one drawn-out conflict. Instead, several conflicts have occurred, involving changes in the nature of the dispute and fighting as well as in the participants. Consequently, no one substantive thesis does justice to the complexity of the story. It is more advantageous to distinguish between three time periods, derived from the clear-cut internal logic of the conflict itself: the French Indochina war from 1946 to 1954, the active years of the Commission from 1954 to 1965, and the American Indochina war from 1964 to 1973. Such a division is useful because it helps clarify the differences between the work of the Commission and the attitudes of its delegations over the years. The work of the Commission in the second period, for example, will be shown to have been entirely different from that in the third, when the conflict had reached a stage where there was no longer any expectation that either side would abide by the terms of the 1954 peace agreement.

It will be useful at this juncture to frame propositions describing national behavior in each period. In the French phase, Canada sought to limit the sphere of its involvement as an Atlantic country; in the Commission, it strove to combine the ideal of impartial peacekeeping with the realities of alliance considerations, but with decreasing success; and in the American phase, its leaders either viewed the conflict entirely in American categories or subordinated their perceptions to dictates of prudence in Canada-United States relations. Indian policy was initially one of benign neglect of the French war, later turning into active opposition to American objectives and techniques; in the second stage, one of playing a mediatory role in the Commission rather than using the Commission to secure the objectives of the Geneva Agreements; and in the third, one of following the maxim that discretion was the better part of valor, until dramatic developments globally in 1971 led to the contrary belief that boldness paid better dividends. For Poland, one could postulate that interest in the French Indochina war was virtually nonexistent, limited to its communist involvement and routed through Moscow. During the second period, the Poles began by working with the Commission in order to secure a political victory for the communists under the terms of the Geneva Agreements. When the settlement failed to materialize, the Poles began to use the Commission solely as a political tool. During the American war, the Poles became enmeshed in the web of Hanoi-Moscow-Peking relations within the socialist world.

Second, the three countries named to the International Commission in 1954 represented the three chief strands of international politics at the time, and were expressions of the international concern over the war in Indochina. As long as there was agreement in the international community that the war should be contained and the Geneva Agreements honored, the three delegations could work together, broadly speaking. The partiality of Canada and Poland would come through not in shielding their respective "sides," but in being vigorous in the pursuit of violations by the opposing side. Once the parameters of the conflict changed, however, the Commission was in trouble: the protagonists had changed and the great powers were deeply implicated. The Commission was unable to deal with the changed situation not because it was inept, but because it was ill-equipped. It was far from being the appropriate forum for the resolution of the new conflict. Its function had been to keep and oversee the peace; it had not been designed to make a fresh peace. In fact, if anything, it was sucked into the cockpit of the new conflict. The two warring parties were interested in the Commission less to preserve the peace than to further their objectives by other than military means.

The third impact that international politics had on Geneva in 1954, and on Vietnam for much of the later period, was through the fact that China was denied membership in the United Nations. The absence of Chinese representation meant that the United Nations was precluded from having a role in the deliberations at Geneva and in the peace system established there. That the United Nations was excluded from the Geneva framework meant in turn that any interested country lacked that international institution to constrain American behavior; that China was not a United Nations member meant that the United Nations lacked the means to moderate Chinese actions. Finally, the exclusion of the United Nations denied the International Commission a continuing political authority to which it could report and under which it could operate.

The last point in turn resulted in the individual delegations lacking even a *pro forma* affiliation with a continuing political body. It was all very well to say that they were instruments of the Geneva Conference; the Geneva Conference was long since dead and its Agreements deeply buried. In this situation, when the Commission itself became an instrument in the new American war in Vietnam, the pressures toward subordinating delegation autonomy to foreign policy objectives became irresistible.

Peacekeeping

International peacekeeping as a conflict management technique is a relatively recent development. Conflict is endemic to international systems; what is new to our times is the manner in which its destructive potential has mushroomed. The urgency its regulation has acquired is to be seen in the efforts at international organization after the two world wars. Both efforts accorded pride of place to collective security; neither met with success. The United Nations was entrusted with the maintenance of world peace in two ways: the search for peaceful settlement where disputes arose, and the enforcement of collective security where states involved in disputes abandoned negotiation to resort to force. Peacekeeping as an institution has evolved in the gray zone between pacific settlement and enforcement. It has yet to be institutionalized, however, to the extent that any one particular force creation is sufficiently durable and adaptable to be of use in other emergency situations.

Peacekeeping grew side by side with preventive diplomacy. The last was practiced and articulated—in that order—by Dag Hammarskjöld. It was an approach derived from his conception of the role that the United Nations ought to play in a world troubled by the cold war.[5] He conceded that the United Nations could not exert any influence on issues in the cold war *per se*. However, he emphasized the fact that although considerable areas of the world lay outside the cold war, they were subject to eruptions of local conflicts. The United Nations was to aim at keeping new conflicts outside the sphere of bloc differences. Preventive diplomacy would be particularly useful for conflict situations that were either the result or a potential cause of a power vacuum in the cold war. The technique was to be used to forestall the competitive intrusion of the rival power blocs into those situations, the first step being to use the United Nations to plug the vacuum. To the extent that the politically impartial organization was not committed to either bloc, it could be used to provide a guarantee in relation to all parties. Hammarskjöld stressed that preventive diplomacy was of service to both the local and the global adversaries. The former averted their region from becoming a great-power battleground, while the latter avoided an escalating confrontation in areas without vital stakes.

Preventive diplomacy differs from peaceful settlement of disputes, then, in that the latter consists of facilitating the reestablishment and maintenance of peaceful relations. The former aims chiefly to confine the conflict within local limits. It is a policy designed to contain the cold war, to achieve a kind of "disengagement before the fact." And preventive diplomacy was given concrete expression by inserting the thin blue wedge between combatants. The linkages between preventive diplomacy and international peacekeeping, established in UNEF, were articulated by U Thant.[6] Both resulted from the impracticality of collective security, which necessitates three elements that are in opposition to peacekeeping requirements: a definition and determination of aggression; identification of the guilty party; and a contribution of forces by the major powers. The need for great-power unanimity is evident in all three conditions. The United Nations failed to fulfill its role as a collective security system not because the system was intrinsically defective but because great-power consensus rapidly broke down.

Once collective security was recognized as being unattainable, states moved to guarantee security through collective defense, while the international community moved to avoid and contain conflicts. The primary purpose of peacekeeping remains a cessation of hostilities. Terminating a crisis does not, however, automatically solve the conflict that produced the crisis.

The Hammarskjöld approach thus focused on noncoercive and facilitative activities rather than on repelling aggression through armed combat. Specific United Nations activities have been varied, ranging from observation and supervision to trying to prevent contacts between opponents, resolving socioeconomic problems, and mediating and conciliating. The theme common to all is to promote international stability and support peaceful change outside the cold-war axis. The viability of the Hammarskjöld approach was a function of the continuing validity of its central assumptions. Specifically, the superpowers had to consent to their mutual exclusion from local conflicts, and thereby forgo opportunities for manipulation on the periphery, while still providing financial and logistical support; the local disputants had to consent to a United Nations presence; and lesser powers had to consent to providing human and other resources.

A general matter that has received some attention is the parallels between municipal and international peacekeeping functions. Swift has argued that peacekeeping operations are more akin to armed police work than to standard combat. They have no military objectives, they are barred from active combat, they are located between rather than in opposition to hostile elements, and they negotiate rather than fight.[7] Nevertheless, few states acknowledge that United Nations peacekeeping requires special training and preparation, and fewer still provide it. Peacekeeping operations are not quite analogous to municipal police forces either, as Mitchell has pointed out.[8] The two operate under entirely different assumptions and conditions, and derive legitimacy from different authorities.

In sum, peacekeeping forces can never *keep* the peace, for they lack both authority and military ability to do so. Moreover, it is not an unfair comment that in Vietnam the ICSC faced conflicts of unprecedented complexity, size, and seriousness. The mix of internal and external factors crossed with political and juridical disputes would have taxed the ingenuity of even experienced national statesmen. It taxes credibility to suggest that the conflicts could have been resolved by international civil and military servants. An analysis of the conflicts *per se* is beyond the scope of the present work. Rather, the object is to summarize the course of the conflicts, examine the nature and effect of the ICSC intervention, and seek to discover lessons pertinent to future peacekeeping operations.

National Foreign Policies

Canada
Prior to the Second World War, Canada's external policy was concerned largely with the problem of status, with establishing rather than exercising the rights of Canada as a sovereign entity. During the war, Canada played a significant military role in the alliance, but did not share in the determination of grand policy. After the war, its leaders accepted that virtually everything in world affairs was of interest to Canada, and were correspondingly willing to assume political, economic, and military responsibility in the international arena. The guiding elements of postwar Canadian foreign policy were spelled out in a lecture by foreign minister Louis St. Laurent on 13 January 1947.[9] He identified five general principles: national unity, the Western conception of political liberty, respect for the rule of law, the Christian conception of human values, and an acceptance of international responsibility commensurate with Canada's role in the world. In the application of the principles, St. Laurent gave special mention to the Commonwealth (particularly Britain), France, and the United States.

In fact, after the Second World War the United States took Britain's place at the center of the Canadian image of the world. Lester Pearson remarked in 1941, "It is inevitable that, as a North American country, Canada should develop North American points of view." Canada could no more remain neutral in a war involving the United States than it had been able to keep out of the European world wars. The problem, Pearson argued, was rather "to ensure that British and American policies do not diverge to a degree which would make it necessary for Canada to choose between them. For such a choice would, for Canada, be an impossible one, fatal to her national unity and indeed to her national existence."[10]

The volume of trade between Canada and the United States is the largest between any two countries in the world. But it is assymmetrical: Canada takes one-sixth of United States trade; the United States accounts for two-thirds of Canada's external trade. In April 1969, Pierre Trudeau told the Washington Press Club that living beside the United States was like sleeping with an elephant: one is affected by its every twitch and grunt. As the remark indicates, problems in American-Canadian relations arise from contiguity, interdependence, homogeneity, and from the difference in size. With the volume and intensity of interactions between the two, differences over the nitty-gritty of low politics are not uncommon, but the general expectation is that they will be peacefully resolved through negotiation. Differences on matters of high policy are rare, but not entirely unknown.

It is tempting to say of Canada and the United States that they have everything in common, including the unguarded frontier, and that the basis of complaints is precisely that they have too much in common. The Canadian identity crisis stems in part from the "flattering, if at times a trifle embarrassing, tendency" of Americans to view Canadians simply "as one of themselves."[11]

The technique chosen to manage Canadian-American relations (as well as relations with other friends and allies) was quiet diplomacy. Because Canada was but a middle power, the best contribution that it could make toward easing world tensions would be limited either to explaining and justifying American policy to others, as with St. Laurent's defense of the United States and NATO during his 1954 visit to India, or to exercising some moderating influence upon its own allies, which could require at times a forthright expression of Canadian views in London, Paris, and Washington.

We recognize, however, that a diplomacy of this kind, depending as it does on the influence Canada can exert with greater Powers, can be carried out successfully only if our interventions are restrained, responsible and constructive; and if we act, in discharging our own obligations, in a way which receives and deserves the respect of our friends in the coalition.[12]

This is the gist of Pearsonian quiet diplomacy, which was to be abandoned only in exceptional circumstances. Canada, explained Pearson, was not naive enough to believe that it could decisively, or even importantly, influence the policies of the great powers. Rather, "I hoped we could influence the environment in which they were pursued."[13] Canada, because of its location, ties, and racial composition, but above all because of its unquestioned allegiance when the chips are down, is uniquely positioned to temper American excesses. But to the extent that he wanted Canadian advice to be given serious consideration, Pearson believed that it should be tendered discreetly, in that it is more difficult for any government to be seen to change its attitudes or course of action in response to public pressure from a foreign government. Considering Canada's limited resources, its diplomacy, in order to be "cost-effective," must be quiet.

Quiet diplomacy was described by one of its leading exponents, Peyton Lyon:[14] "For Canada the best foreign policy is one that makes the most of its unusual relationship with Washington, something that can best be accomplished by tactics now generally described as 'quiet diplomacy'." The arguments in support are as easily stated. The United States, because of its power, is a significant factor in every situation, including those in which it chooses not to act. Because of geographic and cultural factors, Canada can exercise a greater influence upon the Americans than any other state of like power. Such influence is generally exercised to stress diplomatic flexibility and emphasize military caution. Canada's close relationship with the United States is a source of influence with other states as well, including the nonaligned and the communist. In other words, Canada's capacity to influence world affairs is increased by its ability to exploit its close relations with Washington in its dealings both with Washington and with other capitals. Public assertions of independence from the United States would eliminate both channels of influence. To break from the Atlantic alliance would be to destroy its claims, believed to be true by others, to having both a special ear in London and Washington and a share in the formulation and awareness of alliance policy. An independent line within the alliance would merely serve to antagonize the allies without removing the stigma of membership.

Lyon accepted the two basic assumptions upon which quiet diplomacy is predicated: that postwar United States foreign policy has been basically responsible; and that "despite errors in judgement in Washington and occasional excesses, the world is a better place than it would have been had the Americans reverted in 1945 to their traditional isolationism."

The historic Canadian distrust of the United States was displaced after 1945 by suspicions of Soviet communism. According to St. Laurent, "totalitarian communist aggression constitutes a direct and immediate threat to every democratic country, including Canada."[15] Pearson himself, while recognizing that the USSR had some legitimate security fears, and that American analyses of the cold war should not be accepted uncritically, nevertheless contended that

> the fact, the indisputable fact, remains that the main and very real threat to world peace during the first years of Cold War was the armed might, the aggressive ideology, and the totalitarian despotism of the Communist empire of the USSR and its satellite states under the iron hand of one of the most ruthless tyrants of all time.[16]

Canada's answer to its two basic foreign policy problems — avoiding an Anglo-American rift and resisting Soviet-communist aggression — was a North Atlantic alliance, which was especially attractive to such a convinced collective security advocate as Pearson. In the 1920s, the Canadian delegate at the League of Nations, Raoul Dandurand, had opposed the Geneva Protocol with these words: "In this association of mutual insurance against fire, the risks assumed by the different states are not equal. We live in a fireproof house, far from inflammable materials."[17] The unfolding of interwar history convinced men like St. Laurent and Pearson of the folly of the approach. After the Second World War, they saw to it that Canada took out an insurance policy and paid its premiums. Indeed, once burnt, twice insured: the United Nations *and* NATO. In his broadcast to the nation on 11 November 1948, St. Laurent argued with reference to the NATO negotiations that "our geographical situation, our historical ties, our material well-being, and, above all, our national security, make it imperative for Canada to take an appropriate place in this Atlantic community."[18]

NATO provided the answer to many of Canada's problems, and gave rise to some of its dilemmas. It brought Canada into a formal alliance with the three countries closest to it historically, politically, economically, and even geographically: France, the United Kingdom, and the United States. The continued viability of the organization would also free Canada of the need to make a choice between America and Britain. Participation in an alliance decreased for Canada the degree of domination by its neighbor; NATO and the Commonwealth could be said to provide military and politico-diplomatic counterweights respectively (or alternative forums) to the United States. NATO resolved one of the problems Canada had encountered during the war, that of lacking a share in the formulation of defense policy. By stressing the multilateral approach to decision making, Canada was in fact arguing for a role in the shaping of policy, instead of being allocated a share in its implementation. Canadian leaders have also repeatedly stressed the need for developing NATO into more than just a military alliance. Springing from the Canadian desire for a cohesive Atlantic community, this concern found expression in the so-called "Canadian article" of the treaty, Article 2.

Once the decision to enter into alliance had been made, NATO membership itself became an independent factor in Canadian foreign policy. In origins, the decision was political: a military organization was established to realize foreign policy objectives. In effect, the process was reversed: one of the goals of foreign policy became not to upset defense policy; that is, to preserve the alliance. The impact of Canada's membership in NATO and, after 1958, in NORAD, is claimed to have conditioned—some would say determined—its other external policies. Krishna Menon of India complained to Michael Brecher that Canada's NATO membership had belied his hopes and expectations about it becoming a Westward-leaning nonaligned state. He also made the argument that Pakistan, by virtue of its SEATO membership, had obtained NATO arms which were then used against India. That is, though Canada's general policy toward India is friendly, "Canada has bloc politics," and is therefore at times part of the hostile environment.[19] His point was well taken, if obliquely, and perhaps incorrectly, made. Canada, because of its military ties to the United States and to NATO, is part of the worldwide network of American military alliances, and, as such, its own policies will inevitably and inextricably be colored by global American military and political postures.

In the early years of Prime Minister Pierre Trudeau's administration, Canadian foreign policy was subjected to its most searching scrutiny. Many Canadians, deeply troubled by the record of American diplomacy, seriously questioned the two premises—of responsible and beneficial American statecraft—supporting quiet diplomacy. They pressed for a reevaluation of Canada's relationship with the United States and a systematic reexamination of the entire Canadian role on the international stage. Trudeau himself, with a penchant for pragmatism and efficiency, proved amenable to the demand for a reassessment of Canadian foreign policy. Canada underwent the unique experience of a proliferating series of debates, discussions, and seminars, involving politicians, scholars, journalists, career diplomats, and the public, on the bases, means, and objectives of foreign policy. The result was a collection of booklets outlining official Canadian foreign policy, one each on foreign policy in general, Europe, Latin America, the United Nations, the Pacific, and International Development, and a supplementary options paper on Canada-United States relations.[20] There is general agreement that the review did not bring forth a new foreign policy so much as provide a thorough scrutiny of the old one. It did, however, mark a shift toward a more nationalist, self-centered approach to world affairs.[21]

In operation the substance and style of Canadian foreign policy has revealed a continuity that perhaps arises from the country's circumstances and political culture. Canadian foreign policy remains subordinate to domestic concerns for national unity; gradualism, compromise, and even quiet diplomacy are still the preferred approaches to problems. In part the style is a function of parliamentary-federal politics that place a premium upon such methods. In part it is also the product of a politico-cultural belief set that emphasizes the need for structures and processes, as well as attitudes and practices, conducive to peaceful settlement activities. If there are basic political and moral differences, it is better to be pragmatic and concentrate on the soluble conflicts of interests. Otherwise, mounting tension will merely entrench rather than resolve basic differences.

A final element of postwar Canadian foreign policy pertinent to this study is the great importance attached to international peacekeeping, especially between the creation of UNEF in 1956 and its expulsion in 1967. Canada has long been an active proponent of establishing a permanent peacekeeping force under United Nations aegis. Pearson spoke of a standby force in 1950, argued for it in an article in 1957, mentioned it in his Clayton lectures at Tufts University in 1958, dwelt on the idea in his speech to the General Assembly in 1963, and in 1964 at a speech in Ottawa proposed that members of the United Nations could at least earmark contingents for peacekeeping tours. Prime Minister John Diefenbaker of the Conservative government also advocated a permanent United Nations force in his address to the Assembly in 1957. During the Conservative years, the Liberals and the NDP pressed for a Canadian buildup of forces suitable for United Nations operations. Although there was considerable pride in Canada about Canadian presence in all United Nations operations, and hence general support for a greater emphasis on peacekeeping, Defense Minister Douglas Harkness explained that it would be difficult to design and maintain a force specifically for United Nations service. In November 1964, Canada hosted a meeting of peacekeeping experts from twenty-three countries to examine and discuss the technical aspects of peacekeeping operations. If the 1967 expulsion of UNEF was a shock to those enamored of the peacekeeping role, the drawn-out exercise in frustration of the supervisory commissions in Indochina too was instrumental in a Canadian reappraisal of the role.

In sum, the central concern of Canadian policy has been to preserve national unity internally. In the external realm, the preeminent emphasis in Canadian foreign policy has been on the furtherance of the Atlantic community. The primary threat to the Western community was seen by Canada's leaders to lie in Europe, from the Soviet Union. It therefore became a dictum of Canadian policy that Asia should not be allowed to destroy the Western unity of purpose and action. Canada in consequence was propelled into a much-cherished role, that encapsulated in Winston Churchill's 1941 description of Canada as "the linchpin of the English speaking world." As for relations with the superpowers, while there have been points of friction in postwar Canadian-American relations, the underlying harmony has not been seriously threatened. Conversely, while there have been points of contact with the two communist giants, the basic adversarial relationship has never been out of sight.

If we bring the above analysis to bear on Canadian policy in the Vietnam conflict, the following points emerge. Canada's initial interests and expressions thereof in the French Indochina war sprang from its ties in the Western alliance, and it perceived the first Vietnamese war as a member of the Atlantic community. With its nomination to the ICSC in 1954, Canada was put in the position of being the Western peacekeeper in the Commission. Two sets of considerations were then involved: its membership in the Atlantic alliance and its pride in the role of international peacekeeper; and its relations with China, France, the United States, and the USSR.

Fortunately, the two were congruent in the initial stages after the Geneva Conference of 1954. France wanted to extricate itself from Indochina and saw in the Geneva Agreements the means toward that end. Canada could, therefore, work to uphold the Agreements and promote French interests in so doing, even if this came into conflict with some American wishes.

In later years, with the Americanization of the war, the two components diverged. At that time, Canada's primary policy dictum became not to let the Vietnam conflict split the Ottawa-Washington axis of the Atlantic alliance. Canada would be among the last to break with the United States on the Vietnam war; it helped that by then Ottawa's perceptions of the war had come to match official American analyses in several details. One could argue that when Canada finally did break with the Americans on Vietnam, it was not because of a shift in Canada's perception of the war *per se* by its leaders, but more because of Canada's anxiety that the long, drawn-out war was sapping the Atlantic resolve against the threats to freedom in other, more important places, and because of the changing domestic and international political climate, as indicated by domestic opposition, dissent in the United States, and reevaluations among allies.

The two components were thus to converge again. This time, Canada's peacemaking role was to be used in aid of American efforts to withdraw from Vietnam with a semblance of honor. By this shift in perception, continued American involvement was the danger to the unity of the West, as unilateral American actions had been in Korea. It also threatened to tear American society apart, not a pleasant prospect for Canadians who identified their security and well-being with that of their neighbor to the south. In Korea, Canada had the advantage of the United Nations forum to exercise a moderating leverage upon Washington, plus a strong London-based voice for reason. Both were nonexistent in the Vietnam case. Lacking such institutional channels for influencing American policy, Ottawa could do little beyond relying upon its traditional technique of quiet diplomacy. Nevertheless, in both Korea and Vietnam, Canada's basic position was quite clear: in the larger scheme of things, a withdrawal of America into its traditional isolationism, not its occasional excesses or errors in judgment, was the greater threat to world order.

India
The issues involved in Vietnam have been more complicated for India. First, there is the matter of the historical Sino-Indian competition in Southeast Asia through the centuries, which has principally borne upon the consciousness of India's leaders, especially Jawaharlal Nehru. Post-independence India did not have a specific rivalry with China in Southeast Asia. At the same time, however, the two were alternative models for the ordering of society and polity, with undoubted relevance for all of Asia. The attempt has been made to cast the conflict in Vietnam in terms of mutually exclusive categories of the same two models. Vietnam was important to India for several reasons. Indian foreign policy as a cluster of orientations is best described as nonalignment. This involves, *inter alia*, anticolonialism, antiracialism, and an extension of the area of peace by undercutting and eliminating the bloc system. On all three counts, India would be opposed to the French and American cause in Vietnam during their respective conflicts. The opposition was strengthened by the fact that India's interests in Vietnam were funnelled through its broader policy of nonalignment. It was affected also by the element of India's relations with the great powers. Relations with Washington, Moscow, and Peking fluctuated over the years, as will be shown later. Naturally, the two components of India's foreign policy functioned not in isolation but in interaction. India's role in the ICSC would, therefore, be subject to simultaneous pulls from the two. As with Canada, so with India: on occasions the pulls would be congruent and mutually supportive; at other times discontinuous and mutually disruptive. But India's policies toward and actions in Vietnam can best be explained by reference to these two elements of its wider foreign policy.

The main attributes of the future Indian foreign policy were outlined by Nehru as early as 7 September 1946, in a broadcast to the nation from New Delhi:

We shall take full part in international conferences as a free nation with our own policy and not merely as a satellite of another nation. We hope to develop close and direct contacts with other nations and to co-operate with them in the furtherance of world peace and freedom.

We propose, as far as possible, to keep away from the power politics of groups, aligned against one another, which have led in the past to world wars and which may again lead to disasters on an even vaster scale.

Independence of judgment, world peace, noninvolvement in blocs — all three essential elements of his foreign policy were included in this early speech by Nehru. He went on to mention opposition to racialism and the desire for friendly relations with Great Britain, the Commonwealth, the USSR, and China. Indians, "too long . . . the playthings of others," were about to make the history of their choice.[22]

It was only later that the several aspects of this policy came to be subsumed under the single heading "nonalignment." According to Krishna Menon, nonalignment was a "residue of historical circumstances." India would not go back to the West with its colonialism, and there was no question of going the Soviet way. Both Nehru and Menon thought aloud simultaneously, "Why should we be with anybody?"[23]

Nonalignment referred primarily to the avoidance of military alliances in the cold war. The nonaligned sought to break through the dichotomy prevailing between alliance membership and withdrawal from international political activity. To the newly emergent states of Asia and Africa, the ideological cleavage that characterized the "world" was in many respects a distant affair with no immediate bearing upon their conditions. The nonaligned attempted friendly relations with all; "the mind of Asia does not fit in with this great crusade of Democracy or Communism." The emotional overtones of nonalignment are clearly brought out in Nehru's outburst, "Why should we inherit the hatred of others? It is bad enough that we have our own burdens." The strong antipathy to European colonialism, and the suspicions of European motives, were clearly evident in Nehru's speech at the conclusion of the Bandung Conference in April 1955:

> I say that Europe has been in the past a continent full of conflicts, full of trouble, full of hatred. Europe's conflicts continue,

its wars continue and we have been dragged into these wars because we were tied to Europe's chariot wheels. Are we going to continue to be tied to Europe's troubles, Europe's hatreds and Europe's conflicts? I hope not.[24]

Nehru provided an explanation of his foreign policy at the 1957 Commonwealth Parliamentary Conference in New Delhi. For each country, he said, "the outlook on the world is different, and depends to some extent on where you are standing, physically standing, and, secondly, mentally standing, if I may say so, that is to say, your mind has been conditioned by past events."[25] In other words, while military noninvolvement was a product of geography and, to a lesser degree, history, ideological independence reflected a particular mentality, in part again influenced by historical circumstances. Similarly, Indira Gandhi also explicitly acknowledged the importance of history and geography in the conduct of foreign policy. According to her, India sees the world from where it is, others from where they are, and the twain do not necessarily meet: it is impossible for them to view the world from the same angle.[26]

Nonalignment is emphatically not neutrality. The latter refers to a legal state of affairs in respect of war, and imposes fairly precise privileges and obligations upon the neutral state. Nonalignment, on the other hand, refers primarily to a political state of affairs during peace, which leaves a country completely free in determining its relations should a war occur.

As for the second element of Indian foreign policy, it might be noted at the outset that India's international relations have been strongly colored by its dispute with Pakistan. Possibilities for conflicts between the two existed from the beginning: while India was secular, Pakistan's *raison d'être* was religion; additionally, Muslims constituted India's most sizable minority (11 percent). One of the central concerns of Indian foreign policy was to stress Asian solidarity; the ideology that created Pakistan emphasized profound and irreconcilable differences between Asians from the same region. Both sought pan-national unity and identity, but competitively—India in Asianism, Pakistan in Islam.

The territorial and ancillary disputes between India and Pakistan stemmed directly from partition: which of the two was to be considered the successor state to British India? The major bone of contention between India and Pakistan was Kashmir, which still stands as the symbol of the Indo-Pakistan conflict.[27] Once the territorial disputes with India surfaced, Pakistan, given its relative military weakness, looked for external support. Western influence and involvement in Pakistan was an acceptable price to pay for alleviating the fear of Indian aggression against, and a perceived Hindu hostility to the existence of, Pakistan. Unfortunately, Pakistan's decision to opt for alliances brought it into direct conflict with the Indian foreign policy of nonalignment. Nehru did not kindly receive the American decision in 1953–54 to arm Pakistan, in part because it brought the cold war to India's doorstep and also because it reintroduced Western domination of Asia in a new form.[28] John Foster Dulles for his part condemned nonalignment as immoral. Leo Rose has also underscored the point that "the selection of Pakistan as the regional focal point of U.S. policy can be understood . . . within the context of American strategic objectives" in West Asia and Southeast Asia.[29] At the same time, alliance with Pakistan involved the United States in the country's internal politics by strengthening the influence of the military, by committing American prestige to a particular group (the army), and therefore to West Pakistan *vis-à-vis* East Pakistan, since most of the officer corps was from West Pakistan. The alliance also reduced American options in the subcontinent in the years that followed. Finally, it made it that much more difficult for the United States not to become involved in local quarrels.

Indian attitudes towards the United States and the USSR were initially ambivalent. In Nehru's own pithy assessment, "all the evils of a purely political democracy are evident in the U.S.A.; the evils of the lack of political democracy are present in the U.S.S.R."[30] Once the cold war intersected with the India-Pakistan axis in Kashmir, as it may be said to have done in 1954, it was natural for India and the USSR to become diplomatic allies on this particular issue. Relations between Moscow and New Delhi progressed cordially from strong Soviet support for India on such sensitive subjects as Kashmir and Goa to a consistent Soviet defense of Indian interests at the United Nations. The Tashkent agreement between India and Pakistan after their war in 1965 was symbolic of the increasing importance of the USSR in the subcontinent.

In the 1970s, the twin developments of the Sino-Soviet split and Sino-American *rapprochement*, when coupled with the India-China conflict, meant for Moscow and New Delhi a geostrategic community of interest. India had been among the first to recognize the new Peking regime. From 1950 to 1955, New Delhi displayed an attitude of caution in its relations with Peking, as for instance in the Chinese occupation of Tibet in 1950. Its policy was two-pronged. On the one hand, it strengthened security measures along the mountains in Bhutan, Sikkim, and Nepal. On the other, it sought to encircle and contain China in a ring of pledges.

Panchsheel, the five principles of peaceful coexistence between India and China, was first formulated in the preamble to the April 1954 agreement between those countries on the status of Tibet. In the agreement India conceded Chinese rights to Tibet. As a result, *Panchsheel* was denigrated by some in India for having been "born in sin." Nehru responded in Parliament the following month that if India tried to maintain its rights in Tibet—rights forced upon Tibet by British imperialism—then India would be compelled to give up everything at point on arms. A few months later, on 29 September, he again vigorously defended *Panchsheel* in Parliament. Conceding that no state could live on trust alone where other states were concerned, he argued nevertheless that Indian policy sought to make it "more and more difficult progressively for the other country to break trust."

By 1962, China and India had little in common beyond a long border. In 1962, that border witnessed major clashes as the *bhai-bhai* ("brother-brother") relations degenerated rapidly into cries of *hai-hai* ("alas-alas"). Conflict with China involved Tibet as well as border disputes. A rebellion in the east by the Khampas, simmering since 1956, broke out into a full-scale revolt in 1958, spread to Lhasa, and continued into the following year. India's response was one of cautious expression of sympathy for the sufferings of the people. The Dalai Lama crossed into India in March-April through Tawang; he was granted asylum but not permitted to form a government in exile. Chinese explanations of the revolt described it as a reactionary upsurge directed by the Americans from Kalimpong in India. Indeed, soon the Chinese were elaborating upon their exposition of Indian expansionism backed by Western imperialism as being the chief explanation for troubles not only in Tibet but along the entire Sino-Indian border—charges that were rejected by Nehru.

The border dispute proper involved three sectors: the North East Frontier Agency (NEFA) in the east, the Indo-Tibetan middle sector, and Ladakh in the west.[31] The government was in determined opposition to the idea of any settlement on the basis of a barter across the sectors. The sequence of events generally was patrol incursions and road constructions in 1957–58, followed by military clashes in 1959. In response, Nehru declared, "There is no alternative but to defend our country's borders and integrity."[32] The years 1959–62 were marked by heightened tension and a barrage of correspondence containing charges and self-justifications, as well as increased military preparations on India's part.

More crucially, India adopted what came to be described as a forward policy: an attempt would be made to regain lost territory by sending patrols behind Chinese posts to establish Indian posts there. In retrospect one can see that India's forward policy was based on a miscalculation both of respective military strengths and of China's probable response. This despite indications to the contrary from the Chinese, who on 30 November 1961 warned that disturbing the *status quo* in Ladakh would give the Chinese "every reason to send troops to cross the so-called 'McMahon line'" in NEFA.[33] China followed up its warning by a patrol incursion in NEFA in January 1962. New Delhi's note of 26 February protested this attempt to reply to charges of aggression "by threatening aggression elsewhere." Its note of 13 March expressed willingness to maintain the 1957, not the 1959, *status quo*.

The Chinese announced a resumption of patrolling in Ladakh toward the end of April, and in May, Pakistan and China agreed to "negotiate a border settlement." The 1954 Tibet agreement lapsed in June. China began to build up its forces in the summer, and on 27 October published its ideological justification for the war. Chinese troops crossed the Thagla Ridge in NEFA in early September, with a major clash taking place on 20 September. On 12 October Nehru publicly warned the Chinese that the army had been told to drive them out. Eight days later, the Chinese launched major offensives in Ladakh and NEFA. They paused on 24 October, resumed on 16 November, and finally announced on 21 November a unilateral withdrawal of twenty kilometers from the 7 November lines of actual control. The result of that brief war is too well known to need retelling.

Since 1962, China's gravitation toward Pakistan has matched burgeoning Indo-Soviet relations. The announcement in July 1971 that Nixon would visit Peking shook both India and the USSR. The consensus in India was that the development would reshape the world's power pattern profoundly, but with a detrimental impact on India's position. The USSR for its part woke up to the realization that "the front line of its diplomacy in Southern and Eastern Asia is suddenly rendered extremely vulnerable."[34] The India-USSR Friendship Treaty of August 1971 may be seen in this context to represent a response by two states to a dramatic shift in the international structure to their mutual disadvantage. A textual analysis shows that the treaty was an additive alliance in seeking to aggregate Indian and Soviet diplomatic-military power, and a preclusive alliance in that it prohibited each party from joining an alliance against the other. In the contextual sense, it was also of course an attempt by Gandhi to forestall a dangerous isolation in the event of a "Bangladesh war."[35]

The years 1971–77 marked a consolidation of the India-USSR axis. The advent of the Janata government raised the possibility of shifts in India's external ties. Both Morarji Desai and foreign minister Atal Bihari Vajpayee were concerned to reverse the drift away from "genuine nonalignment" and thereby extend the range of flexibility in India's foreign relations. There were limits, however, to how much even the Desai government could move Indian foreign policy away from the USSR and toward the West. Nevertheless, Moscow could only have been pleased with Indira Gandhi's return to power. Reactions to the Soviet invasion of Afghanistan were symptomatic of the differences in emphasis between Gandhi and her predecessors. The Lok Dal and the Janata censured Soviet action as the scale of the intervention became apparent. By then, however, Gandhi was back at India's helm, and she seemed to condone or at least accept the need for the Soviet move. She said in the Lok Sabha on 30 January that "we do not approve of foreign presence or intervention anywhere in the world. However, we do not believe in one-sided condemnation." Indian policy on the subject of Soviet interventions thus maintains a continuity in refusals to censure the Hungarian, Czechoslovakian, and Afghan adventures. If it was not prepared to antagonize Moscow needlessly, New Delhi also carefully refrained from endorsing the Soviet presence in Afghanistan.[36]

Bilateral Relations
A simultaneous study of Canadian and Indian policies in Vietnam leads to one observation that runs counter to expectations. Because

neither Canada nor India was involved in the Vietnam war, it would be surprising if either allowed the conflicts *per se* to sour its broader relations with the other. Yet, this is precisely what happened to Indo-Canadian relations. In Vietnam, and in Indochina generally, Canada became increasingly exasperated with India; this contributed significantly to the demise of their special relationship.[37] Relations between India and Poland, on the other hand, have grown steadily closer over the period. The volume of Indo-Polish trade has risen from a meager Rs 4 million in 1953 to Rs 1.2 billion in 1980. Poland today is India's second-largest trading partner in Eastern Europe, next only to the USSR.[38] But it is doubtful that much of this can be attributed to shared experiences in Indochina.

Canadian-Polish relations have been governed largely by the general state of East-West relations and the fact of a significant ethnic presence of Poles in Canada. Thus during the cold-war years relations between the two countries were generally tense, and produced skirmishes at the United Nations over such matters as Polish art treasures in Canada and allegations of mistreatment of Polish immigrant workers.[39] Canada explored expanded contacts after 1956 as a means of encouraging Wladyslaw Gomulka's liberal and nationalist tendencies. Polish candidacy for a Security Council seat received Canadian support in 1959; ambassadors were exchanged in 1960; and the Polish art treasures were returned by 1961. These years also saw the conclusion of large grain deals. In the years of East-West détente, technological, scientific, and cultural exchanges also proliferated, culminating in the reciprocal visits of foreign ministers in 1975–76.

In short, Canadian-Polish relations have been growing steadily and modestly since the Second World War. This is reflected in the value of trade between the two countries: C$5.8 million in 1948, C$297.2 million in 1978.[40] Moreover, in contrast to the Indo-Canadian relationship, shared peacekeeping experiences in Indochina and the Middle East have had no appreciable adverse impact upon Ottawa-Warsaw ties. Perhaps a realistic appraisal of each other's role from the beginning was helpful, in that there was not much scope for disillusionment and disenchantment.

Poland
The mainsprings of Polish foreign policy are at once more simple and more tragic than those of Canadian or Indian foreign policy. The lessons of history indicate that Poland should distrust both

Germany and Russia. Neither should it rely on the West for its territorial integrity and political independence; reasons of state dictated that post–Second World War Poland would be in unequal alliance with the USSR.

The basic parameters of Polish history have been its modest size and geographical location, a strategic zone of conflict between the great European powers. As a result, Poland's international position was a function of German-Russian relations. Its history is testimony to the dependence of lesser states on the outcome of great-power struggles over which they have little influence, but from the consequences of which they cannot escape. For more than a century (1795–1918) the Polish nation existed only in the hearts and minds of Poles. In 1918, Allied victory, President Woodrow Wilson's self-determination plank, and a temporary power vacuum in Central and Eastern Europe combined once again to give stately expression to the nation. At Locarno in 1925 Poland received notice that Anglo-French concerns were limited to securing Germany's western frontiers, and that Germany was far from reconciled to its eastern losses in the Treaty of Versailles.

Russia too was a revisionist country in the interwar years. Vyacheslav Molotov was to remark in 1939 that Poland was "an ugly offspring of Versailles."[41] Suspicious of both its neighbors, Poland in these years tried to balance the two. However, the aggressive revival of Germany under Adolf Hitler, his realpolitik alliance with Joseph Stalin, and the loss of Western nerve in the policy of appeasement once again served up Poland to its two traditional enemies. The ultimate defeat of Germany and the decisive role of the USSR therein produced a reconstitution of Poland but with its borders moved westward. In the changed balance of power, Poland's international position shifted from being a function of German-Russian relations to being determined by relations between the two superpowers. It was Poland's particular misfortune that one of these should be the USSR.

After the Second World War, and despite the entire historical legacy, Polish frontiers could be secured only in alliance with the USSR. To the west, only the USSR could protect Poland's encroaching territory against a potentially revisionist Germany. For this reason, the alliance was strongly supported by communists and noncommunists alike.[42] To the east, Western disinterest left Soviet goodwill as the sole guarantor of Polish territorial integrity, and

Moscow would not suffer an anti-Soviet Poland. The fate of Poland was sealed in Allied discussions during the war, when there was both a military need of the immense Soviet capability and, in the West, a political belief that only great-power understanding could guarantee a peaceful world after the war. Poland was simply an irritant and a nuisance, if not an actual threat, to this body of opinion.

Hence the steady stream of concessions to Soviet demands on "the Polish question." If the Treaty of Versailles had been damned for being both unjust and unwise, Poland could now be disposed of in terms of political wisdom without recourse to abstract principles of justice. Poland was possibly the chief target of Soviet territorial revisionism. Stalin's interest extended beyond the frontier question, moreover, to the nature of the postwar government in Poland, and its attitude to the USSR. During the twenty-year armistice, Poland had allied first with France (in the Little Entente and in the Locarno system), then with Germany (1934), and finally with Britain (1939), but never with the USSR. In real terms, the USSR has exercised effective subjugation of Poland since 1944 without interruption, except perhaps for a brief flicker of hope in 1956.

Interpretations of the "October spring" of 1956 range from describing it as the outcome of a factional power struggle or as a reversion to true "socialism with a human face," to explaining it as an untempered reaction of the Polish nation against Soviet communist domination and exploitation.[43] In the result it brought Gomulka to power against the wishes of an irate Nikita Khrushchev and on the tide of mounting nationalist feelings expressed in anti-Soviet anger. A program of de-Stalinization was effected immediately, and the right to the Polish road to socialism vehemently asserted. The party newspaper *Trybuna Ludu* declared that the correct sequence of the new program was "sovereignty, democracy, socialism," while Gomulka assured his countrymen that relations with the USSR would henceforth be based on independence, equality, and freedom, even "mutual criticism." This was evident in the Hungarian crisis. When Gomulka paid a visit to Moscow (15–18 November 1956), the joint communiqué at the conclusion of his talks with Khrushchev stressed the similarity and unity of views on the subjects of Suez, China, and the United Nations. On Hungary, however, "the delegations had *exchanged* views."[44] In addition to his right to an independent assessment of events in Eastern Europe, Gomulka extracted three significant concessions from his hosts: a repatriation of Polish citizens still living in the USSR under compulsion; a confirmation of Polish sovereignty on the matter of stationing Soviet military units on Polish territory and an abolition of their extraterritorial rights; and a termination of economic tributes being paid by Poland to the USSR.[45]

At the same time, Gomulka the pragmatist Pole and dedicated communist well understood the scope and limits of Polish foreign policy. The October spring did not modify the need for an unconditional continuance of the alliance with the USSR. No harm would be permitted to the cause of building socialism in Poland or to the vital interests of the Polish state. The concessions outlined above were a significant achievement *within* the framework of existing treaties; they were a confirmation of Poland's position in the eastern bloc. The Hungarian crisis showed clearly that the denunciation of the Warsaw treaties by Imre Nagy on 1 November 1956 was of decisive importance in the Soviet calculations to invade Hungary. If the Gomulka government refused to condone the Soviet intervention, it also refrained from condemning it in public. Gomulka was at all times careful not to lead Poland beyond the limits of its independence. The Soviet intervention in Czechoslovakia in 1968, along with its *ex post facto* enunciation of the Brezhnev doctrine of limited socialist sovereignty, must have come as a vindication of his policy of caution. Poland's participation in the 1968 invasion was perhaps the ultimate reversion to pro-Soviet policies.

Furthermore, the central question in Polish foreign policy remained the assertion of sovereignty over the "recovered territories." The rearmament of West Germany within the NATO framework had intensified Polish apprehensions. On 24 October 1956, three days after his return to power, Gomulka affirmed to the citizens of Warsaw that Soviet troops were needed in Poland as long as "there are Atlantic Pact bases in Western Germany, as long as the new Wehrmacht is being armed there, and chauvinism and revisionism with regard to our frontiers is fomented there." The continuing West German claim in law to the Oder-Neisse territories underwrote the Polish-Soviet alliance at the Warsaw end more potently than any other political or military consideration.

The joint Soviet-Polish statement of 18 November 1956 thus accepted that a temporary stationing of Soviet troops on Polish soil was still advisable because of possible German militarism and challenges to the existing western boundary of Poland. "The Soviet-Polish alliance," it said, "is a paramount factor in strengthening the independence of the Polish People's Republic and guaranteeing the inviolability of its frontiers on the Oder and Neisse."[46]

The accession of Gomulka to the Polish leadership in 1956 did not therefore result in any fundamental break with the central principles of Eastern European socialism. Poland and the other countries in the region are still an integral part of a centralized empire controlled by, for, and from Moscow. Yet, Poland is probably the weakest link in this imperial chain. The historical enmity toward the USSR is one explanation for this. Thus an invocation of Soviet military support would spell the political demise of any Polish regime. A second explanation for Poland's delicate role in the Eastern European system lies in its geographic position. The facts of geography impart strategic vitality to Poland for the defense and security of the USSR, for the perpetuation of Soviet military control over East Germany, and for future Soviet military plans in or against Western Europe. Finally, Poland's population represents almost one-third of the Warsaw Pact peoples outside the USSR. For these reasons, it is not surprising that in one study, Polish conformity to Soviet policies or objectives on a weighted seven-index score for 1956–68 was less than that of East Germany, Bulgaria, and Hungary. Excluding the events of 1968, Poland was even more deviant than Czechoslovakia. On the index of conformity to Soviet policy regarding relations among communist states, relations between communist states and the West, and major developments within the USSR, Poland was more deviant than the above four countries for the entire period (including 1968). At the same time, though, Polish conformity was at its lowest point from 1956 to 1958, and increased markedly after that.[47]

For the purposes of a study of Polish policy toward Vietnam, perhaps China is a more important point of reference than Eastern Europe. Poland recognized the People's Republic of China on 4 October 1949. Peking initially supported Gomulka's experiment along the Polish road to socialism. When Chou En-lai visited Poland in January 1957, having just been to the USSR, Prime Minister Jozef Cyrankiewicz remarked that the Chinese fully understood that "the coexistence of nations should not be like the coexistence of various fish . . . living in one lake, the bigger devouring the smaller ones."[48] The joint statement of 16 January accepted that relations between socialist countries should be "shaped by principles of proletarian internationalism," but on the basis of "the principles of respect for their sovereignty, non-interference in internal affairs, equality, and mutual benefit."

The position was reversed in the summer of 1957, possibly as the result of a factional struggle in the Chinese leadership.[49] For their part, the Poles sided unequivocally with Moscow in the great schism between the two leading socialist states from 1960–61 onward. But Polish leaders refrained from attacking China directly until September 1963. In that year, the Poles must have begun to shudder at the seeming Chinese preference for Armageddon over peaceful coexistence; Poland was in wholehearted agreement with Khrushchev's point that nuclear weapons did not respect class differences. On 8 September 1963, Gomulka expressed "bitterness" at China's "negative attitude toward the Moscow agreement on banning nuclear tests." "The Chinese," he said, "blinded by the desire to possess their own nuclear weapons," were splitting the socialist community and "thus doing a service for the enemies of socialism and warmongers."[50] In its China policy, Edward Gierek's Poland retained the evident solidarity with the USSR and condemned China for the socialist split.[51]

At the same time, nevertheless, the split encouraged tendencies toward socialist polycentrism, and thereby increased the importance of Poland as an ally of the USSR. Precisely because Polish loyalty to the USSR remained above suspicion, the Poles were permitted to explore contacts with the West. These two objectives of Polish foreign policy—alliance with the USSR and improved relations with the West—are complementary rather than in conflict. If Polish security is a function of East-West relations, then Polish vital interests are served in any improvement of those relations. Poland's cultural and historical links with Western Europe make it a useful ally in the promotion of Soviet collective security plans for the continent.

There is thus a strong foundation for the Polish policy that the security of Europe is better built on political cooperation than on military confrontation. Hence the sincerity of the Polish plans to reduce tensions in Europe, beginning with the Rapacki plan of 1957 for an nuclear-free zone in Central Europe, and including the Gomulka plan of 1963, which suggested a freeze on the production of nuclear weapons.

In some respects the crowning glory of Gomulka's reign came with West German Chancellor Willy Brandt's signing on 7 December 1970 of the draft treaty between Poland and West Germany. In the treaty, West Germany formally accepted Poland's western boundary (with East Germany) and agreed to the establishment of diplomatic relations between the two countries. By the same token, and in conjunction with the West Germany-USSR treaty of August 1970 and detente in Europe, reconciliation with West Germany removed the most compelling reason for Polish-Soviet alliance.

But it would be a mistake to conclude that the visits symbolized a departure of Polish policy from Soviet objectives. Poland would no doubt have noted that the Bonn-Warsaw treaty came after the Bonn-Moscow treaty which first accepted the territorial *status quo* in Europe, and that opposition in the Bundestag was stronger to ratifying the former. In other words, Polish collaboration with the West is likely and possible only within a continuing Soviet-Polish alliance, not outside of it.

The policy implications of the above to Polish foreign relations are simple. Poland today has no realistic alternative to continued alliance with the Soviet Union. But its freedom of maneuver internationally is increased with improved superpower relations. Conversely, and more seriously, its very existence, like that of Canada, would be threatened in a central confrontation between East and West. It must therefore remain Polish policy as well as Canadian to temper alliance support at the core with cooperative feelers at the periphery of East-West relations.

2 The French Indochina War

This chapter will set the stage for developments in the field in Indochina *per se,* as well as for the relationships that were to emerge between the ICSC delegations in the field. Canada, India, and Poland were involved in Vietnam only after the Geneva Agreements of July 1954. It is a truism to say that their policies toward the war in Indochina prior to the Agreements were determined by foreign policy objectives and priorities. At the same time, an examination of attitudes toward the Indochina war even before formal involvement in the supervisory commissions serves as a useful reference point for subsequent behavior.

Attitudes Toward the War

Canada
Canada's policy toward the Franco-Vietminh war was a reflection of its isolation from Indochina. About the only contact Canadians had with Indochina prior to the Second World War was a missionary presence. Because Canada did not have any direct interest in the region, its initial involvement was entirely a product of broader Western concerns. The official *Foreign Policy for Canadians*, published in 1970 in the light of developments of the preceding twenty years, stated that "Canada's awareness of the Pacific world has been determined by facts of geography and economics, the links of history and political realities."[1] Geographically, Canada is as much a Pacific as an Atlantic state. Nevertheless, in politico-diplomatic terms it is almost completely Atlantic. In 1968, for instance,

Trudeau spoke of his country's "ring-side seat on the Pacific," suggesting, as Thomson and Swanson noted, a spectator rather than participant role.[2] Economics connects Canada to Japan; history links it to Australia and New Zealand. Canadian interest in the Pacific reflects Canadian foreign policy's shift from Britain to America in this century:

> American influence in the Pacific, in virtually every sphere of activity, is so very great and all-pervasive that it must be regarded as one of the most significant "givens" in any consideration of alternatives; Canadian interests and policies are almost everywhere affected by it.[3]

That is to say, in the Pacific as elsewhere, Canadian policy must be guided by the inescapable reality of its ties to America. With this "retroactive" introduction, which formed the context of Canadian policies in Indochina throughout, it is possible to examine Canada's statements and actions with respect to the Franco-Vietminh war.

Canada evinced no interest in the war until the emergence of its international dimensions with the establishment of the People's Republic of China in 1949, and the cold-war recognitions in 1950 of the governments of Ho Chi Minh and Bao Dai. On 22 February 1950, Pearson stressed the political importance of Indochina by describing Vietnam as the greatest communist effort in Asia, adding that Canadian interest arose from its relations with France. Even while refraining from recognizing either regime, Pearson wished success to the Bao Dai government. By 1951, the government, spurred by the Conservative opposition, was applying the two-value cold-war logic in its analysis of Indochina. Pearson enunciated the domino theory in Parliament as early as 2 February 1951, albeit with reference to the British concerns over Southeast Asia and the subcontinent. At the same time, however, the Canadians were not keen to participate in Pacific security arrangements. Speaking to the proposed Pacific defense pact, Pearson argued that Canadian involvement in such a pact would not be wise, because "a particular procedure in regard to one region of the world is not necessarily the best procedure in regard to another," and because conditions in the Pacific were not analogous to those in the Atlantic.[4]

Its consciousness heightened after the outbreak of hostilities in the Korean war, the United States intertwined the French colonial war in Indochina with the global Western fight against communism. On 17 December 1952, the North Atlantic Council resolved that resistance to aggression in Southeast Asia was in keeping with the aims and ideals of the Atlantic community, and that "the campaign waged by the French Union forces in Indo-China deserves continuing support from the NATO governments."[5] Support from the Canadian government took the form of according recognition on 30 December 1952 to Vietnam, Laos, and Cambodia as Associated States of Indo-China within the French Union.[6] Considering that both the United Kingdom and the United States, among others, had given such recognition in February 1950, there is no rationale other than the North Atlantic Council decision for Canadian recognition at this time. Such an interpretation is supported by Pearson's observation in Parliament on 11 February 1953 that the three Indochinese states were now recognized by all NATO and British Commonwealth countries.

As for the American role in Indochina, it, too, merited favorable mention. Pearson emphasized that the United States was the cardinal factor "in this area of the world where *we* are defending ourselves against communist aggression."[7] The one troubling doubt concerned the impact of the war upon the Western alliance. In 1953, Pearson cautioned that the Far East constituted the greatest threat to Western unity of purpose and action. The threat, he wrote, "arises out of differences of viewpoint over the scope and nature of the menace of communism in Asia and the measures which should be taken to meet it." That the differences often found America and Britain ranged on opposing sides was "a result which causes special anxiety to a Canadian."[8]

The Asian point of view was not entirely unrepresented in Canadian parliamentary circles, even if it remained a neglected one. M. J. Coldwell, leader of the CCF party, argued on 5 May 1953 that Indochina "is a colonial area and the primary issue is whether French colonialism is going to be strengthened in its attempt to maintain its control over the natives." Similarly, on 28 May 1954, during a debate on the Geneva Conference then in progress, his analysis of the background to the conflict closely followed Nehru's description of the war as being one between the forces of nationalism and European colonialism.[9] Roland Michener of the Conservative party expressed the Asian concern most succinctly. Reporting to Parliament on his attendance at a conference in Lahore, Michener on 31 March 1954 referred to the "common Asiatic view that the European has no right or place in dominating the people of Asia. . . . The presence of France in Indo-China was of more concern to them than the threat of communism." NATO assistance to France, he said, would therefore be interpreted as Western support to an imperialist struggle against a nationalist movement.

Such, then, was the Canadian position on the eve of the Geneva Conference: official support for the French and American efforts at combating international communist aggression in Indochina, but without active Canadian contribution to the fight; with a few barely noticed voices arguing the case against France. As for the Conference itself, Canada did not expect to play a major role. In a CBC interview on 23 April 1954, Pearson stated that Canada was interested in the pacification and stabilization of Indochina, and in the strengthening of Southeast Asian security. It would, therefore, follow the discussions on Indochina "with great care and interest." Beyond that, however, Canada would not go: it was not an invitee to the Geneva Conference on Indochina; it was not directly involved in Indochina; and Indochina had not even been taken up at the United Nations.[10]

India
Indochina has been a historical battleground for the rivalry between Indian and Chinese influences. Nehru has written how "amazed" and "excited" he was at the discovery of Indian influences in Southeast Asia. According to his assessment, "as a rule the methods of government and the general philosophy of life came from China, religion and art from India."[11] The current Asian revolt against the West was the product of three related forces: a claim for self-determination, expressed as anticolonialism; a revolt against the social and economic order that seemed to perpetuate poverty and its attendant misery; and antiracialism, the determination that the destiny of Asia was to be charted by Asians. The second point called for planning, which in turn required a choice between coercive and persuasive strategies. It is on this score that China and India reacquired importance as models for Southeast Asia. The Korean war was significant in this connection. It brought the two

Asian giants forcefully to the world scene, with Asia's military might evident upon the battlefields of Korea, and its diplomatic weight evident in the world councils.

The conflict in Indochina attracted early attention in India because the Congress party, with a legacy of concern with world affairs, took an active interest in external events. In Nehru's words, "the Congress gradually developed a foreign policy which was based on the elimination of political and economic imperialism everywhere and the co-operation of free nations. This fitted in with the demand for Indian independence."[12] This also meant that the party would identify with the Vietnamese struggle for freedom against French rule.

British troops dispatched to Saigon in September 1945 to disarm the Japanese included Indians from the Twentieth Indian division. When these were deployed to suppress nationalists in the guise of maintaining "law and order," there was a predictable storm of protest in India. The All India Congress Committee (AICC), in a series of resolutions in 1945–46, expressed itself strongly against attempts at continuing political and economic subjection of the Indochinese and other peoples. Nehru himself declared on New Year's Day, 1946, "we have watched British intervention" in Indochina "with growing anger, shame and helplessness, that Indian troops should be used for doing Britain's dirty work against our friends who are fighting the same fight as we. . . . " Nehru sent greetings to Ho Chi Minh in October 1946. On the other side, in December 1946 he let France know that "the attempt to crush the spirit of freedom in Indochina has deeply moved the Indian people." The sentiment would acquire relevance again two decades later, in the American phase of the Vietnam war.

Ho Chi Minh sent a representative to New Delhi in 1946, aiming for an Indian condemnation of French policy, as well as a more substantial obstruction of French purchases, overflights, and refuellings in India. These requests were only partially met. Limits were placed on the number of French overflights, and combat aircraft were prohibited. However, the restrictions were far less comprehensive than those enforced against the Dutch vis-à-vis Indonesia.

If Nehru and his government were wary of extending support, Indian public opinion was firmly behind the Vietnamese nationalists. Official India's sense of restraint was not shared in other quarters. K. P. Karunakaran, in his survey of the period, writes that Indian public opinion "vigorously championed the cause of Ho Chi Minh and asserted that only the republican government was representative of nationalist aspirations of the people."[13] Acharya Kripalani, president of the Congress, compared French repression in Vietnam to Hitler's tactics. The Trade Union Congress asked that French goods transported to and from Indochina be boycotted. The All-India Students' Congress urged that 21 January 1947 be observed as Vietnam Day. On that day, student processions in Calcutta resulted in violence and death.

Earlier, Sarat Chandra Bose, a leading member of the AICC, had issued an appeal for a volunteer brigade, funds, clothing, food, and medical supplies for Indochina, on the grounds that the struggle there was part of the wider Asiatic struggle agianst European domination, and therefore part of India's struggle. The response to his appeal was flattering and widespread: from Bombay, Delhi, Karachi, and Pondicherry in India; from Burma, Ceylon, and Singapore abroad, came men and material. In February, Bose requested transport facilities and passports from the government, reminding Nehru that the "freedom of Asia is one and indivisible." Nehru refused, explaining that international issues were involved, and that "so long as the Government of India is not at war with another country, it cannot take aggressive action against it." To this, Bose retorted in anger that if the government, "for reasons of its own," wished not to interfere, it should at the very least "allow Indian Lafayettes to proceed to Vietnam."[14]

Indian official attitude toward the Vietnamese question was similarly cautious at the Asian Conference in New Delhi (28 March–12 April 1947). India, anticipating the Geneva formula of 1954, invited two delegations from Indochina, Ho's DRVN and the French-supported regimes of Cambodia, Laos, and Vietnam. At the conference, Mai The Chau, the DRVN representative in New Delhi, addressed the National Freedom Movements Group to the effect that material aid and action should accompany moral support and verbal protest. He stressed that "at the moment when the very existence of my country is threatened, it is not good words which can save my country but action. . . . We have used enough words about Asian unity. Now let us act." The DRVN delegation was interested in persuading the Indian government to recognize the DRVN, to get the United Nations to take up Indochina, and to take measures to stop French reinforcements. The DRVN and

Indonesian delegations jointly appealed: that colonialism and Vietnam be put on the Security Council agenda; that their two republics be recognized; that joint Asian action be undertaken to liberate occupied Asia; that joint Asian action be initiated to prevent Dutch and French reinforcements from reaching Indonesia and Vietnam; and that Asian medical aid and volunteers be sent to the battlefields.

Nehru, in attendance at the Conference, was not convinced of the propriety of outside intervention in Indochina. Reiterating the Indian people's sympathy for the Vietnamese freedom struggle, he nevertheless pointed out that India was not about to declare war on France. The concern rather was to limit the area of conflict. Pressure would be brought to bear on France, but only by methods of quiet diplomacy, for it could not "obviously be done by governments in public meetings."[15] Similarly, India did not act on the requests for recognition and for helping to raise the Indochinese issue at the United Nations.

A secret study by India's consul-general in Saigon confirmed that Ho's forces controlled 80 percent of the countryside. On the basis of this report, India indicated to Britain its inability to recognize the Bao Dai regime. Ho Chi Minh's representative to New Delhi was received on arrival in April 1948 by such prominent Indians as Nehru, Sardar Vallabh Bhai Patel, and Rajendra Prasad; Bao Dai's representative, seeking recognition, was not granted an audience with Nehru in January 1950. "He does not represent anybody to us," said Nehru, "he has come here in his private capacity and officially he is not accredited to us, nor do we recognize him in any capacity." He reiterated India's policy as being "not to give official recognition in Indochina to any government."[16]

The recognition of the two claimants to Vietnam along cold-war lines in 1950 produced the reaction from Nehru that "it is not for me to criticize other governments. . . . But, we have, after very careful consideration of the situation in Indochina, come to the conclusion that we should not jump into the fray."[17] He thought that recognition by India would make Indochina's "fight for independence" more difficult. He also wished to stay clear of internal conflicts, and exercise influence only in favor of peace. Nor was he convinced that either government satisfied the criteria for recognition established in international law. Rather, he was of the opinion that Vietnam was "in a state of civil war," and therefore it could not be ascertained which government prevailed there. In a speech in Parliament on 17 March 1950, he described India's policy as "one of absolute non-interference," because any kind of interference was intolerable to nationalism. In the same speech, however, he did refer to "a country struggling for freedom," which is a good indication of how he perceived the conflict.

On 17 December 1952, Nehru in Parliament explained his policy of circumspection in Vietnam by referring to the "extraordinarily complicated situation" as well as "larger considerations." Such larger considerations were four: the communist character of the Vietminh leadership, the emergence of a communist China that bordered on the communist-led part of Vietnam, the fact that at the time France was with Britain the chief source of weapons supply to India,[18] and the continued presence of French colonial outposts in India until after the Geneva Agreements. On the first consideration, a complication in Vietnam arose from the fact that communism and nationalism appeared to have fused into one movement. Nehru's India would have preferred to see democratic institutions established with the achievement of independence, but even communist independence was to be favored over continued colonial domination. This was quite clearly stated by Nehru in 1950: "No argument in any country of Asia is going to have weight if it goes counter to the nationalist support of the country, Communism or no Communism."[19]

A more important consequence of the internationalization of the Indochinese conflict was that it propelled India into peacemaking efforts. In 1954, India took advantage of the fact that the Berlin Conference had reversed its earlier policy of aloofness, and placed Indochina on the Geneva agenda. On 22 February, Nehru issued a "very earnest appeal" in the Lok Sabha for a cease-fire in Indochina. St. Laurent, on a tour of India at the time, was present in Parliament when Nehru made this appeal. At a press conference two days later, St. Laurent lent unhesitating support to the appeal—an action that may have angered Britain and infuriated the French.[20] This was followed on 24 April by a six-point proposal for the restoration of peace. As important as the proposals were Nehru's analysis of the Indochinese situation and his statement of India's motives in becoming involved.[21]

India, Nehru said, was not a participant in the hostilities, nor would it be one in the conference at Geneva. Nevertheless, it was "interested in and deeply concerned about the problem of Indo-China," and apprehensive that war in "our proximate regions" might spread and escalate. Peace was to be achieved only if basic realities, historical, political, and military, were appreciated. Nehru then proceeded to delineate these realities. Again, what is important for us is not the accuracy of his analysis, but its substance, as indicative of his perceptions of the problem. According to Nehru,

> The conflict in Indo-China is, in its origin and essential character, born of a movement of resistance to colonialism and to attempts to deal with it by the traditional methods of suppression and divide-and-rule.
>
> Foreign interventions have made the issue more complex; nevertheless, it remains basically anti-colonial and nationalist in character. The recognition of this aspect as well as the reconciliation of national sentiments for freedom and independence and safeguarding them against external pressures can alone form the basis of a settlement and of peace.

Nehru traced the origins of the Vietminh movement to the resistance to Japanese occupation, and described the beginnings of the war between France and the Vietminh. The war acquired ominous overtones, he said, with the polarization of communist military aid to the northern half and American supplies to the French effort. The decision by the Berlin powers to negotiate peace at a conference was welcomed, but was followed, first by dangerous talks of instant and massive retaliation, of extending the scope and intensity of the hostilities, and second by calls for united action. There was an impression conveyed that a kind of Monroe Doctrine had unilaterally been declared over Southeast Asia. India, he said, deeply regretted that the conference "should be preceded by a proclamation of what amounts to lack of faith in it, and of alternatives involving threats of sanctions." His misgivings were increased by the stepped-up aid to both sides.

As for India's motives in proferring the proposals for peace, Nehru explained that "peace to us is not just a fervent hope; it is an emergent necessity." Further, the implications of an internationalization of the conflict "impinge on the newly-won and cherished independence of Asian countries." The end of colonial rule, and the maintenance of independence and sovereignty of Asian countries, was necessary for Asian prosperity and world peace. While this would be true as a general principle of world politics, "Indo-China is an Asian country and a proximate area." It therefore fell within India's efforts "to seek to keep ourselves and others, particularly our neighbours, to a peace area and to a policy of non-alignment in world tensions and wars." Hence India's desire to avert an extension and intensification of the conflict, and to strive toward limiting it. For this, India suggested the following: all should desist from threats, and the combatants should not step-up hostilities; a cease-fire; unequivocal and complete independence of the Indochinese states by French proclamation; direct negotiations between the parties; an agreement on nonintervention, of any kind and by any means, between America, Britain, China, and Russia; and the good offices of the United Nations for purposes of conciliation. In other words, Nehru was advocating, in addition to a cease-fire, the principles of *Panchsheel,* which were to be announced within a week of his Indochina proposals. Acceptance of the proposals would not only lessen tension in an area close to India, it would also keep the various powers out of the region. Additionally, inclusion of the United Nations, however obliquely, in the Indochina negotiations would provide India with an "entry." Nehru's suggestions formed the core of the proposals issued by the Colombo Powers[22] a week later. The conference in Colombo (28 April –2 May) was used to register publicly Asian resentment that vital Asian affairs should be decided upon almost exclusively by Europeans, meeting in Europe.

The Eastern Bloc

Poland had no involvement in Indochina whatsoever. But the USSR and China had long-standing interests in the growth of communism in Indochina. The Soviet regime focused its attention on the east only very gradually. In the 1920s, even this little attention was confined to a preoccupation with China. Initial responsibility for guiding Vietnamese comrades lay with the French (Ho Chi Minh* was a founding member of the French Communist Party in 1920). With the formation of the Communist Party of Indochina in 1930, and its formal admittance into the Comintern in April 1931, the region received greater Soviet doctrinal interest which was not, however, matched by an operational program in support of it.[23] Soviet influence was channelled principally through Ho's association with the Comintern, and his presence in Moscow from 1922 to 1925. Reasons for the modesty of Soviet interests include

---

*For the sake of simplicity, only the name Ho Chi Minh is used in the text of this study. See Appendix IV for details.

lack of easy access, ignorance of the region, greater commitment elsewhere, and the Eurocentric cast and orientation of the Comintern at the time.

The Chinese communists for their part were, understandably, too taken up with their own affairs to pay much attention to Indochina. Their influence on Vietnamese politics derived more from example and alleged successes than from intervention or active liaison. One aspect of Sino-Vietnamese relations deserves special mention for the purposes of this study: the duality of Vietnam's relations with China. On the one hand, Vietnamese culture has preserved a distinct identity; the Vietnamese have put up a fierce and largely successful resistance to domination and absorption by the Chinese, despite periods of subjection to Chinese rule and intense sinicization. On the other hand, Vietnam had itself been an active agent of sinicization in Indochina. In the third century, Vietnam was involved in both a series of revolts against China and the beginnings of conflict with the Chams. The complication arose from the fact that Chinese help was needed to repel the Chams. This has an "allegorical" relevance; in recent times, the North Vietnamese have had to resist losing their political identity to the Chinese even while desperately in need of Chinese aid in the fight against the Americans.

By identifying themselves with the anti-Japanese movement during the Second World War, the Vietminh effected a rise in their fortunes. By cutting their links with the returning colonials with precision timing, and reidentifying with the forces of national liberation, they further enhanced their prestige after the war. On 11 November 1945, a final communiqué announced the formal dissolution of the Communist Party of Indochina, in order to "destroy all misunderstandings, domestic and foreign, which can hinder liberation of our country." At home, the Vietminh were concerned to maintain a broadly united national front and to consolidate their hold in the "liberated" areas. Abroad, the two major Soviet considerations affecting their Indochina policy were France and China. In general, Soviet interests in national liberation movements were secondary to their policies in the West. Soviet attitudes to the movements were accordingly a function of their nuisance value against the European metropolitan powers, with whom Moscow was soon engaged in mounting hostility.

In France, however, the communists were within sight of political power. A communist France was a more glittering prize than a communist Indochina. In order to appease nationalist (or imperialist) sentiment in France, therefore, both the communist character and the militancy of the Vietminh demands for independence had to be toned down. Thus on 10 December 1946, less than ten days before the eruption of war in Indochina, Ho affirmed "the sincere desire of the Vietnamese Government and people to collaborate fraternally with the French people" and "to be part of the French Union."[24] During the civil war in Vietnam, Soviet commentaries were careful not to attack the French government of Leon Blum as long as it included the communists. Even afterward, while Soviet comments were no longer circumspect as to the official French role in the war, and while sympathy for the Vietminh cause was unsparing, the USSR would not commit itself to any specific course of action.

Soviet caution in Indochina may in part be attributable to developments in China and the probable American responses to them. If a combined China-Vietnam revolution would be a mighty blow to Western imperialism, Vietnam could equally be used as a base against China. The United States was seen by Soviet analysts to be Bao Dai's chief supporter. His installation as Emperor in June 1949 was taken as proof of the growing French dependence on the United States. Hence Moscow's unease at the prospects of escalation in the Indochina war. With Mao firmly established in Peking in October 1949, one need for restraint was removed. On 14 January 1950, Ho Chi Minh requested recognition of his regime from all countries. China and the USSR did so on 18 and 30 January respectively, with Poland following suit on 3 February. The reasoning behind the Soviet recognition[25] failed to indicate any new circumstance that justified the act more than five years after the proclamation of the DRVN. But after recognition Peking and Moscow were able to present the Vietminh struggle not as an insurgency but as legitimate national defense. The Korean war of June 1950 intensified communist apprehensions of American designs on the region. On 12 December 1950, *Pravda* endorsed a Chinese argument that attack on North Korea was one part of an American "three-pronged invasion" of mainland China—Formosa and Vietnam being the other two. In 1950 the

Vietminh began receiving modest assistance from China, the tempo of which accelerated as the pace of the war picked up.[26] There has been speculation that at one stage China was considering openly intervening in Indochina.[27]

In Europe, in the meantime, the USSR became increasingly alarmed over the prospects of a United States-led defense alliance incorporating within its structure a remilitarized Germany. Many seemed to believe that Moscow agreed to aid France to disengage itself from Indochina in 1954 as a *quid pro quo* for a French veto of the European Defense Community.[28] Another reason behind Moscow's desire for caution was the danger of American military intervention, in which Indochina could become an American base. Finally, prolonging the war could extend Chinese penetration into the area and reduce Soviet maneuverability. Peking's prestige was at its height after the rout of the Kuomintang in China and the paralysis of United Nations forces in Korea. A common Asian identity gave China yet another edge over the USSR in their competition for influence. All this helps explain the Soviet interest in the forthcoming Geneva negotiations in 1954, and its restrained coverage of the Indochina war in the months leading up to the Conference.

Indochina was similarly expendable in the Chinese scheme of things. The possibility of American bases at its frontier as a result of a continuing war was naturally even less attractive to the Chinese than to the Soviets. On the other hand, a complete military victory for the Vietminh could result in the creation of a moderately powerful Vietnam that looked to the USSR to balance Chinese preponderance. Alternatively, a negotiated settlement that established the Vietminh along China's borders but denied them all of Vietnam could neutralize both of China's concerns. Moreover, a conference at which China was an invited, indispensable, and equal participant with the great powers would be a stunning diplomatic coup for the infant communist regime in Peking.

Soviet and Chinese interests in the Geneva Conference were thus complementary, not identical. But they dovetailed in such a manner as to make the convening of the Conference propitious insofar as prospects for a negotiated end to the Indochina war were concerned.

The West
It remains but to mention a few key Anglo-American statements before taking up the Geneva Conference proper. After the recognition

accorded to the DRVN, an American State Department spokesman commented on 31 January 1950 that Ho had "a long record under various *aliases* as a Moscow agent." He declared further that "the fact of recognition by Moscow should destroy any illusion of Ho Chi-minh as a purely Nationalist leader, and place him in his true position as an agent of world communism." In response, twenty-five Western countries, including the United Kingdom and the United States, but not Canada, recognized Bao Dai's State of Vietnam on 7 February 1950. The Americans upgraded representation to a legation in Saigon in 1950, and exchanged ambassadors in July 1952.

In March 1954, American Secretary of State John Foster Dulles declared that "the imposition on Southeast Asia of the political system of Communist Russia and its Chinese Communist ally, *by whatever means*, would be a grave threat to the whole free community." This "possibility should not be passively accepted, but should be met by united action."[29] The statement disturbed Nehru greatly because of its hints of extending and intensifying the war, and transforming it into an international war. In Canada, Pearson declined to comment, on the grounds that he would prefer an analysis and an explanation of the statement before commenting.[30]

Great Britain welcomed the idea of a permanent collective defense organization for Southeast Asia, but was opposed to discussions on the subject until after the Geneva Conference, for reasons similar to Nehru's. There was some confusion created on this score by the Dulles–Anthony Eden London communiqué of 13 April 1954. The statement deplored the intensification of communist activities on the eve of the Conference, and asserted a readiness to examine "the possibility of establishing a collective defence" for Southeast Asia. "We believe," said Dulles and Eden, "that the prospect of establishing a unity of defensive purpose throughout Southeast Asia and the Western Pacific will contribute to an honourable peace in Indochina."[31] This was succeeded by a similar Franco-American statement the following day. Eden explained on 25 April (that is, the day after Nehru's attack on the call for united action) that the London communiqué did not commit Britain to immediate discussions on Allied intervention in Indochina. In fact, Britain was not prepared to give any undertakings in advance of the Geneva Conference for military action in Indochina, but would join in a collective defense organization after the Conference in order to guarantee any settlement that was reached.[32]

To remove any lingering doubts, Churchill tersely stated in Parliament on 27 April that

> Her Majesty's Government are not prepared to give any undertakings about United Kingdom military action in Indo-China in advance of the results of Geneva. We have not entered into any new political or military commitments.

Eden was very concerned about the stands taken by Asian nations, in particular India, because he believed that China would be reluctant to offend India and Asia at that early stage. He recognized that "India had an abiding interest in the outcome of the conference and could play a considerable part at Geneva behind the scenes." He therefore held it to be an essential minimum that India not be alienated in a part of the world that concerned it closely. He was aware, too, of the widespread suspicion in India that the Americans were determined to wreck the forthcoming Geneva Conference. Hence the British position that discussions on a defense organization should not proceed until after the Conference. Eden believed also that India should be given the opportunity to participate in such collective defense, and be kept fully informed of the discussions. "If they could not be with us, we must not put them against us," was his motto.

Dulles, however, given his strong antipathy to Nehru and to nonalignment, was firmly of the opinion that any indication that India might be invited to join must be avoided. When on 20 April Dulles convened an ambassadorial meeting of the United States, the United Kingdom, Australia, New Zealand, France, Philippines, Thailand, and the three Indochinese Associated States, to investigate setting up an informal working group to study collective defense of Southeast Asia, Eden was upset. He thought the timing poor, was sorry that neither India nor Burma had been consulted, and felt the meeting would be insulting to them both and therefore harmful in its effects on the Geneva Conference.

Eden's instruction to his ambassador in Washington makes interesting reading: "Americans may think the time past when they need consider the feelings or difficulties of their allies. . . . We, at least, have constantly to bear in mind all our Commonwealth partners, even if the United States does not like some of them. . . . "[33] It was too late to cancel the meeting, but Eden did succeed in turning it into a general briefing on the upcoming Geneva negotiations. The interesting part of the statement is the revelation that Eden was attracted so strongly to India because of its Commonwealth connection and his commitment to the principle of Commonwealth consultations.

The Geneva Conference

The Geneva Conference on Indochina held its first formal session on 9 May 1954, and its last on 21 July. There were a total of eight plenary and eighteen restricted sessions. Participants were China, France, the United Kingdom, the United States, the USSR, Laos, Cambodia, and the two governments of Vietnam. Krishna Menon of India also assisted, while Canada kept itself informed of developments through contacts with several delegations.[34] Eden and Molotov alternated as chairmen.

One of the issues at Geneva, one that would have recurring importance for Canada, was the question of alliance solidarity. The Korean phase of the Conference involved differences of opinion between the Americans and the British Commonwealth members of the United Nations side. The British, according to one member of the Canadian delegation, considered the Korean conference less important than the Indochinese, and were not, therefore, prepared to split with the Americans. The Canadians and New Zealanders fought against the American and South Korean points of resistance, but accepted the majority position for the sake of unity.[35] To another member of the Canadian delegation, the Americans appeared to be intent upon proving that there could be no political solution by negotiating with communists.[36] In the end, Canada faced the choice of breaking with the Americans and South Koreans, or going along with them in the name of unity and breaking up the Conference. Canada was the last in the United Nations group to give its reluctant consent to termination of the conference "due to United States persuasion or pressure—depending on your point of view."[37] Regarding the Indochina conference, Anthony Eden has written of intense American pressure to maintain Western unity. Britain, however, was determined not to "endorse a bad policy for the sake of unity," and Eden's Commonwealth partners supported his position. He writes that the Americans "seemed deeply apprehensive of reaching any agreement, however innocuous, with the communists."[38]

Anglo-American differences persisted, especially on the question of possible military action in Indochina. The garrison of Dien Bien Phu fell to the Vietminh on 7 May, on the eve of the Geneva Conference. Canada, in response to this "tragic ending," conveyed a message to France in which, along with "all free men," it saluted the heroic defenders; George Drew, the Opposition leader, expressed approval of the message.[39] The American response was stronger. Dulles stated on 7 May that "The United States and other countries immediately concerned are giving careful consideration to the establishment of a collective defense."[40] Eden read in the Swiss papers of 15 May that France and the United States were discussing the possibility of American military intervention in Indochina, either after the failure of the Geneva Conference, or earlier if the French so desired. In the event, France decided to wait while the Conference was in session. Eden also reports how the Americans wanted to go back to plenary sessions when no progress was made at two restricted sessions. He was "flabbergasted" and refused. On 15 June, Bedell Smith, the American delegate, received a telegram from President Dwight Eisenhower directing him to terminate the Conference as rapidly as possible.[41] In the opinion of John Holmes, a member of the Canadian delegation at Geneva, "Dulles did not really want the Geneva negotiations to succeed."[42]

Earlier, at a news conference on 8 June, Dulles accused the communists of deliberately dragging out negotiations while stepping up the military effort. He in effect dissociated himself and his country from the Conference decisions even at this early date by stating that the United States "is playing primarily the role of a friend which gives advice when it is asked for. . . . " Three days later, he spelled out the conditions that would justify American intervention: invitation from the legal governments, complete independence to the Indochinese states, evidence of United Nations concern, collective regional defense, and persistence by France.[43]

The reasons for British hesitation about military intervention were expounded in Parliament by Eden on 23 June. He explained that air action alone would not have been effective (in saving Dien Bien Phu), that military intervention would have destroyed the chances of a settlement at Geneva, and that it might have led to a general war in Asia. The Churchill-Eisenhower communiqué of 28 June indicated, nevertheless, that Britain and the United States were discussing possible consequences of success and failure at Geneva: "We will press forward with plans for collective defence to meet either eventuality."

The sustained and consistent American opposition to the Geneva negotiations was merely confirmed with the publication of the Pentagon Papers documents in 1971. The President's Special Committee on Indochina concluded on 17 March 1954 that "no solution to the Indochina problem short of victory is acceptable." If the French decided nonetheless to accept a negotiated settlement at the Geneva Conference, the United States was to dissociate itself from such a settlement.[44] On 5 April, the committee reaffirmed its previous policy and urged that "all possible political and economic pressure on France" be exerted to ensure a continuation of the effort.[45] On 12 May, Dulles cabled presidential instructions to his delegation that the United States would not associate itself with any agreement that gave recognition or territory to the Vietminh.[46] On 10 July, Dulles informed Pierre Mendes-France of American fears that France would accept a settlement that fell short of the minimum acceptable; the United States could not endorse such a settlement.[47]

The Geneva Agreements on Indochina[48] comprised three bilateral cease-fire arrangements, eight unilateral declarations, and the Final Declaration of the Conference. The last remained unsigned; the Americans would not associate themselves with it, and China insisted that everyone else sign before affixing its own signature. The declaration escaped the problem by merely listing the conference participants. In summary, the Geneva settlement recognized the independence of Laos, Cambodia, and Vietnam. While Vietnamese unity was accepted in principle, the country was temporarily placed under two separate administrations, with the 17th parallel constituting the line of demarcation. The country was to be reunited by means of elections in July 1956.

Cease-fires were to be effected in the three countries on different dates, and French and Vietminh forces were to be withdrawn from specified regions within prescribed time limits. There were provisions regarding the exchange of civilian internees and prisoners of war. Recrimination and foreign military bases in Vietanm were prohibited (bases for self-defense were permitted in Laos and Cambodia). The contending parties were given primary responsibility for the execution of the Agreements, under the supervision of an international commission in each country consisting of Canada, India, and Poland, with India presiding.

The Americans were obviously displeased with the results of the Conference, and issued instead a Unilateral Declaration. At a news conference on 21 July, President Eisenhower expressed satisfaction that bloodshed had been stopped, but reiterated that the United States" has not itself been party to or bound by the decisions taken by the Conference."⁴⁹ He revealed that discussions were under way toward the rapid organization of collective defense for Southeast Asia. Two days later, Dulles conceded that the Agreements "contain many features which we do not like," a reflection of the military situation in Indochina. The lesson to be learned was that collective defense needed to be arranged "in advance of aggression, not after it is under way. . . . The important thing from now is not to mourn the past but to seize the future opportunity to prevent the loss in northern Viet-Nam from leading to the extension of communism throughout Southeast Asia and the Southwest Pacific."⁵⁰ Perhaps the most significant word in his statement, from the point of view of understanding American policy, is "loss" with respect to the establishment of a communist regime in northern Vietnam. The point was underlined in the classified intelligence assessment of 3 August 1954 that the Agreements had "accorded international recognition to Communist military and political power in Indochina and [had] given that power a defined geographic base."⁵¹

The feelings in India were strikingly opposite; the Geneva Agreements were seen to be triumphs of Asian generalship and Asian opinion over American-supported European colonialism. It was a matter of pride that the Agreements, apart from the cease-fire, were Indian ideas, as incorporated in *Panchsheel:* independence, neutralization, noninterference by foreigners. As a corollary, failure of the Geneva Agreements would be a failure of *Panchsheel* in Indochina (that is, within Asia), so India was doubly committed to their implementation. Even the cease-fire had been appealed for in February by Nehru. By reason of the Agreements, France (that is, European colonialism), was to withdraw from Indochina, and China and the United States were not to intervene. India, for its part, without having to guarantee the Agreements, was provided with an institutional channel in the supervisory commissions for exercising influence in the region. Not surprisingly, India would consistently argue for a return to the Geneva Agreements, and for the "Geneva spirit" as opposed to legal technicalities.

What part did India play at Geneva? We have seen how Anglo-American discord was based on differences, first on the question of military intervention, and second on the role of India. It was shown earlier how 1954 was one of the worst periods for Indo-American relations and remarkably good for Indo-Russian and Sino-Indian. In early 1954, for instance, Nehru reacted harshly to a speech by Walter S. Robertson, the American Assistant Secretary of State, where he argued that the United States must "dominate Asia for an indefinite period." Asia was not prepared to be dominated, by America or anyone else: "the countries of Asia, and certainly India, do not propose to be dominated by any country for whatever purpose."[52] Speaking about the *loss* of a part of Vietnam would only reinforce suspicions about Western motives. In Southeast Asia specifically, Indian and American approaches were mutually exclusive, advocating extensions of the areas of peace and collective defense respectively, and led to mutual irritations.

The British position was that a peace settlement, to be viable, would have to be guaranteed by the major Asian powers, including at least the benevolent neutrality of India. Eden maintained a close accord with other Commonwealth members throughout the Geneva Conference. He maintained communication also with the Colombo powers, three of whom belonged to the Commonwealth. In fact, Eden suggested that the supervisory tasks be entrusted to the Colombo countries, who were both Asian and neutral; they were also largely Commonwealth. During the Colombo Conference, Eden inquired by telegram on 29 April how far the Colombo states would be prepared to associate themselves with any settlement reached at Geneva.

Eden was to some extent responsible for assuaging Asian resentment at exclusion from Geneva. His courting of India was based on the realization that since communism was as much a political problem as a military menace in Asia, Western intervention in order to be militarily effective must have Asian political support. He felt, too, that Nehru's statement of 24 April indicated that Indian endorsement of a negotiated settlement could be obtained. Churchill himself promised to keep in close touch with the Colombo powers to give their views every consideration. The promise was kept to the end. As late as 17 July, for instance, Eden sent a message to Australia, New Zealand, and the five Colombo powers suggesting that if a settlement were reached at Geneva, they should quickly associate themselves with it. Conversely, if a settlement could not be reached, then they should consider joining in a collective defense organization.[53]

Nehru's reply to Eden's query of 29 April was reassuring but noncommittal. Eden, however, persisted, till finally on 15 May Nehru agreed to Indian assistance in "promoting and maintaining a settlement in Indochina," provided that any agreement received the backing of all parties, and that obligations did not counter its policy of nonalignment or stretch its limited resources. Nehru explained his decisions on the grounds that India could not simply wash its hands of the affair: "We cannot shed the responsibilities that go with a great country."[54] In fulfillment of the undertaking, Nehru dispatched Krishna Menon to Geneva. Menon arrived in Geneva on 23 May, and stayed for three months. In his own inimitable language, "we didn't stand on dignity; we just stood on the doorstep and tried to be helpful."[55] It is impossible to state with precision what and over whom Menon's influence was; suffice it to say that "for all practical purposes, Menon was a participant in the Geneva Conference."[56]

Also significant was the three-day visit to India of Premier Chou En-lai in June. It was Chou's first visit to a noncommunist Asian country, a prestigious Chinese debut into the Afro-Asian world so far denied to it by American diplomacy. The Nehru-Chou talks, which coincided with the Churchill-Eisenhower meeting in Washington, naturally centered on Indochina. *Le Monde* described the New Delhi talks as "an extension of the Asian Conference of Geneva" between China the unwelcome invitee and India the official outcast.[57] The Chou-Nehru communiqué of 28 June 1954 reaffirmed the five principles of peaceful coexistence, and urged their application in the settlement of the Indochina conflict. For India, *Panchsheel* was a means to get China to commit itself publicly to noninterference in Southeast Asia, and thereby to obviate any need for American intervention. For China, the doctrine could be helpful in keeping a hostile America away from its southern borders, as well as in ensuring Indian nonmembership in any regional defense organization that might be established.

The Geneva settlement was hailed by all in India. A year later, Nehru was to speak of the Agreements as symbolizing the achievement of peace in Asia through coexistence. It was a matter of pride for Indians that their country should have been included in all the three main proposals regarding the composition of the international commission. The initial Chinese and Soviet proposals suggested four "neutrals": Czechoslovakia, Poland, India, and Pakistan. Eden strongly favored the five Colombo countries. The Conference finally decided on 19 July to accept the Chinese proposal submitted the day before. Nehru pointed out that "a place for India on the Commissions was proposed by every participant and on every occasion," and India could not therefore decline invitation to ICSC membership. Since "India's chairmanship of the Commissions became one of the necessities for a settlement," he said, "our refusal would have meant imperilling the whole agreement." India had no illusions about the task, not after its experiences in Korea. Nehru thus spoke of India's having to "shoulder this heavy and onerous responsibility." A mitigating factor, however, was that "we have been fortunate in our colleagues and in our relations with the parties in Indochina." Two additional factors favoring Indian acceptance of the ICSC membership were that "Asia has greater hopes of peace and stability as a result of the Indo-China settlement," and that the Indochinese states were precluded from joining military alliances and thus "bid fair to find a place in collective peace rather than in war blocs."[58] Finally, Nehru did not fail to point out that the Geneva Agreements were "remarkably" similar to the Colombo proposals, which were in turn based on his own, and that this placed a sort of responsibility and obligation on India to participate in the execution of the Agreements.[59]

Canada, like India, was not a participant in the Indochina half of the Geneva Conference. Nevertheless, again like India, it was fully abreast of developments at the Conference. Chester Ronning of the Canadian delegation had the unique distinction among Western delegates of being able to speak to Chou En-lai in Chinese, while Pearson, described by some Americans as "Swami Pearson" because of his suspicious partiality toward India, could "mediate" between the Americans and Krishna Menon.[60] The Canadian position tended generally to follow British rather than American leads.

In a detailed statement of Canada's position vis-à-vis the Geneva Conference, Pearson explained in Parliament that Canadian interest arose from a material consideration. If the Indochinese situation deteriorated into conflict, he said, the consequences "would certainly concern us and might involve us." He could see two short-term problems: how to terminate the conflict on terms acceptable to France, and how to secure free Asian participation in a guarantee of the settlement. The long-range problem was to establish a security system in the region with a maximum of free Asian participation. The British emphasized that war must first be terminated and the question of collective security left for future consideration, but the Americans pressed for treating the two concurrently. Pearson did not indicate the Canadian preference, but chose rather to warn that "it would be the greatest possible tragedy if Asia were allowed to split the West." His suggestions for a settlement included a recognition of communist advances in Southeast Asia, whose danger "cannot be exorcised by comforting interpretations of Asian communism as merely agrarian reform or as nationalism painted red." Regional collective defense arrangements were therefore needed, but within the United Nations Charter and embracing more than military means. Because of its limited size and resources, Canada would be unable to participate in such a scheme.[61]

Canada came out of the Geneva Conference more involved in Indochina affairs than it had been at the start. It was named as one of three delegations to the supervisory commissions in Laos, Cambodia, and Vietnam, with India and Poland being the others. Ottawa accepted the invitation after a week's deliberation, and with public reluctance. In a press release on 28 July,[62] the government demonstrated an awareness of the complexities and difficulties that lay ahead. Indochina was geographically distant, the United Nations was not associated with the settlement or its aftermath, and Canada had to bear in mind relations with the United States, which had withheld support. "In the early stages the Americans offered us neither support nor understanding, going no farther than to say that if there was to be a Commission they would prefer to have us on it."[63]

It was recognized, however, that the composition of the commissions had been one of the most delicate points of negotiations at Geneva.[64] Ottawa appreciated, therefore, that a refusal on its part could jeopardize the whole settlement. Even so, the Canadian statement of acceptance was full of cautions. It emphasized that the primary responsibility for execution of the Agreements lay with the parties themselves, and that the commissions were supervisory, with no enforcement obligation. Canada believed that the commissions had a reasonable chance of operating effectively, but if hopes were belied, then "no useful purpose would be served by continuing their existence." In short, as the Department of External Affairs put it, acceptance "did not mean that Canada was called upon to guarantee or enforce the Indochina cease-fire or undertake any new military or collective security commitments."⁶⁵ The caveats did not facilitate a Canadian withdrawal from a commission moribund in Vietnam in the 1960s; but they may have paved the way for the withdrawal from the second supervisory commission in Vietnam in 1973.

Canada's public utterances were underlined in Pearson's personal messages to Eden and Nehru. He assured Eden that Canada would not evade its new responsibility, "which may, however, turn out to be as onerous as it certainly was unsought." His letter to Nehru is interesting in that it shows their respect for each other. As it was with regard to India, so it was with respect to Canada; the Canadian decision to participate, wrote Pearson, was "determined in no small measure by the knowledge that in this onerous task we will be collaborating with India, with whom we enjoy close, friendly relations."⁶⁶

Conclusion

In Article 6 of the Final Declaration, the Geneva Conference recognized that "the essential purpose of the Agreement relating to Viet Nam is to settle military questions with a view to ending hostilities," arguing that execution of the provisions of the Geneva Agreements "creates the necessary basis for the achievement in the near future of a political settlement in Viet Nam." The Geneva Agreements were a success in that they terminated the eight-year war in Indochina, and provided the mechanism for extricating France from Indochina. They might also be said, as Eden did say, to have achieved the best that was possible under the circumstances of the time: the British position of amputating the infected limb had carried the day.

The Geneva settlement failed, however, to produce a final political solution to Vietnam, even though it provided the framework within which a solution could have been achieved. At the heart of the political problem was the Conference's implicit recognition of two Vietnamese governments, both exerting claims to what continued to be recognized as one national territory. The problem would dog efforts at peace in Vietnam in the years to come, and would be solved only by force of arms in 1975.

The prospects for the political future were not made any brighter by the fact that neither claimant to Vietnam was happy with the outcome of Geneva. The *New York Times* reported on 25 July 1954 that the DRVN delegation at Geneva believed that it could have won all of Tonkin and most of Annam, Cochin China, Laos, and Cambodia within a year if the war had continued, but that the Soviets and the Chinese had pressured them to acquiesce in the settlement. Indeed, there would be no quarrel with the statement that the Vietminh gained less at Geneva than their military possibilities in the field would have gained them, because of Chinese and Soviet concessions to the West. On the question of the demarcation line, for example, France demanded the 18th parallel, while Pham Van Dong began by claiming the 13th, then moving up to the 14th. The Chinese shifted it to the 16th, and on 20 July, Molotov settled on the 17th. Similarly, on the question of elections, France had wished to avoid specifying any dates, while the Vietminh demanded elections within six months. Molotov proposed sixteen months on 15 July, and then suggested two years on 20 July.

In the meantime, on 15-16 June, Chou En-lai informed Eden that he could persuade the Vietminh to withdraw from Laos and Cambodia, and would even be prepared to recognize their royal governments, in return for a promise that no American bases be permitted in these territories.[67] After his New Delhi visit, Chou traveled to the Sino-Vietnamese border to meet Ho Chi Minh (3–5 July). In all probability he used the occasion to obtain Ho's assent to the settlement shaping up at Geneva. Their communiqué was surprisingly brief and curt; perhaps there had been disagreement. The three-sentence communiqué merely stated the fact of the talks, listed those present, and recorded that Chou and Ho had exchanged views on the Geneva talks on Indochina.[68] With the divergence of Soviet and Chinese policies, North Vietnamese freedom of maneuver would be greatly enlarged in the American phase of the war.

Ngo Dinh Diem, strongly nationalist and pro-American, became Premier of Bao Dai's State of Vietnam in June 1954. On 4 July 1954, France had by a treaty recognized Vietnam's independence for the fifth time, but on this occasion as a sovereign and fully independent state "endowed with all the powers recognized by international law." Since there were two claimants to Vietnam, however, the French were able to negotiate at Geneva over the heads of the South Vietnamese. At the eighth (concluding) plenary session at Geneva on 21 July, Tran Van Do, leader of the South Vietnamese delegation, declared that the French High Command exercised power over the Vietnamese forces only by a delegation of powers from their Chief of Staff, and protested against several clauses of the agreement "of a nature seriously to compromise the political future of the Vietnamese people."

> In consequence, the Government of the State of Viet-Nam asks that it be officially noted that it solemnly protests against the manner in which the armistice has been concluded and against the conditions of that armistice, which do not take into consideration the profound aspirations of the Vietnamese people, and that it reserves for itself complete liberty of action in order to safeguard the sacred right of the Vietnamese people to territorial unity, national independence and liberty.[69]

At the time, such declarations could be dismissed as ravings not reflecting the military realities. In fact, the South Vietnamese confidentially agreed with the Americans at Geneva that their position was "not practicable," but felt they must make their "moral position" clear to the world and to the Vietnamese people.[70] Nevertheless, South Vietnam had served notice that provisions of the Geneva Agreements could be executed only on its sufferance; what would be their status after the French High Command withdrew in 1956? Were they binding on South Vietnam? Or on any other third parties, for example, the United States? The Final Declaration, the legal status of which is itself subject to interpretation since it was not signed, envisaged elections in 1956; was it France or the State of Vietnam that would undertake consultations from July 1955 with the DRVN for the holding of the elections? The Final Declaration, in Article 11, reaffirmed the independence and sovereignty of the three Indochinese states, and in Article 10 provided for a French withdrawal of troops "at the request of the Governments concerned." France reiterated both points in its own declarations. Was this consistent with the fact of its actions as the sovereign at Geneva, and with the responsibilities it undertook in respect of the Agreements? Also ominous was the fact that of the nine participants at the Geneva Conference, only four positively endorsed the Final Declaration: China, France, the United Kingdom, and the USSR. That is, none of the immediate parties in the war that followed had endorsed the Final Declaration of Geneva in 1954; none of them were countries whose territories had been directly involved; and only one of them had been a party in the preceding war: France.[71]

The South Vietnamese attitude would assume concrete significance in later years because of American reinforcement. The United States did not join in the Final Declaration. Instead, it issued a declaration of its own on 21 July, wherein it took note of paragraphs 1 to 12 of the Final Declaration. By dissociating itself from paragraph 13, the United States washed its hands of any responsibility for ensuring the implementation of the Geneva Agreements. It also undertook to refrain from the threat or use of force to disturb the Agreements, but declared that it would regard any renewal of aggression with grave concern and as seriously endangering international peace and security. With respect to the South Vietnamese declaration, the United States "reiterates its traditional position that peoples are entitled to determine their own future."

The United States was not entirely displeased with the Geneva Agreements. The record of a telephone conversation between Eisenhower and Dulles (20 July) reveals that in the Administration's view, the two-year delay in elections gave the United States "fairly good time" to get ready. Moreover, Canada's presence on the ICSC would enable the United States to "block things."[72]

In sum, the Geneva Conference ended the hostilities in Indochina. Conditions for their resumption, however, had not been eliminated, for a political solution was left to the uncertain future.

The American involvement increased in later years. The British, on the other hand, steadily withdrew from international postures. After 1954, and in particular after the Suez Crisis in 1956, British interest and prestige in the Far East declined. This would have several consequences. To begin with, an important restraining factor on American decision-making would be removed. Britain with its Commonwealth structure had been at the center of diplomatic activity in Geneva. The removal of the British-cum-Commonwealth base would affect India and Canada as well. India would simultaneously lose an important medium to Washington and free itself of one restraint in criticizing America (if it so desired). For Canada, the removal of British influence on Far Eastern questions would mean the removal of its one substantive mechanism, outside of the United Nations, for moderating American policies. On its own, Canada could not realistically expect to mold American policies significantly. Another possible consequence could lie in Canadian-Indian relations bilaterally. In a very important sense, their deep friendship had been built upon the London-centered Commonwealth; would it survive the removal of the cement of British unity and direction of the Commonwealth's international postures?

And what of Canada and India directly? India's initial interests in the conflict stemmed from its perceptions of the war as one of anticolonialism; its later concern sprang more directly from its policy of nonalignment, to limit the area of conflict, to extend the area of peace, and to remove great-power involvement from an Asian region. Nevertheless, Nehru's statement in 1952 to an Indian cultural delegation going to China is germane: "Never forget that the basic challenge in South-East Asia is between India and China. That challenge runs along the spine of Asia."[73] For Canada, too, interest was directly a function of the internationalization of the conflict, but more through the fear of possible consequences upon the Western security system. At the same time, in their perceptions and sympathies, Canada and India had been on opposing sides regarding the Vietminh. The three members of the commissions in Indochina were quite definitely representatives of the three chief strands of international politics in 1954; Canada the Western, Poland the communist, and India the neutral. Clearly, the various proposals for commission composition had this in common, that they strove to achieve some sort of balance of world political forces. In 1954, if Canada was to be the spokesman for anyone, it would be for France, not the United States. The commission in Vietnam could be expected to be subjected to severe strains when the parameters of the conflict changed: the disputants were different; the international political structure had changed; and two of the ICSC members, India and Canada, which themselves underwent transformation, were caught in the crosscurrents.

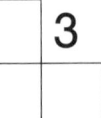 # 3 The Commission in Action
The Military Record

The Field Machinery

The ICSC was among the concrete achievements of the Geneva Agreements. It lasted until replaced by a new Commission pursuant to the Paris Accords in 1973. The Geneva Conference on Indochina was concerned to negotiate an armistice between the French Union Forces (FUF) and the Vietminh. In this it succeeded. The bulk of the ICSC activities during its first year of operation involved matters pertaining to the establishment and maintenance of a cease-fire, disengagement of forces, transfer of territories, and regroupment of units in zones assigned to the belligerents by the cease-fire agreements. Because the extrication of French forces from Vietnam was actively desired by both parties in the conflict, little dispute arose within the Commission in this early phase of its work.

The powers at Geneva, recognizing the dispersal of forces and the tenuousness of the communications links in the field, allowed for a graduated cease-fire in Vietnam. It came into effect in northern Vietnam on 27 July, in the central part on 1 August, and in southern Vietnam on 11 August 1954. At 8 A.M. on 11 August all of Vietnam was at peace. At that precise moment, in Hanoi's Hotel Metropole, representatives of Canada, India, and Poland "constituted" themselves into the International Commission in execution of the Geneva wish that the ICSC "shall be set up at the time of the cessation of hostilities." At its first meeting, the Commission dispatched a note of its constitution to the Geneva cochairmen, and adopted a simple set of procedures on the basis of the draft prepared at the preliminary meeting in New Delhi (1–6 August 1954). One of the rules stipulated that the ICSC "shall operate" with all three members present. At the conclusion of the meeting, the Commissioners traveled forty kilometers north to Trung Gia, where the Central Joint Commission was based.

The Two Commissions
On the basis of the Geneva Agreements, the Joint Commission was to ensure execution of the cease-fire, regroupment and demarcation lines, and demilitarized zones provisions. (The structure of the Joint Commission is shown in Figure 1.) Some of the control and supervision tasks of the International Commission were listed in Article 36, but its work by and large was left undefined. In practice, the International Commission was quite happy not to question the competence of the Joint Commission in respect of any matter with which it was seized, and thereby to minimize its own role. Unfortunately, however, the Agreements also provided for referral to the International Commission of any disputes on which the parties on the Joint Commission failed to agree. The predicament arose, therefore, that where the Joint Commission was able to agree, the International Commission was not required; but where the Joint Commission failed to agree, it merely transferred the locus of its intractability to the International Commission. Furthermore, it could be expected that the greater the strength of the differences in the Joint Commission, the more uncompromising would be the stands taken by the warring factions in the ICSC. Yet another implication was that the latter became a reactive body, responding to complaints rather than initiating investigations. Finally, and with increasing importance, the fact that the Joint Commission comprised Vietminh and *French* (rather than South Vietnamese) forces was to create complications of considerable difficulty.

The French High Command withdrew completely from South Vietnam in June 1956; the Joint Commission did not resume its functions in the Demilitarized Zone (DMZ) after May 1956. After that date, all matters that should have been dealt with by the Joint Commission were instead referred to the International Commission. The latter remarked in its seventh report that provisions of the Geneva Agreements pertaining to the DMZ and the PDL (Provisional Demarcation Line) would be jeopardized if the Joint Commission did not resume functioning. In the eighth report, the ICSC expressed concern at the failure of the Joint Commission to resume. Finally, in the ninth report of 10 March 1959, the ICSC reported the South Vietnamese view that it could not participate in Joint Commission activities at all, not being a signatory to the Geneva Agreements. The International Commission decided, therefore, that the FUF having withdrawn, the Joint Commission could not be revived.

FIGURE 1
Structure of the Joint Commission in Vietnam, 1954–55

(Renamed the Sub-Commission for the Demilitarized Zone, July 1955)

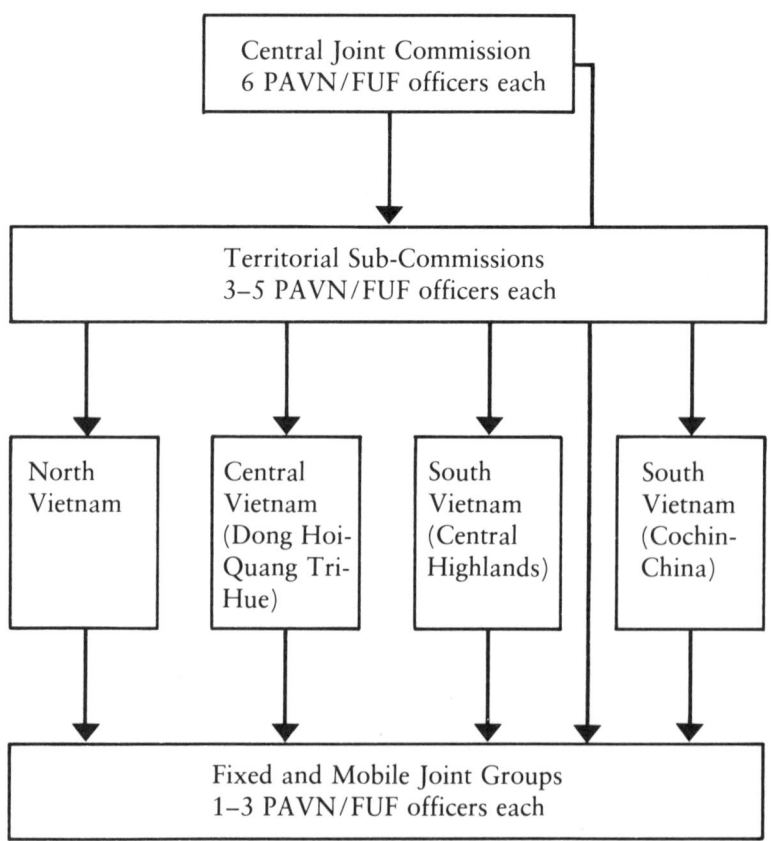

An example of the kinds of problems that arose in the confused situation is to be found in the ninth report. The Commission decided that in thirteen instances Saigon had violated Article 7 of the cease-fire agreement by issuing permits to enter the southern part of the DMZ, in that only the Joint Commission had the authority to decide on permits. South Vietnam's position was that in the absence of the Joint Commission, the chief of the Quang Tri province must have the power to issue permits, since to decide otherwise would be to effectively sever the relations of the DMZ with the rest of South Vietnam.

In this circular situation, then, South Vietnam would not agree to participate in the Joint Commission because it was not a signatory to the Agreement setting up the Joint Commission; and it would then arrogate to itself the functions given to the Joint Commission on the argument that since the latter was inoperative, someone had to perform the functions. In the meantime, there was no let-up in the number of complaints from either side about the alleged violations of the DMZ by the other party.

The ICSC was established in Hanoi on 11 August 1954, transferred its headquarters to Saigon on 31 March 1958,[1] and on 28 September 1972 it reverted to Hanoi for the final four months of its life. It comprised three delegations, one each from Canada, India, and Poland, with India presiding. The head of each delegation was accorded the personal rank of Ambassador. The additional members in a delegation consisted of a senior official known as alternate delegate, plus political and military advisers.

The various committees and teams set up by the Commission were also manned from among its delegations. There was an operations committee, composed of military advisers, which dealt with matters military; a freedoms committee of political advisers to deal with petitions; an administration committee; and a legal committee. There were in addition *ad hoc* committees to meet specific requirements. (The organizational structure of the ICSC is depicted in Figure 2.)

The Indian member, in addition to being the ICSC chairman, was the *ex officio* Secretary-General. The international secretariat was divided into three main branches, each headed by a Deputy Secretary-General: an administration branch, headed by an Indian, responsible for personnel, logistics, and liaison with the two high commands; an operations branch responsible for the Commission's

FIGURE 2
Organizational Structure of the ICSC Vietnam

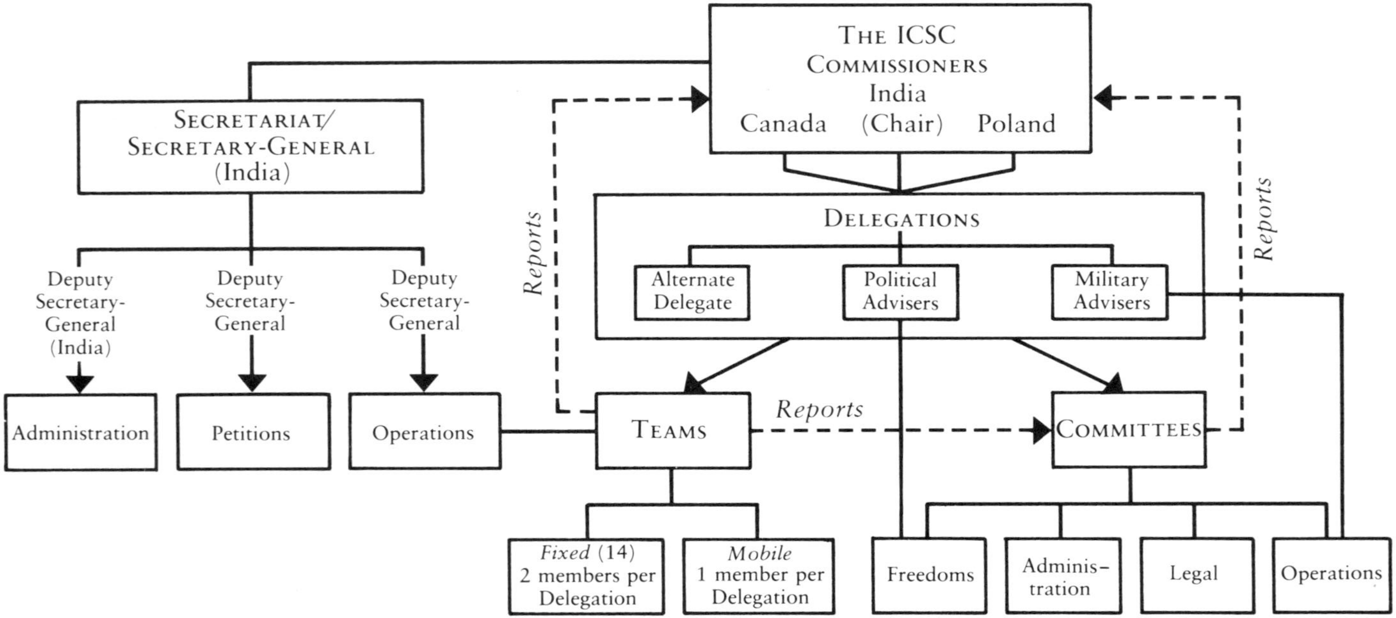

THE ICSC COMMISSIONERS
India (Chair)
Canada   Poland

DELEGATIONS
- Alternate Delegate
- Political Advisers
- Military Advisers

COMMITTEES
- Freedoms
- Administration
- Legal
- Operations

TEAMS
- Fixed (14) 2 members per Delegation
- Mobile 1 member per Delegation

SECRETARIAT/SECRETARY-GENERAL (India)
- Deputy Secretary-General (India) → Administration
- Deputy Secretary-General → Petitions
- Deputy Secretary-General → Operations

Reports

teams; and a petitions branch in charge of handling petitions from the public. (There was also a fourth, a public relations branch.)

The Commission teams were presided over by the Indian member well. In addition, their communications system with headquarters, as also with the four capitals of Hanoi, Saigon, Phnom Penh, and Vientiane, was operated entirely by the Indian Signals Corps. The bulk of the Commission's personnel were thus Indian. In March 1955, for instance, there were 160 Canadians (of which 135 were military personnel), about the same number of Poles, and 1,086 Indians (of which 941 were military personnel). This was in keeping with the decision at the New Delhi preparatory meeting that personnel of the international secretariat and the staff for the three ICSCs in Indochina would be provided principally by India. The proportion remained the same throughout the life of the Commission, even while the actual numbers declined sharply. The strength of the Commission dwindled from a peak of approximately 1,500 at the end of 1955 to some 300-odd by the end of 1971; as good an indication as any of the declining fortunes of the International Commission in Vietnam.

The mandate of the ICSC was supervisory, not executive; responsibility for the latter rested "with the parties." The tenure of the Commission was nowhere specified, though there is considerable plausibility to the argument that it was not expected to last much beyond two years. After 1956, the Commission subsisted with a progressively reduced staff, on sufferance. Yet the mandate was also too broad, in that the extent of the Commission's supervision was unlimited. As for decisional procedures, the general recommendations of the ICSC were to be made by majority vote. Certain classes of decisions required unanimity with respect to making recommendations to the parties; the Commission was still free to submit majority reports and minority statements to the members of the Geneva Conference. It was also required to inform the Geneva powers of refusals by the parties to implement ICSC reccommendations, as well as of cases where its activity was being hindered.

The Control System: Fixed and Mobile Teams and Their Movements
India's position in the control system was thus quite critical. It chaired the International Commission, presided over its teams,

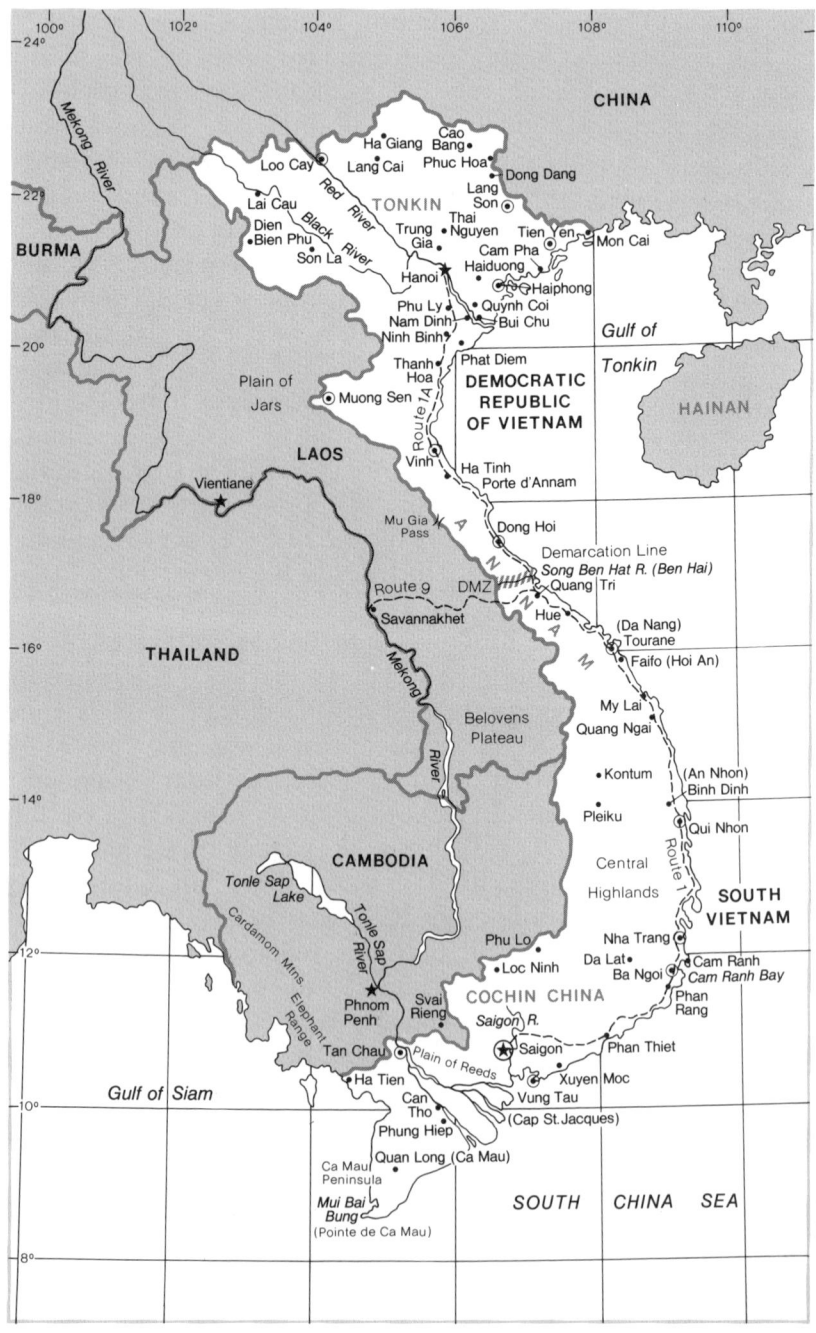

Vietnam after Geneva Agreements of 1954   ⊙ ICSC fixed team sites

was responsible for reporting the team findings to headquarters, and its citizens staffed the communications signals system. Article 35 of the Geneva Agreements declared that the International Commission "shall set up fixed and mobile inspection teams" composed of representatives of the three delegations in equal numbers. At the New Delhi preparatory conference, the delegations had decided upon the size of a fixed team at six and a mobile team at three. In addition, India provided ancillary personnel without any supervisory function. Although the size of the teams was supposed to have been left open to readjustments in the light of experience, they became almost fixed, both because of the difficulty of securing unanimous agreement to an amendment and because of the reluctance of all delegations, especially Canadian, to strain their resources even more by any further investment of manpower in Indochina.

Fourteen "legal" points of entry were specified as the locations for the fixed teams (see Map). The ICSC was also empowered to form mobile teams that would have complete freedom of movement in the border areas, along the demarcation line, and in the DMZ. For movement beyond these "zones of action," mobile teams could function only "by agreement with the command of the party concerned." To the extent that the Commission would have to declare a team's destination and purpose, the element of surprise would be lacking, and its verification effectiveness reduced. Along with the reductions in personnel strength, the number of mobile teams set up by the ICSC is also a good barometer of the pace of its activities. From an average of ten per month in its first year of operation, the Commission authorized only one investigation in two months for the last year of its regular report (1961). While some mobile teams had a life of only hours, most remained in the field for about a week; one, Mobile Team 76, formed on 12 July 1955 to supervise the PDL, was in existence until 1 April 1968. Undoubtedly, the chief reason for the decline in mobile investigation teams was that the main military provisions of the Geneva Agreements were required to be executed within three hundred days.

A second reason for the steady decline in the frequency of investigations concerns, not a lessening of complaints, but the issue of the rights and duties of the teams. The Commission's teams, its "eyes and ears," needed complete freedom of maneuver, including logistical, if their verification role was to have credibility. The effectiveness of the control and supervisory functions of the ICSC, in turn, depended on the credibility of the investigative procedures of the inspection teams. At the same time, however, the principle of respect for the sovereignty of the local states clashed with the principle of total freedom of movement, without let or hindrance. In Vietnam, where the advantage in the field lay with the Vietminh forces, and where it was the Vietminh who had suffered political losses at Geneva in comparison with their military situation, a rigid adherence to the military *status quo* would work to the advantage of North Vietnam. Preserving the *status quo* would also, however, enable a better consolidation of South Vietnam. By the same token, the temptations to test the truce would in the military sphere have to be resisted by the PAVN forces, especially any local units that chafed at the Geneva losses. Furthermore, if the key political provisions of Geneva were to be dishonored, North Vietnam was the more likely candidate to take to the military offensive again.[2]

It was, therefore, in the North Vietnamese interest to limit the scope of ICSC investigations of disturbances of the military truce, with the important exception of the clauses that prohibited changes in the *status quo* in regard to the military potential of the two sides. Conversely, it would be in South Vietnam's interest to press for detailed investigations—until the American military machine started rolling in. As for France, it was only natural that it should be in favor of absolute control over the military truce so as to facilitate and not endanger its extrication. As a reflection of these interests in the Commission itself, one would expect Poland to be lukewarm to proposals for strengthening the investigative machinery. (That is, unless the Geneva pattern was to be repeated, of coercing the DRVN into executing all provisions scrupulously in the larger interests of the great powers.) Canada could be expected to push for an active and effective Commission role in searching out violations of the truce agreement. India one would expect to be ambivalent. There was clearly a strong commitment to ensuring the success of the Geneva Agreements, for reasons given in the preceding chapter, but there would be an equally strong reluctance to enforce the authority of an international body *over* the wishes of the local government(s), for fear of precedent-setting repercussions on its own border problems.

There was never any doubt that the Commission's teams would not have *complete* freedom of movement; the question rather was the extent to which the teams would be permitted operation even with fetters. At the twenty-fourth meeting of the Geneva Conference, the Soviet delegate had put forth the prevailing communist view that the teams must work on the principle of respect for the sovereignty and independence of the two parties. Since the question of reinforcements was of equal concern to both sides, the teams were permitted unfettered operation in the border regions, but not beyond. Nor could there by any alterations in the fixed team sites without the consent of the party concerned.

The debate over the rights and duties of its teams occupied the Commission until early 1955, and resulted in a progressively narrower view of its authority to act independently of the parties. Indeed, procedural and jurisdictional wranglings over the competence and terms of reference of the teams became a favorite mode of frustrating the intent of investigation. As the Commission was to report before too long,

> the provisions of Article 35 which require the concurrence of the High Command for Mobile Team investigations except along the frontiers and the dependence of the Commission's teams on local civil and military authorities for logistic and security arrangements has led to delays and even obstruction in some cases which have retarded the implementation of various Articles of the Agreement.[3]

The first test was not long in coming. Early in October 1954, two fixed teams (Dong Hoi and Lang Son) of the three established in the north reported restrictions on their movements. On 12 October, the ICSC unanimously took the position that the fixed teams should have complete freedom of movement in Vietnam. The Indian view, with Canadian and Polish concurrence, was that Articles 16–20 presupposed freedom of movement in the entire country. Moreover, the Commission took the debatable position that Article 35 specified the zones of action of only the mobile teams, and therefore implicitly recognized the whole country as the zone of action of the fixed teams. The Commission, therefore, divided Vietnam into fourteen administrative zones, for each of which one fixed team would be responsible. (Poland's position came as quite a surprise to Ottawa, which had been hoping for an early maximalist position by the Commission. Ottawa's strategy was to be able to clearly place the burden of noncooperation on Hanoi's—and Poland's—shoulders.)[4]

Poland began to retreat from the 12 October position before the month was out. While the FUF accepted the Commission's interpretation, the PAVN did not. The latter offered a more logical interpretation of Article 35, that a fixed team was to operate only at its location. North Vietnam suggested, however, that a fixed team could be transformed into a mobile team to carry out special duties, but that the movements of such mobile teams would be subject to the limitations of Article 35, namely, prior concurrence of the party concerned.

At the fifty-fourth meeting on 4 November, Poland withdrew from its earlier support of the Commission's position, to accept the PAVN interpretation. Canada and India resisted. Canada sought to move beyond the legalistic interpretation in seeking to derive the teams' mandate from the argument of the effectiveness of the Commission's supervisory role, and India tended to agree. In practical effect, the two pointed out, seeking to obtain local concurrence before acting on complaints or suspicions would give enough time to local parties to rectify offending situations. In Chairman M. J. Desai's words, a restrictive interpretation would inevitably mean "action after the event." With the Polish refusal to budge from its total support for the PAVN view, the Commission agreed to a Canadian compromise proposal, that fixed teams be allowed *observation* beyond their headquarters, but not investigation and inspection.

When the teams continued to experience "bureaucratic" frustrations in the field, it became necessary to tackle the question of specifying and delineating the "zones of action" of Article 35. In Commission debates during December, Canada argued for including all motorable roads within the teams' zones of action; Poland pressed for the principle of uniform width corridors. And it was in December that India began a cautious retreat to compromise solutions, from its earlier broad interpretation. Canada again argued from the premise that the most important consideration was the effectiveness of international supervision, and that the competence of the Commission should be presumed to extend accordingly in fulfillment of tasks clearly designated to it. Poland turned the statement on its head: the jurisdiction of the Commission must be presumed to stop where restrictions placed by the Agreements came into force. The Commission was not competent to impose greater restrictions on the sovereignty of the parties than they had accepted at Geneva, and in case of doubt, the Poles argued, the rule of restrictive interpretation should apply. That is, the interpretation that placed the *lesser* obligation on the sovereign state was to be accepted.

The Indian compromise was that it was better to start modestly than not at all, and therefore a restrictive interpretation should be accepted rather than the whole task imperiled in the quest for perfection. The chair put forward its practical solution to break the impasse on 21 December 1954. The zone of action in which the fixed teams would have unfettered freedom of action would be a ten-kilometer-wide strip of land following the land and sea frontiers of Vietnam. To satisfy the Canadians, communication routes that lay outside the strip were designated "spheres of action," through which mobile elements could travel freely to reach otherwise inaccessible points of their zones of action, but within which they could observe and record, but not inspect and investigate.

Canada and Poland accepted the formula, no doubt reluctantly. Canada's association was qualified with the reservation that the Commission retain the freedom to broaden its competence in the light of experience; this never materialized. The Commission did, however, uphold its broader definition of observation powers in the spheres of action in the face of restrictive attempts by the PAVN. Not that this translated into changing PAVN behavior in the field, where its interpretation carried *de facto* authority.

The zone of action, in sum, had been narrowed from the whole of Vietnam on 10 September to a ten-kilometer-wide strip on 21 December 1954. The debate also set the pattern for the positions of the three delegations in the ICSC: Poland would agree with North Vietnam, Canada would seek to shape the Commission into a forceful body willing to assert its authority, and India would move away from an initial broad view to a position of searching out the highest common factor, if necessary by compromise.

There were other problems that the teams faced in the field, all in themselves minor, but cumulatively cutting into the Commission's credibility. For example, each fixed team was served by a liaison officer, a military officer representing the party in whose territory the team operated. The Commission would naturally prefer its teams to act as independently as possible of the local parties, but it also needed the liaison officers to ensure the necessary services and protection. The latter in turn necessitated "time notice," advance notification to liaison officers of a fixed team's trip to observe or inspect. But the time notice requirement obviously contradicted the need for surprise for an inspection to be genuine. The dilemma was perhaps intrinsically insoluble. Its effect was to render the control system seriously defective: the teams could be immobilized by as simple an expedient as the liaison officer suffering from or feigning illness, or even vanishing for a day. The more cause a party had to hide anything, the less likely was its liaison mission to cooperate with a team's investigation. Not surprisingly, a party would rather be cited for not offering all possible cooperation to the ICSC, than to be found guilty of a gross violation of one or more of the substantive provisions of the armistice agreement. The former could also be explained away as being due to differences in the interpretation of "all possible assistance and cooperation."

The Commission reports did not devote much attention to the problem of the control system. Nevertheless, some of the later reports did hint at the difficulties encountered. In the August to December 1955 period, for instance, the Commission decided to send out sixteen mobile teams: twelve to PAVN territory, three to FUF territory, and one to the DMZ on both sides. Of the teams sent north, one (Mobile team F-44)[5] the Commission reported as having been hindered in its task by delaying and obstructionist tactics. All of the three teams sent to the French zone were referred by French authorities to the Government of the Republic of Viet Nam (RVN). The RVN, in turn, declined to grant concurrence to the dispatch of any of the three teams.[6]

The RVN was also cited for its insistence on forty-eight hours' or twenty-four hours' notice for the movement of ICSC teams, fixed or mobile respectively, in the south. Saigon argued inability to comply, on grounds of security, with the two-hour time notice required by the Commission. This was undoubtedly frustrating, in that it seriously hampered the movement of teams in the south, and there were instances of actual humiliation. Members of Mobile Team 76 were, within its own sphere of action, arrested by a village headman with the help of local inhabitants; the headman declared that he was acting on orders.[7]

The Commission went into some detail in its next report with respect to Mobile Team 88 at Phuc Hoa on the Sino-Vietnamese border. On 25 January 1956, the team had to be withdrawn from Phuc Hoa because of PAVN insistence that the tenure of the team could not be extended any further, and that logistic support to it was to be discontinued. On 8 February, Team 99 was established at Phuc Hoa, only to be withdrawn on 16 May 1956, due to the refusal of the PAVN High Command to implement Commission recommendations. For purposes of supervising and controlling execution of Articles 16–20 of the armistice, pertaining to a ban on the introduction of fresh troops and arms, and on the establishment of new military bases, the mobile element of the fixed team at Lang Son was given the additional task of controlling the area during the absence of mobile teams from Phuc Hoa.

The Commission's position was that continuous control by a mobile team at Phuc Hoa was essential to ensure the supervision of most of the important lines of communication near the border between North Vietnam and China. The PAVN position was even simpler. Maintenance of a mobile team for an indeterminate period, it argued, changed its character to that of a fixed team, which was contrary to the provisions of Article 35. In other words, the battle lines were being drawn again on the 1954 basis of different premises. The Commission sought to derive its mandate from the initial premise of effective supervisory capability, and the PAVN countered by defining the limits of supervisory jurisdiction according to explicit Agreements provisions.

There was, however, one crucial difference from 1954. This time the battle lines were made public, there was no compromise, and Poland broke ranks. The Commission held, over the dissenting voice of Poland, that it had full authority under Article 35 to keep mobile teams in operation in their zones of action for such periods as it considered necessary, and that such mobile teams did not constitute *de facto* fixed teams irrespective of the length of time they were kept in operation. In early 1956, then, on a substantive question of crucial importance, Poland refused to sign a citation against North Vietnam, and India acted firmly in a matter that could see increased Chinese involvement in the Vietnamese conflict and provide the Americans with a pretext for intervention.

The long ICSC-DRVN dispute on the status of indefinite mobile teams was apparently due to Hanoi's intention to smuggle tanks and trucks into North Vietnam. The USSR resisted DRVN demands on the Polish delegation on the subject of border control. In the Soviet view, the transport of tanks was not of sufficient military value to justify the political risks in having themselves and the Poles shown up as parties to violations of the Geneva Agreements at this early date (1955–56). Mieczyslaw Maneli writes that "Warsaw sent us instructions supporting the Soviet point of view," *viz.*, not to vote against the Indians and Canadians. In his opinion, Hanoi had been put up to the struggle with Moscow by the Chinese, who emerged with the appearance of being more concerned with Vietnam's military future than was the USSR.[8] After July 1956, Moscow began to lose ground to the Chinese, and the Polish delegation began to defend DRVN interests in the ICSC more actively.

Determining that it had the competence did not, of course, provide the Commission with the means to continue with a team at Phuc Hoa. It conveyed its decision to the PAVN High Command, but it also withdrew Mobile Teams 88 and 99. Nevertheless, it did state publicly, and in no uncertain terms, its version of the story:

> The Commission had made it clear that the decisions to withdraw the team were forced on the Commission because of the refusal of the P.A.V.N. High Command to implement the recommendations of the Commission and to extend the necessary cooperation to the teams.[9]

At the Commission's insistence, the North Vietnamese agreed on 19 July 1956 to the deployment of a new mobile team at Phuc Hoa. This they agreed to without prejudice to their own interpretation of Article 35; the question of tenure was simply left for later discussion. When, in subsequent months, the mobile team at Phuc Hoa continued to be opposed by the PAVN, the Commission decided to take action under Article 43 for nonimplementation of its recommendation.

The Polish delegation once again dissented, but failed to deter the Canadians and the Indians from recording a citation against North Vietnam. The problem remained, however, in that action under Article 43 was less than forceful: all that the Commission could do was "inform the members of the Geneva Conference" of the failure of a party to implement a recommendation. Since in practice "members of the Geneva Conference" was taken to mean the cochairmen, and since by July 1956 attitudes in and on Vietnam had become quite rigid, neither party in Vietnam was likely to be intimidated by an invocation of Article 43. It could virtually take for granted a split along ideological lines in any international body. Also, by August 1956, with the date for the all-Vietnam elections having passed, North Vietnam was not likely to be deterred by words alone from its efforts to begin the long preparation for the even longer war that was sure to come over the right to determine the destiny of Vietnam. It therefore continued its defiance of the International Commission. The Commission thus reported in its ninth report the inflexible attitude of the PAVN on Phuc Hoa. In the absence of a mobile team there, the mobile element of the fixed team at Dong Dang went out once a week in attempts at ICSC control of the northern boundary up to and including Phuc Hoa.

In a letter to Commissioner David Johnson on 23 March 1956, John Holmes conceded that the ICSC was unlikely to operate any more with unanimity. The Canadian delegation in Vietnam was therefore instructed to "shape the record" wherever possible, "so that we still have good grounds—relating to both north and south—for our decision to refuse further participation in the Commission's less useful functions."[10] The Phuc Hoa controversy was pressed by the Canadians to shape the record. In substantive terms it was immaterial—the ICSC control system in the north was clearly seen to be inadequate. Phuc Hoa was important, however, as a symbol of the ineffectual Commission control system. Moreover, a "rump commission" could serve quite well as a symbol of Geneva. A full complement of teams was unnecessary if they were unable to execute duties assigned to them; it would also be misleading in contributing to the illusion of ICSC control.

By 1959, South Vietnamese attitudes had hardened as well, and Canada's position on the Commission could be identified more closely with South Vietnam. Saigon persisted, for instance, in its view of time notice restrictions on movements of teams to certain areas in its zone. Not only that, one fixed team was unable to go out on control duties even after the Commission revised its time notice regulations. The Commission decided, therefore, that South Vietnam had failed to afford all possible assistance and cooperation under Article 25, as a result of which the Commission was unable to exercise control and supervision in terms of Article 36(d) at several places.

The RVN government was also informed of the Commission's intention to take action under Article 43. This time, Poland was able to join in the Commission's decision, while Canada found it necessary to dissent from the citation against South Vietnam. India was still soldiering on in its efforts to provide a semblance of international control of the cease-fire agreement. The ninth report also mentioned continuing difficulties in both zones in obtaining logistical support for inspection teams. The see-saw action continued when in the following year the PAVN rejected a Commission request for a visit by its fixed team to a point on the China-Vietnam border. In January 1960 the Commission converted its request into a recommendation, against the better judgment of Poland, but in vain.

The Commission's last public statement on the matter was continued in its famous special report of 2 June 1962. Therein, it brought to the notice of the cochairmen a recent and deliberate tendency on the part of both parties to deny or refuse controls to its teams, with a consequent near-complete breakdown in recent months in the Commission's supervision of Articles 16 and 17.[11] The Commission had thus gone through the full gamut of debating, declaring, and deploring, with no discernible impact upon the disputing factions at any point.

Preserving the Status Quo: Articles 16–20

The Geneva Agreements were predicated on the principle that until political differences could be resolved, military strengths should be frozen at existing levels. The technique adopted to maintain the military *status quo* was to deny the two sides means to increase military potential, while permitting them opportunities to replace men and material. Chapter III of the cease-fire agreement addressed itself to the problem by prohibiting five things: troop reinforcements and other military personnel outside of a "man-to-man" rotation program (Article 16); war material beyond a "piece-for-piece" replacement (Article 17); new military bases (Article 18); transfer of existing bases to foreign control (Article 19); and adherence to any military alliance or allowing the use of a zone to resume hostilities or further aggression (Article 19). Article 20 listed the fourteen points of entry, seven in each zone, for rotation of personnel and replacements of material. In other words, the Agreements did not demand nor even envisage a demobilization or demilitarization of the country, but merely sought to ensure a freeze in military strengths in order to facilitate the settlement of political issues. The Agreements failed even in this modest objective, but not before registering for the record, through reports of the International Commission, that the fault lay not in themselves but with the parties, in the plural.

Articles 16, 17
At the time of the Geneva Conference, the Vietminh forces either enjoyed supremacy in the field, or, at the very least, were precluded from being defeated at existing force levels. This, coupled with anxieties about possible American intervention, led the communist side to press more closely on the provisions prohibiting an increase in military strength after the cease-fire. The provision formed part of Pham Van Dong's first set of armistice proposals. The communist side also pressed for a tighter international supervision of these provisions, drawing in both respects — prohibition and supervision — on the Korean precedent. It should be borne in mind too that for reasons of geography and topography the ban on importation of men and material would be easier to supervise in the south than in the north.

A direct consequence of the differential rights to freedom of movement given the Commission's teams in the frontier and nonfrontier regions of Vietnam was an increased ability to supervise the ban on reinforcements relative to other clauses in the cease-fire agreement. The task would not be easy, however, in that Vietnam's frontiers comprise over 3,000 kilometers of land borders with China, Laos, and Cambodia, and almost 2,500 kilometers of coastline along the Gulf of Tonkin, the South China Sea, and the Gulf of Siam. In effect, at its peak coverage (fourteen fixed teams plus three special mobile teams on border supervisory duty) the Commission was attempting to control a complex 5,500-kilometer land and sea frontier by means of a surveillance strength of ninety-three personnel. In 1958, economizing measures reduced the size of the fixed teams to one member each from the three delegations.

A related problem the Commission was forced to grapple with early concerned the procedures to be followed by the teams in the course of their duties. Two problems that particularly vexed the Commission were notifications and inspections of shipments. The parties were required to notify the Commission (and, by ICSC requests in September and October, the appropriate fixed teams) two days in advance of any entry or egress of military personnel or material. By the end of 1954, it was clear that the control system was ineffective at the legal ports of entry themselves, let alone in zones beyond. The Commission received no notification of the arrival or departure of material until early 1955, because the Central Joint Commission in Trung Gia could not agree on a definition of "war material" under Article 17 or on the notification procedures.

The question was important because of the provision that, to facilitate rotation of personnel and replacement of parts in order to keep the military balance at the Geneva 1954 levels, credit be given to parties for exports against which corresponding imports could be permitted. In December, therefore, the Commission instructed its teams to inspect any shipment they wished to check, even if it was said not to contain any war material, and pressed the two sides to come to an agreed definition of "war material." In early January the Secretary-General prodded the two parties yet again, threatening that the Commission itself might be forced into determining what constituted war material. The Central Joint Commission finally reached agreement on the meaning of "war material" and on the means of implementing Articles 16 and 17 on 14 January 1955,[12] almost six months after the cease-fire agreement.

The difficulties caused by the delay in agreeing to terms of execution of Articles 16 and 17 are well illustrated with respect to French actions in southern Vietnam. In January 1955, the French Liaison Mission began to supply the Commission directly with "retroactive" schedules for movements of material dating back to October 1954. In their schedule of retroactive notifications, the French claimed to have exported more material between October and December than was replaced. The question arose whether they should be given a corresponding credit on their ledger. The Commission query as to why notification had not been received at the time brought the obvious response that no definition of war material had existed. Poland argued that no credit should be granted, because mandatory provisions of Article 17(e) had been ignored. Canada believed that credit should be given, if with a mild rebuke. India leaned toward the Polish view, but not very firmly, and decided that the French be asked whether they wanted credits. The French, apparently, never answered.

The question was of considerable import to the South Vietnamese, however, and they persevered in their efforts to obtain credit under Article 17(b) for war material exported by the French High Command from the time of the cease-fire until 30 June 1956 (when they left). The Commission did finally work out principles and procedures under which claims for credit were to be granted. Poland officially dissented from the granting of credit for war material taken out of Vietnam by the withdrawing French forces. The Commission sent a letter on the matter to the cochairmen, and forwarded copies of its decision to both parties. The PAVN High Command responded on 14 June 1958 that the Commission's decision was contrary to the spirit and letter of the Geneva Agreements as well as to Protocol 23 of the Central Joint Commission, and further, that it was beyond the competence of the Commission. The DRVN government had placed the matter before the cochairmen and requested a review of the ICSC decision. The Commission should, therefore, defer implementing its decision pending a recommendation by the cochairmen on the subject.

The Commission's answer to this apparent attempt at intimidation was a show of firmness. It informed the PAVN High Command that no communication had been received from the cochairmen, that it had considered all relevant opinions in coming to its decision, that it could find no provision in the Agreements for an appeal by the parties to the cochairmen against a decision of the ICSC, and that there was no provision for a deferral by the ICSC of an implementation of its decision pending such an appeal. The Polish delegation simply reiterated its earlier negative stand with regard to granting credits for war material withdrawn from Vietnam by the French Expeditionary Corps.[13] The effect created by the show of firmness was enhanced by the fact that the show was public.

The story of supervising Articles 16 and 17 beyond the ten-kilometer zone of action, in addition to the usual frustrations in both zones, is interesting in that it highlights two particular problems, namely, the principle of reciprocity and the politicization of technical issues. In its sixth report, the Commission pointed out the difficulties encountered in the reconnaissance of airfields because of South Vietnamese insistence on numerical parity in both the number and frequency of investigations in the two zones. The ICSC position was that action would be taken on the merits of each case individually, pursuant to specific complaints. South Vietnam responded by withholding full cooperation. For example, foreign aircraft would taxi directly to the military section of an airport, access to which would be denied to the ICSC team.[14]

The South Vietnamese position was generally supported by Canada. In the Canadian view, North Vietnam was in a better position to make specific complaints by virtue of its channels of information, including covert channels. Therefore, South Vietnam should not be vicitimized for seeking, in its insistence upon the objective principle of parity, to overcome the handicaps of an open society relative to a closed one. The Canadian delegation accordingly dissented from ICSC decisions of South Vietnamese violations of Article 25.[15] But when the Commission decided to accept the majority report of its Air Advisers' Team that no night landing facilities existed at Tourane airport in South Vietnam, it was Poland's turn to dissent.[16] In other words, by 1959–60, the delegations could not agree even on such technical matters as the existence of night landing facilities. Their positions were determined more by political alignments than by technical veracity.

Finally, the USSR shared the Indian position that airports should be under complete Commission control. Hanoi, however, failed to be persuaded by Soviet and Polish arguments. Therefore, for the first and only time, the Indians found themselves confronting a united Canadian-Polish stand in the legal committee. The Indian delegate remarked that "I never supposed that the Chinese intended to build so many airports in the North."[17]

The Southern Zone

SEATO
In the fall of 1954, the United States moved in two ways to stem the "loss" of Indochina to communist control. Multilaterally, it created the Southeast Asia Treaty Organization (SEATO) at Manila on 8 September 1954; bilaterally, it offered aid to the Indochinese

"free" states to bolster their capacity to resist both internal and external threats to security and stability.

Although SEATO died a natural death in 1977 without having fired a shot in anger, its creation in 1954 caused many a major problem. In a protocol to the treaty, signed the same day, the parties to the treaty unanimously extended to Cambodia, Laos, and "the free territory under the jurisdiction of the State of Vietnam" the protection of Article 4 against armed aggression and internal subversion. The three countries were thus brought under the protective umbrella of SEATO's collective defense without formal membership, in an effort to satisfy both the letter of the Geneva Agreements and the American call for a collective defense scheme in advance of aggression.

In the bilateral sphere, the United States bypassed France in providing aid directly to South Vietnam. President Eisenhower wrote Diem on 23 October 1954 about American readiness to enlarge its aid program. The declared objective was "to assist the Government of Viet-Nam in developing and maintaining a strong, viable state, capable of resisting attempted subversion or aggression through military means," in return for reforms to be instituted by Diem. Direct American financial aid to the three Indochinese governments began on 1 January 1955, in implementation of the agreement between General J. Lawton Collins and the French in December 1954. On 12 February, Diem announced that the American Military Assistance Advisory Group (MAAG) was taking over the training of the Vietnamese National Army. While the size of MAAG remained unchanged, its role was expanded from equipping to training the South Vietnamese forces, barely six months after the cease-fire; the French, under American pressure,[18] had begun their unexpectedly early withdrawal from South Vietnam.

While American objectives and Canadian interests in Vietnam were complementary (preventing the Vietminh from capturing South Vietnam through armed might), American and South Vietnamese interests were identical: at a minimum, averting a communist takeover south of the 17th parallel by any means, and, at the maximum, recovering the territory to the north. Hanoi, well aware of the coincidence of interests between Saigon and Washington, could not but be disturbed by the evident rising fortune of South Vietnam, rid of its dependence on the outgoing exhausted French, brought under SEATO's protection, cultivating ties with the Americans, and increasingly assertive of its authority in its zone and in its relations with the International Commission.

Hanoi's reaction came in the form of a fourteen-page letter from General Vo Nguyen Giap on 5 December 1954. While it included a few references to violations of political rights in South Vietnam, it concentrated on the Collins mission (the General had been to Saigon as President Eisenhower's personal representative) and the Manila Pact. Giap described the latter as an aggressive military bloc designed to further American imperialist aims in Southeast Asia. He charged further that the treaty was in violation of the Geneva Agreements. The purpose of the Collins mission, according to Giap, was to funnel men and weapons into South Vietnam in violation of Articles 16 and 17, and to use the southern zone to engage in acts of aggression in violation of Article 19 of the Agreement and Article 5 of the Final Declaration. The acts had the one common objective of "integrating the south of our country into the aggressive military bloc of Southeast Asia, led by the United States," and preventing the reunification of Vietnam through elections. While denying that the PAVN had violated the Agreements by enlarging its armies since the cease-fire, Giap was careful not to lay blame on the French in the southern zone, but on the Americans and the South Vietnamese. The Canadians concluded that a principal purpose of the Giap broadside was to drive a wedge between the French and the Americans. Such Canadian concern was quite in keeping with earlier Canadian apprehensions about the potential of Far-Eastern issues to divide Western unity.

The PAVN sent the letter to the ICSC, and later—publicly—to the cochairmen, with the request that the Commission "pay particular attention" to the violations alleged and that it undertake "appropriate measures to ensure" respect for the Geneva Agreements. The Commission was uncertain of how to react. Canada and India objected to Hanoi having made the memorandum public before the Commission was able to discuss it. Ottawa was particularly unhappy with the tone and contents of the letter and, since no evidence was presented to substantiate the charges, did not believe that the Commission should take them up for consideration. Chairman Desai tried unsuccessfully to persuade the North Vietnamese not to publish the letter; they merely delayed publication by a day. The Commission then asked the French to comment on Giap's charges with respect to SEATO and the Collins mission. The French reply, received six weeks later on 23 January, was a point-by-point refutation of Giap's charges. Principally, General Grout de Beaufort stated that, first, the strength of MAAG was in fact lower than its cease-fire level, and second, SEATO was designed to *prevent* aggression and had adopted a formula that did not violate Article 19.

In the ensuing Commission debate, Canada again argued that Giap's letter was patently a piece of propaganda and, therefore, undeserving of Commission action. Poland demanded that the Commission treat Giap's charges as formal complaints and rule on the legality of SEATO and the Collins mission. Desai faithfully worked out a middle ground. Giap would be asked to clarify whether the PAVN wanted a Commission investigation. The Commission reply (28 January 1955), therefore, indicated to Giap that it would take action only on the basis of specific requests for investigation establishing a *prima facie* case. The Commission was thus once again defining its role in reactive terms. Giap was asked whether the PAVN memorandum was to be considered "a definite complaint" under Article 37. If it was, then Giap should "communicate to the Commission . . . the specific articles of the Agreement, violations in respect of which require investigations under Article 37 and full particulars in support of this request." The French comments on the Giap memorandum were attached, along with a statement that the Commission through its teams was doing its best "to secure full compliance with Articles 16 and 17 along *all* the frontiers of Viet-Nam" (emphasis added). In a concession to Lett, the Canadian Commissioner, Desai further noted that the Agreements had not been fully implemented by *either* party, "due to ignorance, misunderstanding or narrowmindedness of officials."

Canada anticipated that the PAVN would take up the Commission offer to investigate the legality of SEATO and the Collins mission. Ottawa, therefore, engaged in detailed legal studies of the issues involved, and the matter of the MAAG training camp, to conclude that the three did not in themselves constitute violations of the cease-fire agreement. MAAG would step beyond legality, it found, only if its strength was increased beyond the cease-fire level, as in itself MAAG had existed since 1950.

The question of SEATO was more complicated. Article 19 of the cease-fire directed that "the two parties shall ensure that the zones assigned to them do not adhere to any military alliance." France was a signatory to SEATO, the State of Vietnam was not. Whether Article 19 had been violated would depend, therefore, on whether the State of Vietnam, whose *de facto* territorial boundary extended north only to the 17th parallel, could be said to possess a distinct international personality independent of France. If France was the exclusive territorial sovereign in Vietnam, then its adherence to SEATO was an undoubted violation of Article 19, since the southern zone, by virtue of its being a piece of French territory, had joined a military alliance.

Canada decided that the parties most competent to determine the relationship between France and the State of Vietnam were the states themselves, who in turn argued that the State of Vietnam had enjoyed full independence from France since before the Geneva Agreements, and had merely delegated certain powers to France in the juridical, military, and economic spheres. Canada decided, therefore, that the State of Vietnam, comprising southern Vietnam, enjoyed an independent personality separate from France, that it had not adhered to SEATO, and that therefore no violation of Article 19 had occurred.[19]

In other words, Canada's position was that while the PAVN continued to be bound by the provisions of the Geneva Agreements, the position with respect to the southern zone was very fluid. The State of Vietnam, which it recognized, was an independent entity, and France was not, therefore, sovereign with respect to the southern zone even in September 1954, at the time of the Manila Pact. But if the State of Vietnam's independence antedated the signing of the cease-fire agreement, then it could not in fairness be held to be a successor to France with respect to functions and obligations undertaken by France in consequence of the agreement.

Which party then was responsible for the southern zone, especially as the State of Vietnam had specifically excluded responsibility at Geneva itself? And what of the propriety—and legality—of French actions at Geneva? If French action in signing the agreements was illegal, and null and void by virtue of incompetence, then were not the agreements themselves illegal, and was not North Vietnam therefore freed of any obligations arising from the

Geneva Agreements? What would be the *political* consequences in Vietnam of such highly technical and legalistic interpretations? Canada was not concerned with such questions; it was quite content to determine that France and the State of Vietnam were separate international entities, and leave the contradictions to the communists.

It would be remiss not to point out the coincidence between the Canadian interpretation and the American perception, as in fact was evident in Eisenhower's letter to Diem (23 October 1954) promising aid "in developing and maintaining a strong, viable state." The Americans, too, were apparently unconcerned about the discrepancy between that particular promise to Diem and the oft-repeated Geneva promise that the partition of Vietnam was a temporary military expedient. Outside the scope of the Commission, Canada was not only not asked to become a member of SEATO, but in fact specifically excluded itself from any commitment. This "clearly reflects the traditional principles of her policy: commitments must bear a precise relation to power, and the conviction that the sole source of her security is the unity of the Atlantic Triangle."[20]

As it turned out, Hanoi did not press charges. Perhaps it had shied away from the risk of having a Commission ruling on such a fundamental question as the legal status of the State of Vietnam *vis-à-vis* France. It was to submit specific complaints, but not until later.

If Canada's reaction to SEATO was legalistic, India's was political. Nehru considered SEATO to be no more than an angry reaction to the Geneva Agreements.[21] He engaged in a bitter attack on SEATO in Parliament on 29 September 1954. The Geneva Conference, Nehru said, brought peace to Indochina; had the Manila conference "relaxed tensions in South-East Asia or increased them?" India had declined the invitation to attend because of its policy of nonalignment and also because of its chairmanship of the supervisory commissions. But it was concerned about the direction the Conference had taken, in particular with the "dangerous extension of the idea of defence" to cover any designated territory within the defensive area. That smacked too closely of colonial spheres of influence to be comfortable.

Nehru was equally concerned that the attempt to cover "a fact or situation created within this area" in addition to armed attack from without encroached upon the integrity, sovereignty, and independence of the countries in the area. SEATO was objectionable because it was an expression of the American concept of world order based on a system of interlocking alliances, which was diametrically opposed to the Indian policy of extending the area of peace by means of nonalignment. "The Manila Treaty comes in the way of that area of peace. It takes up that very area that might be an area of peace and converts it almost into an area of potential war." A more immediate concern, of course, sprang from the fact that Pakistan was a member of the organization. NATO, said Nehru, had begun as a defense pact for the security of the North Atlantic, but had then spread geographically to the Mediterranean and by Portuguese desire to Goa. SEATO embraced "certain colonial powers, certain powers not colonial in themselves but interested in colonialism, and certain associated countries, all of which try to decide or control the fate of this great area of South-East Asia." If NATO could extend to cover Goa, where might the scope of SEATO not reach, especially as it could unilaterally extend its defensive area? SEATO was the embodiment of all that India strove against: colonialism, racism, military alliance systems, and Pakistan's adherence to the system of military alliances.[22] Small wonder then that India should react with such sharpness.

India believed that the Geneva Agreements had effectively neutralized the Indochinese states, and prohibited them from joining military alliances. Furthermore, India interpreted the neutralization in terms of nonalignment. As Nehru expressed it in the Rajya Sabha on 26 August 1954:

> In the decisions at Geneva in regard to the Indo-China countries — Laos, Cambodia and Vietnam — it has been specifically laid down that they should not have military alliances with other countries. That is to say, they should be more or less unaligned and should more or less belong to what we call the area of peace.

The Geneva Agreements were held to have been the result of *Panchsheel*; the system they established was, therefore, predicated upon nonalignment; and the intrusion of SEATO was as much as challenge to India's foreign policy as a threat to Indochinese peace. Indians were not unaware of the uncertain legal foundations of their interpretation. Rather, it was Nehru's view that the context of Geneva, and in particular the Anglo-French assurances to China *vis-à-vis* American bases,[23] were of greater political import than the letter of the Agreements. The view was extended into the argument that to attack the political foundations of Geneva was to risk destroying the far from secure legal structure that rested on it. In Nehru's own words:

> One of the basic things of the Geneva Conference decisions was— *not interpreting it strictly legally*—that the Indochinese countries should remain neutral. That is a very vital thing. In fact, the Geneva Conference almost broke down on that issue. On the one side . . . France and others could not tolerate the possibility of those countries being used against them in the future. On the other, China could not tolerate those countries being used against her as bases. . . . Now if anything is done which affects that basic position of Indochina as a neutral area, the whole conception of the Geneva decisions is shaken. . . . If SEATO does something which shakes that position it again shakes the basis of this agreement, not only psychologically but practically.[24]

The statement is a very good illustration of India's twin concerns. To attack the political base of the Geneva peace was a risk to the peace system itself, and to risk the system of peace established so delicately at Geneva was to risk great power involvement in Indochina. And, if the great powers were to fight their war in Indochina, then the Indochinese would be the most likely to suffer. As Vijaya Lakshmi Pandit put it, "the purpose of SEATO is not peace, but war. Asians will become implements of war."[25] The concerns were repeated by Nehru in his survey of the international situation on 31 March 1955.[26]

American Military Missions
In the event, SEATO turned out to be less important than United States missions in South Vietnam in increasing the American presence there. In 1956–57, the PAVN complained to the Commission that MAAG was a "factual military alliance" in contravention of Articles 16 and 19 of the cease-fire agreement and Articles 4 and 5 of the Final Declaration. Saigon replied that MAAG was not a military alliance, that it had been in existence since 1950, and that there had been no change in its activities, statute, or structure. Nor had it at any point exceeded its original strength.[27]

The Canadian position on the subject of American military advisers was in part dictated by a desire to preserve a balance of forces in North and South Vietnam. At the 354th meeting on 25 October 1956, Acting Comissioner Bruce Williams observed that "failure of the control system in one part of the zone . . . invalidated the entire control of the zone." The case for an effective control system in the South was correspondingly weakened. Regarding MAAG specifically, the Canadian stance was that since the Agreements prohibited additional rather than existing forces, the American presence was consistent with a continuation of the cease-fire *status quo*. Thus at the 535th Commission meeting on 27 June 1959, the combative Canadian Commissioner J. P. Erichsen-Brown argued that Article 16 was so general in its prohibition that one could not clearly conclude that the MAAG ceiling could not be raised to the level of "total military advisers." In this context, only 342 technical advisers remained of the original 150,000 foreign (French) forces. The MAAG ceiling of 342 was therefore a "self-imposed limit" set by the United States-South Vietnam side.

This interpretation of the Agreements assumed importance on 23 February 1960, when South Vietnamese Foreign Minister Vu Van Mau requested that the MAAG ceiling be raised from 342 to 685. Saigon pointed out that the increased strength would still be below the combined strength of 888 MAAG and French instructors present in Vietnam at the time of the armistice. The request was discussed at the 571st meeting of the Commission on 8 April 1960. Commissioner T. Wisniewski of the Polish delegation noted that the Canadian proposition could lead to 150,000 American personnel replacing the original French forces. Erichsen-Brown argued that the MAAG increase was necessary because of organized subversion against the Saigon government, and was justified because the Geneva Agreements were meant to maintain "the balance of forces." Nevertheless, according to a document declassified by the American State Department in January 1975, Ottawa had been dubious about the legality of the proposed increase. The ICSC decision was ultimately favorable largely as a result of an Indian initiative.[28] Thus at the 572nd meeting on 13 April 1960, Chairman S. S. Ansari ruled in favor of the Canadian argument that Article 16 could not definitively be read as either permitting or prohibiting replacement of foreign military personnel in Vietnam by other foreign personnel of a different nationality.

On 19 April 1960, therefore, the Commission acceded to Saigon's request to raise the MAAG ceiling to 685 — but only over

Polish objections. When Giap complained that South Vietnam had requested the Commission to allow entry of American arms and personnel as replacement for the French Expeditionary Corps that had invaded Vietnam, the Commission answered simply that no such request had been made. In May 1960 Giap returned to the charge, complaining that the Commission decision to accede to Saigon's request contradicted both the spirit and the letter of the Geneva Agreements. In June, Prime Minister Pham Van Dong wrote directly to the cochairmen (with a copy to the Commission), requesting that they direct the Commission to reconsider and repeal its decision. The Commission instead reaffirmed its decision. It also reiterated that there was no provision in the Agreements for an appeal to the cochairmen against a decision of the Commission. Poland again dissented: MAAG was indeed in violation of the relevant articles of the Geneva Agreements, and the Commission's decision to permit a doubling of MAAG personnel contradicted Geneva in letter and spirit.[29]

The next installment in the story of increasing American military personnel in Vietnam may be taken up with documents declassified in 1974–75. In February 1961, the United States examined various contingencies for further troop increases in South Vietnam, with a view to their relationship with the Geneva Agreements. The existing complement at the time was 685. An additional 203 military personnel could be justified by claiming that there were 888 foreign military advisers in Vietnam at the time of the cease-fire. If still more American personnel were required, the figure of 888 would be replaced by 1,847 "on the ground that subsequent information has disclosed that the latter is a more accurate figure regarding foreign military advisory personnel in Viet-Nam at about time of conclusion of Geneva Accords." If more than 1,162 additional personnel were to be required, "justification would then have to be that we were replacing French combat personnel withdrawn from Viet-Nam."[30]

Also of interest is the fact that the United States anticipated that Hanoi and the Polish delegation would demand an ICSC condemnation of any fresh increases. In response, "the U.S. would wish to be able, through the Canadians and the GVN to refute such charges and to argue that the introduction of additional military personnel does not violate the Geneva Accords."[31] By May 1961, however, Washington had decided against justifying each increase in military personnel as being consistent with the Geneva Agreements. Instead, justification would be sought through renouncing Articles 16 and 17 of the cease-fire agreement after accusing Hanoi of having violated the Agreements. Close allies of the United States were informed of this change; the Embassy in New Delhi was to inform the Indian government four days after South Vietnamese concurrence had been obtained.[32]

The American strategy faltered somewhat with Diem's refusal to consent to it.[33] Then the Canadian ICSC Commissioner joined Diem in opposing the American plan to renounce Articles 16 and 17. Commissioner C. J. Woodsworth and his senior military adviser called on United States Ambassador Frederick E. Nolting on 20 June 1961. The Canadians were in full agreement with increased American support for Saigon and wished to be helpful. But they argued that openly confronting the problem would render the ICSC position untenable, make the DRVN denounce the entire Geneva Accords, and lead to the demise of the Commission. A more satisfactory approach might be for the United States to exploit various techniques to escape ICSC attention. Thus additional MAAG personnel could be introduced as civilians, or could arrive on unscheduled military flights synchronized with the absence of ICSC airport control teams, or could be brought into areas where ICSC teams did not operate. Since ICSC control was effective only in respect of observed arrivals and departures, the new arrivals could easily merge into existing MAAG personnel once they were in the country. Similarly, materiel could be introduced through ports beyond ICSC control; once introduced, they would be indistinguishable from that already in the country. Or they could be claimed as credits for materiel outshipped by France: "This would permit Canadians stall question for year or more." (Woodsworth also informed his American friends that under Canadian pressure the Indians had agreed to investigate specific terrorist incidents and possible subversion.)[34]

Another problematic American mission was the Temporary Equipment Recovery Mission (TERM). On 25 April 1956, the French Liaison Mission and the Government of South Vietnam requested ICSC permission for the entry of 350 American military personnel into South Vietnam in the form of TERM. Its duties were said to be to examine war material and military equipment lying in South Vietnam toward the end of May. The Commission's response was that it would consider the matter, and that no entry of the Americans should be effected pending an ICSC decision. The Commission learned, however, that 290 TERM personnel were already in the southern zone, and was thus faced with a *fait accompli*. The Commission took exception to this method of procedure; it sent a letter to Saigon on 29 May 1956, in which it (1) asked to be assured that TERM's functions would be limited to selecting materiel for export; (2) requested details of number and names of personnel, as well as their postings and the task assigned to each man; and (3) proposed that the acceptance of TERM personnel would be subject to a fortnightly progress report of the mission, to notifications of the entry and exit of its personnel, to the right of the Commission to control their exit and entry, and to the right of the Commission to conduct checks on the spot at any place where TERM personnel were stationed.[35]

The South Vietnamese government subsequently failed to comply with the Commission request to furnish fortnightly reports, although it did permit Commission teams to visit TERM sites. The Commission then asked for an updated report on TERM, with fortnightly reports to be furnished thereafter, and it asked further for a list of TERM sites. South Vietnam thereafter furnished the Commission with monthly reports, although not always on time. It gave a list of eight TERM sites, of which four were spot-checked. The Commission believed that, with respect to TERM, as well as MAAG, Saigon had failed to supply all the information that had been requested of it. It therefore expressed grave concern that all assistance and cooperation in terms of Article 25 was not being offered, and asked the Liaison Mission to supply the necessary information.

The Canadian delegation dissented from this citation of Article 25 against South Vietnam, because in its view all the essential information had been supplied. Saigon's answer to the Commission citation was to send it a copy of the MAAG agreement of 23 December 1950. In 1958–59, the Commission decided that TERM should be able to complete its mission by the end of June 1959 and that, since it was only temporary, it should cease to exist thereafter and its personnel leave South Vietnam. In the same period, the Commission pursued continuing Hanoi complaints about the number of American military personnel in South Vietnam. By checking its own team records, the Commission was able to establish that between 7 January 1956 and 28 December 1957, 759 more Americans had entered than had left South Vietnam (2,002:1,243); the Saigon government agreed to check the matter.[36]

With respect to the Commission directive that TERM cease operations by July 1959, Saigon declared that the mission would have to continue until approximately the end of 1960. The Commission agreed to this grace period for South Vietnam, but only over Polish dissent.[37] Poland argued that to have introduced TERM into South Vietnam in 1956 was in itself a transgression of the Geneva Agreements. Its activity, not subject to Commission control, was also in violation of the Agreements. The Commission had earlier decided that TERM should be wound up by July 1959, which Saigon found impossible allegedly because of continuing discoveries of additional quantities of materiel. The Polish delegation was willing to extend the termination deadline by two months, but a period of eighteen months beyond the deadline set by the Commission itself was quite unacceptable.

Saigon explained the 759 Americans unaccounted for in South Vietnam by saying that the Americans entered in military clothes and planes, but left in civilian clothing in commercial flights that were not subject to Commission control. The Commission's reaction to the South Vietnamese explanation was a gentle rebuke. In Article 16(f), it informed Saigon, the cease-fire imposed a duty on the parties to notify it of entries and exits of all military personnel irrespective of their dress and mode of transportation.[38]

The Commission referred briefly to TERM in its last regular report. In the first two months of 1961, the PAVN had thrice alleged to the Commission that TERM had not in fact ceased to exist, but was instead extending the scope of its activity under the assumed name of the Logistics Section of MAAG. The Saigon government for its part informed the Commission that TERM was disbanded on 31 December 1960, and that out of its total strength of 350 men, 261 had left South Vietnam in 1961. The remaining 89 had by virtue of their technical expertise been transferred to MAAG. The Commission requested more detailed information on the evacuation of TERM personnel and the distribution of MAAG personnel. Poland again found the Commission reaction to be inadequate. In its view, the transfer of men from TERM to MAAG was tantamount to a failure to implement a Commission recommendation that all TERM personnel be evacuated by the end of

1960. Its concern was strengthened by the PAVN charges that all TERM personnel continued to operate in South Vietnam, in violation of Articles 16 and 25. Canada and India replied to the Polish observation with the simple comment that the matter was still under consideration.

Thus, on a substantive matter of critical importance to the viability of the Geneva system, Poland was insistent throughout in its demands that South Vietnam be called to account. Canada was equally consistent in its inability to cite either Saigon or Washington for a violation of the Agreements. India, and therefore the Commission, began by attempting to assert some control after the fact in 1956. It parted company with Canada in 1957-58 by declaring that South Vietnam had failed to meet Commission requests for information, repeated the attempt to assert some control over TERM in 1958, and then virtually accepted "defeat" in 1959 at the cost of a parting of ways with Poland. Between 1959 and 1961, despite Polish prodding, India refused to act against South Vietnam for transparent failures to obey Commission directives: the matter was still under (Canadian and Indian) consideration.

The positions of the delegations were identical with respect to the equally critical issue of MAAG. According to the Pentagon account, the decision in May 1956 to send 350 additional military men to Saigon in the guise of TERM was an example of the United States ignoring the Geneva accords. It was a "thinly veiled device to increase the number of Americans in Vietnam." The temporary TERM personnel stayed on as a permanent part of MAAG, "and provided a convenient cover for a larger intelligence effort."[39]

It would appear that Ottawa had been informed initially that the operation was to be carried out regardless of ICSC opinions and judgments. The Americans were unwilling to accept ICSC supervision for fear of thereby conceding the validity of the Agreements *vis-à-vis* American actions in Vietnam.[40] The Canadians found such attitudes dismaying, in that compliance with ICSC procedures would have been relatively simple. Otherwise, had unilateral American actions resulted in an ICSC crisis, the Canadians would either have to side with the Indians or be prepared to withdraw from the Commission. However, Washington had learned directly of Indian nonobjection.[41] At the 442nd meeting of the Commission on 8 November 1957, the Poles had pressed for a mandatory exit of TERM. Chairman T. N. Kaul frustrated them by ruling that "it is customary for the Commission to take the Party at its word until anything is proved to the contrary."

By mid-1958, the Canadians were prepared to stretch the cease-fire agreement considerably in order to accommodate Saigon's stance and military needs. At the 489th meeting on 17 October 1958, Poland demanded that the ICSC impose 1 January 1959 as the terminal date for the Mission. Commissioner T. Le M. Carter responded simply that "it is true that TERM is staying here longer than was originally envisaged. It is also true that the Commission is staying longer than was originally envisaged." Privately, the Canadians did not consider their position to be partisan. They had been assured by American sources that the United States was indeed exporting more equipment from Vietnam than it was importing.[42]

The Commission returned to the question of Saigon-Washington military relations in urgent detail in its special report of 2 June 1962.[43] It referred to PAVN complaints alleging direct American military intervention in South Vietnam, as well as the increasing and accelerating import of war material and military personnel. Six allegations were especially important: of a bilateral agreement of a military nature between President Diem and Ambassador Nolting; of a gradual introduction of 5,000 American personnel into South Vietnam, with a target of 8,000 in the near future; of four aircraft carriers (*Core, Breton, Princeton,* and *Croaton*) having brought men and materiel; of visits to South Vietnam of a large number of high-ranking American military experts, including Generals Maxwell Taylor and Lyman P. Lemnitzer, and Admiral Harry D. Felt;[44] and of the establishment of the United States Military Assistance Command (MAC) with General Paul D. Harkins as its chief (8 February 1962).

The Commission reported that South Vietnam had persistently denied its teams the right to control and inspect since December 1961. On 9 December 1961, Saigon in a letter to the Commission justified the introduction of American men and arms on grounds of the right to self-defense in the face of subversion by Hanoi, but failed to meet Commission requests for control. Nor was the Commission request for details on MAC met by South Vietnam. Nevertheless, on the basis of its own observations and authorized statements in South Vietnam and the United States, the Commission concluded that the Republic of Vietnam had violated Articles 16 and 17 in receiving increased military aid from the United States.

The Commission further believed that while there was no formal military alliance between Saigon and Washington, the establishment of MAC in South Vietnam, as well as the introduction of a large number of American military personnel beyond the stated strength of MAAG, "amounts to a factual military alliance, which is prohibited under Article 19 of the Geneva Agreement." Canada *was* a signatory to this finding against the South Vietnam-United States alliance. This despite the fact that within the Commission, at its 652nd meeting on 2 June 1962 to sign the special report, Canadian Commissioner Frank G. Hooton did differ from the Indians on one important point. He observed that military assistance that was limited in scope (advice and material) and time (duration of subversive aggression) could not constitute "a military alliance in the normally understood sense of this term." As will be made clear later, this difference, not made public in 1962, contained the kernel of the Canadian minority statement in 1965.

The Northern Zone

The Chinese Border

The Commission received a complaint from General de Beaufort of the French Liaison Mission on 27 November 1954 alleging that "important quantities of war material have been delivered to the PAVN since the entry into force of the Geneva Agreements." The complaint further charged that existing Commission supervision of the Chinese frontier was quite inadequate and should be supplemented by creating two more fixed teams at Cao Bang and Lai Chau.[45] Pending the establishment of two fixed teams, the French Mission requested that traffic in the areas be controlled by mobile teams.

The French complaint served as a catalyst in bringing to the surface dissatisfactions with the effectiveness of the Commission's control system along Vietnam's northern border. Reports that the Vietminh were importing arms across the Chinese border without fear of Commission detection began to receive public circulation as early as November 1954. In Britain, there was a statement by Eden to his Parliament on 8 November, describing major increases in North Vietnamese military strength. At a press conference on 20 November, the chairman, M. J. Desai, seemed to imply that the Commission's control of the northern border was in the main adequate to prevent a significant clandestine importation of arms.[46] Ottawa, disturbed by the story, instructed its Commissioner to have the ICSC correct the misleading impression that effective investigations had been carried out. That the chairman was well aware of the problems involved is more than evident in his comment at the 27 September 1954 press conference, that a thorough check along the entire border would require an army.[47] All the same, the French complaint of 27 November did serve to bring into the open Canadian unhappiness with the existing state of affairs. The Canadians concluded that either the Commission's control system should be tightened, or the lack of one be made public. Otherwise, the credibility of the Commission, and in particular of Canada as the guardian of southern interests, would suffer.

The dilemma, however, was precisely the fact of Canada's duality as an impartial delegation and as an adversarial advocate entrusted with guarding the interests of one side. The two could be combined in a *Commission* judgment; a unilateral Canadian condemnation of the control system could serve to cast aspersions on Canada's rather than the Commission's credibility. The dilemma would haunt Canada for all its years in Vietnam. It would also contribute no little share to increasing Canadian anger with the Indians, in that India, not Poland, was the inevitable target of persuasion in efforts to arrive at a Commission decision in favor of the Canadians' perceptions.

An equally serious dilemma concerned the consequence of condemnation for the Geneva Agreements themselves: what if an official statement of the ineffectiveness of the control system in the north produced a volatile reaction in an already distant south, resulting in permanent damage to the fragile Geneva peace structure? Indian support was crucial for such a serious step, since no one delegation wished to assume the responsibility for wrecking the Geneva structure. The paradox there, in turn, was that if the dilemma was sharp for Canada, it was unbearable for India. By virtue of the tripartite composition of the Commission, the burden of any controversial decision fell on India. The more important or serious a question, the more likely were Poland and Canada to be adamant, and the more likely were their delegations to seek India's support. By the same token, the stronger would the disappointment be of the side that failed to secure India's vote. To complete the equation, the more serious the gulf that separated Canada and

Poland on the Commission, the greater the probability that India would avoid committing itself on the matter, other things being equal. In other words, because attacks on the Commission would in practice be directed against India (Canada and Poland would receive formalistic criticism, of course), India was more than likely to make efforts toward consensual Commission decisions or no decision at all—except that the latter course of action presented its own dilemma: the failure of the Geneva Agreements. And a failure of the Agreements would be taken to be a major failure of Indian foreign policy. The dilemmas would return repeatedly for India as well in future years.

In this context, the French request for reinforced control on the northern border would provide the test of Canadian, Indian, and Polish policy in the Commission, and of North Vietnamese policy toward Commission directives, in an area of substantive importance. The Commission first considered the French complaint at its seventy-third meeting on 30 November 1954. India's position was that, with a minimum of dissension within the Commission and with minimal damage to relations with Hanoi, gaps in the control system must be plugged. It suggested, with Canadian support, that France be asked to provide evidence to prove its charges, and that a mobile team investigate the existence of any gaps on the Chinese border. Poland objected on two different grounds, that reconnaissance should not be initiated until after evidence had been obtained from the French, and that the existence of gaps could have been a deliberate point of negotiations in Geneva. (France never presented its evidence, either because there was none, or because the French did not wish to compromise their sources.) When Desai persevered, however, Poland acquiesced in a mobile team reconnaissance.

The survey and its study by the Operations Committee took two months. Three mobile teams were dispatched; all three were hampered by varying degrees of noncooperation from the PAVN authorities, but persisted in their task. The Ha Giang and Lai Chau teams returned reasonably satisfied with the Commission's control system in the two areas. However, the Cao Bang team, Mobile Team 29, came across two motorable roads between Cao Bang and the Chinese border. In the Operations Committee, India was in favor of a mobile team for continuous control of the Cao Bang region. Canada took the position that once the road linking Cao

Bang with Thai Nguyen and Hanoi was completed, a fixed team would be necessary at Cao Bang. Canada also favored installing a temporary mobile team at Dong Dang, pending a relocation of Fixed Team Lang Son at Dong Dang, on the reasoning that a fixed team at the latter junction could control the Dong Dang-Thai Nguyen road as well as the road and railway currently under Fixed Team Lang Son control. Poland argued that a mobile element of the team at Lang Son would suffice to control the whole region, and that to station a team at Cao Bang on a permanent basis would be tantamount to the creation of a new fixed team and would, therefore, require an amendment to the Agreements. The Committee also discussed its control system on the South Vietnam-Cambodia border north of Saigon. India and Poland agreed that a Saigon-based mobile team would be adequate control, while Canada, to maintain consistency, favored the creation of a special mobile team to be located at Loc Ninh.

The ICSC debated the divided report of its Operations Committee in January-February 1955. Desai probed his colleagues repeatedly in efforts to preserve unanimity and avoid a Hanoi-ICSC confrontation. Ultimately, the three delegations accepted Lett's proposal that the mobile element of Lang Son be posted to the Dong Dang junction for four weeks. When the Operations Committee tried to arrange implementation of this, however, Poland appeared to retract its previous agreement, but yielded to a firm Canadian stance in the Commission. As for Cao Bang, continued Polish obstructionism finally exasperated Desai to the point where he sought and obtained concurrence directly from Giap for installing a mobile team there.

Mobile Team 41 was dispatched to Loc Ninh on 8 February, and Mobile Team 40 to Cao Bang and Mobile Team F-17 of Fixed Team Lang Son to Dong Dang on 11 February. While none of the teams uncovered illegal shipments of arms, observations did confirm the need for continuous control at Dong Dang and Cao Bang. After their withdrawals (8 and 11 March), the Operations Committees studied the question of recommending to the Commission the establishment of permanent control at Dong Dang, Cao Bang, and Loc Ninh. The Commission concluded that Fixed Team Lang Son should be relocated at Dong Dang, a course of action that the Canadians had pushed for a few months earlier, subject to PAVN concurrence as per Article 35.

Concerning Cao Bang (and Loc Ninh), Desai was still wary of trying to amend the Agreements, and postponed the matter till after the expiry of the three-hundred-day period. In the meantime, he again opted for the "temporary expedient" of seeking concurrence of the parties to a further two-month installation of mobile teams at the two sites. The French concurred quickly in the installation of Mobile Team 59 at Loc Ninh, but its dispatch was held up with the PAVN declaration that the team at Cao Bang would have powers of observation only in Cao Bang and other areas outside the ten-kilometer strip of unfettered control. The teams were dispatched in mid-April while the debate still continued. Later in 1955, the team at Cao Bang was forced to move to Phuc Hoa, from where in turn it had to be evacuated finally in January 1958.

The intensity of the debates in the Commission on the question of the freedom of movement of its teams was not made public in the first three hundred days. Toward the end of its first report, for instance, the Commission noted that while logistical support to fixed and mobile teams had been generous in the two zones, "both sides have preferred narrow legalistic interpretation of the Articles of the Agreement regarding the tasks and the spheres of movements of the Commission's teams."[48] The subsequent sorry story of the Commission's team at Phuc Hoa was, however, publicly told in later reports, as noted earlier. The Canadian government went considerably farther than the Commission even during the initial stages. Thus Pearson said in Parliament in early 1955 that the Commission had tried to maintain a check on men and materials entering Vietnam, but that establishing the inspection machinery had taken some time, and its effectiveness he could not predict. He alluded to Canadian experience elsewhere "with the difficulties encountered by international commissions with communist representation," and warned that while the inspection system could render violations more difficult, a determined party could nevertheless circumvent provisions of the Geneva Agreements.[49] Yet after a lengthy visit to Vietnam in June 1955, John Holmes discounted charges that the North Vietnamese had grossly violated Articles 16 and 17.[50]

Subversion
Because of diminished opportunities in North Vietnam flowing from a more tightly controlled society, or a less visible boundary

zone, or even a lesser interest in the south in enforcing the ban on increases in the military potential (or all three), the volume of complaints to the Commission alleging PAVN violations was significantly lower than that directed against Saigon. In its seventh report, for instance, giving the particulars of violations of Articles 16 and 17 against South Vietnam, the Commission pointed out that it had not considered any violations by the PAVN because there was no team report, notification, or complaint to warrant a consideration. Nevertheless, there were some complaints. The French alleged, for instance, that in October 1955, fourteen railway wagons carrying armaments had reached Hanoi from Moscow via Peking. A Commission investigation uncovered no evidence to support the claim.[51]

The most serious charge that Saigon leveled against the DRVN was Hanoi's alleged complicity in subversive activities in the southern zone and, following from that, Hanoi's aggression against South Vietnam. In 1959 the Saigon government requested the Commission to take up its complaints alleging sabotage, subversion, and espionage. The Commission informed Saigon that its complaints were being examined to ascertain whether any of the provisions of the Geneva Agreements had been violated. Poland attached a dissenting note to even this reaction by the Commission. In its view, the complaints should have been considered as communications concerning cases beyond the scope of the Geneva Agreements. According to the Polish delegation, "Such communications cannot be referred to in the Interim Report, and in this connection paragraph 24 should have been left out of this Report."[52] The Commission's stance had undergone a transformation since 1956, because India's position had changed. Military action against the other zone by either party was expressly forbidden by the Agreements, but the question of subversive activities was far from clear.

The ICSC received the first complaints on the subject in 1955. By mid-1955, Lett had already identified subversion as a probable major threat if the electoral negotiations did not begin on schedule in July 1955. But he also believed that Commission teams could not operate effectively enough to uncover hard evidence of attempted subversion. In September 1955, External Affairs' legal advisers in Ottawa concluded that Article 24 of the cease-fire agreement could be construed as prohibiting guerrilla operations.[53] The Canadian delegation then began to press for Commission investigations of

French-South Vietnamese allegations of subversion. After 1956, Canada's Indochina policy was guided by three objectives: support for the ICSC, which as a symbol of Geneva helped avoid a reversal to fullscale war; furtherance of South Vietnam's defensive build-up by frustrating ICSC condemnations of American military assistance; and exploration of the ICSC legal committee's potential for inhibiting North Vietnamese subversion south of its border.

The Commission first discussed the allegations of subversion on 26 August 1955. It unanimously referred the matter to its legal committee to ascertain whether the ICSC was competent to entertain such charges. The committee reported back on 30 January 1956 with a Canada-India majority position, wherein it held that Article 10 of the cease-fire and "the Geneva Agreement taken as a whole" *implicitly* forbade subversive activities against the proper administration of a zone. The International Commission was, therefore, "both competent and under an obligation to entertain and settle complaints" alleging subversion.

The Commission rejected the legal committee report on 2 November 1956. India and Poland concurred that the Commission was not competent to examine the matter of subversion because it received no specific mention in the Agreements. When complaints about subversion continued, the Commission finally gave in on 4 July 1958 to repeated Canadian requests to refer the question once again to the legal committee. The committee this time decided, on 17 October 1959, that "instead of any hypothetical discussion of jurisdiction each case should be considered separately on its merits." Once again, this was a Canada-India majority report.[54] The Commission accepted the legal committee report the second time, and responded to Saigon accordingly.

In 1960, Saigon alleged a direct and open North Vietnamese aggression in the provinces of Kontum and Pleiku during October 1960, routed through Laos. The Commission forwarded the allegations to Hanoi for comment; the Polish delegation did not participate in the decision because in its view the South Vietnamese had failed to establish a *prima facie* case, their complaint in fact being entirely groundless.[55]

In 1960 and 1961, the Polish member resorted to many diversionary tactics in the legal committee, effectively stalling any consideration of the question of subversion.[56] The frustrated Canadians and Indians finally decided, on 13 June 1961, to take up the issue directly in the Commission. The full Commission discussed the matter at its 610th meeting. Chairman Gopala Menon took the position that while subversion was not cognizable under the Agreements, the Commission did have a "right and an obligation to enquire and investigate . . . complaints" that alleged "acts which might be detrimental to the peace and security of Viet Nam, and which *prima facie* fall under Articles 10, 19 and 24 read with 27." As far as the Indian government was concerned, "it would be difficult for the Commission to divest itself of the responsibility of ascertaining whether or not the alleged acts have been fomented by either Party against the other in violation of the Geneva Agreement." The points were reiterated in a "statement of principle" communicated to the two parties by the Commission, albeit over Polish "dissent and protest."

The Commission took up the two South Vietnamese complaints in its 1962 report, once again over Polish objections. In September 1961, Saigon had again alleged an attack in the Kontum region on the first of the month. Hanoi's response to the South Vietnamese allegation was that the question of "subversive activities" in South Vietnam bore no relevance to the Geneva Agreements. The PAVN would, therefore, reject any Commission decisions on the matter, and reject also any Commission requests for comments on allegations pertaining to such matters.

On 28 November 1961, the Commission referred the charges to its legal committee for examination "with a view to determining whether the allegations and evidence therein *prima facie* attract any provisions of the Geneva Agreement." From 4 December 1961 onward, progress in a series of committee meetings was not possible because of Polish delinquencies and obstructionism.[57] In consequence, on 2 February 1962 G. Parthasarathi chaired a most acrimonious 644th meeting of the ICSC, when remarks by Commissioner Hooton implied a lack of balance in Indian chairmanship of Commission activities. In February 1962, the Indians finally agreed to press ahead in processing and evaluating the cases of subversion in the legal committee even without Polish participation.

Its Polish member dissenting, the legal committee reported that an examination of the complaints and the supporting material warranted

> the conclusion that in specific instances there is evidence to show that armed and unarmed personnel, arms, munitions and

other supplies have been sent from the Zone in the North to the Zone in the South with the object of supporting, organizing and carrying out hostile activities, including armed attacks, directed against the Armed Forces and Administration of the Zone in the South. These acts are in violation of Articles 10, 19, 24 and 27 of the Agreement on the Cessation of Hostilities in Viet-Nam.[58]

The legal committee further concluded that "the P.A.V.N. has allowed the Zone in the North to be used for inciting, encouraging and supporting hostile activities in the Zone in the South, aimed at the overthrow of the Administration in the South," in violation of Articles 19, 24, and 27 of the cease-fire. It also believed that the 1 October 1961 kidnap-murder of Colonel Hoang Thuy Nam, late chief of the South Vietnamese mission to the ICSC, might have been part of the campaign of subversion and aggression against the South. The legal committee concluded, therefore, that there was *prima facie* evidence to warrant a full investigation of the case by the International Commission. The Commission ruled that it

> accepts the conclusions reached by the Legal Committee that there is sufficient evidence to show beyond reasonable doubt that the P.A.V.N. has violated Articles 10, 19, 24 and 27 in specific instances. The Polish Delegation dissents from these conclusions.

The Polish delegation was not content with dissenting; it attached a minority statement as well. In it, Poland charged that the majority report

> does not correspond with the real state of affairs. It places on the same level doubtful and legally unfounded allegations of one of the Parties, on the one hand, and grave and undeniable violations of the Geneva Agreement substantiated by records and findings of the International Commission on the other.

In the opinion of the Polish delegation, the "artificial allegations" against Hanoi merely served to mask the seriousness of the charges against South Vietnam and the United States. The cause of Polish unhappiness is understandable. By June 1962, the only purpose that a public Commission report could serve was to inform world public opinion. And, on the bar of world opinion, there was bound to be a qualitative difference between a citation against Saigon for having entered into a *de facto* alliance with Washington (which had been publicly conceded by both Saigon and Washington already in December 1961), and a finding of aggression and subversion against Hanoi. Indeed, given the coincidence of the two findings in one report, the latter could be used to justify the former, and was in fact so used extensively, not the least by Canada. Not surprisingly, therefore, the special report drew praise from Washington and Saigon, and strictures from Hanoi and Peking.[59]

In sum, then, Poland consistently denied the competence of the Commission to consider complaints of alleged subversion, while Canada equally consistently pressed the Commission to take them up. India's position in the Commission changed over time, even though its opinion in the legal committee did not vary. The pattern of change, as with other issues, was that it refused to entertain complaints from Saigon on the matter in 1955–56, agreed to consider the cases in 1958–59, and established findings against Hanoi in the 1959–62 period.

Before leaving the subject, it should be pointed out that the Commission decision against Hanoi was the culmination of a process initiated in New Delhi to strengthen the Commission with respect to subversive activities. During Nehru's United States tour in November 1961, senior American officials had publicly impressed upon him the need to have India play a greater role in the fight to save South Vietnam from communism. Nehru in response decided to send the veteran Parthasarathi, who had previously served with the ICSC in Vietnam as its second chairman and headed the Indian embassy in Peking, to chair the Commission in Vietnam. He was to determine the matter of subversion and inform New Delhi of his findings.[60] Before Nehru had his talks with John F. Kennedy, in fact, India's Ministry of External Affairs scheduled a meeting on 4 November between its special secretary Badr-ud-din Tyabji and the heads of missions of the *United States, the United Kingdom, Canada, and South Vietnam* with a view to improving the effectiveness of the Commission's role in Vietnam.

Thus, as 1961 drew to a close, India was still trying to avert a resumption of hostilities in Vietnam. Toward this end, New Delhi was prepared to have the Commission play a more active role in seeking out instances of subversion by the Hanoi regime. But, and again in the interests of preventing a wider conflagration, it did not believe that American combat troops in Vietnam would be the best means to save South Vietnam from communism. It was the considered opinion of Nehru's government that the opposite effect was more likely, that the presence of American troops shoring up Saigon would aid Hanoi's political cause while escalating the level of military support to Hanoi from Moscow and Peking. In a public interview with Adlai Stevenson in New York on 12 November 1961, Nehru expressed his belief that the Soviet Union had no particular motives in Vietnam and should not, therefore, be foolishly provoked into countering American moves.[61]

Miscellaneous

The Military Provisional Demarcation Line and the Demilitarized Zone
Negotiations at Geneva on the Military Provisional Demarcation Line (PDL) had involved parallels rather than existing physical or administrative boundaries. The Demilitarized Zone (DMZ) was formed by drawing lines five kilometers wide on each side of the PDL, but taking into account such features of human and physical geography as villages and streams. Duties with respect to the Line and the Zone were supervisory for the International Commission, and executive and administrative for the Joint Commission. In point of fact, however, even though the International Commission expressed general satisfaction with their execution, it engaged in little supervision of the provisions pertaining to effecting the cease-fire, disengagement of troops and their withdrawal into provisional assembly areas, and demilitarization of the DMZ or delineation of its borders.

Supervision of the DMZ was one of the Commission's principal responsibilities under Article 36, but received low priority. The delegations had agreed at their preliminary New Delhi meeting to establish a token presence in the Zone in order to "show the flag," but were content to leave the Joint Commission to deal with the Zone for most of 1954. In early 1955, differences developed between the French, who urged supervision, and the PAVN, who argued that to place a mobile team in the Zone would be to convert it into a fixed team and would, therefore, require an amendment to the agreement. In the Commission, Poland supported the PAVN line.

When the three hundred days were over, supervision of the PDL and the DMZ remained a principal responsibility, and the Commission sought to come to grips with it. On 25 May 1955 the Commission considered a majority report from the legal committee wherein Canada and India rejected the North Vietnamese position that an amendment was necessary before the Commission could locate a mobile team in the DMZ on a continuous basis. They further argued, and against Poland again, that concurrence of the parties was not required. In the Commission, when Canada and Poland stuck to their respective legal committee positions, the Indian chairman opted for the compromise that the High Commands be informed of, rather than requested to concur in, the Commission's decision to station a mobile team in the DMZ pursuant to obligations under Article 36(b). The initial stationing period would be three months. Mobile Team 76 was installed in the DMZ on 12 July 1955, and remained until 3 March 1967 when hostilities forced a move south to Hue.

Regroupment

The armistice at Geneva was achieved on the basis of a temporary partition of Vietnam into two "military regroupment zones." Movement of the forces of the two parties was to be completed within a period of three hundred days. The two zones were in theory placed under *military* authority to avoid creating the impression that two separate *political* entities existed. The creation of two zones was not an easy task, in that there was no one continuous fighting front, but rather a "leopard spot" division of teritories between the forces of the two combatants. The criteria guiding the regroupment operation were evacuation of all PAVN and FUF forces to the north and south of the 17th parallel, transfer of territory in the two zones to the appropriate party, and protection of Vietminh supporters in the south and government supporters in the north. To meet the last requirement, the agreement provided for the free movement of civilians during the regroupment period to the zone of their choice, and prohibited reprisals against those sympathizers of one zone who chose to remain in the other.

The regroupment process, large and complicated as it was, was carried out with relative success, involving 250,000 troops, a little short of a million civilians (refugees, dependants, freed internees), and up to one-third of the land area of Vietnam. The International Commission recorded that the two parties were able to deal in the Joint Commission with problems of withdrawal of armed personnel, and withdrawals and transfer of civil administration; ICSC help was successfully given with respect to transfer of public properties and essential services. Regroupment of the two forces north and south of the PDL, the Commission noted, was completed within the three-hundred-day period, and civil administration of the parties concerned had been established in the regroupment areas in accordance with Article 14(a).[62] The general satisfaction with the Commission's work in the regroupment of troops was clearly expressed by Pearson in 1955. According to him, "That very difficult and complicated job is now almost complete, and it was pretty successfully done. That was the primary job of the commission—the implementation of the military clauses of the armistice agreement."[63]

The first important test for the Geneva Agreements came with the transfer of Hanoi to the Vietminh.[64] The transfer was of immense symbolic importance to both sides. It was also a potentially explosive event since it involved the transfer intact of a well-equipped major city. The transfer modalities were sorted out largely by the High Commands directly, and encompassed withdrawal of FUF forces; the transfer of administrative and police functions, without interruption in the civil administration; and the transfer of public utilities and services, also without a break in continuity. Although there were some minor problems, such as jurisdictional claims over equipment and material required to operate services the owners of which were private companies withdrawing to the south, these were smoothed over, and the Hanoi perimeter was transferred with some efficiency on schedule between 6 and 10 October 1954.

A good example of the methodical efficiency was the transfer of Hanoi proper on 9 October, between 7 A.M. and 5:30 P.M., zone by zone, to a minute-by-minute timetable. Joint officer groups from both sides watched and presided over the operation. The French suggestion was acceded to by the International Commission in instructing five of its mobile teams to show the flag in the streets of Hanoi. The three Commissioners were also in personal attendance to observe the transfer. The "loss" of the city was felt most immediately in South Vietnam. In a speech broadcast to mark the occasion, an intense and uncompromising Diem provided a hint of things to come. "At the moment when Hanoi is to pass under the Communist yoke," he pledged to the citizens of Hanoi, "I send you all . . . a message not of farewell but of *au revoir*."

The last French enclave in the northern zone, and the largest of the provisional assembly areas to be turned over to DRVN control, the Haiphong perimeter, was transferred on 18 May 1955. (FUF forces pulled back from the Haiduong perimeter on 28–30 October 1954.) The Commission was forced against its wishes to intervene in the transfer of Haiphong, because the PAVN and the FUF failed to come to an agreement on the question of preparing inventories of publicly owned equipment. Time would work to Vietminh advantage, in that the French would simply have to abandon equipment after the 18 May deadline. Therefore, while the French sought to secure ICSC intervention, the Vietminh attempted to drag negotiations in the Joint Commission. The protracted dispute continued in the latter forum through December and January. The International Commission on 24 January 1955 referred the dispute to an *ad hoc* committee, and subsequently drew up a list of seven suggestions based on the committee's report delineating points of agreement between the parties.

The suggestions, submitted to the parties on 29 January, were accepted with a minor complaint by the French. The PAVN accepted them in principle, but wanted to discuss the modalities of their implementation in the Joint Commission. At this point Desai's frustrations at PAVN delaying tactics came through, and he decreed that in the absence of *agreed* amendments from the two High Commands, the suggestions would stand, and work would begin forthwith toward putting them into effect. To the apparent bewilderment of the PAVN, and the equally apparent delight of the Canadians, Desai had by his chairman's fiat converted the "suggestions" into Commission Recommendations, even without prior consultation with his fellow Commissioners. Once involved, however, the Commission found it impossible to extricate itself from the operation, and found itself confronted with a number of thorny issues. The four most important dealt with American aid equipment, private property, the Haiphong Chamber of Commerce, and property owned by the state of France. In its efforts to resolve the problems, the Commission sought to provide practical solutions to problems with large legal ramifications. With respect to American aid equipment, for example, the Commission determined that lend-lease equipment could be removed since their ownership remained with a foreign country, but that property provided under American aid whose ownership had passed to the Vietnamese, and which were integrated into the public services network, must remain. The actual transfer passed without incident on 18 May, the three-hundredth day.

The transfer of the central Vietnam provisional assembly area, comprising the provinces of Quang Ngai and Binh Dinh, from the DRVN to the French, took place in three installments on 10 October 1954, 30 October 1954, and 18 May 1955. The graduated transfer led to some disagreements on the proportions to be handed over at each installment, but no serious incident. The Commission again dispatched teams as an expression of its presence, seven for the final transfer. In the Ham Tan-Xuyen Moc assembly area, the transfer to South Vietnam was completed on 10 October 1954. The last, and the largest in size and population, of the Vietminh provisional assembly areas in South Vietnam, Ca Mau, was turned over to French forces on 7 February 1955. The Commission's role was once again limited to observation by mobile teams.

The completion of regroupment was marked by speeches at the Commission's 176th meeting on the three-hundredth day. The tone was one of relief and satisfaction, even if the Commission's influence had been unevenly exerted in the implementation of the regroupment provisions pertaining to the withdrawals of forces and transfers of territories. The Agreements had required regroupment only of regular armed forces, and this had been successfully completed. There was no obligation in the Agreements for the regroupment of political cadres, guerillas, families, and sympathizers. To the contrary, the Agreements in fact sought to guarantee them certain rights in consequence of their continued residence in the southern zone. The story of these rights and the Commission's role will be taken up in the next chapter. For now, it is sufficient to point out American efforts to subvert even the military clauses of the Agreements between 1954 and 1955.

The Pentagon Papers carry verbatim excerpts from the report of the Saigon Military Mission, established covertly in Saigon in *June* 1954, that is, while the Geneva negotiations were still in progress.[65] The Mission was born of a Washington policy meeting in early 1954 when Dien Bien Phu was under siege; its objective was "to prepare the means for undertaking paramilitary operations in Communist areas." Paramilitary operations were to include both sabotage and psychological warfare. The Mission used MAAG cover to establish its personnel strength in South Vietnam before the 11 August cease-fire deadline. Operations in Hanoi in September 1954 included distributing forged Vietminh leaflets so as to frighten the people into seeking refuge in the south, to enhance the appeal of the "voting by foot" argument, and sabotaging rail and bus operations in the city after the PAVN took over control of the services.[66]

With respect to the Haiphong perimeter, the report reveals smuggling of "arms and other equipment including explosives . . . into Saigon . . . for shipment north by the Navy task force handling refugees." The result was that "Haiphong was taken over by the Vietminh on 16 May. Our Binh and northern Hao teams were in place, completely equipped." The most interesting part of the report at this point, however, is the statement that the operation "had to be kept secret from the Vietminh, *the International Commission with its suspicious French and Poles and Indians*, and even friendly Vietnamese" (emphasis added). The omission of Canada is interesting. The statement also confirms the communist assessment that threats in the future would come from the Americans rather than from the French; the latter were quite anxious to implement the Agreements and leave.

The 1965 Special Reports

The Commission signed its last two reports on 13 and 27 February 1965. The subject exercising its attention in the first was the matter of American-South Vietnamese military action against North Vietnam, specifically bombing. The Poland-India majority report itself was very short, with the Canadians expressing a minority opinion in an extended statement thrice as long. The Americans and the South Vietnamese had in a joint communiqué on 7 February informed the Commission of "military action . . . against military installations in the Democratic Republic of Vietnam." Further, this action had been taken because these installations had been employed in the direction and support of those engaged in aggression in South Vietnam, culminating in the attacks earlier that morning against installations and personnel in the areas of Pleiku and Tuy Hoa.

On the same day, Hanoi issued its own communiqué on the bombing and strafing. Further air action against the DRVN was officially announced on 8 February. Hanoi notified the Commission of the bombing and strafing on that day, and requested it "to consider and condemn without delay these violations of utmost gravity and report them to the co-Chairmen."[67] In the Commission's view, the documents "point to the seriousness of the situation and indicate violations of the Geneva Agreement."

> The International Commission is examining and investigating these and connected complaints still being received by it concerning similar serious events and grave developments. . . .
> In the meanwhile, this Special Report is submitted for the earnest and serious attention of the co-Chairmen in view of the gravity of the situation. The International Commission requests the co-Chairmen to consider the desirability of issuing an immediate appeal to all concerned with a view to reducing tension and preserving peace in Vietnam and taking whatever measures are necessary in order to stem the deteriorating situation.

The Canadians argued that the situation in Vietnam was "dangerously unstable," but insisted that "*events* since February 7" must be viewed "in context." By concentrating on a very limited aspect of the situation in Vietnam, "the majority report runs the serious risk of giving . . . a distorted picture of the nature of the problem in Vietnam and its underlying causes." Viewed "in their proper perspective," the events "are dramatic manifestations of a continuing instability which has, as its most important cause, the deliberate and persistent pursuit of aggressive but largely covert policies by North Vietnam directed against South Vietnam." In support of this conclusion, Canada recalled the Commission verdict in its 1962 report that North Vietnam had allowed its territory to be used in support of aggressive and subversive activities against the government of South Vietnam.

The 1962 Commission report was in turn based on conclusions of the legal committee, which the Canadian delegation proceeded to recite in detail. The gist of it was that "the Legal Committee concludes . . . that it is the aim of the Vietnam Lao Dong Party (the ruling Party in the Zone in the North) to bring about the overthrow of the Administration in the South." Canada then gave instances of continuing complaints from Saigon alleging similar serious violations of the Agreements, including Saigon's contention that the RVN "has found itself compelled to take appropriate military actions against the North Vietnamese strategic bases which, as known to everyone, have been utilized actively for the training and infiltration of Viet-Cong elements into South Vietnam." Canada also pointed to South Vietnamese restraint, in that "the retaliatory operations were limited to the military areas which supplied men and arms for the attacks against South Vietnam."

The Canadian statement concluded:

> It is the considered view of the Canadian Delegation that the events which have taken place in both North and South Vietnam since February 7 are the direct result of the intensification of the aggressive policy of the Government of North Vietnam. In the opinion of the Canadian Delegation, therefore, it should be the chief obligation of this Commission to focus all possible attention on the continuing fact that North Vietnam has increased its efforts to incite, encourage, and support hostile activities in South Vietnam, aimed at the overthrow of the South Vietnamese administration. These activities are in direct and grave violation of the Geneva Agreement and constitute the root cause of general instability in Vietnam, of which events since February 7 should be seen as dangerous manifestations. The cessation of hostile activities by North Vietnam is a prerequisite to the restoration of peace in Vietnam as foreseen by the participants in the Geneva Conference of 1954.[68]

The Indian and Polish delegations attached separate but very brief responses to the Canadian statement. Poland simply asserted that the Canadians were responsible for distorting the causes of events in attempting to justify American military actions against North Vietnam. It also pointed out that Poland had not subscribed to the terms of the 1962 report. M. A. Rahman of India qualified the Canadian reference to the 1962 report by saying that the latter had established "only specific cases" of aggressive and subversive activities. He then added the intriguing statement that "the other quotations . . . purporting to be 'conclusions' of the Legal Committee have neither been presented to, nor have the sanction of, the Commission or any of its Committees."[69]

The discrepancy between the Canadian and Indian records of the legal committee was left unexplained in the Commission report, but "cleared up" by Paul Martin in the Canadian Parliament a month afterward. While tabling the Commission report, Martin stated on 8 March that Canada did not deny the facts of the majority report, but did believe that the report itself was an oversimplification. As far as Canada was concerned, "the factor which underlies the grave situation" in Vietnam "is the determined and long standing attempt of the Hanoi regime to bring South Viet Nam under its control through the pursuit of aggressive policies." This much was evident in the 1962 special report, at which time the Commission undertook to take action on the basis of a fuller report to be prepared by its legal committee.

> Faced since then with the unwillingness of our commission colleagues to act on these promises, we have decided that it was necessary to go ahead on our own to fulfil these obligations.
>
> The most significant conclusions of this legal study have therefore been quoted in paragraph 3 of the Canadian statement of February 13.

Martin's clarification is not entirely satisfactory. Where the Canadian statement of 13 February had implied that it was quoting conclusions of the legal *committee*, upon which the 1962 report had been based, Martin's statement of 8 March would seem to indicate that the conclusions were more likely those of the *Canadians* on the committee, undertaken *after* the 1962 report, pursuing their study unilaterally in impatience with their colleagues. Martin reintroduced confusion two paragraphs later, when he rejected Polish and Indian questioning of the status of the extracts quoted in the Canadian statement of 13 February:

> I cannot agree that a document which has been carefully prepared by a properly constituted committee of the commission,

acting on a majority basis, in pursuance of commission instructions, and on the basis of material referred to it by the commission, has no status.[70]

In other words, the implication now was that it was a (presumably Canada-India) majority report in the legal committee to which the Canadian statement had referred; except that the Indian statement in response had said the conclusions did not have the sanction of any of the Commission's committees. The confusion is compounded by Maneli, head of the Polish delegation (1963–64). He writes that when, after the 1962 report, he suggested a special mobile team investigation (which would necessarily include PAVN officers), the whole issue of Saigon's charges of aggression and subversion was quashed.[71]

Thus by the time of the 1965 bombing of North Vietnam, the gulf between Canada and the other two delegations on the International Commission was complete. Poland and India believed that the action introduced a new and dangerous element into an already volatile situation; Canada argued that it was but a symptom of the instability, which had its root cause in North Vietnamese aggression and subversion. The differences in perception were to persist for a few years. There are already in the 1965 report items in the Canadian statement to which attention should be directed. To begin, the statement does not refer to bombing in North Vietnam; the euphemism is "events." Moreover, the Americans are not referred to at all. Second, Canada accepted the American-cum-South Vietnamese case in its entirety. Hanoi was guilty of aggression, and the bombings were only a limited response. The Canadian delegation failed to recall the second half of the 1962 report, documenting a military alliance between Saigon and Washington in violation of the Geneva Agreements. In the Canadian view, the Commission ought to concentrate its attention on the aggression from the north. Finally, with respect to reestablishing peace, the prerequisite in the Canadian view was a cessation of hostile activities by North Vietnam. The pattern was to persist for a few years, as will become clear.

On 27 February 1965 the Commission informed the cochairmen of a PAVN request to withdraw all teams from North Vietnam. In view of the tension and gravity of the situation, the PAVN felt itself unable to guarantee the security of the team personnel. The

Commission pointed out that such a withdrawal would have far-reaching implications for the work of the Commission under the Agreements. It was prepared to take reasonable risks in the conduct of its tasks, but would reluctantly withdraw if the PAVN reiterated its decision. Poland voted against the Commission decision asking the PAVN to reconsider its request. In the Polish view, Article 35 quite clearly dealt with the alteration of the teams' locations, not with their withdrawal for security reasons, and was therefore inapplicable. The PAVN was responsible for the security of the teams. However, it could not be expected to shoulder the responsibility when the causes of the dangers lay beyond its control, that is, in American bombings. Hanoi repeated the demand for withdrawal by cable on 20 February, and the teams were withdrawn by the next day.[72] In an independent press release on 5 April, the Canadian government charged that the reason adduced by Hanoi for the withdrawal of teams was insufficient. Recalling how ICSC teams had been denied "meaningful controls" in the north for years, Ottawa concluded that their withdrawal in 1965 was "an obvious and very serious illustration of the way the work of the Commission [had] been hindered by North Vietnam."[73]

Summary

The fluctuating fortunes of the military clauses worked out at Geneva can be gleaned from the general comments that the International Commission permitted itself in its reports. In the first, in 1954, the Commission concluded that "the provisions of the Agreement which are of a military or semi-military nature have on the whole been carried out according to the time schedules and directions given in the Agreement." In cases of dispute, the Commission urged the parties to approach problems in a practical spirit and to avoid a narrow, formalistic manner. In its fourth report, in 1955, the Commission remarked that the parties were giving it full cooperation in purely military matters, while civil administration matters were problematic because of questions of sovereignty. The eleventh report, in 1961, closed on a pessimistic note, pointing to the worsening situation with respect to the DMZ and the failure to make headway in the matter of reconstituting the Joint Commission.

In its special report in 1962, the Commission directed the cochairmen to "a recent and deliberate tendency on the part of both Parties to deny or refuse controls" to its teams, with a consequent "near-complete breakdown" in Commission supervision of Articles 16 and 17. The concluding paragraph drew the attention of the cochairmen to the seriousness and gravity of the situation in Vietnam: "Fundamental provisions of the Geneva Agreement have been violated by both Parties, resulting in ever-increasing tension and threat of resumption of open hostilities." The role of the Commission was further hampered by a lack of cooperation. The Polish minority report challenged the majority position by laying the blame solely at the doors of Saigon with its American connection. In the 1965 special report of 13 February, finally, India and Poland attempted to draw the attention of the world to the gravity of the situation created by the American bombing, while Canada sought to place the bombing in the context of North Vietnamese subversion and aggression.

In paragraph 13 of the Final Declaration, members of the Geneva Conference had agreed "to consult one another on any question which may be referred to them by the International Supervisory Commission in order to study such measures as may prove necessary to ensure that the Agreements on the cessation of hostilities in Cambodia, Laos and Viet Nam are respected." Paragraph 13 was the only paragraph of the Declaration of which the United States had refused to take note.

The preceding text chronicles ICSC efforts to implement the Geneva cease-fire agreement, showing shifting nuances between the delegations and over time. Essentially, the disengagement provisions applied largely to the war of 1946–54, and the Commission was able to oversee their implementation in its first year.

Analysis of the Commission's voting record clearly demonstrates that the Vietnamese policies of the ICSC delegations were subsumed under or subordinated to their wider foreign policy considerations. Between 1954 and 1956, Canada, India, and Poland did try to keep the peace to the best of their abilities. This was in furtherance of the peacekeeping ingredient in their foreign policies generally, and their overlapping desire (if for different reasons) to prevent a great-power conflict developing in Vietnam.

After July 1956, when the freeze had set in Vietnam and there were no prospects for a final settlement, their policies locally were increasingly subordinated to their international considerations. For Canada, this meant a declining ability to concur in findings against South Vietnam, especially as South Vietnamese and American interests converged. For Poland, the same was true in regard to North Vietnam. For India, with its variable relations with the great powers, the freeze in Vietnam with the resultant rigidity in the Commission meant that its stance on the Commission would be taken as responses to questions of fundamental importance in relations between the two blocs. It therefore behooved India at the very least to take this into account when dealing with any matter before the Commission, and to be correspondingly cautious. It also meant that India ought not, at a minimum, to allow its involvement in a complex and drawn-out situation to adversely affect the evolution of its own relationships with the great powers. If the direction of the relationship is reversed, it can be argued that the more extensive the big-power involvement in Vietnam, the more likely would India's attitude toward the conflict be conditioned by features of its own relations with the same big powers.

Differences in delegation perceptions and behavior are thus discernible even on the relatively less difficult military issues. It would be rather surprising if they were anything but sharper in the political realm, an analysis of which follows.

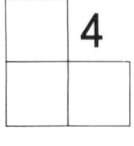
4 The Commission on the Descendant
Human Rights

In a sense, the Western half of the international community assembled at Geneva in the summer of 1954 was concerned mainly to find the means to extricate France from a bloody mess. As one senior Indian official put it in 1975, "that is always what colonialists want." Any peace conference may be said to aim for the realization of three broad objectives: a cease-fire agreement; the creation and maintenance of conditions that ensure the continuation of the cease-fire; and a final political settlement. A cease-fire in Vietnam was one of the mechanisms written into the Geneva Agreements for attaining the second and third objectives. As a matter of analytical convenience, it is useful to separate the second military objective of a peace conference — to ensure through disengagements that a cease-fire does not collapse — from the third, to achieve a lasting resolution of the political essence of a conflict.

In Article 6 of its Final Declaration, the Geneva Conference had recognized that "the essential purpose of the Agreement . . . is to settle military questions with a view to ending hostilities . . . ." The military clauses of the Geneva Agreements thus established a cease-fire in Indochina and created the mechanism for the final French withdrawal from the area. The International Commission was one part of the mechanism, in that in supervising the implementation of the cease-fire, disengagement, and regroupment provisions, it helped to establish the conditions for the French departure.

A permanent political solution, on the other hand, was inherently more difficult. Supervising clauses in the Agreements that had political content, such as those touching upon civil administration, amnesty in the form of freedom from reprisals, movement of peoples, democratic liberties, successor governments to France, and national elections, could be very delicate for the International Commission or any authority. A successful implementation of the military half of the Geneva accords was a necessary but not sufficient condition for an eventual political solution. The failure to execute the political clauses of Geneva created the necessary—and perhaps sufficient—conditions for the eventual breakdown of the cease-fire agreement itself. In effect, the failure to realize the political settlement envisaged in the Geneva accords is the link between the largely successful implementation of the military clauses and the later renewal of the war, albeit with different protagonists.

To Be or Not to Be Political

The cease-fire agreement stipulated in Article 36 that the ICSC would be responsible for supervising the proper execution of the agreement by the parties, by means of control (verification), observation, inspection, and investigation. These functions were charged particularly with respect to regroupment, the demarcation line and demilitarized zone, exchange of prisoners of war and civilian internees, and provisions regulating importation of military men and material. The Commission regarded these as its four unavoidable tasks. It failed, therefore, in the initial stages, when working out its organization and procedures, to anticipate investigative mechanisms for other provisions of the agreement, especially those political in nature. Similarly, expecting a supervisory and control role, the Commission failed to provide for means to investigate complaints of alleged violations of the agreement. In time, the investigation of complaints was to become the Commission's principal and ultimately sole preoccupation. The supervision of the political provisions also began to drain most of its energy before long.

On 3 August 1954—that is, before the ICSC was established—the FUF and PAVN High Commands signed Decision No. 3 in the Central Joint Commission. Therein, they agreed to a general supervision in the implementation of the agreement, reversed the Geneva Agreements by arrogating to the Joint Commission residual supervisory power (which is the position the communists had favored at Geneva), and left to the International

Commission responsibility only where the two sides failed to agree in the Joint Commission.

Decision No. 3 was probably based on the assumption that concentration on the four specific tasks of Article 36, which were military in nature, would be the Commission's wish. Yet, supervision of the political clauses was a residual power. At the New Delhi preparatory conference, the Commission had hoped to avoid involvement in the supervision of the political agreements. The military tasks enumerated in Article 36 were practicable, calling for technical skills to deal with the tangibles of troops, munitions, and territorial lines.

With respect to the political clauses, however, the Commission could easily find itself ensnared in definitional disputes about "reprisals," "discrimination," "democratic freedoms," and even what constituted "help" to refugees (Article 14[d]), and "interference in local civil administration" (Article 15[d]). The problems could easily give rise to political disputes within the International Commission, comprising delegations with totally different legal, political, and moral points of view, and affect its performance in the military sphere. A further complication in the southern zone was that the French forces would accept competence only in military matters, while the Saigon government, on whom responsibility for the execution of the political provisions fell, had all along dissociated itself from the Geneva decisions. Finally, the political clauses involved passing judgment on such sensitive issues as the relations between a government and its citizens, and thus impinged on questions of sovereignty. In the beginning, therefore, as the Canadian delegation put it to Ottawa, the Commission "perhaps conceived its role to be more that of an adviser than an umpire."[1] If so, the Commission's tranquillity lasted less than six weeks, during which, having given tacit consent to Decision No. 3 and its reversal of the Geneva concept, the Commission became set in a reactive role. It would intervene only where the parties failed to reach an agreement and sought its assistance, rather than control and investigate on its own initiative.

The Commission's calm with respect to the political provisions was broken in September 1954; one of the unanticipated consequences of the break was to confirm the Commission's reactive role. The dispute arose over which of the two Commissions should be the first-instance investigative authority with respect to alleged violations of the agreement. In practice, once the Joint Commission was itself unable to resolve disputes, the two High Commands began to take their cases to the International Commission directly. The frequency and volume of complaints from the parties increased steadily to the point where the International Commission focused almost entirely on dealing with complaints from the two sides, each alleging violations by the other. Eventually, the Commission engaged in action only after a formal complaint, specific in allegation, had been received from one party. Perhaps more importantly, when the tranquillity was shattered in September 1954 the Commission found itself plunged well and truly into the sea of political troubles.

The Commission had initially formulated procedures that referred petitions from the public pertaining to Articles 14 and 21 to the appropriate High Command for an internal investigation and comment. The advantage here was that the Commission avoided both implying a lack of faith in the parties, and overextending its resources.

In September, the PAVN complained in the Joint Commission about incidents in south and central Vietnam that had resulted in violent clashes between the Franco-Vietnamese troops and civilians.[2] The Joint Commission reached an impasse when the High Commands accused each other of responsibility for the incidents: the PAVN alleged a massacre of innocent civilians; the French forces retorted that Vietminh agents had provoked confrontations. While the two parties agreed that the incidents deserved thorough investigation, they differed as to how and by whom the investigation should be conducted. The PAVN, in accordance with Decision No. 3 and precedent, demanded that the investigations be principally in the hands of Joint Commission officers. The French in effect repudiated Decision No. 3 and returned to their original Geneva position, that residual powers were vested in the International Commission.

Faced with this dispute, the Indian chairman of the International Commission suggested that "as a matter of practical urgency," but "without prejudice to any views expressed by either party," the two get together and either request an investigation under Article 37 by the International Commission or propose an alternative solution. The French stuck rigidly to their position. The PAVN suggested a compromise: the ICSC teams investigating the incidents should be accompanied by a representative Joint Commission team to "aid and assist the investigation and help the Commission's team get a proper appreciation of the facts." Canada and India pressed for the International team to have investigative and reportorial responsibilities, and the Joint team to have a liaison-cum-support role. By this means, the ICSC could retain its privacy even while having representatives of the two parties present. Its proposal thus declared:

> The International Commission . . . have, without prejudice to the legal positions taken up by the Authorities in respect to the interpretation of the Agreement regarding the functions of the Joint Commission and its Joint groups, decided in view of the urgency of the matter, to have the alleged incidents investigated through their Fixed and Mobile Teams assisted by a Liaison Officer and Interpreter from each side.

It was thus that the Commission became involved in first-instance investigations of alleged violations of the political clauses. Later, the sending of mobile teams accompanied by liaison officers and interpreters who were not allowed to aid in assessments of findings became routine practice. In October, the decision was taken that all mobile teams would be accompanied by an interpreter from each side to ensure the accuracy of interpretations, and that a request from a High Command to attach a liaison officer would receive automatic Commission approval. Thus, while the French fears that witnesses might be intimidated had not been quite eliminated, at least the statements by witnesses could be taken to be accurate in translation. The French were perhaps also apprehensive that the presence of PAVN officers in the midst of South Vietnamese populations might merely serve to excite the latter, and that the officers could serve as contact points with the Vietminh cadres remaining in the south. The PAVN for its part might have desired to maintain an official presence in the south, possibly for the reasons the French suspected. Also, excluding international involvement would have maximized their own freedom in the northern zone, given the differences in political conditions between the two zones.

Article 15(d): Civil Administration
After the withdrawal of troops into appropriate zones had been completed, and designated territories transferred as per schedule,

there was a series of five bloody clashes in central Vietnam between mid-August and the end of September 1954, involving troops and civilians in Vietminh strongholds now under Vietnamese National Army (VNA) control. The incidents posed some serious political questions about the relationship between the military and civil administrators taking over enemy-held territory and its residents. Specifically, at what point did the democratic liberties guaranteed under Article 14(c) become license in need of suppression? When—and to what extent—could the occupying authority justifiably transcend the Article 15(d) prohibition against damage to the life and property of civilians in the name of law and order?

Before the case was over, the Commission had ruled on all these questions. Investigations of the incidents had a four-fold significance: they were the first mobile team investigations; they were the first Commission venture into the political domain of the Geneva Agreements; they led to the first Commission finding of a cease-fire agreement violation; and they established responsibility for the incidents on *both* parties. The last point, however, was possible only because the incidents had occurred as part of the withdrawal process, and were therefore examined by the Commission under Article 15(d). Later incidents would be examined only under Article 14(c), which dealt with the rights of civilians *vis-à-vis* the authorities in charge of the zone. In the southern zone, then, later investigations of incidents under Article 14(c) would not consider whether the authorities had been provoked; they would be limited to examining the behavior of the Franco-Vietnamese authorities.

The incidents in central Vietnam occurred against a backdrop of continuing hostility and deep enmity between the communists and their adversaries. The incident at Ai Nghia, involving an attempt on the part of a crowd to prevent VNA troops from taking down DRVN flags, resulted in death and injury. A similar incident in Ngan Son and Chi Thanh resulted in the death of about eighty people, with half as many injured. For the Commission, determining the facts of the incidents was in itself delicate, as indeed equivalent exercises would be for most governments within their own territories. In the opinion of the Canadian delegation, the Polish team members were more concerned to indict the South Vietnamese authorities than to establish the facts, and the Canadians had therefore to make a concerted effort merely to ensure that the reports of the teams were balanced documents.

The ICSC formed an *ad hoc* committee to investigate the incidents, and took up the committee's report for consideration in December 1954. Desai urged his fellow Commissioners to bear in mind that the areas were coming out of years of warfare, that there was a tension between the political sympathies of the populace and their new government, and that "this was a period of adjustment when events moved too fast for reorienting the psychological attitude of the local population." He pointed out also that political differences and government-population clashes over them were not unknown "even in normal conditions." "The existence of the Geneva Agreement," he reminded them, did "not, by itself, render every incident involving a clash between the civil population and the authorities a violation of the Agreement."

As a general conclusion, the committee had established that the use of force *per se* had been justified in all five cases, but that the amount tended to be excessive. The Commission began by finding both parties to have been lax with respect to implementing the disengagement provisions of the cease-fire agreement. As for provocation by the civilian population, impossibility of proof did not deter the Canadians from being satisfied that Vietminh agents had actively instigated the incidents. The Commission noted that a normal procedure of expressing grievances in groups had been "intensified or exploited by certain persons or groups to give a political colour to these demonstrations." It noted further the inexperience and inadequate training of the French forces in the light of the prevailing conditions. The effect of the two notes was to exonerate both parties from a concerted plan to sabotage the Agreements.

The Commission was able to establish that excessive force had been applied in three of the five incidents. On the question of what action to take where excesses were established, the Commission could recommend that the French High Command punish the officials under its command who had been responsible for the excesses. The task of fixing responsibility and taking suitable punitive measures would be left to the French Command. Poland and India wanted to recommend such action. Canada, however, with respect to action against the southern authorities, pointed to the inadequacy of the evidence, and suggested in its light that the Commission merely ask the French to institute their own investigations and decide upon appropriate measures thereafter. It was ultimately persuaded to recommend punishment upon receiving assurances that the Commission would reconsider its decision if the French furnished evidence to justify the conduct of their officials.

The various conclusions and recommendations were conveyed in a letter dispatched to both parties on 22 December 1954, which concluded with a plea to prevent a recurrence of such incidents. The Franco-Vietnamese authorities were resentful that greater emphasis had not been given to Vietminh provocation, but implemented the recommendation by punishing the responsible officials through reprimands and relieving of commands. Hanoi was pleased with the Commission condemnation of the behavior of the VNA troops, but unhappy with the conclusion that certain persons had exploited the demonstrations to give them political color. In the end, the Commission's decisions were fair, practical, and constructive. In the process, though, the Commission came to recognize that the cease-fire had failed to usher in an era of conciliation. The weight of distrust and suspicion hung heavily enough on both sides to augur ill for the political future of the country.

Amnesty: Reprisals, Migrations, Internees

In the cease-fire agreement, the parties had accepted obligations not only concerning relations with each other but also in respect of their own citizens. Complaints about possible violations of the agreement could, therefore, be expected to come from two sources: the opposing party or private individuals. The latter could thus petition the Commission for redress of grievances pertaining to reprisals, discrimination, democratic liberties, movement from one zone into the other, and civilian internee status. The Commission ruled in its instructions of 21 December 1954 that teams should accept any petitions submitted by individuals—by hand, through the mail, through liaison officers, or through special boxes installed for the purpose at team headquarters. The teams were free to engage in preliminary investigations and on-the-spot solutions, but all petitions had to be forwarded to the Commission. The teams had perforce to guard petitioners' identities from local authorities. At the same time, however, cooperation of the parties was essential in providing the public and the teams access to each other. Such cooperation was not readily forthcoming in either zone by mid-December, as the 21 December instructions recognized. The Commission, therefore, decided on that date that liaison officers be informed that "free accessibility to the team by members of the public is one of the fundamental principles which the Commission is keen to enforce."

Article 14(c): Reprisals and Democratic Liberties
As noted above, beyond the initial incidents in the southern zone, the Commission approached violations of people's freedoms under Article 14(c) of the agreement rather than 15(d). The latter article covered only the process of disengagement of the combatants and the withdrawals and transfers of military forces, equipment, and supplies. The more general "political and administrative measures in the regrouping zones" were covered under Article 14 of the agreement, clause (c) of which obligated each party "to refrain from any reprisals or discrimination against persons or organizations on account of their activities during the hostilities and to guarantee their democratic liberties." The clause was necessary because of the fact that people in the regrouped areas in particular would be living under a regime to which they had been unsympathetic if not actively opposed. The principle of prohibiting reprisals under the circumstances was important enough that the Geneva Conference sought to reinforce it in its Final Declaration with respect to all of Indochina (paragraph 9).

Article 14(c) was thus eminently political. It was also extremely sensitive, requiring an appreciation of the optimal balance between orderly administration and repression which even the Anglo-Saxon democracies have found difficult to achieve *within* their political systems. It was sensitive also because in this instance *outsiders* would be required to pass judgment on the balance struck by the governments in the two zones with respect to their own citizens. Article 14(c) was, therefore, a prime example of the political clauses in the agreement that the Commission had hoped fervently to avoid, for the three delegations represented different types of political regimes. Central to the defining attributes of regimes is the relationship between the government and its citizens. If, therefore, any one of the home governments of the three delegations found it difficult to achieve a harmony between the rights of its citizens and the duties owed to the State (and all three have), what hope was there that they could be brought to agree on a common perception in Vietnam? Even with the best of intentions, and with a total absence of affiliations on the part of any of its delegations with either party, the Commission would have found it an extremely delicate task at best and an impossible one at average to supervise a clause that was of such political content as Article 14(c). As it turned out, the second condition was never met (Poland recognized only Hanoi, and Canada only Saigon), and the first was generally — and increasingly — qualified.

As already shown, the wish to avoid the political provisions was not granted the Commission for long. The disappointment of the Commission comes through in its very first report. Both sides, the Commission noted in its concluding section, "have been sadly lacking in a sense of purpose and urgency in dealing" with the matters pertaining to democratic freedoms. Giving up on its earlier wish, the Commission on 19 October 1954 set up a Committee on Freedoms, to control and supervise action taken under Article 14. Table 1 gives the statistical details of the Commission's role with respect to complaints and investigations in cases of damage to life and property in its first year. The table establishes quite clearly the pattern of Commission activity insofar as alleged violations of Article 14(c) were concerned. The Commission was to expend a considerable portion of its energy in reacting to complaints lodged by the Hanoi authorities alleging reprisals and denials of freedoms in the southern zone. From December 1955 to July 1956, for example, the Commission received 102 complaints from the PAVN alleging a total of 281 reprisal incidents in the south, to five complaints from the French alleging eighteen incidents in the north.[3]

TABLE 1

Statistical Details of Cases under Article 14(c), 1954–55

	FUF	PAVN
1. Number of complaints received by the ICSC, alleging violations of Article 14(c), from	12	66
2. Number of complaints, in which ICSC teams undertook investigations, from	3	38
3. Number of investigations pending, in territory controlled by	10	0

TABLE 1 continued   FUF   PAVN

4. Number of cases in which loss or damage to   15   0
   life and property established, against
5. Number of cases in which corrective action   13   0
   recommended, to
6. Number of cases in which the recommenda-   7   n.a.
   tions were implemented, by

Source: ICSC, *Fourth Interim Report,* Appendix III.

The sixth report marks an open acknowledgment of the many problems besetting the Commission in supervising implementation of Article 14(c), especially in the southern zone. The Commission decided upon three mobile teams to investigate the allegations in the south, but met with "delaying tactics." Concurrence of the French High Command, requested for all three in March 1956, was finally received for two in July 1956. However, the Saigon authorities were not eager to cooperate. The Commission was unable to send out any teams in the southern zone, despite the fact that the allegations and complaints regarding violations of Article 14(c) were many and serious. In the circumstances, it found itself unable to confirm or refute the charges, "as it has not been permitted to verify them through the machinery laid down in the Agreement." Mobile Team 47 had, however, succeeded in conducting an inquiry in April 1955 in the Chi Hoa Prison, on complaints that the French had violated Article 21. During the inquiry the team discovered the arrest of twenty-five prisoners since the cease-fire. A Commission examination determined a violation of Article 14(c) in fifteen cases, the immediate release of all being recommended by the Commission. Its recommendation was not implemented. A similar recommendation on 26 June met an identical fate.[4]

Implementation of Article 14(c) continued to be one of the major problems confronting the ICSC. The Saigon government soon decided not to reply to complaints under the article. It also decided to deny permission for mobile team investigations of such complaints. Between August 1956 and April 1957, it refused to concur in the deployment of eight mobile teams the Commission wished to dispatch, and it also prevented the deployment of two mobile teams to the investigation of which concurrence had already been given. The Commission was able to determine by a majority decision, with Canada dissenting, that the detention of one prisoner constituted a violation of Article 14(c).[5] When the government in Saigon declined to implement the Commission's recommendation for his release, the Commission decided upon action under Article 43 and informed the Geneva members of South Vietnam's disobedience.

The invocations of Article 43 failed to produce any change in Saigon. The story remained essentially the same. At first, Saigon furnished some particulars but failed to implement ICSC recommendations for release of detainees. Soon, however, Saigon simply ignored requests for comments upon PAVN allegations of violations under Article 14(c). The Commission equally stubbornly persisted in its exercise in futility by finding South Vietnam guilty of not having afforded all possible assistance and cooperation under Article 25.[6]

Canadian attitudes to South Vietnamese transgressions of Article 14(c) were in part a product of their earlier experiences regarding Article 14(d) in the north (see pp. 130ff.). At least the Saigon authorities did not imitate Hanoi's tactics of deception and obstruction in order to frustrate ICSC investigations. Instead, South Vietnam stood on a point of principle and refused to permit the investigations. The results, according to Canadian representatives, were that the Saigon government was punished for its integrity rather than rewarded for it.[7] The Indians concluded that the violations recorded against the north were technical and those against the south substantive.[8]

The extent to which the Canadian delegation had become combatively partisan by 1959 is shown in the Phu Loi affair.[9] Phu Loi was a South Vietnamese "civic re-education center." There was a scandal of sorts concerning rumors of poisonings in the center in December 1958, and Hanoi took its complaints on the score to the ICSC. The Commission discussed the complaints at its 507th meeting on 14 February 1959. Commissioner J. P. Erichsen-Brown did not simply reject the complaints. Instead, he took to the offensive and attempted to have the Hanoi authorities put in the dock. In his view, Hanoi had deliberately fomented the scandal through its agents in the south, and it would therefore be appropriate for the Commission to censure the DRVN authorities.

The Commission's role with respect to Article 14(c) was not all, however, "fun and futility." It did make one major ruling that was quite indicative of the positions of the three delegations by 1959–61. In 1959, the PAVN complained to the Commission about the antisubversion law, 10/59, passed by the South Vietnamese National Assembly in May 1959.[10] Hanoi alleged that the law was in violation of Article 14(c). Saigon briefly abandoned its stance of indifference, and communicated to the Commission its view that Law 10/59 was not contrary to any of the provisions of the Geneva Agreements. The Commission decided, over Canadian dissent, to inform both parties that it had requested and received the text of the law and was in the process of examining it. In the meantime, the Commission drew the attention of parties to its letters of 5 March 1956, and reaffirmed that

> no law, regulation or order in either of the two Zones can, in any way, supersede the obligations which the two Parties have undertaken under the provisions of Article 14(c) of the Agreement on the Cessation of Hostilities in Viet-Nam, namely, to refrain from any reprisals or discrimination against persons on account of their activities during the hostilities and to guarantee their democratic liberties.[11]

Canada was willing to accept the principle in theory, but did not deem it appropriate for the Commission to cite it in the context of Law 10/59 just yet, when the law was still under consideration by the legal committee of the Commission. It was the view of the Canadian delegation, moreover, that Articles 1, 10, and 24 of the cease-fire agreement provided the legal framework within which Law 10/59 could operate as long as it did not violate Article 14(c) in application. These were in addition to Commissioner Erichsen-Brown's contention that Law 10/59 was a municipal law and thus beyond the competence of the Commission. The response of the Indian and Polish delegations to the Canadian minority statement was threefold. In the first place, they held it necessary for the Commission to reaffirm the principle because of the seriousness of the allegations. Second, they pointed out that the principles had received fresh affirmation with respect to *both* parties. And third, they stated that irrespective of the final findings on any subject, the Commission was free at any time to affirm principles that clearly followed from the Agreements and which had been unanimously accepted by the ICSC.

In other words, Canada was demurring from even appearing to hint that South Vietnam's tough new antisubversion law[12] was questionable by reaffirming principles it had agreed to three years earlier. When it came to the actual decision, however, it was Poland's turn to dissent and record a minority statement. At its 574th meeting on 25 April 1960, the Commission decided that Law 10/59 did not in itself violate Article 14(c) or any other provision of the Geneva Agreements. If, however, the law was applied in such a way as to conflict with Article 14(c), then the latter would prevail. The Commission conveyed its interpretation to both parties. In the Polish view, the law constituted a "flagrant violation of Article 14(c) of the Geneva Agreement and of paragraph 7 of the Final Declaration," especially in its provision for the establishment and organization of "Special Tribunals." The Canadians and Indians rejected the Polish contention as being "untenable." They referred back to a December 1956 decision by the Commission to the effect that it was not concerned with the "quality" of regimes but rather with their implementations of the Agreements:

> The Commission cannot lay down a standard of democratic liberties applicable to the whole of the population in both Zones, as this would depend on the laws, rules and regulations in force in either of the Zones. . . . [I]t cannot go into the nature of the regimes in either Zone.

The Commission declined a request from Hanoi to reconsider its decision. Referring to the fact that the DRVN had addressed the cochairmen of the Geneva Conference directly on the matter, the Commission reiterated its position (Poland dissenting), that there was no provision made at Geneva for an appeal against a decision of the Commission.

The North Vietnamese submitted five specific complaints alleging applications of Law 10/59 in violation of Article 14(c). They charged that reprisals, including execution, had been carried out against former resistance members under Law 10/59. Saigon denied the accusation and submitted its own version of the incidents. When Hanoi challenged the "correctness of the facts" as reported by its rival, the Commission requested the South Vietnamese government to submit the complete dossiers and judgments. This was held necessary to sift through the two conflicting versions. It also expressed concern that South Vietnam had not responded to allegations of mopping-up campaigns, and recommended that comments be forthcoming within a month. In its final report, the Commission found South Vietnam guilty of noncooperation under Article 25 in the case of alleged reprisals and mopping-up operations against former resistance members in eastern Nam Bo, and decided to take action under Article 43; the Canadian delegation dissented. In another specific complaint where reprisal against a former resistance member had been alleged under Law 10/59, the Commission decided to close the case after it had examined copies of the relevant dossiers. This time, predictably enough, Poland dissented from the Commission decision.

In the 1962 special report, the Polish delegation argued that the majority report had ignored violations of Article 14(c) by the RVN. In the Polish view, persecution of former resistance members, followed by a persecution of all democratic elements, had given rise to a widespread movement against the Saigon government. In other words, Poland was arguing for an appreciation of the political context within which the alleged subversive acts were taking place. Also, before leaving Article 14(c), it should be mentioned that as early as 31 December 1954, Diem had issued a directive that was actually a plan developed by the covert American Saigon Military Mission for the "pacification of Vietminh and dissident areas."[13]

Article 14(d): Freedom of Movement
The Geneva Conference guaranteed the Vietnamese residence in their traditional homes, free from the fear of reprisals at the hands of a different set of authorities. The Conference recognized, however, that despite the guarantees, the prospect of living under a hostile or alien regime would be unpalatable enough to many that they would wish to transplant themselves across the zones to be able to continue living under a compatible regime. The Geneva Agreements, therefore, provided that in the three-hundred-day period between the signing of the Agreements and the movement of the troops, "any civilians residing in a district controlled by one party who wish to go and live in the zone assigned to the other party shall be permitted and helped to do so by the authorities in that district" (14(d)). The question of determining what constituted adequate help could be expected to be particularly vexatious. The

substance of the provision was again sought to be shored up in the Final Declaration, paragraph 8 of which decreed that "the provisions of the agreements . . . must, in particular, allow everyone in Viet Nam to decide freely in which zone he wishes to live."

The problem in the Declaration formulation was the use of the word "freely." The sight of thousands of refugees (60 percent of them Catholic) fleeing from the communist regime, "voting with their feet," exercised a powerful appeal for Canadians, as it would not for Indians or Poles.[14] As it turned out, the movement of population was overwhelmingly from the northern zone to the southern (Table 2). Not surprisingly, the number of complaints alleging violations of Article 14(d) could be expected to be larger from the south, and transgressions of the provision could be expected to be greater in the north. Thus, by the end of the first quarter of 1955, the Commission was complaining that while Article 14(c) was being retarded in implementation in the south, Article 14(d) was suffering the same fate in the north.[15] A major reason why there was no exodus from the south to the north may have been that communist followers were directed to stay behind for the elections and the campaign for popular power in the south. Only those well known to the authorities migrated north.[16]

TABLE 2
Figures of Movement of Population in Vietnam under Article 14(d), up to 20 July 1955

	North to South	South to North
Figures given by South Vietnam	888,127	
Figures given by PAVN	892,876	4,269

Source: ICSC, *Fourth Interim Report*, Appendix IV

The Canadians were from the start vigorous proponents of an activist Commission role in supervising implementation of Article 14(d). The Indians were more reluctant for fear of alienating one party completely. At the eighteenth ICSC meeting on 4 September 1954, the Indians described their policy as a "parallel approach in respect of similar problems," implying a balanced criticism of both sides, not a unilateral condemnation of one. Thus at the thirty-ninth meeting on 12 October, even while agreeing to send a team to monitor the refugee evacuation, chairman M. J. Desai stressed that "The team's mission should be fact-finding, not fault-finding. This would in general apply to all investigation teams."

At the forty-first ICSC meeting on 14 October 1954, Acting Commissioner Marcel Cadieux proposed that refugees could be sheltered in regular Commission camps pending inquiry into their cases. Commissioner P. Ogrodzinski in reply pointed to the complex juridical aspects of the proposal, and advised the Commission "to avoid any diplomatic embarrassments." Desai rejected the asylum camp proposal. But at the next meeting the following day, he also rejected PAVN denials of ICSC competence in the matter (Colonel Ha Van Lau, the PAVN Liaison Officer, wanted the subject left to the Joint Commission forum).

At the fifty-first meeting on 31 October 1954, the freshly arrived Sherwood Lett opposed Ogrodzinski's demand for "parallelism" of investigations in the two zones. He stressed the mandatory language of the Agreements. Desai did not dispute this, but pointed out the physical necessity of working out a system of priorities. At the meeting the next day, Desai further remarked that the Commission had avoided "lengthy judicial debates, and concentrated mainly on finding practical solutions to build up an atmosphere of effective cooperation." On the other side, on 30 November Desai rejected Polish demands that investigations be numerically balanced in the two zones. "Reciprocity" was out of the question; every issue had to be considered on its merit. The subsequent Indian stand on controlling airports in South Vietnam was thus at least consistent.[17]

On 1 February 1955, Desai accepted Canadian complaints that Article 14(d) procedures needed to be improved, and an Indian-Canadian majority forwarded a fourteen-point recommendation to both parties to facilitate implementation of the provision. The Canadians remained dissatisfied with the response. On 12 March, Lett proposed that the Geneva powers be informed of 14(d) nonfulfillment because of DRVN intransigence and obstruction, and that three roving mobile teams investigate how far the recommendations of 1 February had been implemented in the north. Ogrodzinski's demand for parallelism was again rejected by Desai: "The number of teams to be sent out depended entirely on the need and not on any basis of reciprocity." But Desai also declined to accept the idea of a special report on a subarticle.

The Commission devoted public attention to the problem of securing implementation of Article 14(d) in its very first report. The South Vietnamese had alleged that Hanoi was hampering the free movement of refugees. The Commission investigated two places, Nam Dinh and Phat Diem. At Nam Dinh, the Commission's mobile team came across not obstacles but pressures from the French and church authorities upon the populace to move south. The team at Phat Diem ran into a congregation of 10,000 refugees, of which the Commission helped transplant 8,268. The Commission also delivered a gentle reprimand, in the form of a conclusion that "the administrative process should not be so clumsy, slow and complex as in effect to defeat the provisions of Article 14(d)."

By April 1955, the Commission had progressed to expressing serious concern at the inadequate administrative arrangements and transport facilities that were causing delays in the implementation of Article 14(d) in the PAVN zone. Nevertheless, at the end of the three-hundred-day period, the Commission was able to report that the bulk of the people who wished to change their zone of residence had been able to do so by 18 May 1955. It described its own role as seeing that transport and administrative facilities were adequate, and that there was no pressure or obstacle to the free exercise of the choice regarding the zone of residence. The Commission had even stressed the importance of sufficient publicity to inform people of their right to change residence. Moreover, it also succeeded in obtaining an extension of the movement period to 20 July. During the grace period, 4,749 people moved south, while 1,671 travelled north. The Commission did establish, however, that an additional, 2,531 persons had wanted to move north because they feared reprisals at the hands of a government in Saigon that was talking tough on communists by the middle of 1955; they were denied permits and facilities for the move. The Commission also investigated, with negative results, PAVN charges that many people had been forced to flee south and would like to return to the north.[18]

Canada was dissatisfied with the Commission's statement of the problem. It attached an amendment twenty paragraphs long, the gist of which was two substantive accusations against Hanoi. First, Canada alleged the PAVN to have resorted to delaying and obstructing Commission teams in the course of their investigations under Article 14(d). Second, the Canadians charged that individuals wishing to exercise their choice to move south were not permitted and helped to do so; they were on occasion prevented and hindered from so doing. As examples of the latter, the Canadian amendment cited group intimidation of those wishing to seek the Commission's help and the physical molestation and forcible dragging away of intending evacuees by hostile crowds. Indeed, the last had at times apparently occurred even in the presence of team officials.[19] While it was impossible to prove that the measures were part of an organized policy by the North Vietnamese authorities, this nonetheless was the Canadian view. Furthermore, the Canadian statement continued, "soldiers, political cadres and local militia were frequently stationed in the houses of the Catholic population with instructions to prevent them from leaving their homes in order to contact the teams."[20]

In April 1955, the French High Command lodged a complaint with the Commission alleging that the seminarists of Xa Doai were not being permitted to move south. The Commission decided to dispatch Mobile Team F-49 to investigate the complaint, but the investigation was stalled when the PAVN refused the team members entry into the seminary. They also failed to implement the Commisssion recommendations that the seminarists be produced before Fixed Team Vinh. The Commission decided to take action under Article 43 and inform members of the Geneva Conference of the PAVN failure to implement its recommendation. By that time (1957), Poland was dissenting from the condemnation of even such obvious cases of noncooperation by Hanoi. Similarly, when in 1956 the Commission decided that of the 149 ex-prisoners of war engaged in North Vietnamese construction yards, 89 should be allowed to exercise their option of zone of residence, Hanoi rejected the Commission decision. The subsequent conversion of the request into a recommendation also met with a rejection from Hanoi. The Commission then decided in 1957, and again over Polish dissent, to take action under Article 43.[21]

The Commission reports invoke Article 14(d) against South Vietnam only once after July 1955. In 1959, with respect to the eight people whose release had been recommended by the Commission on the basis of the report by Mobile Team 103, the Commission further recommended that the choice of residence be permitted to four of the eight who had expressed their desire to go to North Vietnam, and that facilities be provided for their move. Saigon did not comply with the recommendation. The Commission therefore held in September 1960 that South Vietnam had failed to provide full cooperation under Article 25, and that action would be taken against it under Article 43. By 1960, Canada was dissenting from findings against Saigon.[22]

A final point worth bearing in mind in the episode of the refugees is the part played by covert American efforts under the direction of Colonel Edward G. Landsdale.[23] It raises the question about how "free" was the exercise of choice by many Vietnamese in the frantic days of 1954–55 when subjected to "psychological warfare" tactics of manipulation.[24]

In conclusion, one may make the simple observation that the concerns of the ICSC delegations with respect to the freedom of movement provision were dissimilar. For Canadians, there were two extra elements of interest in that the refugees were mainly Catholics, and were escaping communism. Pearson declared in 1955 that the provision "has been a matter of great concern to us in view of our responsibility on this commission, because it has involved the fate of many thousands of Christians who have suddenly found themselves under the hard and intolerant rule of a communist administration." The Canadian delegation made every effort to facilitate freedom of movement, Pearson said, despite obstructive tactics of the communist government.[25] Discussing the matter two months later, he pointed to the inherent difficulties in the agreement, in the need to gather evidence, in the need to reach agreed interpretations, and in the lack of enforcement powers. The Commission's reports, he added, reflected the positions of the Commission as a whole, and as such "do not reflect entirely our dissatisfaction with the freedom of movement position."[26] At the very least, nevertheless, the Commission's investigations had represented a steady pressure on the parties which made nonimplementation that much more difficult.[27]

"Dissatisfaction" is an understatement. In retrospect, in the light of the Commission's failures in other more important respects, its record on 14(d) is regarded as something of a modest triumph. At the time, however, it was probably the single most decisive element in socializing Canadian officials into a lasting posture of determined anticommunism. As one former ICSC representative explained, the problem of Catholic refugees was a moral dilemma. Everyone assumed that Ho Chi Minh would win the 1956 elections.

But in that event, "the refugees we had helped would be much worse off than if they had never moved, since their disloyalty to the new government would be a matter of record. It was a moral problem. But Diem took it out of our hands" by refusing to accept elections, and for that reason he "was worthy of our support."[28] The sincerity of the agonized soul-searching of Canadian officers was due to it being literally a matter of life and death for thousands of people committed to opposing communism. The first year of the ICSC, and the refugee issue in particular, was thus a most important factor in the educative experience of Canadians in Indochina. They would neither forget the repression and conformity of communist rule in North Vietnam, nor condone the brutality and callousness of communist behavior toward would-be refugees.

But because of vigorous Canadian prosecution of the matter, Indians, led by Krishna Menon, categorized the Canadians as "Western Poles" by March-April 1955.[29] The Canadians were quite upset. They, in marked contrast to the Poles, had made every effort to act judiciously and impartially. In the process, they had scrupulously avoided colluding with the Franco-South Vietnamese authorities. Could the same be said of the Polish-DRVN relationship?

The reasons for Canada's position being different from its colleagues' are not far to seek. India would not be particularly affected by the fact that most refugees were Christian; would be indifferent as to the regimes in the two zones, if not actually favorable to the north; and would probably consider the Canadian concerns sentimental in the light of its own experience of partition and the attendant carnage and mass migrations.

Connections between the coexistence of Church and State in Poland and the attitude of the Polish delegation in the ICSC toward Catholics migrating from North to South Vietnam can at best be speculative and tenuous. Nevertheless, it is not implausible to suggest that the delegation in its official role would be sensitive to possible repercussions at home, while some members of the delegation in their individual capacities may also have been sympathetic to the plight of the Catholics. At the same time, the Polish delegation's concerns would be opposite those of the Canadian delegation insofar as the refugees were fleeing from communism.

The DRVN faced a dilemma in that if the Catholics were allowed to migrate south, they would strengthen Diem's political base. If, however, the Catholics were compelled to remain in the north, they would be obdurately uncooperative and weaken the political base of the communist regime. Hanoi began by requesting Moscow's help in containing the politically embarrassing exodus to the south. Specifically, the Soviets were to use their influence to dampen Indian eagerness in the matter. Instead, the Soviets in talks with the Poles suggested that the Polish delegation should cooperate with its colleagues in solving the refugee problem. Maneli notes that Hanoi, concerned not to damage prospects for the 1956 elections, decided ultimately to let the Catholics leave. However, local authorities in many instances sabotaged central directives.[30]

Article 21: Prisoners of War, Civilian Internees
Article 21 of the cease-fire agreement attempted to govern the conditions under which the "liberation and repatriation of all prisoners of war and civilian internees" was to be effected. They were to be released within thirty days of the cease-fire in each theater (21(a)), and "surrendered to the appropriate authorities of the other party, who shall give them all possible assistance in proceeding to their country of origin, place of habitual residence or the zone of their choice" (21(c)). "Civilian internees" was defined to include any person who had been arrested in consequence of "having in any way contributed to the political and armed struggle between the two parties" (21(b)). The first of the three clauses was a relatively simple matter, of determining the "facts" of the situation. The definition of a civilian internee, however, made it incumbent to establish the cause of detention before ascertaining the status of a *détenu*. There could also be the further problem of an internee being released and then rearrested on a purportedly nonpolitical charge. The third clause provided an escape against just such a possibility, by requiring that the release be effected to the other party. However, clause 21(c) had its own problems. If a prisoner wished to remain in the southern zone, for example, what was the sense in his being handed over to the PAVN authorities first, and where was the guarantee that the latter would return him to the southern zone as his preferred choice of residence? The International Commission could not hope to escape the problem, as one of its specified "particular" tasks was to "Control the operations of releasing prisoners of war and civilian internees" (35(c)). Although supervision of Article 21 was not among the more prominent tasks

reported by the Commission, it did provide as sharp a division between the delegations as any other provision. Moreover, of the public references to Article 21 by the Commission in its reports, all with an early and a final exception dealt with violations alleged against the southern authorities.

The reference to allegations of violations of Article 21 by the PAVN authorities occurs in the fifth report. The French had brought to the attention of the Commission five cases of detention where they believed the *détenus* to be entitled to claim prisoner of war status under Article 21. A Commission team investigated the allegations and concluded that they had not been proved. The Canadian delegation, however, did not subscribe to the Commission position. In its view, the five prisoners should have been handed over to the French High Command. While the Canadians conceded that it could not be established with certainty that the five were detained as prisoners of war for a year after the cease-fire, they did find sufficient evidence to indicate that the prisoners were under restrictions that effectively negated their right to live in their preferred zone of residence. With respect to another French complaint, that 141 Vietnamese officers had been detained in prisoner of war camps since the cease-fire, the Commission again failed to find the allegation proved. Nevertheless, the Commission did believe that the 141 ex-prisoners, by being employed in construction yards upon release, had been unable to exercise their choice of residence. The Canadian delegation in this instance concluded simply that the general allegation was neither proved nor disproved. The last reference to Article 21 in the Commission reports is in its final regular report (1961). It had received a petition from M. B. Zagur through its suboffice in Hanoi claiming that he was entitled to Commission asylum because he was a prisoner of war. The Commission, however, determined that he was a *rallie* (deserter), not an escaped prisoner of war, and that the provisions of Article 21, therefore, did not extend to him. Canada, from a quite understandably different political perspective, could not be expected to share in a decision that condemned a person to life as a prisoner under a communist government, and recorded a dissenting vote.

The story of the difficulties encountered by the Commission in its attempts to supervise implementation of Article 21 in the southern zone is taken up in the sixth report.[31] The Saigon government denied that a case of nineteen civilian internees was covered by Article 21(b). According to Saigon, they were former members of the National Armed Forces who had been detained or punished under the military law applicable to them. They could not, therefore, be classified or considered as civilian internees. The Canadian delegation found Saigon's statement quite acceptable. However, after examining the legal aspects, the Commission by a majority decided otherwise. When it was clear that a person had been arrested and convicted because he had contributed to the political and armed struggle between the two Vietnamese parties, the Commission concluded, his case was covered by Article 21, irrespective of the law he was convicted under and independently of his status at the time of arrest and conviction. The Commission decision was conveyed to the French High Command, but South Vietnam adhered to its own interpretation of Article 21(b).

The Commission ran into trouble with the French as well. The two cases of Tran Quy Minh, alias Hamaide Francois, and Nguyen Truong Sinh, alias Tangavelou, had been with the Commission since mid-1955. The Commission concluded that both were civilian internees under Article 21(b), and informed the French High Command accordingly in February 1956. The two were believed to be in custody in France. The Commission directed that they be produced in Saigon in order that their choice of zone of residence could be ascertained. The French, however, took the position that the two were French nationals and that their cases were not, therefore, covered under Article 21. They accordingly refused to implement the Commission's recommendation. The Commission then drew the attention of the cochairmen to the matter in its sixth report.[32]

The Commission continued to be severely hampered by the lack of cooperation from the South Vietnamese government. In the 1956–57 period, for instance, it was unable to judge the cases of 122 alleged prisoners of war or internees because Saigon refused to produce the relevant dossiers or documents. Nevertheless, the Commission did conclude during the period that in one instance a prisoner in South Vietnam was a civilian internee, and recommended his release. Canada did not assent to this decision. When its recommendation was not implemented, the Commission subsequently held, again over Canadian dissent, that South Vietnam was guilty of a violation under Article 25 for not having offered full assistance, and that the Commission would take action under Article 43 and inform members of the Geneva Conference of the failure on Saigon's part.[33] The pattern held until the end of Commission reports.

Conclusion

The difficulties besetting the Commission arose from the inherently problematical nature of human rights as much as from deliberate obstructionism. Clearly, the Commission attempted to carry out its mandate even in this tricky field. However, a detailed look at the Commission's own reports shows that by the late 1950s and in the 1960s a distressing pattern had emerged. The position of the two alliance delegations in the ICSC had become polarized, with the result that the nonaligned chairman's decision became the *de facto* arbiter of the Commission decision. This naturally placed strains on India different in kind and magnitude from those on Poland and Canada. At the same time, in the immediate aftermath of the Geneva Conference, the Commission was able to function with some effectiveness even in regard to politically sensitive matters. These early successes had a dual basis. First, there was sufficient give-and-take behind the scenes between the three delegations to produce a working cooperation and an outward appearance of smoothness. Second, consensual decisions of the ICSC translated into execution in the field because neither of the two original belligerents wished to give offense to or act in defiance of the Commission in the early stages.

The chief political provision of the Geneva Agreements, nevertheless, was not the clauses on human rights, however admirable they may have been as expressions of sentiments. Rather, it was the call for Vietnamese reunification through countrywide elections. On this provision, it was not too difficult to foresee problems. Whichever side feared losses in the elections could be expected to resist holding them at all. This was indeed the case in regard to the southern regime in Vietnam. The northern regime, by the same token, would fight to hold elections, in order to consummate the Geneva Agreements. Ultimately, the fight raged on the juridical, political, and military battlefields.

5 The Commission in the Background
Vietnamese Reunification

The clause of greatest consequence in the Geneva Agreements pertained to the general elections that would reunify the country. They were scheduled for July 1956, but not held, because South Vietnam demurred and then flatly refused to honor the elections pledge. The strongest ground Saigon put forward for its refusal was that it could in no way be construed to be a successor regime to the French.

Divorce of Authority from Responsibility

Article 27 of the cease-fire agreement seemed unambiguous in its specification of the "signatories . . . and their successors in their *functions*," and mandatory in its language: the parties "*shall* be responsible for ensuring the observance and enforcement" of the agreement. The problem, however, arose because of that one difficulty the Geneva Conference had tried to sweep under the carpet, *viz.*, the status of the State of Vietnam (South Vietnam), *at the time of the signing of the Agreements*. The French, in their urgency to secure a release from Vietnam, had managed both to have their cake and eat it at Geneva. Vietnam was already a fully independent and sovereign state and recognized as such within the French Union; but France still had the competence to sign an agreement on behalf of the State of Vietnam even over its most explicit protests.

In order to maintain the argument that the 17th parallel was a temporary military demarcation line, not a permanent political boundary, the Geneva Conference had assigned responsibility for execution of the agreement to the *military* authorities, the High Command of the PAVN and the FUF. Article 27 continued:

> The Commanders of the Forces of the two parties shall, within their respective commands, take all steps and make all arrangements necessary to ensure full compliance with all the provisions of the present Agreement *by all elements and military personnel under their command.* (Emphasis added.)

The civil authorities were thus left unspecified, and the question of the relationship between the competent military commanders and their respective political governments was ignored. Yet the question was clearly of fundamental importance, one that was to lead very soon, in the Commission's own words, to a "divorce of authority from responsibility in the South."[1] The confusion was compounded (or the separation made irreparable and divorce inevitable) by the French Declarations at Geneva on 21 July 1954. In the first Declaration, France agreed to withdraw its troops from Indochina if the latter's governments so requested. In the second, the French promised to base their policies in Indochina on "respect for the independence and sovereignty, the unity and territorial integrity" of the three countries of Indochina. The Geneva Conference as a whole took note of these in its own Final Declaration. Although the contradictions of the Geneva formula were to take on their sharpest form with respect to the question of general elections for Vietnam, other problems arose from the divorce, including custody of the ICSC.

The essence of the dispute was stated most succinctly by President Diem in a declaration broadcast on 16 July 1955:

> We did not sign the Geneva agreements. . . . We are in no way bound by these agreements. . . .[2]

The Commission underscored the point that because of the categorical attitude of South Vietnam, the French were unable to fulfill obligations in the southern zone. In the Commission's view, the attitude of South Vietnam required an early consideration by the Geneva co-chairmen to resolve the uncertainty regarding the sanction for the continued operation of the Commission, and the probable duration of its activities. (The Canadian delegation was quite understanding of the French predicament, and sought to exonerate the French High Command in its amending statement in the fourth report.) The response of the cochairmen was far from helpful to the appeal by the Commission. The United Kingdom and the USSR declared in December 1955 that their responsibilities were "neither more nor less than those of the other Powers adhering to the Final Declaration of the Geneva Conference."³

Legal Arguments
The juridical issues can be summarized as follows. In 1954, neither the cease-fire agreement nor the Final Declaration of the Geneva Conference provided for the resolution of a stalemate during the prospective consultations for general elections. Nor did either document foresee the type of problem that ultimately arose — the refusal of the competent authority in one zone to consult about and then participate in the general elections. The validity of South Vietnam's refusal to engage in either consultations or elections hinged on the question of whether it was bound by the Geneva Agreements. The answer to that was in turn related but not limited to whether South Vietnam could be construed to be the successor in functions of the French colonial regime. A similar problem had been addressed in 1953, when the Korean armistice agreement provided that "responsibility for compliance with and enforcement of the terms and provisions of this armistice agreement is that of the signatories hereto and their successors in command." The Korean clause was thus more specific in assigning responsibility to the military commanders.

An exhaustive analysis of the legal aspects has been undertaken by Robert F. Randle.⁴ He concluded, first, that if on 21 July 1954 the State of Vietnam was the duly constituted government of a sovereign state, then it was free to withhold its consent to be bound by any of the provisions of the Geneva accords, unless its subsequent conduct implied consent; in fact, South Vietnam had officially protested against both the Agreement and the Declaration at the time. Second, if the State of Vietnam was not sovereign on 21 July 1954 (in which event, which entity was the legatee of a French bequest of sovereignty: the Democratic Republic of Vietnam or the Republic of Vietnam?), but became so before July 1956, it — or its successor the Republic of Vietnam — was free upon the assumption of sovereignty to refuse to be bound by the Geneva Agreements, unless it was the successor of France. Even in the latter case, the legal rule according to which obligations survive state succession does not extend to internal political arrangements, as opposed to, say, external commercial or cultural questions.

Randle, distinguishing between juridical and functional sovereignty in terms of *de jure* and *de facto* exercise of authority, establishes that South Vietnam exercised neither in July 1954. By July 1956, however, the Saigon government was functionally sovereign in the southern zone (and remained so until insurgency in 1959), and even its juridical sovereignty was plausible on the basis of French declarations and formal recognition by more than thirty states. For the DRVN, *de jure* sovereignty was plausible in early 1954, and probable in July 1956; *de facto* sovereignty was probable in July 1954 and certain in July 1956.

Further, the cease-fire agreement did not bind either the government or the High Command of the army of the State of Vietnam. In fact, the explicit theory of the State of Vietnam was that the French High Command maintained command over South Vietnamese troops only through a delegation of authority from Bao Dai, the Vietnamese chief of state. The French High Command, according to this theory, could not bind the State of Vietnam to the terms of an arrangement as significant as the cease-fire agreement without prior consent, which neither had been obtained nor would have been given.

The question of South Vietnam's obligations under the Geneva accords was not limited to the determination of its status as a successor state. Even if it was the successor in functions to France, it is axiomatic that it could not be bound by obligations additional to those imposed by the accords upon France. And the question of what obligations were binding on France is itself unclear. The problem arises essentially because of the status of the Final Declaration.[5]

On the basis of the cease-fire agreement, one can assign to France the responsibilities to implement the cease-fire, not introduce arms and soldiers into Vietnam, and recognize the unity, independence, and territorial integrity of Vietnam. Beyond these responsibilities, however, the position is ambiguous, especially as regards the articles of the Final Declaration. Was the Declaration an unsigned treaty, the terms of which were binding upon the Conference participants? Or was it more in the nature of a minute of the Conference? Since neither written nor verbal consent of *all* nine participants was given to the Declaration, it cannot be said to have created *collective* conference obligations. Furthermore, in paragraphs 1, 4, 5, 10, and 11 of the Declaration, the Conference *took note* of the several documents produced at Geneva. Does the phrase "takes note" indicate a statement of intent with respect to certain courses of action, or does it impose legally binding obligations? The point of all this is that the questions are at least legitimate, and the answers to them are not self-evident.

Washington consistently argued that South Vietnam did not sign the cease-fire agreement and did not adhere to the Final Declaration. As such, its status as a successor state to France, bound by all the provisions of the Geneva accords, was unclear. A more rigid attitude was taken by John Norton Moore. France had granted substantial independence to the State of Vietnam prior to the Geneva accords, he noted, and the two had entered into a series of independence agreements which would in international law take precedence over later inconsistent treaty obligations. Therefore, "there was at least substantial question whether France had capacity to bind the state of Viet-Nam." There was also the element of the political background. By the time of the Conference, the State of Vietnam was recognized by more than thirty countries, was a member of specialized United Nations agencies, had been endorsed since 1952 by the General Assembly as a state qualified for United Nations membership, and had a presence at Geneva separate from France.[6]

Daniel G. Partan concedes that there is disagreement over the extent to which a new state may be bound by obligations accepted prior to independence by the state responsible for the conduct of its foreign relations. At Geneva, nevertheless, he pointed out, it is clear on the basis of articles in both the Agreement and the Declaration that the Conference understood that France would be leaving Indochina. It is equally clear that the Conference contemplated that the Agreements would be implemented in the southern zone by the successors to the French authorities. Therefore, Partan concluded, "it would make better sense to regard the obligations of the Geneva Agreements as the type of obligations that devolve upon successor states than to permit a successor state to avoid these obligations because it was not a party to the agreements."[7] Two comments are in order. First, the last sentence is essentially a political conclusion based upon an interpretation of the intent of the Geneva Conference rather than upon a reading of the specific obligations and the relevant law. Second, Partan's analysis is considerably vitiated by the fact that he failed to confront the question of the extent to which even a clearly recognized successor state can be bound by the parent in its *internal political arrangements*.

Canadian and Indian Positions
The uncertainties in Canada's Department of External Affairs on the question of the juridical status of South Vietnam *vis-à-vis* France was referred to earlier, when the legality of SEATO was debated. There is no need to repeat the arguments; suffice it to say that Canada believed the legal position to be fluid rather than clear-cut as to South Vietnam being a successor to France. Pearson addressed the question publicly in May 1955. He pointed out that the Vietminh had signed the Geneva Agreements on their own; the South Vietnamese government had not. But he also implied that Diem's government should accept the obligations France had assumed at Geneva as the representative authority.[8]

By April 1956, however, Ottawa had succumbed to British moral and American material support for Diem. The Canadian delegation was instructed to interpret the Agreements so as not to disadvantage South Vietnam, and Polish-style obstructionism was implicitly approved. Two years of involvement in Indochina had thus transformed Canadian objectives in respect of the region. The Canadian goal at the start of its ICSC involvement had been to secure a strict implementation of the Geneva Agreements as the best means of defusing the Indochina crisis. By the middle of 1956 the protection of South Vietnam had become a more important goal than having the Agreements implemented.[9] Not surprisingly, T. N. Kaul, who chaired the ICSC in Vietnam from the end of 1956 to the summer of 1958, concluded that "Canada usually took a pro-Western stance while Poland adopted a pro-Soviet posture."[10]

The changed Canadian position had become quite firm by the mid-1960s. In June 1965, in testimony before the House committee, Paul Martin was asked explicitly by T. C. Douglas if "the Canadian Government is taking the position that the 1954 Geneva Agreement does not apply to South Viet Nam?" Martin's response was that South Vietnam and the United States had cooperated in the implementation of the Agreement, and that the Commission had "acted toward South Viet Nam as though it had a legal obligation." Strictly speaking, however, the Agreement was signed by France, which had withdrawn. Douglas then questioned the value of Canada's presence on the Commission, if the Commission was without jurisdiction in South Vietnam. Martin answered that the Commission "has a jurisdiction that has been consented to by the South," even though "there was no legal compulsion on him [Diem] or his government to accept it."

Douglas pressed Martin still further. If Canada believed that South Vietnam was not under a legal obligation to observe the terms of the Geneva Agreements, he asked, then how could it have joined India in subscribing to the 1962 special report, paragraph 20 of which held that South Vietnam had violated the Geneva Agreements in receiving increased military aid from the United States? He observed that it was "extremely difficult to see how the Canadian representative can say that the Government of South Viet Nam has violated the Agreement if it is not bound by the Agreement." Furthermore, Douglas continued, if South Vietnam was not bound by the armistice, then it was hypocritical of both Martin and American President Lyndon Johnson to insist that their objective was a return to the Geneva Agreements.

Martin replied that in his opinion "the position that the President has taken is a very sound position." By virtue of Saigon's own attitude, the Commission had been allowed to treat South Vietnam as though it were legally obligated. He conceded that the language of the 1962 report "is such as to warrant the belief that there was a clear legal obligation on the part of the South. I can only say that as the South did not sign, there is no legal obligation." He elaborated:

> Legally, it would have been correct in paragraph 20 to make the indictment France, France being legally obligated. However, that does not alter the fact that South Viet Nam did not sign, and gave its reasons for not signing, one of them being that it was opposed to division of the country. That was predicated on the knowledge of the intentions of the North. I must say if I had been living in that country I would have shared the same view.[11]

The gratuitous comment toward the end, perhaps a slip, is a significant revelation of the essentially political base on which the juridical superstructure was being constructed to defend Saigon's position. Martin was still arguing in 1967 that the government of South Vietnam, not having signed the Agreements, was not bound by them.[12]

It is a sign of fluidity of the situation that where Canada had difficulty in maintaining that South Vietnam was *not* legally bound by the Geneva Agreements, India had problems insisting that it *was* so bound. At a press conference on 19 July 1955, on the eve of the date for consultations, Nehru conceded that "it is true that the South Viet Nam authorities did not sign the Geneva Agreements," but added that "they had no business to sign them either." France was the controlling power, and signed the Agreements on behalf both of itself and of its successor governments. The government of South Vietnam was a successor government, he continued, and "they have to take the agreements, responsibilities and liabilities. . . . It would be an impossible position if every successor Government denied the Agreements arrived at by its predecessor." But then, the question was raised, are all governments of former colonies bound by the pacts signed by their colonial masters? Nehru's response was that the answer depends upon whether independence was achieved by consent or revolution:

> If it is by a revolutionary process, there is no binding. But if it is by consent, then certain terms of consent are laid down. But what binds it and what does not bind it, broadly speaking, may be a matter of detail.[13]

It is pertinent to recall a 1921 Congress Party resolution which had urged foreign countries not to enter into agreements with the Government of India, as the government did not represent the people of India.[14]

At any rate, India too was concerned less with the juridical position than with the political consequences. Specifically, it was concerned with the threat to the entire Geneva system if South Vietnam was not bound to the terms of the Agreements. This was explicitly stated by Nehru at the press conference. In India's opinion, South Vietnam was bound by the Agreements as a successor state to France. "That is the legal question. Practically, the question is of giving effect to the Geneva Agreements or putting an end to them and facing the consequences." The Agreements were the end-product of delicate and difficult negotiations; peace had come to Indochina in consequence of these Agreements; to upset the structure that brought peace was, therefore, a course fraught with danger.[15]

India was far from happy with the idea that the Commission could continue to operate *as if* the government in Saigon was legally obligated. Nehru declared in the Lok Sabha on 21 March 1956 that the Commission was a creature of the Geneva Agreements, and "if the Geneva Agreement goes, then the Commission has no place or function left." The South Vietnamese stand of acknowledging a *de facto* position without accepting responsibility, therefore, was "very unsatisfactory." On 6 April, Diem declared that while South Vietnam was not legally obligated by the Agreements, it would continue a policy of cooperation with the Commission as "an agency working for peace." In effect, Diem made the Commission's continuance a matter of Saigon's pleasure. The British acquiesced in this interpretation. London's position was not warmly received in the Indian press. The *Indian Express* commented that Britain, two years after having chaired the Geneva Conference, had made the "strange discovery" that the RVN was not obliged to observe the Geneva Agreements.[16]

Political Developments
On 5 April 1956, the ICSC received a letter from the French High Commission in Saigon giving notice that the French Command would withdraw completely from South Vietnam by the end of the month. (The move was delayed until June.) The Commission once again turned to the cochairmen for directions as to its future. The Government of India had on its own sent another note to the cochairmen on 23 March, which stated that

> the Commission views with serious concern the prospect of having to supervise an agreement which will cease to have any legal basis since one party to the agreement—the French High Command—will have disappeared. It is clear that the Commission will be unable to hold the Government of South Viet Nam accountable, unless it accepts the full residuary obligations undertaken by the French High Command.

The Commission, therefore, desired that the two cochairmen "resolve the legal lacuna . . . to enable the Commission to discharge the functions entrusted to it by the Geneva Conference on Indo-China."[17] India was thus putting its own diplomatic weight behind the Commission request to the cochairmen.

South Vietnam also sent a note to the United Kingdom on 3 April 1956. In its note, Saigon recognized the Commission as "an organization working for peace." The Government of the RVN promised, therefore, that it

> will continue to extend effective co-operation to the Commission, will ensure security of its members and will, to the fullest extent possible, facilitate the accomplishment of its mission of peace, although the Government of Viet-Nam still consider the Geneva Agreement as *res inter alios acta*.[18]

That is, South Vietnam viewed the Geneva Agreements as "transactions among others," agreements concluded by two parties (France and the DRVN) that could not bind a third party (South Vietnam).[19] At the same time, however, in the interests of peace, it was prepared to assist the Commission. The International Commission, for its part, was very unhappy at the prospect of continuing not on the basis of a sanctioned right but on Saigon's sufferance; but there was nothing it could do.

The cochairmen met in London on 8 May 1956 for discussions, following which they dispatched messages to the ICSC, the French government, and the Vietnamese governments.[20] The cochairmen urged the implementation of the political provisions of the Geneva Agreements and full assistance to the International Commission. The latter was asked to persevere in its attempts to secure implementation of the political clauses of Geneva. The Commission in response lamely declared its readiness to "persevere in its efforts to maintain and strengthen peace in Viet-Nam on the basis of the fulfillment of the Geneva Agreement," despite the difficulties it faced.[21]

The difficulties, however, continued, and were severe enough that the Commission was forced to bring them to the attention of the cochairmen. It sent a message to them on 14 September 1956, requesting that they urgently consider the problems arising out of the fact that the FUF had been disbanded in Vietnam. The Saigon government was prepared to offer effective cooperation to the Commission; but it was not prepared to accept responsibility for the implementation of the Geneva Agreements. As a specific instance, the

Commission sent yet another letter on 11 April 1957, urging the cochairmen to consider the difficulties arising out of Saigon's intransigence and noncooperation with respect to Article 14(c).[22] Once again, no help was forthcoming.

Elections/Reunification

The uncertainty about the successor to the French in Vietnam became urgent when deciding who was to implement the election provisions of Geneva. The legal situation was made murkier by the fact that the cease-fire agreement, which was signed by the PAVN and the FUF, does not have an article requiring the holding of elections; it merely *assumes* that elections will be held, and that they will constitute the only means to reunify the country. The sole reference to elections is in Article 14(a), which begins, "pending the general elections which will bring about the unification of Vietnam," and then enumerates conditions of civil administration during the disengagement process. In other words, *the* Geneva Agreement has no provision for holding elections, and provides no mechanism for reunifying the country; it is limited to stating, albeit unequivocally, that the demarcation line is both military and provisional.

If there is no provision for elections and reunification in the Agreement, there is no dearth of them in the Final Declaration. The problem with the Declaration, however, is that it was not signed by anyone, not completely acceptable to the United States, and not endorsed by the immediate parties to the conflict (with the sole exception of France). In the Declaration, the Geneva Conference expressed "its conviction that the execution of the provisions" of the Agreement and the Declaration "creates the necessary basis for the achievement in the near future of a political settlement in Viet Nam" (paragraph 6). The next paragraph stated the requirement for free general elections by secret ballot in unequivocal terms.

However, there was an element of tension between the two clauses of paragraph 7. The first provided for "democratic institutions established *as a result* of free general elections"; the second implied that "all the necessary conditions obtain for free expression of the national will" *prior* to elections—hence the two-year pause. The South Vietnamese, Americans, and Canadians were to focus on the second clause, while ignoring the first. Once again, there is an apparently insoluble contradiction within the same article of the

Final Declaration of Geneva. The purpose of the elections was to enable the Vietnamese people to determine for themselves the type of political system they desired—but could elections be free under conditions of communist rule? What was the alternative? The contrary interpretations were to confront the Commission squarely before a year had passed.

At Geneva, the communist delegations had pressed for elections at the earliest possible time, while their adversaries had attempted to postpone them as long as possible. The reason for this is clear. Under the military and political conditions of 1954, Ho Chi Minh would undoubtedly have carried the day in any elections in Vietnam. It was perhaps in this expectation that the South Vietnamese delegation protested so bitterly about the political clauses of Geneva. The United States shared their fears. As early as 7 July 1954, Dulles was urging that the United States seek to delay the elections, and to require guarantees so strict that the communists would reject them. Dulles cabled instructions to Bedell Smith at Geneva that

> since undoubtedly true that elections might eventually mean unification Vietnam under Ho Chi Minh this makes it all more important they should be only held as long after cease-fire agreement as possible and in conditions free from intimidation to give democratic elements best chance.[23]

A detailed exposition of the Western position on elections is given by Philippe Devillers and Jean Lacouture. They write that as early as 12 August 1954, one of the most trusted advisers of Mendes-France was reporting with respect to the consolidation of the south: "The test of success in this case would be the continued partition of Vietnam beyond 1956." Several close advisers had by then concluded that if the Agreements were implemented and free elections held, the southern zone of Vietnam would be "lost" as well. As for the Americans, the French Ambassador to Berne, Jean Chauvel, reported to the French government on 30 *July 1954* that general elections, in the American view, must be prevented by any excuse whatsoever. For them, the only purpose of the Geneva Agreements was to provide cover for the political, economic, and military preparations for the reconquest. In May, Dulles had assessed the preparatory time at two years. The reconquest was to be achieved either through war or the threat thereof, and the proposed Southeast Asian defense pact would be the instrument to either wage the first or make the second credible. On 6 November 1954, General Paul Ely, commander of the French forces in Vietnam, pointed out the discrepancy between French and American attitudes towards the 1956 elections. France supported South Vietnam unreservedly and would attempt to enable it to face the elections in as favorable conditions as possible, but would not rescue it from the confrontation at the polls.

> I fear that Washington, on the other hand, is repelled by the idea of general elections, if it is not determinedly hostile to them. . . . The American correspondents . . . say that such elections are out of the question. Finally, Diem and the members of government are telling everyone that elections will not take place.[24]

American intentions and objectives are transparent even on the public record. In his letter of 23 October 1954, President Eisenhower had written to Diem that the purpose of the American offer of aid to Saigon was "to assist the Government of Viet-Nam in developing and maintaining a strong, viable state." In other words, just a few months after the Geneva Agreements, the United States was openly proclaiming its purpose to subvert the central political decision of the Geneva Conference. Its stance remained unchanged throughout. Thus the White Paper of February 1965[25] declared that "in Vietnam a Communist government has set out deliberately to conquer a sovereign people in a neighbouring state." It avoided referring to the elections provision, saying merely that "Hanoi's original calculation was that all of Vietnam would fall under its control without resort to force." But, it continued, "South Vietnam's refusal to fall in with Hanoi's scheme for peaceful takeover came as a heavy blow to the Communists." In South Vietnam, "hope rose that their nation could have a peaceful and independent future."

The 1961 White Paper[26] had mentioned the elections, but in the form of a "well-laid trap" by the communists into which South Vietnam refused to fall. The idea of South Vietnam as an independent country was repeatedly emphasized by President Johnson in his John Hopkins speech in April 1965: "The first reality is that North Vietnam has attacked the independent nation of South Vietnam";

"Our objective is the independence of South Vietnam"; "peace demands an independent South Vietnam."[27]

The Western fears that Diem could lose the elections were matched by communist expectations that Ho would win them. Indeed, that was the argument used to justify signing the Geneva Agreements and thereby giving up in the diplomatic field what the Vietminh had so bloodily gained in battle. In an appeal broadcast to the people of Vietnam on 22 July 1954, Ho Chi Minh declared that

> the Northern, Central and Southern Viet-Nam are integral parts of our territory, our country will surely be unified and our compatriots throughout the country will certainly be emancipated. . . .
> We must endeavour to fight for the holding of general free elections throughout the country to realize national unification.[28]

The Pentagon Papers refer to agreement among most estimates that the Vietminh would win the general elections in 1956, if the Diem-headed South Vietnamese government did not collapse of its own accord earlier.[29] As it turned out, Diem was able to stabilize his regime with American aid, and successfully resist all attempts at holding elections, again with American support.

Legal Arguments
The signatories of the Geneva cease-fire agreement had understood that elections would be held. The delegation of the State of Vietnam, a nonsignatory, had protested the competence of the French High Command to bind it to political provisions, including specifically fixing a date for elections, without its prior consent. It was to be expected that the Vietnamese would demand that civil control over the southern zone be transferred completely to themselves before the date of elections. It was also to be expected, given the position and declarations of France, and the attitude of the United States, that the Vietnamese demand would be met. Saigon's substantive position on elections differed from the statement of the Conference in paragraph 7: it did not want a fixed date; it would have liked a United Nations verification of conditions of stability and order before agreeing to a date; and it would have called for United Nations supervision of the elections, since India had not exactly been sympathetic to its point of view, thereby putting a

Commission majority against it. Therefore, South Vietnam did not consent to the elections clause in July 1954. The United States similarly, by its unilateral declaration of 21 July, obligated itself to free elections under United Nations, not ICSC, supervision.

Nor did South Vietnam's subsequent behavior give implied consent to the elections provision. Saigon consistently refused to be drawn into negotiations about elections, refused to consult with Hanoi's representatives in July 1955, and refused finally to hold the elections in July 1956.[30] By the last date, South Vietnam was functionally independent, while in legal theory both it and the DRVN were provisional governments pending resolution of the status of each in a political settlement that would follow from countrywide elections.

The legal theory is compatible with the principles enunciated by virtually every interested state in July 1956. Also, if in July 1956 the Diem government is held to have been the duly constituted government of the sovereign state of the Republic of Vietnam, *even* as a successor state to France, it could exercise sovereignty to disavow obligations incurred by the parent state with respect to internal political matters. "This is certainly true of political arrangements that might affect the structure or form of the government of the successor state and of political questions whose resolution might affect the pattern of competition among rival political groups for offices and authority."[31] If, on the other hand, the RVN is held never to have been a legitimate entity, then the responsibility for implementing the provisions of Geneva must have remained with France (to the extent that France itself was obligated).

The United States sought to provide a detailed justification in law of Saigon's refusal to participate in elections. In its legal memorandum of March 1966, the State Department began by pointing out that the extent to which South Vietnam was bound by the elections provision was unclear. However, even on the assumption that Saigon was bound, its failure to consult towards and hold elections was not a breach of obligation, for the simple reason that "the conditions in North Viet-Nam during that period were such as to make impossible any free and meaningful expression of popular will." North Vietnam was a terrorist police state, and "a nationwide election in these circumstances would have been a travesty."[32]

The argument in defense of Saigon was extended still further by John Norton Moore. With respect to the "expectations" of the

Geneva Conference, he wrote, the context of the settlement becomes as pertinent as the terms of the accords. In the political context, the chief objective of the West was an armistice and a partition; the State of Vietnam was given a separate presence; and the State of Vietnam as well as the United States clearly expressed their unwillingness to be bound by the elections provision. Even on the text, the elections provision is surprisingly vague given the importance of the clause. Therefore, to infer that Hanoi could have had reasonable expectations on the basis of the Geneva Conference that elections would be held in July 1956 *is* debatable. Further, if it is permissible to speak of Hanoi's expectations, then the expectations of others at Geneva must also be allowed.

The totality of evidence suggests that the Western nations, particularly the United States and Britain, desired that the settlement would lead to a non-communist South and expected that it had some chance of doing so, that the Vietminh desired that the settlement would lead to unification under Northern control and may have expected that takeover by political settlement or military activities would be feasible if the regime in the South proved nonviable, and that the Diem government expected that the agreement would lead to de facto partition because the election provisions were unacceptable to them.

That the USSR attempted later to admit both North and South Vietnam to the United Nations, Moore says, reinforces the proposition that partition was the core of the settlement. In any case, his basic point is that there were only minimal shared expectations on the political settlement among the participants at Geneva in 1954.[33]

Richard A. Falk elected to confront Moore head-on. First, one consults the context of the agreement only if the provisions themselves are unclear; the election provisions are unambiguous, even with respect to dates and auspices. In any case, the context cannot take precedence over the text. Second, the rhetoric of partition is consistent with a temporary period of division. Third, the question of American approval of the accords is not legally pertinent. Fourth, that the Final Declaration was unsigned does not detract from its character as a binding legal instrument. Fifth, Saigon was bound by the Geneva accords as a successor to France. Sixth, there is agreement among experienced and impartial observers that unification through elections was part of the Geneva settlement, and that elections would have resulted in the consolidation of Vietnam under Ho Chi Minh. And seventh, the United States was from the beginning discontented with the Geneva settlement, refused to endorse it, and set about almost immediately to frustrate it.

That is, partition was expressly temporary in the written agreements, and unification by elections was the essential political bargain that allowed France to disengage and withdraw. Therefore, "once it became clear that the election provision would not be carried out recourse to coercion by Hanoi was both predictable and permissible." It was predictable because in 1954 Hanoi could have attained its objectives through military means, and it was reasonable for Hanoi, given the stakes and outcomes of the 1946–54 war, to act on the basis of *status quo ante* 1954 in the face of Saigon's intransigence.[34]

Quincy Wright made essentially the same points, with two additional arguments. First, he noted that the Geneva powers were well aware of the nature of the regime in the northern zone when they provided categorically for elections in the Agreements. Therefore, one could not subsequently argue that the provision was rendered inoperative because of communism in the north. That was a constant, not a changed condition altering the Agreements. Second, "it is incredible" that Ho Chi Minh "would have agreed to the cease-fire . . . unless he was convinced that unification would shortly be effected by the peaceful method of elections." Wright observed, therefore, that the "material breach" principle invoked by the State Department in its memorandum seemed more applicable to North Vietnam's suspension of the cease-fire obligations after the south's failure to hold elections. Or, to put Wright's argument differently, the demarcation line was temporary, the provision to erase it was the clause for elections, and when elections were denied the demarcation line became suspendable. The official legal memorandum failed to address itself to "the question of whether the cease-fire line in Viet-Nam became suspendable after frustration of the conditions which induced its acceptance by one of the parties."[35] The International Commission did not take up the question either, but, to the extent that it continued to examine allegations of violations of the agreements, it implied that the cease-fire was still operative and binding on the parties.

If we move from the legal technicalities to the political realities, the reason for the American support of South Vietnam's refusal to hold elections is contained in the following well-known passage from Eisenhower: "had elections been held as of the time of the fighting, possibly 80 per cent of the population would have voted for the Communist Ho Chi Minh as their leader rather than Chief of State Bao Dai."[36] The Pentagon Papers account argues that Diem's refusal to hold elections was his own initiative rather than a consequence of Saigon-Washington connivance.[37] Nevertheless, it was United States policy to seek maximum postponement of the elections.

The American declaratory policy was stated by Assistant Secretary of State Walter S. Robertson on 1 June 1956. Diem's policy, openly stated, was to seek reunification by peaceful means.

> In this goal, we support them fully. . . . For our part we believe in free elections, and we support President Diem fully in his position that if elections are to be held, there first must be conditions which preclude intimidation or coercion of the electorate.[38]

This, then, was the American policy on the provision for elections to reunify Vietnam: the declaratory component, to claim that elections were impossible because free choice could not be guaranteed in the communist zone, *qua* communist zone; and the action component, to delay and circumvent the provision because of the high probability that Ho Chi Minh would win.

Canadian Position
Canadian policy closely followed American policy, with one difference. The Canadians seem to have genuinely believed that the Vietminh might lose the elections. In a message to Lett on 24 August 1954, Pearson wrote that "it may . . . be in the interests of the Viet Minh to violate the terms of the cease-fire agreements since the agreements, if successfully implemented, will prevent them from taking over the whole of Indo-China as they had hoped to do." After a month in the field, the Canadians were becoming aware of the fact that the communists at least believed to the contrary. R. M. Macdonnell, the first (temporary) Canadian Commissioner in the ICSC, wrote to Pearson on 9 September 1954 that "my provisional hypothesis, for what it is worth, is that the Communists have decided that as far as Viet Nam is concerned, the Viet Minh can observe the Geneva Agreement and still win in a walk."[39] By 1967,

Canadian perceptions of the 1954 provision were somewhat more realistic. Paul Martin in a speech at Columbia University on 27 April declared in reference to the elections envisaged in the Geneva Agreements that "with the wisdom of hindsight, we can see how the dragon's teeth were sown."[40] Presumably, the imagery of the dragon was more than coincidence.

The turning point in Canadian policy on Vietnamese elections has been dated as 1955.[41] Until early 1955, Canadians expected that elections would be held as scheduled and that the communists would be victorious. Between then and January 1956, the Indians grew increasingly irritated at the course of events in Vietnam, but the Canadians resisted attempts to pressure Diem into acceding to the entire Geneva package. The emerging Canadian strategy aimed instead to "split" the package: the cease-fire agreement deserved full ICSC support, but the more political Final Declaration was the responsibility of the parties and the Geneva powers. In early 1956, the Canadians did put pressure on Diem to acknowledge a binding commitment to the armistice as the successor state to France. But it was too late by then.[42]

The political basis of the Geneva Agreements was quite changed by mid-1956. Diem had defied virtually all expectations in consolidating his regime, and partition had become a realistic alternative. Moreover, in the context of American support for Diem and problems within the north, Vietnam did not seem to be a major threat to general peace.

The Canadian position was conveyed to India at the Commonwealth Prime Ministers' Conference in London in February 1955. Canada expressed the hope that an electoral law would emerge from pre-electoral negotiations, but pointed out that the initiative for conducting the latter did not properly lie with the ICSC.[43] In contrast to this restrictive interpretation which attempted to avoid any electoral entanglements if at all possible, the Indians pursued an activist role for the ICSC regarding its electoral responsibility. In the words of T. N. Kaul, the Indian view was that South Vietnam "wanted all the advantages from the presence of the international body but they would not submit to its supervision and control . . . except when and where it suited them."[44] At a meeting with Sherwood Lett in London in April 1955, Krishna Menon argued that the Final Declaration *was* a major part of the original Geneva settlement. In reporting the conversation to Ottawa, Lett for the first time expressed fears that the Canadian delegation might find it impossible to reconcile the twin objectives of preserving good relations with both New Delhi and Washington.[45]

The same thought must have occurred to Escott Reid, the Canadian High Commissioner in New Delhi. In the fall of 1954, acting under instructions, he had reported to the Indian government that the Canadian views on Vietnamese elections were substantially in accord with India's. Toward the end of January 1955 he was asked to inform New Delhi of the substantially altered Canadian views on the electoral commission for Vietnam. But he did not appreciate the full extent of the divergence between Canadian and Indian views until the summer of 1955. In his report to a meeting of senior DEA officers, Reid expressed agreement with the Indian view that the Geneva Agreements had meant to draw the line against communism at the borders of Laos and Cambodia, not along the middle of Vietnam. "The roof fell in on top of me. Officer after officer at the meeting attacked me for my callous, immoral proposal which would betray millions of anti-communist people in South Vietnam into the clutches of the communists of North Vietnam."[46]

In the autumn of 1955, Canada made continual efforts to moderate Indian determination to force the elections issue. In January 1956, Lester Pearson, through Reid in New Delhi, expressed appreciation of Indian anxiety that the ICSC might be blamed for the failure to realize the Geneva settlement. He suggested that the Commission could be absolved if the cochairmen of Geneva formally acquiesced in the continuation of the *status quo*. India's response was that any jettisoning of the Final Declaration would relieve the DRVN of obligations under the armistice agreement. To expect Hanoi to accept the greater sacrifices voluntarily (having done that once already in signing the Agreements) was politically naive.[47] Yet the cochairmen in their messages of 8 May 1956 in effect accepted the Canadian approach in bowing to the political realities of the French withdrawal, a functionally sovereign South Vietnam, and an indefinitely postponed election.[48]

This is the context in which Canadian public statements must be read. Official DEA attitudes in Ottawa were reinforced by sentiments of officers in the field in Vietnam. By the beginning of 1956, Canadians on the ICSC were so embittered by DRVN bad faith that they were not likely to recommend coercing Diem into agreeing to elections. Moreover, once the Diem regime had stabilized in the south, the Canadians could use the ICSC and the cease-fire agreement as protective shields against northern communist designs.

Lester Pearson described Canada's position at length in public testimony in May 1955. While the specific responsibility of the Commission for ensuring implementation of the election provisions was uncertain, he said, Canadian interpretation in general differed from that held by its colleagues. Nevertheless, Canada would have to be extremely careful that the will of the people was expressed in conditions of reasonable freedom and without hindrance. In other words, "they would have to be free elections." Even free elections, however, would not solve all the problems, though Pearson did not say it as such. "The governments concerned," he pointed out, without further specification, had pledged themselves in the armistice agreement to reunite Vietnam by means of free elections.

He then pointed out that those who had fled from the north would be in an uncomfortable position if in a couple of years they found themselves inhabitants of a united Vietnam "under the type of government from which they had fled." Holding elections would be a rather difficult task because of the disturbed conditions, but Canada was pledged under the agreement to securing them. "I must say, however, that the government of Vietnam is not pledged because it did not sign the armistice agreement." Thus, as early as May 1955, Canada was arguing that prevailing conditions made general elections difficult, and that in any event South Vietnam was not bound to hold elections. Pearson concluded with the observation that "I am very much afraid of the fact that there will not be elections of a kind which we would consider free. *I am even more afraid that we might be manoeuvred into the wrong kind of elections.*" Some consolation, he said, was to be derived from the realization that South Vietnam would not enter into elections unless they were free.[49]

Quite clearly, then, Saigon had only to express an unwillingness to participate, and Canada would defend its right to that course of action. There was no mention made of the consequences flowing from a refusal to implement the essential political half of the Geneva Agreements. When Pearson did refer to the question again in the following year, it was only with reference to the impact of no elections on Canada's obligations *apropos* the Commission.[50]

The government's stand was generally supported by the Conservative opposition. Thus, after the date for elections had passed,

Diefenbaker spoke of "the continuing delays and procrastinations imposed by the *communists*" in Vietnam as "just another example of duplicity on their part." Pearson's reply was to reiterate that elections were not possible because South Vietnam was not willing to accept the legal responsibilities that had been undertaken by the French. He added that "the other difficulty is the understandable reluctance on the part of the Diem government to take part in any elections unless they can be given absolute assurance that these will be free elections, in our meaning of the word."[51] And, by 1962, the Conservative government in Ottawa was quite explicitly speaking of two "separate countries."[52]

Canada's position was being articulated quite succinctly by June 1965. Paul Martin declared in committee on 10 June that South Vietnam did believe in one Vietnam, but that elections for reunification could be "meaningful only if they were absolutely free, and with a Communist regime installed in Hanoi this condition seemed unlikely to be fulfilled in that half of the country."[53] This had been confirmed for Martin in the course of conversations with the mainly Christian refugees from communist rule. Martin suggested that the situation in Vietnam might have been avoided had the equivalent of NATO been established in time to provide for Asian security.[54]

In any event, South Vietnam had not signed — had in fact rejected — the Geneva settlement, and the elections envisaged therein did not take place because, as the French withdrew, "it became clear that the government in Saigon had no intention of passively accepting the absorption which Hanoi had planned for it." Once Hanoi realized that South Vietnam was not going to "disappear as anticipated as a result of manipulated elections," it decided upon "a more active and aggressive policy" in order to establish control over the whole country.

Three comments are in order about Martin's 1965 statement. First, there is the point that Quincy Wright raised in the debate in the United States, that the Geneva powers knew very well in July 1954 that the regime in the north was communist, and the fact of a communist regime in the north, therefore, could not invalidate the election provisions. Second, in almost every respect, and certainly in every important respect, Martin's statement paralleled American and South Vietnamese positions. Third, Martin by implication conceded, perhaps unwittingly, that *Hanoi's aggression was in response to and subsequent to failure by South Vietnam to comply with the election provisions.* In this again Martin mirrored the American position as per the White Paper of February 1965:

> After 1956 Hanoi rebuilt, reorganized, and expanded its covert political and military machinery in the South. . . . In short, Hanoi and its forces in the South prepared to take by force and violence what they had failed to achieve by other means.[55]

This aspect of the situation was quietly ignored in the American legal memorandum of March 1966. By that date, Canada had publicly declared itself in favor of two Vietnams. Pearson suggested in Parliament on 20 January 1966 that "perhaps the ultimate solution will have to be, as it has been in other cases since world war II, the acceptance of two Vietnamese communities, neutralized, with other countries staying out." The two zones had developed along different lines for over a decade, he said. This was not to say that any settlement would "preclude the possibility of reunification of Viet Nam." In other words, a country pledged to supervise the implementation of agreements which declared repeatedly that the demarcation line was military, temporary, and provisional, was recommending that the line be converted into a secure political border. The essential political provision was to be changed to a possibility that should not be precluded.

Martin repeated the position five days later. He declared that "*in principle we appreciate and support the purposes and objectives of the policy of the United States,*" and that "the people of *South* Viet Nam must be left to work out their own future free from outside pressure or intervention" (emphasis added). Canada could not deny the right of self-determination to the South Vietnamese. Further, "our policy in this situation represents our own honest assessment of the position and is not a reflection in any way of pressure imposed upon us by the United States or by any other country." There is no reason at all to doubt the last statement; there is reason to believe it, in the form of the anticommunist and antiappeasement attitudes of Pearson and Martin. Martin reiterated in 1967 that the path to a final solution in Vietnam lay in letting the people of South Vietnam decide their own future.[56] Again, he did not attempt to reconcile this position with the Geneva Agreements of 1954.

Indian Position

India's policy during the 1954–56 period was to insist upon a full implementation of the Geneva Agreements, including elections. This is quite clearly evident in a number of documents in the official *Foreign Policy of India: Texts of Documents*, including joint communiques with DRVN, Soviet, and Polish officials.[57]

The United States had never accepted the election obligations for South Vietnam; Great Britain took the position that while it was prepared to advise Diem to hold elections, the RVN was under no legal compulsion to respect the Geneva Agreements; and France declared in February 1956 simply that it lacked the "practical means" to do anything. In other words, well before the scheduled two years were up, the three major Western powers had effectively washed their hands of the most important remaining clause of the Geneva Agreements. The USSR put its own seal on this in May 1956, at the conclusion of the talks between the cochairmen.

In a joint message to the two Vietnamese governments, as well as to France and the International Commission, the cochairmen noted that the principle of reunification by means of national elections was accepted by both sides. They were concerned that consultations had not yet begun, creating "a threat to the fulfilment of this most important provision of the Geneva Agreements." Saigon and Hanoi were requested to submit, jointly or separately, views on the time required on the opening of consultations. The two were also urged to give the Commission all possible help in the exercise of its functions under the Geneva Agreements. The two cochairmen had thus accepted the reality of the Republic of Vietnam. Henceforth, the International Commission was to be "an agency for peace," "a symbol of Geneva," a *de facto* relegation from its earlier status as the instrument of Geneva for overseeing implementation of the Agreements. D. R. SarDesai has observed how the cochairmen's message marked the triumph of the Canadian view over the Indian, that the Commission's functions were limited to the cease-fire and did not embrace a political settlement. He also refers to the fact that the message was ill-received in the Indian press, not the least because it consigned the Commission to an indefinite period of responsibilities.

Nevertheless, "in the middle of 1956, after prospects of the reunification of Vietnam had become distant if not dim, India joined most other countries in recognizing the *de facto* partition of Vietnam along the seventeenth parallel."[58] In Parliament, Nehru expressed the hope in May 1956 that elections could perhaps be arranged to everyone's convenience at a later date, but rejected the idea of bringing diplomatic pressure to bear on South Vietnam. To the suggestion that the French foreign minister's presence in New Delhi could be utilized for the purpose of putting French pressure on Saigon, Nehru responded that the state of relations between Paris and Saigon did not lend feasibility to the suggestion. To an equivalent proposal with respect to the United States, Nehru responded that the United States was not an immediate party to the Geneva Agreements.[59]

By the end of the year, however, the Indian stand had altered slightly. On 6 December, Krishna Menon used the General Assembly forum to address the problem of Vietnam. Partition remained in that country, he said, and his government regretted the failure of South Vietnam to accept the Geneva Agreements. "We believe that the future of Viet Nam rests in free elections in the country, internationally supervised and held under conditions of secret ballot and free speech." India, therefore, would like the West to use its influence with South Vietnam, and China "and others" with North Vietnam, toward the attainment of that end.[60] Significantly, the mention of South Vietnam was balanced by a reference to North Vietnam.

The changed Indian position is also evident in the Indo-Polish communiqué of 28 March 1957. Their statement two years earlier had deemed it essential for world peace that the Geneva Agreements should be fully implemented and the elections clause observed. By 1957, their position had been diluted to the expression of "the hope that the problems with which the Commissions are concerned and are still outstanding will be solved by negotiation and co-operation in accordance with the Geneva Agreements of 1954." Elections were not mentioned. Absence of any reference to elections was even more conspicuous in the Nehru-Diem statement of November the same year. The two simply expressed "the hope that the problems of Vietnam will be solved peacefully and in the best interests of the people of Vietnam." India implicitly conceded the reality of two Vietnams in the sentence that stated the decision "to continue and increase the co-operation between their two countries."[61] Taya Zinkin wrote in the wake of Diem's visit that "the Indians begin to say and to write that the reunification of Vietnam is not as simple a question as they thought, and that there is a real moral problem, and they begin to admit that Mr. Diem and his party represent the people of the South as much as Ho represents those of the North."[62]

The damage was not entirely undone by Ho Chi Minh's visit to India in February 1958. He played as much as possible to the Indian sentiments on reunification and colonialism. On 6 February, for example, he compared Vietnamese reunification to Goa's liberation. The joint communiqué issued a week later did not unequivocally endorse Ho's position. It reaffirmed rather the cochairmen's hope of May 1956 that the International Commission would persevere in its efforts to secure implementation of the Agreements with a view to reunification through elections. "In this connection," the communiqué added, the two leaders "stressed the need for promotion of mutual understanding between the two zones in Viet-Nam in accordance with the purposes and provisions of the Geneva Agreements."[63] This was patently less than total commitment.

Elections and the Commission: The Hapless Referee

The DRVN as early as 4 February 1955 declared its readiness to reestablish normal relations between North and South Vietnam, and appealed to the State of Vietnam to do the same. The proposal elicited no response from Saigon; Diem's government had severed almost all ties with the northern zone in the midst of a crusade against communism. North Vietnam's position on the issue of elections and reunification was quite clearly expressed by Pham Van Dong to Western journalists in Hanoi on 30 December 1954. Asked about rumors that Diem was preparing to announce his refusal to hold the elections in 1956, Pham replied, "That would be a very serious decision." But, he continued, the responsibility to ensure their implementation was France's, the signatory to the agreement. He then declared in a raised voice:

> Vietnam will be united one way or the other, with France or against it. . . . The Saigon government, however, cannot refuse to hold these elections, because it would thereby show itself up as an unpopular regime. The Vietnamese people demand elections so that their voice may be heard, and the elections will take place.

Ho Chi Minh, in an interview with the *Observer* on New Year's Day, 1955, denied that the north would hold separate elections prior to the general elections of 1956, which should be "universal, free, democratic, and secret." Nevertheless, by January 1955 both the USSR and China were insisting to Hanoi that they could expect nothing more from the Geneva Agreements. The French would continue to execute the military clauses, they said, but South Vietnam with American encouragement would disregard the political settlement. Their "catch" was that France being helpless to take any corrective action, Moscow and Peking were the only sources of help left open to Hanoi, since only global politics could create the circumstances for the reunification of Vietnam.[64]

On 6 June 1955, with no progress in consultations for elections having been made, Pham publicly declared Hanoi's "readiness to hold the consultative conference with the competent representative authorities in South Viet-Nam from July 20, 1955 onwards in order to discuss the organization of free elections throughout the country in July 1956."[65] This was followed by a statement by the government of the DRVN on 7 June. A week later, New Delhi sent an *aide-memoire* to the cochairmen, endorsing the idea of a "consultative conference." It also indicated that in its view, the State of Vietnam was the proper representative authority for the south. "Having regard to the relations between the parties and the circumstances prevailing in Viet-Nam, it appears to the Government of India that consultations may not take place without some initiative being taken by the two co-Chairmen." The Indian government, therefore, asked the cochairmen to request the two parties to begin consultations.[66]

North Vietnam made its first formal approach to Saigon for the opening of the consultative conference on 19 July 1955, in the form of a letter to Bao Dai and Diem. The way the wind was blowing in South Vietnam was only too evident the next day. The anniversary of the Geneva Agreements on Indochina (20 July) was observed as a "day of shame" in South Vietnam. In Saigon, demonstrations against the Agreements developed into attacks on the two hotels housing members of the ICSC; the target of the attacks was the Indian contingent. On 9 August, South Vietnam declared that "the Government does not consider itself bound in any way by the Geneva Agreements, of which it was not a signatory."[67] The next month, the Congress of the National United Front (*Lien Viet*) in

Hanoi established the Viet-Nam Fatherland Front. In the southern zone, a referendum was held on 23 October on the matter of deposing Bao Dai. Of the votes cast, 98.2 percent were said to be in favor of establishing a republic, with Diem as President; only 1.1 percent favored retaining Bao Dai as the head of state.

The Republic of Viet-Nam, with Ngo Dinh Diem as President, was established on 26 October 1955, and recognized as such by the United States the same day; the American consulate in Hanoi was closed on 12 December 1955. The rigidities were setting in, the temporary military demarcation line was acquiring the permanence of a political boundary, and the coming struggle was shaping up. To be sure, Diem was as dedicated to uniting Vietnam as Ho, but on his own terms, and not in 1956. In his broadcast of 16 July 1955, Diem promised: "To those living beyond the 17th parallel I would say: Do not lose faith. With the support and agreement of the free world, the national government will bring you independence in freedom."[68]

Efforts at producing some progress towards elections continued in 1956. On 25 January, Chou En-lai wrote a letter to the British Foreign Secretary condemning the RVN for its failure to hold election consultations. Chou further proposed a second Geneva Conference, whose members would include the three supervisory countries, to discuss the question of the implementation of the 1954 agreements. The USSR endorsed the Chinese proposal in a note delivered to the British Embassy in Moscow on 18 February. Britain responded on 9 March that to propose a fresh Geneva Conference would be "premature," and suggested instead that the two cochairmen confer with each other.[69] As mentioned earlier, the messages the cochairmen finally dispatched on 8 May simply urged implementation of the political provisions of the Geneva Agreements.

Three days later, Pham Van Dong in a note to Diem repeated the call to a consultative conference that would discuss the all-Vietnam elections. The Foreign Minister of South Vietnam, Vu Van Mau, replied directly to the cochairmen on 22 May 1956: "the absence of all liberty in North Vietnam makes the question of electoral and pre-election campaigns practically unattainable."[70] Almost exactly a year later, on 19 May 1957, after a two-week visit to the United States by Diem, a Diem-Eisenhower communiqué promised that the United States and South Vietnam would work towards a "peaceful unification" of Vietnam.

On 17 August 1955, Pham had appealed to the cochairmen, requesting them to take measures to implement the Geneva Agreements. He had followed this up in November by writing to Molotov to urge Britain to secure implementation of the Agreements. In a note to the United Kingdom on 30 March 1956, Moscow accused the Saigon government of sabotaging Vietnamese reunification, demanded full implementation of the Agreements, and called for a new conference of the original Geneva powers plus the three supervisory states, with preliminary talks between the cochairmen. The proposal for preliminary talks was accepted by Britain on 5 April. Four days later, however, the British challenged the substance of the Soviet note: the RVN was not obliged to hold elections, even though the British had hoped and advised that it do so.[71]

The story of nonelections in Vietnam has been considered separately from the International Commission because that is where the story unfolded. The Commission itself was little more than a passive if unhappy spectator to the events. It was not directly concerned with a political settlement. Its jurisdiction was limited to ensuring conditions of freedom before elections; the actual supervision of the elections had been entrusted to a special commission that was to be drawn from the constituent states of the ICSC. In 1957, the Commission reported that a major difficulty facing it was the failure to hold consultations between the two parties for free nationwide elections that would reunify Vietnam. In the same paragraph, the Commission referred to the continuing problem of the parties tending to give their own interpretations of the Geneva provisions. In 1958, the Commission again noted that consultations on elections had not been held, but permitted itself an element of positive thinking: "The Commission is confident that this important problem is engaging the attention of the co-Chairmen and the Members of the Geneva Conference."

Its stance by 1959 was more sober and realistic, with perhaps just a trace of resigned pessimism. "There has been no progress in the field of political settlement as envisaged in the Final Declaration of the Geneva Conference," it said. Consultations between the parties for holding elections with a view to reunifying Vietnam were yet to start, raising the prospect of an indefinite continuance of the Commission and its activities. The Commission, therefore, *"hopes"* that the matter was engaging the attention of the Geneva powers, "and that they will take effective measures to resolve this problem." In 1960, the Commission simply repeated that there had been no progress in either a broad political settlement or even in the specific provision for "nationwide elections." Similarly, the Commission concluded its last regular report (1961) by reiterating that there had been no progress in the field of a political settlement in Vietnam. In the 1962 special report, it was left to Poland to argue in a minority position that the cause of the extensive movement against the government in Saigon was to be found in the refusal of Saigon to act toward reunification, and that American military assistance had been requested in order to cope with the movement.

John Holmes has written:

> I don't think any of us who watched the Geneva negotiations up close . . . had any doubt at the time that the whole settlement was a package deal. The Communists, who were winning the war, were persuaded to stop fighting in exchange for certain things most important of which was the promise of elections in two years.

Holmes believes that the South Vietnamese and Americans, in jettisoning the elections, "conceded a propaganda point to the adversary which has cost them dearly." The reasons for Diem's refusals to put forward proposals for elections were possibly an unwillingness to acknowledge the validity of Geneva, a reluctance to communicate with "the loathsome regime" in the north, and a fear that once he had made proposals he would be pressured into compromises.[72] It is possible also that consultations could have upset the delicate balance or political equilibrium that Diem had achieved in the south, and perhaps lost him the support of the strongly anticommunist segments; the last comment would be particularly relevant to the small Catholic population that was the backbone of Diem's support in Buddhist South Vietnam. The contrary interpretation is given by Gettleman: "The clear implication is that they feared a Vietminh electoral victory no matter how carefully prepared and supervised the elections were."[73]

Conclusion

The International Commission was not very successful, as is only too obvious, in supervising the implementation of the political provisions of the Geneva Agreements. It tried, at least initially. As with the military clauses, so with the political; the attempt was made in the early stages to translate the Geneva theory into reality. Nevertheless, there was a difference between the military and political issues. To begin with, military clauses were inherently simpler to agree upon, involving largely technical questions of fact. The political provisions were far less susceptible to definition by any one of the delegations, let alone to a common definition for three delegations representing three different types of political systems. Within this constraint, the delegations did make the effort to work out solutions to the best of their abilities.

A good summary of the situation is captured by SarDesai. He is quoted at length both because of the accuracy of his description of North Vietnamese behavior and because the extract helps explain why India would be sympathetic to Hanoi's position:

> Between 1954 and 1956 the DRV's record in the implementation of the Geneva Agreements and in cooperating with the ICC was incomparably superior to that of the government of South Vietnam, not because the northern Communist regime had any natural higher regard for international agreements but because it was intent on securing through elections in 1956 the prize that had slipped from its hands in 1954. To those foreign visitors who doubted that the elections would be held at all, Pham Van Dong said: "Make no mistake. Those elections will be held." If not, the DRV leaders indicated their readiness to fight for the reunification of Vietnam.[74]

This was a line of political argument Indians could understand,[75] but Canada would find unconvincing.

The Commission itself paid tributes to the Agreements in its first year of operation. It referred to the Geneva Agreements as "a balanced document" which "attempts to reconcile the interests and the sovereignty of the authorities in control of the two zones."[76] The rock that ultimately dashed the efforts of the Commission was the impossible juridical position of South Vietnam *vis-à-vis* the Geneva Agreements. Was it or was it not a successor government to the French in the southern zone; and was it or was it not bound by the terms of the Geneva Agreements?

South Vietnam, with unqualified American support, used the uncertainty to escape the most serious political requirement, that of nationwide elections as the means of reunification. It used the same escape route also with respect to some other political provisions, as we have seen. But the elections provision was the crux of the political future of Vietnam. Once this was ignored, the North Vietnamese could be expected to abandon the Geneva Agreements and the Commission for all but propaganda purposes, and revert to the more traditional means of achieving objectives—military and political warfare. Once the Geneva structure lay in ruins, and first the political and then the military war raged ever more fiercely, the three delegations were hopelessly divided. For at the heart of the war lay two conflicting conceptions of political order, with Canada and Poland subscribing to the rival conceptions. The more crucial any dispute, therefore, the more likely would Poland and Canada be to adopt a rigid stance in support of the sides representing their respective conceptions, and the more bitter would the disappointment be with India for the party that lost the vote. In other words, by the time the Geneva Agreements had fallen (July 1956), the Commission was itself a political weapon, in that the parties would make maximum use of their political affiliations with the Commission delegations. This became even more the case as American involvement in Vietnam increased.

However, the two disputants used the Commission to further their own purposes even in the beginning. Before the first six months were over, the Commission realized that the close cooperation of the parties that it needed for effective implementation of the Agreements was lacking. "Each party is more keen to get the Commission to denounce the other than to take reasonable measures to get the Agreement implemented," the Commission noted in its second report. Subsequently, the Commission blamed both sides for delays, obstructions, and grudging cooperation. In most cases, the Commission said, strong representations resulted in a removal of obstructions, but delays could not be remedied. The French authorities were also hindered in remedial attempts by the independent attitude of the State of Vietnam, and difficulties increased as a result.[77]

By July 1956, the Commission was alarmed at the ease with which it could be ignored. It complained that

> the Commission views with concern cases . . . where a party refuses to implement the recommendations of the Commission due to difference of interpretation of the Agreement. If the Commission

is to fulfil its tasks of supervision and control adequately, it is essential that the Commission's authority on interpretation must be accepted by the parties as final.

It distinguished between two types of difficulties being encountered with respect to cooperation of the parties: a hindrance of Commission activities, and a refusal to implement Commission recommendations. The Commission pointed out that the distinction was contained in Article 43 of the cease-fire agreement. Its activities were being hindered in South Vietnam, it reported, largely in connection with the operations of its teams and implementation of Articles 16 and 17; in North Vietnam, mainly with respect to Article 14(d) and reconnaissance of airfields and coastal areas. Non-implementation was a problem in the south in the matter of releasing civilian internees, in the north in the matter of the Mobile Team at Phuc Hoa. Neither party, therefore, had "fulfilled in their entirety" the obligations to afford full cooperation and all assistance.[78]

The Commission penned a reminder two years later that it was finding it difficult to supervise implementation of the Geneva Agreements because the parties persisted in not accepting Commission interpretations. In the following year, the two sides intensified their tendency to reject Commission interpretations and decisions in favor of their own; the Commission reiterated that its effectiveness was correspondingly impaired.

In what was to be its final regular report, the Commission concluded rather appropriately with a series of pessimistic observations: the situation in the DMZ had deteriorated; there was no progress in the matter of reconstituting the Joint Commission; the financial position of the Commission was worsening; and no progress had been made toward a political settlement in Vietnam. The ground could not have been more fertile for the Americans to intervene in force.

6 The Commission Record
A Summing Up

Chapters 3–5 have analyzed the International Commission's efforts in the context of the Geneva accords, and their results. The efforts, without regard to results, can be given a precise grounding by a tabular analysis of the ICSC reports. The first section of this chapter accordingly is a tabulation of *all* the public decisions by the Commission. The advantage of this method is that it gives us an objective measure, in however limited or qualified form. Recognizing that undiscriminating quantification gives an incomplete picture, the first part is supplemented by a discussion of some of the more crucial or representative issues to confront the Commission.

The Commission Voting Record: A Tabular Analysis

Tables 3–6 are a computation of the Commission's decisional patterns as expressed in its reports from 1954 to 1965.[1] Although the tables do not in themselves tell the whole story, they come surprisingly close. In particular, the tabular documentation and analysis of the Commission's voting record substantiates the following points: that there was an honest if qualified attempt to keep the peace between 1954 and 1956; that the weight of the Commission judgments was overwhelmingly against South Vietnam; and that Poland's position in the ICSC froze into a rigid support of the North Vietnamese case only after the date for elections had passed, with the consultative process not having been even initiated.

The tables are forceful and eloquent enough not to require detailed elucidation. Nevertheless, some salient features deserve comment and analysis. One of the enduring public perceptions about the ICSC is that it was always a failure, not the least because of being perennially a house divided. That this perception is false for the initial period is revealed in the first two complementary tables. After July 1956, as the Geneva Agreements became increasingly meaningless, the consensus among the delegations correspondingly diminished. Reinforcing this trend was the fact that as the Vietnam war acquired an increasingly international character, the positions of the two alliance delegations became correspondingly rigid. The fault for the failure of the Commission, therefore, lay not in the admittedly less-than-perfect Agreements, but in the belligerents and their allies.

The detailed voting record in Table 5 also confirms the attempt by all three delegations—and therefore by the Commission—to assess cases at least somewhat on their merits between 1954 and 1956. All three were prepared to concur in findings against both parties with respect to breaches of the Geneva Agreements. There is no doubt that all three were affected by their respective political biases but not, initially, to the point of being overwhelmed. Within the constraint of differing political perspectives, they did attempt to work together in supervising the implementation of the Geneva Agreements.

On the matter of the voting patterns of the three delegations individually, the sharpest break in 1956 occurs in Poland's behavior. This supports the view that once the chief factor in the North Vietnamese adherence to the Agreements, *viz.*, the provisions for elections to reunify the country, was rendered inoperative, the battle lines would be drawn again in Vietnam for military and political warfare. Canada's record on balance was only marginally more sympathetic to the South Vietnamese side. The break for Canada came in January 1959, thirty months after the Polish break. This lends documentary credence to the oft-repeated but not as frequently believed claim by Canadian spokesmen that they were forced into presenting the southern case just to retain a semblance of balance in the Commission reports. Once the Polish position had frozen, the Canadians could take one of two courses. They could continue trying to be impartial, in which event the Commission would record "n" instances of violations against South Vietnam with the authority of a unanimous decision, without having the same hold true against North Vietnam. Or, the Canadians could become rigid as well, in order to prevent the Commission record from being imbalanced on grounds other than merit. Not surprisingly, they chose the second course. Insofar as the public record is concerned, the sequence of rigidities by Poland and Canada supports the contention that Canada's lack of balance was a response to Polish bias.

In an address at Columbia University on 27 April 1967, Paul Martin conceded that the troika arrangement worked out at Geneva in 1954 had implicitly cast Canada as the Western representative. He contended, however, that from the outset Canada had decided upon impartiality rather than a rigid advocacy for the West. The reason he gave for this is instructive: Canada would not simply represent Western interests because to do so would contradict its broader goal, as a major participant in United Nations peacekeeping operations, to promote the United Nations as an impartial and objective agency for the settlement of international disputes. He observed further that to the extent that Canada had tried to be impartial in Indochina, the burden of the arbiter on India had been lessened, "but not, unfortunately, to the point where it can act without any reference at all to the implications on its own national position."[2] That Martin's claim to objectivity is no idle boast is clear from the letter of instructions issued to Sherwood Lett.[3]

The contention that Canada's bias was reactive indicates that the catchy phrase, that Canada could be the Poland of the Western world rather than neutral,[4] should be turned on its head. That is, if only Poland had been prepared and able to be the Canada of the Eastern European world, the Commission might have functioned differently, and India's predicament in the Commission would have been considerably eased.

India's voting record reveals even more interesting facts. To complete the picture of sympathies first: India on balance took the North Vietnamese side on two of three occasions (Table 5). This should not be surprising. From the time of the Franco-Vietminh war, India's sympathies lay almost entirely with the Vietminh, and it tended to view the conflict generally from their perspective. Within this constraint, India was at first glance prepared to search out and record violations of the Agreements conscientiously. But there is a difference when India's voting is broken down into time periods. As Table 6 shows, in the first two years there was almost a rough parity in India's voting. For the 1956–59 period, when South Vietnam was seen to have jeopardized the whole Geneva structure by its refusal to agree to reunifying elections, India's votes were overwhelmingly in favor of North Vietnam. In India's view, jettisoning the political settlement imperilled the entire Geneva framework for peace in Vietnam, increased the risks of a wider conflagration, and therefore militated against India's foreign policy. A word of caution is in order. The strength of India's voting towards Hanoi's view may well reflect the fact that after July 1956 Saigon began to more openly defy the Commission and its attempts at supervision, as much as it reflects Indian displeasure at Saigon's noncompliance with elections. It is almost impossible to differentiate between the relative causal weight of the two elements.

After 1959, when the ruins of India's policy lay scattered on the Himalayan ranges, India ceased to attach much symbolic importance to the Geneva Agreements as an expression of *Panchsheel.* In the 1959–62 period, most critical to India in its relations with China, India's votes in numerical terms were only slightly more favorable to Saigon's interpretations than to Hanoi's. The shift to the South is very dramatic, however, in the *pattern* of voting. In the 1965 reports, India returned to a semblance of equivalence.

There are some discontinuities in the data by category of issues. The tabular documentation and analysis of the Commission's voting record shows that the weight of military disturbances to the Agreements came from North Vietnam, and political violations from South Vietnam. This had an impact upon delegation behavior in the ICSC. On military issues, the Commission overall split almost evenly between South and North (52 percent for North Vietnam). Its record on political cases demonstrates that it favored the northern cause overwhelmingly (78 percent). The reasons for the latter would be two: South Vietnam would be the more likely to transgress the political clauses; and India, from the beginning, was in sympathy with Vietminh objectives. The individual delegation voting records exhibit the same tendencies. Thus the overall percentages of votes in favor of Hanoi on political issues were 56 for Canada, 78 for India, and 89 for Poland. The corresponding figures on military issues were 34, 53, and 77. All three delegations were agreed then that South Vietnam was more often in transgression of the political provisions than North Vietnam, and that the north's record on military clauses was not as good as on political clauses.

Discriminating by category of issues permits a further differentiation in alignment patterns among the delegations. India was twice

TABLE 3
ICSC Decisions, Delegation Divisions

Period	Unanimous	Canada + Poland	Poland + India	Canada + India	Total
11/8/54–10/8/55	36	0	8	0	44
11/8/55–31/7/56	25	0	3	4	32
1/8/56–30/4/57	18	0	6	3	27
1/5/57–30/4/58	19	0	3	2	24
1/5/58–31/1/59	17	0	9	2	28
1/2/59–31/1/60	3	0	6	6	15
1/2/60–28/2/61	2	0	5	11	18
1962	0	0	0	12	12
1965	0	0	3	2	5
Total	120	0	43	42	205

Source: ICSC, *Reports*, 1954–1965.

TABLE 4
Minority Positions on the ICSC

Period	Canada	India	Poland
1954–55	2	0	0
1955–56	1	0	1
1956–57	2	0	3
1957–58	3	0	2
1958–59	5	0	2
1959–60	6	0	6
1960–61	5	0	11
1962	0	0	4
1965	2	0	2
Total	26	0	31

Source: ICSC, Reports, 1954–1965.

TABLE 5
Decisions in Favor of North Vietnam/South Vietnam
(Zero Sum Assumption)

Period	For North Vietnam				For South Vietnam				Total			
	Canada	India	Poland	ICSC	Canada	India	Poland	ICSC	Canada	India	Poland	ICSC
11/8/54–10/8/55	30	30	30	30	21	17	17	17	51	47	47	47
11/8/55–31/7/56	12	14	16	14	19	17	15	17	31	31	31	31
1/8/56–30/4/57	16	22	25	22	9	3	0	3	25	25	25	25
1/8/57–30/4/58	19	22	24	22	5	2	0	2	24	24	24	24
1/5/58–31/1/59	15	24	27	24	13	4	1	4	28	28	28	28
1/2/59–31/1/60	3	9	14	9	12	6	0	6	15	15	14	15
1/2/60–28/2/61	2	7	17	7	15	11	0	11	17	18	17	18
1962 Special Report	4	4	12	4	6	6	0	6	10	10	12	10
1965 Special Reports	0	3	5	3	16	2	0	2	16	5	5	5
Total	101 (47%)	135 (67%)	170 (84%)	135 (67%)	114 (53%)	68 (33%)	33 (16%)	68 (33%)	215	203	203	203

Source: ICSC, Reports, 1954–1965.

TABLE 6
Pattern of Voting by India/ICSC in Four Periods
(*Percentages in Brackets*)

Period	For North Vietnam	For South Vietnam	Total
11/8/54–31/7/56	44 (57)	34 (43)	78
1/8/56–31/1/59	68 (88)	9 (12)	77
1/2/59–1962	20 (47)	23 (53)	43
1965	3 (60)	2 (40)	5
Total	135 (67)	68 (33)	203

Source: Table 5.

as likely (20:9) to agree with Canada as with Poland in the event of a divided Commission on military issues; but it was much more likely (17:11) to disagree with Canada in the event of a divided Commission on political issues. The disagreement can be traced to contrasting perceptions of the preceding Franco-Vietminh conflict. Where Nehru felt that Ho Chi Minh had been fighting a nationalist war against European colonialism, Pearson believed that France had been engaged in fighting the democratic battle against "a serious communist menace." Once the bulk of the military provisions had been implemented, and as consensus broke down, the split on political issues found Canada ranged against India and Poland.

It is interesting that the above pattern shows up in the first year of the Commission's activities. By August 1955, the ICSC had recommended remedial action in military issues to the northern command in six cases, to the southern in two. In political issues, on the other hand, corrective action was recommended to the northerners in only two cases, compared with seven to the southern command.[5]

The voting record in its totality confirms that India was the arbiter in the Commission. In *all* tables, India's and the Commission's votes are identical; this is seen most strikingly in Table 5. In effect,

India's vote was the Commission's vote, not because India could always persuade the others to act as it saw fit, but because where Canada and Poland agreed, India would not break that agreement, and where both Canada and Poland opposed any decision, India would again preserve unity. Thus the Indian chairman of the ICSC for 1956–58 has recently written that "I used to give a *carte blanche* to my Polish and Canadian colleagues that I would agree to anything that both of them accepted."[6]

There is a corollary. Because of the tripolar structure and troika composition[7] of the Commission, both Canada and Poland would seek to win over India rather than each other to their cause. As Paul Bridle expresses it, "in the nature of things no action desired by Canada could be taken without Indian support."[8] This of course meant that in any matter involving a dispute in the Commission, India was always under pressure. Furthermore, the amount of pressure varied directly with the intensity of the dispute. India in response chose to tread cautiously, and achieved some sort of a balance between the Canadians and the Poles. Most strikingly, India's balance between the two disputants is an almost exact mean of the balance that Canada and Poland struck (Table 5). Where between the parties Canada's is the most balanced voting record, India's record is an almost perfect balance between the other two delegations to the International Commission.

The difference is crucial to understanding the respective involvements of India and Canada in Vietnam. Canada took pride in its peacekeeping expertise, at least until the 1967 expulsion of UNEF, and sought a reputation for objectivity. Up until 1964–65, when the last Commission report was submitted, this general aspect of its foreign policy did not conflict much with the particularities of its relations with the United States in Vietnam. India's role in the Commission was more sensitive. Poland and Canada could be expected to look after the interests of the northern and southern zones, for which they had been chosen. Nor would this necessarily create a problem for India, as long as rough consensus could be achieved and the Vietnam war was relatively free of international involvement. Once the great powers were deeply involved, however, India found itself in the unhappy position of having to referee between Canada and Poland on the Commission. India's vote then became the *de facto* Commission vote. It was a heavy responsibility to shoulder, in that India's vote would be taken to reflect a judgment on the fundamental issues of international politics. Not surprisingly, the Indians would try to side with one or the other delegation in roughly equal instances. This role was explicitly recognized by a former chairman of the ICSC upon his retirement from the foreign service: "As Chairman and Secretary-General of the ICSC, India had a most difficult and delicate job in trying to hold the balance between Canada and Poland . . . and between North and South Viet Nam."9

Strong Canadian frustrations developed because of a perceived failure on India's part to act against the communist menace. Canadian officials complained that India sided too often with the Poles. According to a Canadian reporter, the Canadian ICSC contingent in Saigon from 1966 to 1972 was "a dispirited group trying to put on a brave front but frustrated and angry at inactivity which, almost to a man, the Canadians blamed on the Indians."10 In part the difference between Canadian and Indian perceptions could be attributed to different traditions of resolving disputes. The adversarial system of legal relationships certainly does not sit very easy in India.11

In a related vein, Indians would view the chairman's role as that of a mediator dedicated to the proposition that consensus can be worked out between opposing factions. As the first chairman of the Commission, M. J. Desai, put it: "The Commission is not a super-body, its role is to get the two parties to co-operate. . . . I would rather change the commission's official name from the Commission for Supervision and Control to commission for supervision and conciliation."12 In the absence of policing machinery, the Commission's effectiveness necessarily depended on authority, which would diminish in the absence of unanimity. It therefore became the Indian chairman's task to seek consensus by means of compromise and conciliation. As early as 16 May 1955, Lett complained in a dispatch to Pearson that Desai "has always had a preference for finding a middle way, almost at all costs, and certainly frequently without due regard for the objective merits of a question, whenever the Polish delegate and I have differed."13

Canadians, however, would see the chair's task as to "get things done," to keep the Commission going when it was in danger of being bogged down. According to the Canadian Press, in 1961–62 officials in Ottawa blamed India, as chair of the Commission, for much of the reluctance to investigate complaints alleging infractions of the Geneva Agreements.14 A comment by the Canadian Commissioner in Cambodia, R. Duder, about his chairman is pertinent, especially as G. Parthasarathi was subsequently moved to Vietnam. On 27 October 1954, Duder wrote to Pearson that Parthasarathi, "like many of his compatriots . . . moves at a pace which is as far removed as possible from that of a go-getter. He believes strongly in the healing influence of time. . . . As a chairman, he is not always firm enough, with the result that matters are sometimes postponed for no very cogent reason."[15]

Finally, Indians would be more aware than either the Canadians or the Poles of the fact that ultimately, whichever side won or survived, Canada would retreat to North America and Poland to Europe, while India would have to carry on relations with its Indochinese neighbours. India would, therefore, be more sensitized to the political context, while Canada concentrated on the mechanics of peacekeeping, and Poland groped its way through the maze of intracommunist relations.

The Commission Record: A Selective Summary

Turning away from the quantifiable and venturing into a selective assessment of the delegations' voting behavior in the Commission, some of the above conclusions need to be modified. In the military category, Canada pressed insistently from the very beginning for instituting an adequate control system on Vietnam's northern border; it did not think that SEATO was a breach of the Geneva Agreements; it often attempted to dilute or deflect Commission criticisms of the southern authorities on noncompliance with Commission directives; and it generally accepted American interpretations of the conflict, as for instance in the report of 13 February 1965, where it argued the American justification of the bombing as a response to North Vietnamese aggression and subversion. On political clauses, Canada tended to indict the North Vietnamese for hindering the free movement of refugees, but was less ready to find South Vietnam in violation of democratic freedoms and reprisals prohibitions.

It was on the critical matters of substance, however, that Canada's record is most significantly modified from the position implied in the tables. Canada did accept the American justification for the bombing campaign; it did find North Vietnam guilty of aggression and subversion; it did not think that South Vietnam was a successor government to the French in the southern zone; it did not, therefore, accept that South Vietnam was legally compelled to implement the provision for elections as the means to reunify the country; and it did in fact accept the United States–South Vietnam argument that elections would be meaningless because of the lack of freedoms in the communist system north of the demarcation line.

Canadian behavior, in other words, could fairly be described as qualified impartiality: Hanoi was deemed guilty until proven innocent,[16] while Saigon was considered innocent until proven guilty. Within this prejudicial framework, Canada was willing in the initial stages to concede that the weight of evidence established Hanoi's innocence or Saigon's guilt. The problem was that both were rather difficult convictions to establish, and in the absence of conclusive evidence, Canada's judgment would err invariably on the side of the southern zone—on occasions to the point of forgiveness. The bigger problem was that with the passage of time even this small concession to the weight of evidence rapidly disappeared, first in the case of Poland and then in the case of Canada. By 1959, neither delegation was willing to accept a citation against "its" side.

Restlessly anxious to establish North Vietnamese culpability, Canada was nonetheless on occasion compelled to concede American guilt or at least withhold support for the American case. The best instance of this is the 1962 special report. With reference to participation in peacekeeping operations, Paul Martin wrote that "unlike the United Nations as an organization, we cannot always be impartial towards the issues themselves. We must and do reserve the right to state our views on these issues in the framework of our foreign policy." On the second point, he recalled that "Canada is also a Western country with a point of view which is shaped by her alliance commitments and responsibilities."[17] John Holmes as well conceded that in the Commission in Vietnam, "Canadian impartiality was, of course, conditioned by Western perspectives and prejudices."[18]

The initial general pattern was in evidence in the Commission's first year, in its investigation of the five bloody clashes in southern Vietnam in August–September 1954.[19] The unfolding of the Commission activities on that occasion is a good example of the assertions that Poland would argue the case for the PAVN, Canada would in response be "compelled" to state the Franco-Vietnamese point of view in order to retain a Commission balance, and India, aiming for consensus, would put forth compromise proposals, rather than rule on the merits between the proposals already before the Commission.

As for India, in the years 1959–62 (the period of open hostility, including violence in India-China relations), it ruled against North Vietnam on a number of extremely critical issues: subversion, Law 10/59 in South Vietnam, and the American military missions in South Vietnam. The Indian chairman is said to have been asked by North Vietnamese officials at private meetings whether the Indian voting on the cases had anything to do with the Sino-Indian dispute. The Indian representative naturally denied any such connection.[20] Nonetheless, as one Indian official serving in Indochina during the period responded to a query as to whether the Sino-Indian dispute had any impact on India's relations with the two parties, "It was bound to. That is only natural."[21] The point was not that India would consciously adopt partiality, but that its changed perceptions of Chinese communism would produce an element of prejudice. As a corollary, North Vietnam maintained the Soviet line of neutrality in the Sino-Indian border dispute in the 1959–62 period, and sided openly with China only after mid-1962. Thus, in October 1960, Pham Van Dong declared in an interview with an Indian journalist that North Vietnam was "an outsider" in the India-China dispute. It was his hope, he added, that the two countries would be able to negotiate a satisfactory settlement.[22]

For perspective, bear in mind that Hanoi's decision to actively intervene in South Vietnam was taken in early 1959. According to the Pentagon study, in December 1958 or January 1959 Hanoi apparently decided that the time had come to intensify its efforts. In December 1958, Hanoi directed its headquarters for the central highlands that the Lao Dong party's Central Committee had decided to open a new stage of the struggle. The use of armed forces in support of political struggle (that is, not aimed at militarily defeating Saigon), was ordered the following month. According to this account, the May 1959 (fifteenth) meeting of the Central Committee was "the point of departure for DRV intervention."[23] The period from 1959 when the Indian voting pattern changed dramatically against North Vietnam coincided with the initiation of an interventionist policy by North Vietnam.

The explanation for the changed pattern of voting by India is, therefore, best supplied by combining the factors of Sino-Indian hostility and increased guerrilla activity in South Vietnam. The combination is to be achieved in the form of a shift of Indian perceptions of China. The cobwebs of *Panchsheel* were finally being blown away, to reveal that China could perhaps be expansionist after all, and its actions as suspect as those of the West. Maneli has written how in 1963 and 1964, Indians in Saigon "could not talk about China without emotional engagement, without spitting out invectives against a faithless friend. Since 1961–62, whatever happened at the Commission was interpreted by the Indians through the prism of their hostility toward China."[24] To put it differently, between 1959 and 1962 the two components of its foreign policy were mutually supportive for India, and worked against North Vietnam.

The above analysis of the Commission's voting record supports the conclusions reached by Paul Bridle. It is useful to recall his appreciation of the three delegations in detail, in that he is a Canadian diplomat with field experience in an Indochina commission. About Poland, he writes:

> The Poles not only brought to the Indochina commissions impeccable military and diplomatic credentials. They were also good communists, particularly well attuned to Soviet international policy. They understood and served the commissions' objectives but were fully prepared to subordinate them to the needs of their Indochinese ideological partners.[25]

With respect to Canada, Bridle distinguishes usefully between the role of judge and advocate. Thus, "Canada tried to act impartially as a member of the commissions," but "it was in the nature of things that Canadians should be alert to the interests of the non-communist side and ready to defend those interests if necessary." That is, Canada was expected to bring a Western outlook, and "Canadians could be vigorous protagonists," but objectivity was attempted in the judgment of particular issues. Bridle also raises the possibility that perhaps Canadians were excessively zealous and overly legalistic.[26]

Regarding India, "the leading proponent in the world of nonalignment," Bridle notes that it carried nonalignment "into the commissions and . . . except for one brief aberrant period after the Chinese 'invasion' of India, it practised as a member of them." In the early days in Vietnam, he says, the Indians "could be very strong in the fight." Once unanimity disappeared, however, India seemed to treat issues collectively rather than in isolation, "the effort evidently being to strike a long-term balance."[27]

Given the approximate coincidence of this analysis and Bridle's, it is not surprising that they agree on the part played by the Commission. Bridle writes:

> During the very early years the commissions displayed energy, ingenuity, and imagination in pursuit of their goals. . . . In the first few months there was a genuine spirit of collective endeavour and, even after this spirit had been somewhat fragmented, the commissions were able to use the procedures provided by the agreements as a basis for useful action, as long as there was still hope of achieving a settlement or at least of keeping the peace. Thereafter, in terms of their mandate, their activities became increasingly futile, and their morale gradually deteriorated.[28]

The tables in this chapter bear out the statement in entirety.

7 The American Intervention

> It would be, I think, quite impossible for us to remain neutral in any major Pacific conflict in which the United States was engaged.
>
> Lester B. Pearson, 31 January 1941.[1]

Background

Virtually all shades of opinion are agreed that the American involvement in Vietnam was a singularly unfortunate one. The reasons for the involvement remain a subject of controversy, but its details are fairly clear.[2] In the initial stages of the French Indochina war, the United States was caught in the dilemma of opposing both Indochinese communism and French colonialism. The contradiction was resolved with the establishment of the People's Republic of China in 1949 and the outbreak of the Korean war in 1950. Possibly the first statement of the "domino theory" was enunciated by the American Secretary of Defense on 6 March 1950, and a decision to grant $10 million in economic and military assistance to the French in Indochina was approved on 1 May 1950:[3] the United States had come down firmly against the communist Ho Chi Minh. By 1954, the United States had assumed 78 percent of the French financial burden in the Indochina war.[4]

In the wake of the Geneva Conference, and after the withdrawal of French forces from Indochina, DRVN and United States clients were locked in a struggle for the control of the territory of southern Vietnam. As the insurgency-cum-civil war intensified, Washington and Hanoi became embroiled in a protracted conflict that eventually engulfed all of Indochina. The legacy of the war was devastation and suffering for the Vietnamese and a deep scar on the American psyche — the death toll alone between 1965 and 1974 was 56,000 Americans and 1.25 million Vietnamese.[5]

The bastion of American power in South Vietnam came to be built around the Diem regime. From 1955 to 1959, Diem waged a merciless and highly effective campaign against communist remnants in the south. Hanoi initially confined cadres in the south to political activity only, in order not to jeopardize the political formula of Geneva. After 1956, Hanoi maintained the policy to promote the Moscow-Peking strategy of peaceful coexistence, as well as because of peasant discontent and rebellion in the north. In May 1959, with Hanoi's acquiescence (partly because it did not wish to lose control over the movement), communists in the south took to the offensive. The National Liberation Front (NLF) was formed on 20 December 1960. As a result both of alienation of much of the populace through harsh rule without land reforms, and of guerrilla militancy, by mid-1961 Saigon was no longer in control of rural Vietnam.

President Kennedy's response was two-pronged. On 11 May 1961, he quietly dispatched four hundred Special Forces and an additional one hundred military advisory personnel to Saigon; and he authorized a clandestine program of "sabotage and light harassment" by South Vietnamese agents in the DRVN.[6] In December, he placed American troops in South Vietnam in a combat-support role. The counterinsurgency program achieved initial successes in early 1962, but the initiative was once again with the guerrillas a year later. Washington concluded that Diem had become a liability, and accordingly did not discourage a military coup plotted with their knowledge. However, its execution shocked them; Diem was brutally murdered. The coup intensified rather than settled political instability in Saigon. It has recently been argued that a number of post-Diem coups were instigated or supported by the United States in hopes of establishing a reliable client regime in Saigon.[7]

Stalemated in its search, the United States decided to take the war to the north.[8] In doing this, it assumed that the insurgency was directed and supplied by Hanoi, and that it could therefore be controlled by punishing the DRVN for its "aggression" as well as interdicting the infiltration of men and material. In the beginning this took the form of increased subversive activity against North Vietnam, approved by President Johnson in January 1964. By March Secretary of Defense Robert McNamara was already reporting that the program was ineffective; he urged air attacks against military and possibly against industrial targets in the north.[9] The plan was finally implemented in the wake of the Tonkin Gulf incidents. On 2 August 1964, North Vietnamese torpedo boats attacked the American destroyer *Maddox* in the Gulf; two nights later, they were alleged to have attacked the *Maddox* and the *Turner Joy* in a second incident.

American provocation of North Vietnam, in the form of espionage and harassment, was concealed from Congress by President Johnson. As a result, he was able to secure from it the fateful Tonkin Gulf Resolution, which gave the President authority to use armed force if necessary to repel armed attacks against American forces, and to prevent aggression against the member or Protocol states of SEATO. Senator Wayne Morse, who cast one of two dissenting votes in the Senate (there were none in the House), criticized the resolution for giving the President blanket authority to wage war. On the basis of this congressional authorization, Johnson launched the United States on its fatal war in Vietnam.[10] Table 7 is an accurate metric of direct American involvement in the war. The air war against North Vietnam began on 7 February 1965; United States marines in Danang were given an offensive role around coastal enclaves in April; on 26 June, General William Westmoreland was authorized to launch "search and destroy" operations anywhere in South Vietnam; and on 28 July Johnson gave him another 175,000 troops to do so. But the insurgents were able to match the increasing American commitment. As an American defense official noted on 18 January 1966, the United States was caught in "an escalating military stalemate."[11] At about that time, the United States decided upon its "ratchet"-effect bombing-halt policy: a pause in the air raids, if it failed to elicit a favorable response, would be used as a means of slackening pressure in order to increase it.[12] Thus the much-publicized bombing pause from 24 December 1965 to 31 January 1966 was accomplished by demands that amounted to "capitulation by a Communist force which is far from beaten," in the words of the United States Assistant Secretary of Defense.[13]

George Ball, Johnson's Undersecretary of State, had been opposed to an American ground war in Vietnam from the beginning.

TABLE 7
U.S. Forces in South Vietnam

30 April 1960	327
31 Dec. 1960	900 (approx.)
31 Dec. 1961	3,205
31 Dec. 1962	11,300
31 Dec. 1963	16,300
31 Dec. 1964	23,300
30 June 1965	59,900
31 Dec. 1965	184,300
30 June 1966	267,500
31 Dec. 1966	385,300
30 June 1967	448,800*
31 Dec. 1967	485,600
30 June 1968	534,700
31 Dec. 1968	536,100
30 April 1969	543,400**
30 June 1969	538,700
31 Dec. 1969	475,200
30 June 1970	414,900
31 Dec. 1970	334,600
30 June 1971	239,200
31 Dec. 1971	156,800
30 June 1972	47,000
31 Dec. 1972	24,200
30 June 1973	less than 250

* RVN troops at the time 600,000
NLF troops at the time 294,000, including 50,000 DRVN regulars

** Peak strength; other allied troops in South Vietnam in 1969 (Australia, Korea, New Zealand, Philippines, Spain, Taiwan, Thailand) - 68,889.

Sources: Cooper, *Lost Crusade*, 507; Schandler, *Unmaking of a President*, 352–53; and Sheehan, *et al.*, *Pentagon Papers, passim.*

By October 1966, McNamara too had begun to have doubts about the course of American policy in Vietnam. Publicly, however, the

Administration continued to be determinedly optimistic about the war. On 2 November 1967, General Westmoreland pronounced that victory was in sight. On 31 January 1968, the guerrillas launched their Tet offensive which gave them temporary control, among other targets, of the United States embassy in Saigon. The offensive was a failure by any military reckoning; its political and psychological impact, however, was devastating.[14] In the midst of widespread insistence that the war was unwinnable, and mounting opposition to American policy both at home and abroad, Johnson faced his moment of truth. He had to choose between increasing the force level in Vietnam by another 200,000, necessitating a call-up of reserves; or seeking to stabilize the war and explore a negotiated settlement. He chose the latter course, and withdrew from the presidential contest, on 31 March 1968.[15] Johnson's decision to cease bombing north of the 20th parallel effectively halted the momentum of the military buildup in Vietnam.

Negotiations for peace began between Washington's and Hanoi's delegates on 13 May 1968 in Paris. In the United States, Richard Nixon was elected President with the promise of a secret plan to end the war. His strategy was revealed to be a progressive withdrawal of American troops through a policy of "Vietnamization," whereby responsibility for the prosecution of the war was transferred increasingly to the Vietnamese themselves. The American political objective reverted to the original aim of securing a viable South Vietnamese government. The "Vietnamization" strategy was shown to be in shambles, however, when in early 1971 a South Vietnamese incursion into Laos retreated in disarray. In the meantime, Nixon reintroduced the bombing campaign against the north. This was enlarged with the failure of the Vietnamization drive, and the military situation in Vietnam seemed to revert to the familiar escalating stalemate. Internationally, however, detente with the USSR and *rapprochement* with China gave the United States an opportunity to bring pressure to bear upon Hanoi via Moscow and Peking. Nixon and Kissinger, through the application of such pressure and through a demonstration of their determination to bomb the north unrestrainedly if need be, secured an end to the war on 27 January 1973. But even the Paris Agreements failed to resolve the political ambiguities in Vietnam. Thus they simultaneously affirmed the "independence, sovereignty, unity, and territorial the political ambiguities in Vietnam. Thus they simultaneously affirmed the "independence, sovereignty, unity, and territorial integrity of Vietnam" in accord with the 1954 Geneva Agreements, and conceded the principle of "the sovereignty of South Vietnam" (Articles 1 and 18c). But they did, in securing the withdrawal of American troops from Vietnam within sixty days, serve to bring to a close one of the major events of recent international history.

Canadian Response
Just before the Commission issued its special report in 1962, foreign minister Howard Green declared in Parliament that to single out the United States for blame in South Vietnam would be quite unfair:

> There have been troops infiltrating from North Vietnam, and *I am certain* that the Communists have been at the root of most of the trouble in South Vietnam. . . . Any action the United States has taken has been in a measure of defence against Communist action.[16]

The communists were condemned on less than strict grounds of evidence; the American intervention was accepted as responsive. The chief blame for the trouble in South Vietnam was pinned squarely on the shoulders of the communists, with the United States completely absolved. Not surprisingly, the External Affairs report for the year claimed that the ICSC special report on Vietnam had "made it clear that the increased military aid which South Vietnam had received since December 1961 was requested for the purpose of dealing effectively with subversion," and that aid would cease when North Vietnam terminated its acts of aggression.[17] This was a rather generous, if not actually unwarranted, stretching of the special report. The latter referred to South Vietnamese and American claims that their actions were in response to Hanoi's aggression, but had not entered into the merits of the claims. Far from accepting the southern case, the special report had described the factual alliance between Saigon and Washington as a transgression of the Geneva Agreements. The External Affairs report, on the other hand, without actually saying so, seemed to imply that the South Vietnamese case had received sympathetic Commission hearing.

External Affairs repeated its position in 1963. In 1964, after the scale of American involvement was such as to change its nature, External Affairs under the new Pearson administration reported that political instability in South Vietnam was directly related to Viet Cong insurgency. It held North Vietnam's determination to interfere in the affairs of South Vietnam to be the root cause of the crisis in South Vietnam: "The Canadian delegation has sought to ensure that North Vietnamese aggression and South Vietnam's resulting need for outside military assistance in legitimate self-defence be kept under review by the Commission."[18] Small wonder that in early 1965 the Canadian delegation felt unhappy with the majority statement, which dwelt solely on the American bombing raids into North Vietnam. Canada tried to moderate the majority view by attaching its own statement, which drew attention to the fact that the causes of American bombing lay in Hanoi's aggression.

Canada's External Affairs reported conscientiously that the Vietnam crisis became more acute during 1965. The scale of the Viet Cong insurgency and North Vietnamese aggression increased, it said, "as did the response from South Vietnam and the countries providing it with the military assistance required for its self-defence." As for the United States, its "*participation* in hostilities had increased substantially" by the end of the year.[19] Paul Martin's ability to avoid reference to the citation against the United States was phenomenal, almost legendary. On 23 March 1965, for instance, T. C. Douglas specifically asked Martin in Parliament why he referred only to North Vietnamese violations in the 1962 special report, when the latter had declared that the Americans and the South Vietnamese were violating the Geneva Agreements as well. Martin's response was to reiterate Hanoi's violations and intransigence. The closest he came to acknowledging the Commission verdict on American transgression of the Agreements was in 1966, when he pointed out that "there was no reservation made in the Canadian position with regard to the Commission's report of 1962."[20] One may wonder whether a Liberal government would not have attached reservations, or preferred the format adopted in 1965: to attach a minority explanatory statement, without denying the facts of the majority report.

Canada, was, of course, part of the Western alliance system, with its own special access to Washington. It would be kept fully abreast of the American position even outside the Commission.

The other side would lack an equivalent opportunity for a hearing in Ottawa, so that there would always be an imbalance of presentation so far as the protagonists were concerned. Moreover, Canadian officers in Vietnam were not experts on the region. As often as not, their briefing prior to departure would be based on American sources. Once in Vietnam, they would be exposed without qualification to Americans serving there, for obvious and understandable reasons. Consequently, American-based perceptions of the conflict would be reinforced rather than diminished. The *Ottawa Journal* carried a report on 3 April 1969 that

> there is something close to unanimity among all External Affairs men who have been stationed in Southeast Asia. They're all for the Americans in Vietnam and the role they are trying to carry out.

The cold war attitudes of the Canadian political leaders would in turn be reinforced; reports from their officials in the field would only serve to confirm their perceptions of the communist menace.

An example of the benefit to Washington of its special status in Ottawa is provided in two statements by Paul Martin in 1964. On 13 April, he reported to Parliament that he had had "very full discussions" with Dean Rusk on American policy in Vietnam, including pressures to use military force. Similarly, on 26 June he reported on the meeting of the Canadian-American ministerial committee on joint defense, held a day earlier. The situation in Southeast Asia had been discussed, including the deep American concern over the manner in which China and North Vietnam were attempting to extend their influence in Laos and South Vietnam through interference. A serious situation could develop if the communist powers continued on their path of subversion. The American objective, said Martin, was "simply the proper execution of the Geneva accords of 1954." Canada had pointed out its special position arising from its membership in the ICSC, and the United States "fully understood the limitation which this fact places on our activities in this area and made no effort to press upon us an alteration of our current policies." These comments illustrate a basic continuity in Canadian policy from the pre-1954 period to 1964: Canada understood and supported the objectives motivating Western intervention but could not itself contribute materially.

Canada was quite prepared for an increased American role even before the Tonkin Gulf incidents. On 22 May 1964, Martin declared in Parliament that the "full-scale civil war" in South Vietnam was "supplied, directed and inspired from communist North Viet Nam." The civil war was in danger of being turned into an international war because of continued and increased communist interference in South Vietnam. The Americans "have responded to the requests of successive South Viet Namese governments for help . . . against this externally organized and supported insurgency." Martin declared on 9 July 1964 that "the North Vietnamese and their friends" should not "underestimate the firmness of the intentions of the United States government."[21] Canada would do everything to bolster the American firmness of intentions, and would be reluctant to say or do anything that might undermine them.

It came as no surprise, therefore, that Canada should express understanding of the American reaction to Tonkin Gulf. Martin observed in Parliament on 6 August 1964 that North Vietnam had violated the Geneva Agreements, and that "if the communists would observe those agreements there might be none of the present difficulties in Viet Nam." Pearson on the same occasion explained that Canada had expressed the hope to the United States that "any retaliatory action required in defence will be limited to the necessities of the circumstances." A day later, in response to a question from H. W. Herridge as to whether he was satisfied with the veracity of the American version of events, Martin shot back, "of course I am; and I suggest to the hon. gentleman that the evidence is such that he should take a similar view."

That Martin's riposte was less than satisfactory has been demonstrated by James Steele. South Vietnamese commandos had been engaged in raids against targets in the north since July, with the occasional collaboration of American patrol boats. North Vietnam had complained to the International Commission on 27 and 31 July about such raids, and on 23 July the *Saigon Post* reported General Nguyen Ky's boast that raids into North Vietnam were taking place. In light of the fact that Canada as an ICSC member should have been aware of the raids, Steele argues, it "might have been more circumspect in its assessment of the episode."[22] Martin's culpability increases with the realization that the facts of South Vietnamese and American provocation were detailed in the

American Senate on 5 and 6 August by Senator Morse.[23] Canada was surely in a better position to be aware of this than a United States senator in the immediacy of the crisis.

In April 1965, Martin denied that the American intervention was illegal;[24] however, the legal position was characterized by doctrinal ambiguities and uncertainties rather than self-evident conclusions. On the question of who was to blame for the crisis in Vietnam, Martin said on 10 June 1965 that "there has been an impartial international judgment on this matter and that . . . judgment is against North Viet Nam." South Vietnam had appealed for help in the exercise of the legitimate right of self-defense, permitted under Article 51 of the United Nations Charter. The Americans had responded to the appeal, and had made it clear that military help would cease when its need ended.[25] Two years later, Pearson attacked the NDP position that the crisis was not one of aggression from the north, but a localized civil war in which the United States had no justification intervening. American policy makers, said Pearson, were men of goodwill and peace. He affirmed that:

> I believe that the purposes and objectives of United States policy in Viet Nam were not agression. I believe that the United States moved into Viet Nam in the first place to help South Viet Nam, at the invitation of the government of that country, to defend itself against military action and subversive terrorism aimed at preventing the people of that part of Viet Nam making their own decision as to their future development and political institutions rather than having one particular solution forced upon them under the guise of a liberation struggle conducted in the interests of a totalitarian communist regime in North Viet Nam which has not allowed and does not intend to allow its own people any choice as to their social, economic or political system.[26]

The Air War

The attempt to systematically justify its bombing campaign as well as stepped-up intervention in Vietnam was published by the United States in the form of a White Paper in 1965.[27] The opening statement declared that "South Vietnam is fighting for its life against a brutal campaign of terror and armed attack inspired, directed, supplied, and controlled by the Communist regime in Hanoi." The rest of the paper sought to prove each of the charges, but above all to establish that "the war in Vietnam is *not* a spontaneous and local rebellion against the established government."

According to the White Paper, a joint South Vietnamese–American analysis of the massive evidence of North Vietnamese aggression showed the hard core of the Vietcong forces to have been trained in the north, their key leadership to have come from the north, and their infiltration and operation to be under direction from Hanoi. It also claimed that much of the arms and ammunition being used in the south had originated in communist countries and been shipped to Hanoi.[28] The NLF was described as a subordinate part of the Central Office for South Vietnam located in the north, and was said to have been formed in 1960 under Hanoi's order. The paper drew attention to the 1962 Commission special report that had established aggression and subversion against Hanoi, in violation of the Geneva Agreements, and added that the DRVN's complicity had increased in the years since the report.

The assertion that the NLF military personnel were North Vietnamese was based on individual case studies of "an illustrative group" of captured soldiers. The charge that war material was North Vietnamese was similarly justified on the basis of an analysis of weapons captured from communist forces in South Vietnam. By virtue of the detailed evidence and exhaustive analysis presented, the White Paper declared:

> The record is conclusive. It establishes beyond question that North Vietnam is carrying out a carefully conceived plan of aggression against the South. It shows that North Vietnam has intensified its efforts in the years since it was condemned by the International Control Commission.

As a result, the Saigon government had been forced into vigorous action to meet the intensified threat. Part of the response was air strikes against those military targets in the north that were being used as assembly points and supply bases for aggression. This "limited response" would continue until such time as the Hanoi intervention was halted or effective steps were taken to maintain peace and security in the region.[29]

The American objectives were reiterated in April by President Johnson in a speech at Johns Hopkins University.[30] It was the American intention to convince North Vietnam that the United States would not be defeated, would not grow tired, and would not withdraw "either openly or under the cloak of a meaningless agreement." Air attacks alone would not accomplish these purposes, but they were "a necessary part of the surest road to peace." The stick being waved in the air was matched by the carrot of reconstruction aid in the event that war stopped. In a revealing passage, Johnson declared that for centuries nations had struggled, but at the same time dreamt "of a world where disputes are settled by law and reason." He recognized that "it is a very old dream. But we have the power, and now we have the opportunity to make it come true." The irony of the statement had obviously escaped him.

Canadian Response

The bombing of North Vietnam was, for a considerable period of time, regarded by Canadian leaders as understandable. Gradually, however, the conviction crept in that talks could not begin and American extrication from Vietnam could not be started unless the bombing stopped. It should be halted not because it was unjustified but because it was an obstacle to negotiations; it was also unpopular with the public. And, as Pearson expressed it, America had to be extricated from the quagmire because of "the ever deepening involvement of the United States and the resultant complication for their role as leader of the Western world."[31]

The Canadian position and attitudes were clearly stated by Pearson on 2 April 1965 in the celebrated Temple University speech in Philadelphia. The United States, he said, had responded honorably to a South Vietnamese request for defense against aggression. The situation in Vietnam could improve only when North Vietnam was convinced that aggression would fail. Nevertheless, there was an acute and intractable dilemma. On the one hand,

> no nation . . . could ever feel secure if capitulation in Vietnam led to the sanctification of aggression through subversion and spurious "wars of national liberation". On the other hand, the progressive application of military sanctions can encourage stubborn resistance, rather than a willingness to negotiate.

Pearson then proceeded very gingerly to suggest a pause in the bombing:

> there does appear to be at least a possibility that a suspension of such air strikes against North Vietnam at the right time might provide the Hanoi authorities with an opportunity, if they wish to take it, to inject some flexibility into their policy without appearing to do so as the direct result of military pressure.

A suspension of air strikes for a limited time would permit the rate of incidents to be measured in order to determine the efficacy of the bombing pause. He repeated that he was not

> proposing any compromise on points of principle, or any weakening of resistance to aggression in South Vietnam . . . resistance may require increased military strength. . . . I merely suggest that a measured pause in one field of military action at the right time might facilitate the development of diplomatic resources which cannot easily be applied to the problem under existing circumstances.

If Hanoi did not respond, its intransigence would at least stand exposed.[32]

The next day, Pearson met Johnson at Camp David, and suffered through a verbal assault from the President: Pearson had made things more difficult by joining the domestic opponents of America's Vietnam policy.[33] Pearson tried to explain that his statement had been a carefully guarded suggestion aimed at helping the Americans in a situation where the stepped-up bombing had failed to achieve the result desired. Besides, in Canada "some of us were having difficulty with public opinion in our complete support of that policy." Johnson failed to follow Pearson's reasoning, but did explain that his policy was a middling compromise between rival pressures and policies. Johnson's plan was to destroy military installations progressively, but not those too near the Chinese border. Pearson believed that the President "is sincere about this limitation of air action." He also recognized that the Canadians too would have been very angry if an American official had commented in Canada on his host government's policy.

After his return to Ottawa, Pearson tried again to explain his position in a letter to Johnson. He wrote:

> I want to assure you that my Government, and I particularly as its leader, want to give you all possible support in the policy, difficult and thankless, you are following in Vietnam in aiding South Vietnam to resist aggression. . . . There is also, however, a feeling of deep anxiety about developments which could lead to wider hostilities.

There was also the "political background in Ottawa," *viz.*, a vocal and critical opposition to American policy which the government was not in a position to ignore simply because it was a minority one. Pearson added that Johnson's

> exposition of the American case for planned and limited air retaliation, designed to do the job intended, with a minimum of loss of life, and without provocation to China or Russia, was reassuring and impressive.[34]

On 10 June 1965, Paul Martin defended the Canadian minority statement in the 13 February special report by the ICSC. He denied that it condoned South Vietnamese and American policies. Rather, "the sole purpose of the Canadian statement was to augment the presentation of facts" in the majority report by inserting material that was as relevant as the bombing strikes. Further, it represented the Canadian assessment of the facts, and reflected the Canadian conviction that a partial report would seriously distort the true situation. The Canadians did not disagree with the majority report; they had merely augmented it.

Toward the end of 1965, the Americans did initiate a bombing pause; the air raids resumed on 31 January 1966 on the argument that the pause had failed to produce results. The Canadian reaction was given by Pearson in Parliament the same day. He regretted that the United States had found it necessary to resume the bombings, and thought that the pause might have been extended until all reasonable possibilities for negotiations had been exhausted. Nevertheless, it was clear that North Vietnam had shown itself "completely intransigent" on the matter of starting negotiations. He hoped that another halt might be instituted when circumstances warranted believing that they would lead to discussions. In essence, Pearson was implicitly—yet not too implicitly—accepting that bombing was the path to peace, with differences as to degree and timing.

Among the opposition parties, the NDP was completely against the bombing; the Conservatives were generally sympathetic to the American position. In May 1967, former Conservative defense minister Harkness argued that there was no evidence to warrant the belief that an end to the bombing would solve the Vietnam problem. He reminded Canadians that the United States had both the better information and the greater responsibility "for maintaining peace and containing communism." A year earlier, however, Diefenbaker had denounced the extension of the air raids to oil installations in the Hanoi-Haiphong perimeter. Martin in response outlined the government position on the same matter. He was concerned about the proximity of civilians to the new target areas, and about the possibility of a reciprocal escalation on Hanoi's part. Nevertheless, if North Vietnam was to halt its assistance across the border, the United States would cease bombing.[35] The Canadian government was in full agreement with the American rationale for bombings.

The official Canadian position on bombing changed in 1967. While Johnson was in Canada for the centennial visit, Pearson put it to him that the bombing could be halted without condition, along with a statement announcing the willingness to enter into immediate negotiations toward an armistice.[36] The first public suggestion for an unconditional halt to American bombing was made by Paul Martin in an address to the United Nations General Assembly on 27 September 1967. On that occasion, he declared that "all attempts to bring about talks between the two sides are doomed to failure unless the bombing is stopped." A halt to the bombing must be accorded first priority in starting the process of de-escalation and moving to a conference room. He reiterated, however, that bombings were only one side of the military equation.[37] Martin confirmed his changed position in Parliament two days later, to NDP congratulations for finally adopting its policy.

One of the last statements on this matter by the Pearson-Martin government was made on 18 March 1968. The House was informed that in January 1967 the North Vietnamese had said that talks "could" take place if the bombing stopped. In December, their position had changed to the point that talks "will" take place once the American attacks on North Vietnam stopped. Responding to these hopeful signs, the Canadian Commissioner in Vietnam, O. W. Dier, had been sent to Hanoi to seek clarification and confirmation of their position. Canada hoped that the Commission could be reactivated in the DMZ in order to facilitate the exercise of military restraint by both sides. Unfortunately, North Vietnam had not replied with any flexibility. Martin recalled that in September last he had declared that bombing must be stopped as a matter of first priority in the search for peace, as a deliberate and calculated risk: "It will be impossible for North Viet Nam to appear to be responding to military pressure." The difficulty was that both sides envisaged different objectives for the talks that would follow the cessation of bombing. Hanoi aimed to bring about the early and complete withdrawal of America from the country. The United States, on the other hand, wanted to secure South Vietnam from military pressure. Hence their insistence upon reciprocal restraint on North Vietnam's part to a cessation of bombing. By 1968, when Trudeau became Prime Minister, Canada had a fairly clear appreciation of the problems involved in Vietnam.

The advent of the Trudeau government in 1968 produced no immediate change in Canadian pronouncements on the war in Vietnam. Campaigning in the 1968 elections, Pierre Trudeau had taken the position that bombing of North Vietnam should cease at once and totally. In an address to the General Assembly on 9 October, however, Mitchell Sharp, even while conceding that bombing must be stopped as a first step, insisted that since a political settlement requires a general military de-escalation, Hanoi too must indicate a willingness to contribute to the process of peace.[38] In 1970, nevertheless, Sharp was able to declare in the House on 4 May that Canada was opposed to a resumption of the bombing, suspended by President Johnson in 1968. Sharp was more forthright on 28 December 1971 in his reaction to the escalation of air strikes: "We condemn any action that may widen the war in Indo-China. I have no hesitation in again saying this with respect to the bombing operations in North Viet Nam." The final Ottawa-Washington parting of ways on the subject came in the wake of Nixon's carpet bombing over Christmas 1972. On 5 January 1973, Mitchell Sharp made a motion in Parliament deploring the large-scale bombings; the motion was adopted the same day.

Canadian Complicity?

For the major part of the war, Canada was not able to separate its pronouncements on the war from its political alliance with the United States. Similarly, and perhaps more crucially, as a participant in American defense networks that were global in reach, Canada could not hope to isolate or shield itself from a measure of military involvement in America's wars. The question of Canadian "complicity" in the American war effort in Vietnam acquired embarrassing prominence in 1966–67.[39] The discomfort to Canadians stemmed not merely from the fact that their arms were ending up in Vietnam in the cause of war, but also that Canada was responsible in part for keeping peace in this particular instance. In 1967, Paul Martin sidestepped a question as to whether Canadian military sales to the United States were consistent with its participation in the ICSC.[40] The most comprehensive statement of the official Canadian position was made by Pearson on 10 March 1967 in reply to representations from university professors against Canadian participation in the war.[41] He put the issue of military sales to the United States "in a somewhat broader perspective than the problem of the Vietnam war alone"; *viz.*, defense integration between Canada and the United States. Such an integration, he said, was "necessary and logical" for economic and security reasons. Imposition of an embargo on the export of military equipment to the United States would be tantamount to a notice of withdrawal from continental and Atlantic defense arrangements, and unleash "far-reaching consequences which no Canadian Government could contemplate with equanimity." Nor could the government reveal the scope of military sales related to the Vietnam war, Pearson said, because items of military purchase went into the general inventory of American forces, and Canada had no control over the purposes or places of their use.

The Trudeau government continued established policy in the matter of arms sales, and defended it with identical arguments.[42] The shadow over Ottawa-Washington relations also hung over questions of Canadian aid to the Vietnamese. In respect of official aid programs, from 1953 to 1967 the Canadian contribution to South Vietnam totalled $5.8 million; to the north, nil.[43] While Ottawa granted all requests to export medical supplies to the south, it refused a permit to the Canadian Unitarian Aid to Vietnam for the export of medical equipment to civilians in the north.[44]

An element of foreign policy that spanned both the Pearson and Trudeau eras is quiet diplomacy. Pearson lectured the professors in a letter on 10 March 1967 that in peace negotiations, "confidential and quiet arguments by a responsible government are usually more effective than public ones." Martin extended the benefits to argue that public diplomacy would only serve to destroy both Canada's influence in Washington resulting from a special relationship, and its credibility in Hanoi as enjoying the special relationship.[45] Three years later, in the context of the American excursions to Cambodia and Laos, Sharp expressed his belief that diplomatic gestures should be avoided in favor of hard and patient work, even "quiet diplomacy." T. C. Douglas retorted that Sharp "seems to place his entire faith in silent diplomacy—a policy of hear nothing, see nothing, say nothing."[46]

For many Canadians, the Vietnam war represents a shameful episode in the history of their country's foreign policy. Charles Taylor summarizes the Canadian experience in these eloquent words:

> At every stage of its involvement in Vietnam, Canada gave active support to the United States and its policies. . . . [F]or nearly two decades, Canada promoted American interests on successive truce commissions, gave public endorsement to American war aims, provided the Americans with political and military intelligence, became diplomatically entangled in the Americans' escalation policies and fed millions of dollars worth of military hardware into the American war machine.[47]

Fluency of writing need not correspond to accuracy in argument, however. The statement is incomplete, erroneous, and harsh. There is force to Taylor's argument, certainly—but only if we limit his comments to the period *after* the Commission had become moribund, not since its inception. His statement is incomplete in ignoring the largely creditable performance of both the ICSC in general and the Canadian delegation in particular in supervising the miliary disengagement that successfully terminated the Franco-Vietminh war.

The statement is also in error on the counts of facts and interpretation. The Commission's reports show Canada to have jointly striven towards an effective peacekeeping role in the first one or two years. From this it follows that the Canadians in the beginning pursued a policy *opposed* to American desires. As the Pentagon Papers confirmed, the United States had set about attempting to subvert the Geneva Agreements even before their completion.[48] Washington was not exactly pleased with the Agreements, associated itself with them only grudgingly, and did not suffer the ICSC lightly. For the 1954–55 period, at least, a charge of Ottawa's collusion with Washington flies in the face of American hostility to and Canadian support for the Agreements and the Commission. Escott Reid perceptively noted in a letter to his children after Pearson's 1955 visit to India that in the 1953–55 years, Pearson "has had to be a sort of leader of the opposition to Dulles in the North Atlantic Community." Canada's special relationship with the United States made it uniquely positioned to "bell the cat."[49]

The mistake in interpretation occurs for the subsequent period, and is a product of confused logic. The coincidence of major Canadian and American objectives represented a convergence in independent points of view, not Canadian subservience. Canadian leaders in the 1960s supported the objectives of securing a non-communist South Vietnam, in keeping with their general foreign policy; the Americans were fighting to secure a non-communist South Vietnam; the objectives of Ottawa, Washington, and Saigon therefore dovetailed. It was not solely or even largely a case of Ottawa supporting Saigon because it supported Washington.

The Taylor position is harsh, finally, for two more reasons. First, it overlooks the rather simple point that ultimately there was little that the Canadians *could* have done to temper American excesses or diminish the warfare; to claim otherwise would be pretentious. Second, it is unfair in its implication that Canadian partiality to one side in the war did violence to the principles of the Geneva accords and the ICSC. To indict Canada for having favored Saigon misses the point that by virtue of the Geneva accords Canadian partiality was both inevitable and, equally important, desirable. It was *inevitable* because of the troika structure of the Commission. Once the Polish delegation became uncompromisingly rigid in its support of Hanoi's side to any argument—which it did almost from the beginning—the Canadian delegation did not have any genuine alternative but to respond in kind. The Commission would else have become completely one-sided. Canadian bias was *desirable* because of the representational philosophy underlying the troika system. Canada was *chosen* to represent the interests of one side, much as Poland was chosen to represent the interests of the other side. The neutral role in the center was left to the nonaligned representative, India. Krishna Menon was led to refer in 1961 to "the Commission consisting of the representatives of Canada, Poland, and ourselves, representing . . . the different points of view, and ideologies, or alignments that exist in the world."[50] To accuse the Canadians of having performed the part they were chosen for in the cast is, therefore, lacking in charity.

A related if hypothetical argument may be advanced here. The South Vietnamese were shabbily treated at the Geneva Conference in 1954, denied even the courtesies accorded to the Vietminh. At the other end of the time frame, opposition to the American role in Vietnam by 1973 stemmed in no small measure from the transparent corruption and brutalities of the southern regime. Whatever else it may have been fighting for, the United States was not defending democracy and freedoms. However: what if South Vietnam had proved a viable experiment in democracy? Would condemnations of the American role—and, in Canada, of the Canadian role—have been so readily forthcoming if Diem had in fact proved a democratic nationalist, as there was plausible ground for hoping in 1955–56?[51]

The unfairness of the Taylor position can be demonstrated in his charge that Ottawa allowed itself to be used by Washington in escalation strategies. In 1964–65, J. Blair Seaborn, the Canadian ICSC Commissioner, carried to the DRVN five messages from the United States, and brought back reactions on three of the occasions. Taylor accords a comprehensive but hostile discussion to the trips.[52] His thesis is that the Americans used Seaborn to convey terms for peace that North Vietnam was bound to reject, and then used the rejection to justify escalating the air strikes. In short, "Canada became an active accessory to Washington's expansion of the conflict."[53] Surely it is more sensible to regard the trips as a courier service that peacekeepers are called upon to provide between opposing parties in a conflict. Similarly, it is easy enough to attack Seaborn for having engaged in political intelligence functions at the behest and on behalf of the United States in his trips. Yet, it is equally plausible that his reports, accurately predicting that North Vietnam would struggle on in spite of escalating American efforts, could have been instrumental in informing the Americans of the futility of their policy, and thereby promoted peace. We can at least give Seaborn—and Ottawa—credit for an honest effort sincerely made, even if it was abused.

The American War and India

India had no military ties with either protagonist in Vietnam. There was never any question of revulsion among Indians for their country's role in the destruction being wrought there. Consequently the attention devoted by Indian officials to the military aspects of the conflict, and their implications for India, are not comparable to the Canadian case. Moreover, for most of the 1960s, India was still recovering from the debacle with China, as well as suffering severe economic problems and food shortages. Criticisms of American intervention in Vietnam were therefore muted. On 22 September 1964, Swaran Singh declared that the Vietnam situation was critical and dangerous. It was India's belief that eventually political, not military, solutions would have to be found. The incidents in the Gulf of Tonkin six weeks earlier "caused us great concern to which we officially gave expression at that time. Fortunately, these have not led to a wider conflict." Three days later, Singh repeated that the search for peace and a political solution to the Vietnam conflict was necessary because of the dangers of great-power involvement.

The concern India felt over the air strikes into North Vietnam that were initiated in February 1965 was clearly expressed in the ICSC report of 13 February. In April 1965, Johnson rejected appeals to stop bombings unilaterally, and followed this by announcing a postponement of Prime Minister L. B. Shastri's visit to the United States. Shastri interpreted the postponement as an expression of American resentment of India's view of the bombing policy. However, he did not cancel the visit to Ottawa, scheduled for June. The Shastri-Pearson communiqué of 14 June 1965 suggested that the belligerents in Vietnam might reduce the scale of hostilities or institute periods of cease-fire that could acquire permanence. It recalled the 1962 special report that had blamed both sides. Perhaps in deference to the hosts, a bombing halt was not demanded as a precondition for negotiations.

Criticisms of American policy were curtailed in the aftermath of the September war with Pakistan. Swaran Singh's statement at the United Nations General Assembly in October, for instance, did not mention Vietnam. Shastri himself observed that "at least the United States has shown some willingness to negotiate, even if it has imposed some very heavy conditions," adding that "I would like to see some sign from China that she is prepared to take steps towards peace there."[54] At the end of Indira Gandhi's visit to the United States in 1966 (28 March–1 April), the joint communiqué asserted that the two leaders had touched upon Vietnam only very briefly. Shortly after, Johnson announced emergency food aid to India. Gandhi's statements at the time emphasized the need for peaceful solutions, but also referred to the sincerity of the American president's quest for peace. There have been suggestions that Johnson's aid was contingent on some appreciation by India of American efforts to defend Southeast Asia from communism.[55]

Indian criticisms of American bombing resumed toward the end of June, shortly after the extension of bombings to POL targets near Hanoi and Haiphong. Gandhi toured the USSR the next month, and her communiqué of 16 July with Alexei Kosygin called for an immediate cessation of the bombings and the resolution of the Vietnam conflict within the framework of the Geneva accords. One observer speculated that India's shift towards the NLF position was attributable to concern over possible Soviet military aid to Pakistan and economic needs. The last was partly answered by a 970 million rouble credit, announced during the visit.[56]

On 30 July 1966, the United States launched air assaults in the DMZ, leading to Commission apprehensions of a fresh crisis. In August, New Delhi reacted by urging a revival of the Joint Commission, and suggested that the International Commission could resume patrolling in the DMZ. (The Commission never formally protested the use of the DMZ for infiltrating and staging purposes by the communists, nor the entry of American forces into the zone in May 1967.) New Delhi was concerned above all with increasing escalation that might involve Chinese and even Soviet intervention. There were fears that the DMZ might constitute the functional equivalent of the 38th parallel in Korea so far as the crossing of ground forces was concerned. The Indian proposal was favorably received by the United States, South Vietnam, Britain, and Canada, but rejected by North Vietnam and its allies. DMZ patrols were almost instituted a little later. With Polish and Canadian approval in the Commission, India asked Washington to suspend bombings in the zone, and requested Hanoi to permit patrols.

Bombings were suspended in the southern half of the zone on 27 September, and two patrols were made by a Commission team. Bombings in the northern segment were then halted, but Hanoi did not permit the Commission patrols to operate, citing a lack of transportation facilities. The Commission allowed on 7 October that patrolling was not possible even with the pause in bombing; on 13 October, Johnson rejected calls by U Thant and indirect appeals from India for an unconditional end to air strikes; and bombings in the DMZ resumed on 15 October 1966.

India went to the polls in February 1967. In early February, Foreign Minister M. C. Chagla welcomed the Tet cease-fire, but appealed to the United States for an unconditional and indefinite halt to the bombings. The basis of his appeal was the DRVN Foreign Minister Nguyen Trinh's statement of 28 January that talks between North Vietnam and the United States could begin after an unconditional halt to the bombing. After the elections, in April, Chagla explained that bombings were counterproductive because they stiffened northern resolve, risked Chinese intervention, and hurt Soviet-American relations. The call for an unconditional bombing halt became a regular feature of India's pronouncements on Vietnam.

By 1970, India's attacks on the American position had again softened. This was the period when the Soviets were briefly flirting with Pakistan by providing military aid, and their theoreticians despaired of socialistic progress in India. On 1 May 1970, Foreign Minister Dinesh Singh, speaking in the Rajya Sabha, "regretted" the massive entry of American forces into Cambodia. The government, he said, was "distressed" at the situation. However, the government failed to meet demands by the communist parties for an outright condemnation of American aggression in Cambodia. Three days later, Gandhi herself expressed "grave concern" at the worsening situation in Vietnam and Cambodia. In a mild reference to the resumption of bombing in North Vietnam, she regretted that "certain good steps" taken by the United States should have been so retraced. She confessed to a sense of "shock and distress," saying that the fact that she had not used strong language did not mean that she did not feel strongly about the developments. Nor did it mean that she did feel strongly about the developments.

Nineteen Seventy-One, the year of the signing of the Indo-Soviet Treaty, and the year of the Bangladesh war, was crucial for India. It marked a formal realignment of India's bias toward the USSR, and a record low in Indo-American relations. The shift in India's attitudes toward the Vietnam war is also very pronounced from 1971 onward. In an address to the United Nations General Assembly on 4 October 1971, Foreign Minister Swaran Singh expressed agony over the continuing war in Vietnam. India regretted in particular the recent resumption of bombing in North Vietnam, he said, especially as the South Vietnamese regime had not progressed towards the ideals for which so many lives had been lost. Singh endorsed the seven-point proposal made in Paris by the Provisional Revolutionary Government of South Vietnam (PRG), and expressed the hope that "American and other foreign troops will finally be withdrawn by a definite date and the people of Vietnam will be allowed to settle their own future."[57] Two points are of interest here. First, in comparison with Canadian and American statements, India was calling for an internal settlement by the people of Vietnam, not South Vietnam. Second, the reference to bombings was still mild: a regret, not a condemnation. It should be borne in mind that Singh's address was given just before the war that clearly loomed, and on the eve of Gandhi's international tour to gain support, including Washington's, for Indian actions.

The war with Pakistan ended with a unilateral cease-fire on 17 December 1971. From then on, there was no pretense at a balance between the belligerents. In a full statement in Parliament on 10 May 1972, Singh addressed himself to the mining of North Vietnamese harbors and intensive bombing raids. He declared that the measures were contrary to the cause of peace and to Nixon's declared objectives, caused unnecessary suffering, and constituted unjustified escalation. He expressed deep regret over the unilateral American action in breaking off the Paris peace talks, and apprehensions of "a bigger and wider conflict." More importantly, from the point of view of a departure in Indian foreign policy, he said: "I am sure this House will join the Government in condemning this latest escalation."

In 1956, Nehru had drawn international and domestic opprobrium because he would not be a party to a resolution that *condemned* the USSR for its actions in Hungary. In 1968, Gandhi had repeated her father's policy and argument in regard to Soviet suppression of tendencies in Czechoslovakia. Yet, in 1972, her government was condemning the United States in Vietnam. Nor was Singh's statement a singular, exceptional instance. The Working Committee of the Congress Party, by a formal resolution on 11 May, expressed its "anguish" at the American measures, declaring them to be "in defiance of international law" which "cannot but be condemned by all peace loving peoples." Since Indians were "peace-loving peoples,"

> the Working Committee condemns these acts of naked aggression. The use of brutal force cannot succeed in subduing the will of the brave and determined people fighting heroically to maintain their national identity.[58]

Finally, on 19 December 1972, Singh expressed distress in the Lok Sabha about the highly intensified bombings, and hoped that there would be an immediate stoppage of all bombings and other acts of war. Three days later, his deputy found the indiscriminate bombings "distressing," and extolled the Vietnamese people as "brave" and "heroic." India welcomed the Paris peace in 1973, but it welcomed the final NLF victory in 1975 even more. Discussion of this appears in the next chapter.

Poland and the American War in Vietnam

Most of Polish policy toward the American involvement is discussed in the next chapter, within the framework of Hanoi-Moscow-Peking relations rather than in direct response to American policy. The Polish position was in any case very clearly expressed in the special reports of 1962 and 1965. The Polish delegation's sentiment as expressed in the 1962 report was mirrored in a Gomulka interview conducted by *Life*, but published in *New Times*. Gomulka charged that the Saigon regime lacked popular support and maintained itself in power only by savage mass terror. In this context, the expanding scale of American intervention was causing widespread disquiet. Colonialism, he said, was an anachronism. If, however, any state interfered in the internal affairs of another state in the pursuit of colonial or neocolonial objectives, then the victim country had the right to appeal for assistance from sympathetic countries. Socialist countries were not in the business of exporting revolution, Gomulka concluded; but they could not be indifferent to counterrevolution being exported by the capitalists.[59]

The Soviet-Polish joint communiqué of 9 April 1965, issued after the aerial phase of the American war, reaffirmed complete solidarity with the DRVN. In December 1965, William Averell Harriman traveled to Poland in an exploration for peace feelers during the Christmas-New Year bombing pause. Gomulka and Adam Rapacki rigidly emphasized the solidarity of their alliance with the DRVN, the culpability of the United States for the war in Vietnam and for propping up a puppet regime in Saigon, and demanded that the United States unconditionally and permanently cease bombing of the north and withdraw its troops from the south. Nevertheless, Rapacki was prepared to forward messages from Harriman to Hanoi.[60] When Paul Martin traveled to Poland the following year (5–9 November 1966), his joint communiqué with Rapacki stated that the two had expressed "deep concern" at the continuation of the conflict in Vietnam, and had "presented their respective views on this matter."

President Nixon was in Warsaw from 31 May to 1 June 1972. A joint communiqué on the visit said that his talks with the Polish leaders had been "frank, businesslike and constructive." The two sides had been in agreement on the Poland-West Germany treaty and on the desirability of a European security conference; but they expressed "divergent" views on the subject of Vietnam. The next month, Foreign Minister Swaran Singh of India was in Poland. In the Indo-Polish communiqué of 11 July, both sides "strongly deplored the bombings of the D.R.V.N. territory and mining of ports." In addition, they "resolutely condemned the outside interference" in Vietnamese affairs.[61] Even in the ICSC, the Polish and Indian delegations found themselves in alliance against the Canadians.

A Matter of Opinion

Canada
The Vietnam war has been prominent enough in the Canadian consciousness for the public image of the war to have been extensively recorded. And, although leaders may have greater freedom of maneuver in foreign policy than in domestic politics, representative governments must still operate within the constraints of public opinion.

In a Canadian public opinion survey in June 1965, 80 percent of the respondents were aware of the American intervention in Vietnam or the Dominican Republic. Of these, 44 percent expressed approval; 33 percent disapproved. Canadian images of the American role in Vietnam turned steadily more unfavorable after the initial intervention. By April 1966, only 1 percent more approved than disapproved of the American handling of the Vietnam situation (35:34). In the same year, an identical multinational poll by the Gallup organization revealed the interesting, if expected, result that the Canadian attitudes stood almost exactly between American and British on the question of whether the Americans should withdraw their troops from Vietnam (Table 8). By 1967, American opinion favoring withdrawal had increased sharply to 32 percent. Canadian opinion in favor of withdrawal had jumped to 41 percent by September 1967, with 16 percent advocating continuation, and 23 percent an increase in fighting. In November 1967, Canadians dissociating themselves from the American effort outnumbered those who were grateful to the United States for its actions in Vietnam (37:35).

TABLE 8
World Opinion on the U.S. War in Vietnam, Gallup Polls, 1966

	Australia	Great Britain	Canada	France	Germany	United States
The United States should withdraw its troops	21	42	31	68	51	18
The United States should carry on as at present	43	17	18	8	19	18
The United States should increase attacks	24	16	27	5	15	55
No opinion	12	25	24	19	15	9
Total	100	100	100	100	100	100

In other words, by the time that Canadian spokesmen began to publicly demand an unconditional halt to American bombing (Paul Martin on 27 September 1967), the gesture had become politically profitable at home. By 1970–71, opposition to the American role had crystallized while support had largely diminished. In 1970, 42 percent stated that their opinion of the United States would go up if it withdrew from Vietnam in the near future; only 16 percent said that the United States would decline in their estimation. Toward the end of the following year, 51 percent believed that the United States had made a mistake in sending troops to Vietnam; only 27 percent disagreed with the proposition.[62] In light of our preceding analysis of the official Canadian pronouncements, it is readily apparent that the government lagged behind its citizens insofar as opposition to the American intervention in Vietnam is concerned.

India

Opinion polls of the Vietnam war *per se* were somewhat scarce in India. The few conducted, however, confirm that Indians by and large identified with the Vietnamese against the Americans. Table 9 gives the results of a parliamentary survey carried out in late 1968. On the matter of the preferred outcome of the war, 35 percent believed that the United States should give up and leave; 36 percent answered that it should compromise even at the risk of probable eventual communism; and only 20 percent wanted it to continue fighting in order to safeguard South Vietnam against communism.[63] In 1969, an overwhelming 62 percent of the literate population of the metropolitan cities of Bombay, Calcutta,

TABLE 9
Attitudes of Indian Parliamentarians Toward U.S. Role in Vietnam, 1968

	Yes	No	Don't Know/ No Answer	Total
Is the United States really trying for peace in Vietnam	28	65	7	100
Should the United States bomb North Vietnam	36	57	7	100

Madras, and New Delhi said that they would be happy with a United States withdrawal; only 23 percent expressed worry. In the same sample, on the matter of Indian policy toward Vietnam there was again general support for the government's low profile (Table 10).[64] Finally, in 1970, in a poll conducted after the American–South Vietnamese incursion into Cambodia, 24 percent of the respondents stated that their opinion of the United States had declined of late; of this, 18 percent ascribed their lowered estimation to American interference in Vietnam and Cambodia. In comparison, the United States had gone up in the opinion of only 15 percent.[65]

TABLE 10
Opinions on Indian Policy Toward Vietnam, 1969

	Yes	No	Doesn't matter	Can't Say	Total
Was the government right in declining recognition to the PRG	39	28	5	28	100
Should India take a leading role in resolving the Vietnam crisis	40	49	–	11	100

If comprehensive surveys of Indian opinion on the Vietnam war are lacking, commendable work has been done in mapping Indian images of international affairs. Since India's relations with the great powers has played a demonstrably important role in its official behavior toward the Vietnam war, public images of the major international actors becomes directly relevant to this study. The strong anti-American frame of mind of official India in 1954–55 coincided with a position on Vietnam that clearly favored Hanoi's interpretations. In an August 1955 survey, a massive 79 percent of respondents in Calcutta thought that American foreign policy might lead to a war of aggression, compared to a meager 6 percent who held that opinion of the USSR.[66] In the 1959–62 period, on the other hand, there was a marked swing in India's Vietnam policy, to the detriment of North Vietnam, related to the dramatic turnaround in India's relations with China. The marked shift away from China and toward the West is reflected in parliamentary surveys taken in 1958 and 1962, just after the war (Table 11).[67]

TABLE 11
Attitudes of Indian Parliamentarians Toward the USA, USSR, and China, 1958 and 1962

	USA 1958	USA 1962	USSR 1958	USSR 1962	China 1958	China 1962
India should cooperate very closely with	21	58	23	24	Not asked	
There is a likelihood of better relations between India and	74	95	76	74	82	13

An equally interesting point about Table 11 is that the image of the USSR remained static—and high—while that of the United States and China underwent major changes. The image of China, it might be added, has since 1962 stayed consistently at the bottom (Table 12).[68]

TABLE 12
Indian Images of China, 1965–71

	1965	1970	1971
Positive Score (Good-Very Good Opinion)	1	9	7
Negative Score (Bad-Very Bad Opinion)	85	66	70

The second striking period in India's great-power relations and Vietnam policies was post-1971. Again, the patterns hold true for Indian images of the United States and the USSR, with the low ranking of China being a constant. Even in a late 1961 survey, 85 percent of urban and 77 percent of rural respondents had said that India should remain "strictly neutral" as between the United States and the USSR in the cold war.[69] In other words, the Indian public too has differentiated between global cold-war issues and bilateral India-China relations.

The pattern of images of the superpowers has, however, been strongly colored by the factor of Pakistan. Both the importance of Pakistan and the general popular bias toward the USSR can be gleaned from the graph (Figure 3). The USSR, it will be recalled, flirted with the idea of equating India and Pakistan in 1968–70, and even gave Pakistan a limited supply of arms. That is the only period in which the image of the United States was higher than that of the Soviet Union. The United States tilted disastrously towards Pakistan in the 1971 Bangladesh war,[70] and in early 1975 lifted the arms embargo on Pakistan. Reactions to all three events are clearly visible in the graph. The pattern of Indian public opinion would seem to be in harmony with official policy toward American involvement in Vietnam and the eventual outcome of the war.

FIGURE 3
Indian Images of the Superpowers:
The USSR-USA Differential, 1966–76

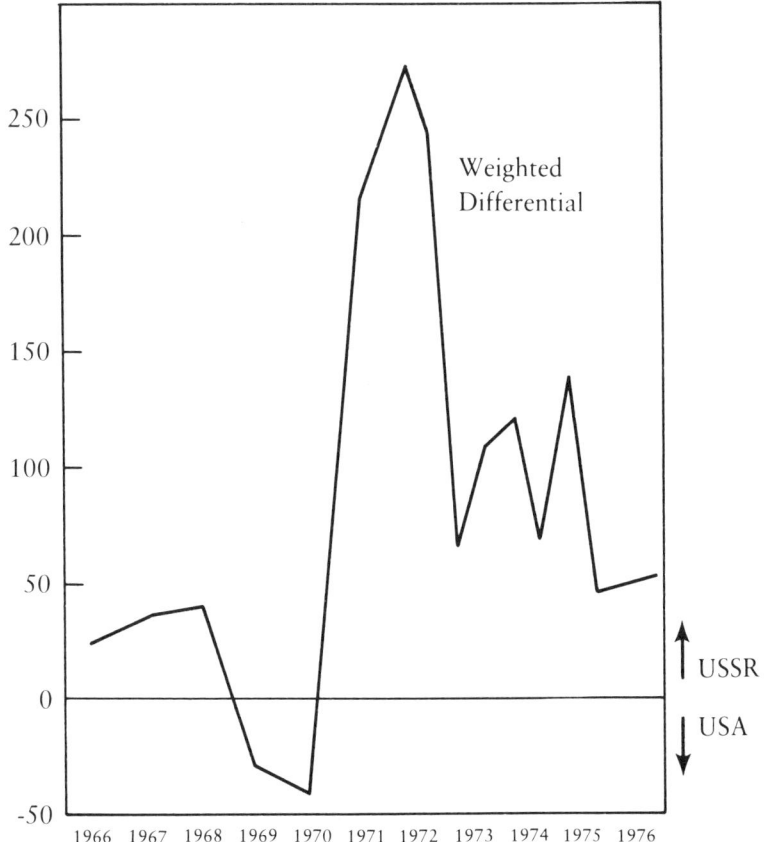

Source: IIPO, *Monthly Public Opinion Surveys* 20 (August 1976): Supplement, pp. III–IV. Computation is author's, based on weighted scores provided by the IIPO.

A Point of Law

Debate over the legality of American intervention in Vietnam was extensive and passionate. Moore asserted "that there is an unlawful armed attack on the R.V.N. by the D.R.V., that third states may lawfully assist in the collective defense of the R.V.N., and the the response of the R.V.N., the United States and other assisting nations is reasonably necessary to the defense of the R.V.N."[71] On the other hand, Wright concluded that "American military action in Viet-Nam has been in pursuit of the policy of containing Communism rather than in fulfilment of any legal obligation." Specific actions, such as the bombing of North Vietnam, violated "international law, the United Nations Charter, and the Geneva Agreement, if the latter were in effect."[72] Faced with these contrary conclusions, it seems safer for us to agree with Wolfgang Friedmann that "we delude ourselves as to the degree to which international law controls the Viet-Nam type of conflict at this time, if we disguise the legal anarchy by the invocation of formulas that merely cloak the nakedness of the political and ideological struggle."[73]

The legal merits of the arguments will not be commented upon; the point here is that there was a controversy within the United States. Official Canadian statements can be placed in the context of the American debate to determine the degree of coincidence or divergence between Canadian views and official and dissenting American views. Three central questions will be discussed: was the war civil or international; was North Vietnam guilty of armed attack upon South Vietnam; and to what extent were North Vietnamese and American actions legal?

The Canadian Brief

Canada's defense of the American intervention began explicitly with the Commission's report of 1962. Before Canada began to shy away from its self-assumed role as the apologist for the United States, it had accepted and stated every major American argument in justification of the American war: North Vietnam was engaged in an illegal armed attack upon South Vietnam; the claim that the uprising was an indigenous rebellion was fictitious; South Vietnam was within its rights in refusing nationwide elections, in attempting to determine its own future, and in resisting aggression by all means at its disposal; the United States was within its rights in aiding South Vietnam to fight communist aggression; and the American intervention was consistent with international law and the United Nations Charter.

Even when Canada finally drew back a little from such close identification with the American position, it was due not to a changed evaluation of American objectives but in response to domestic political conditions, a hardening of world attitudes, and the strengthening of dissent within the United States. Even so, the Martin-Pearson position changed in September 1967 only to the extent of demanding unilateral cessation of the bombing of North Vietnam as the first necessary step to peace in Vietnam. It is also arguable that by September 1967 the possibility of a split within the Western alliance of purpose and resolve, and a sapping of the American will, were considered by Canada to be more dangerous to world peace and stability than the abandonment of the struggle in Vietnam.

In March 1965, Martin declared that the Vietnam war had features both of a civil war and an international war mixed together.[74] He entered into a more detailed defense of the American role on 2 April 1965. According to him, "in 1954 the Geneva powers determined that until such time as there could be free elections, until such time as there could be unification of North and South Viet Nam, each territory would be regarded as having the attributes of sovereignty." Martin was clearly at fault for translating functioning governments in specified temporary zones into sovereign territories; he was also guilty of having glossed over the delimited time for elections, to imply that the question had been left open. At any rate, he continued that Saigon had called for American support in its effort to resist infiltration and aggression from the north. "No one can suggest that the intervention of the United States in these circumstances is illegal"; it was also "pursuant to Article 52" [sic] of the United Nations Charter. News of the bombings was disturbing, but so was "the chronicle of communist murder and armed attacks against innocent civilians." The fact of North Vietnamese interference had been established by Canadian observers. While the guerrilla movement might contain domestic elements, he concluded, it would not have the same strength without North Vietnamese "encouragement, supply and direction."[75] The last statement in particular is an interesting demonstration of the propensity of Canadians to arrive at facts from their prior perceptions of aggressive communism: that the movement was strong was automatically taken to mean that the northern regime was involved, rather than demonstrating the extent of disaffection with the Saigon regime.

On the question of two Vietnams, Martin stated in his speech of 2 April that the division was not a Western creation, but resulted from native political forces. Specifically, "its continued existence represents the conviction of those Vietnamese who were concerned that a communist Viet Nam under Ho Chi Minh would be little more than a province of China, a fate which the Vietnamese people have feared and rejected throughout their history." Martin asserted, without offering evidence, that elections "would not have been fairly carried out." South Vietnam, therefore, refused to fall under northern control through elections, and Hanoi then decided upon a more aggressive policy to accomplish its ends. "Violations of the Geneva accords were begun following aggression by the north *in the early part of 1955*" (emphasis added). This, Martin claimed (quite wrongly insofar as the chronology is concerned), was the conclusion of the 1962 majority report and the 1965 minority (Canadian) report. The chronological insistence was necessary in order to avoid the charge that North Vietnam's actions were in response to material breaches of the Geneva Agreements by Saigon, in refusing elections in July 1956 and consultations for elections in July 1955. (American intelligence estimates were quite realistic on this score. On 19 July 1955, an intelligence assessment pointed out that if the Diem government persisted in refusing to enter into election discussions, Hanoi would likely conclude that South Vietnam could be won only by force.)[76]

Addressing himself finally to the American role, Martin declared that it was bearing a heavy responsibility in its global defense of freedom. Canada ought, therefore, "to consider and exercise care over any disagreement with the United States in a matter of such importance, in the light of our own national interest." Martin then proceeded to give a very clear enunciation of the domino theory.

Martin's speech of 2 April 1965 has been dwelt on because, in the immediate aftermath of the full-scale American involvement (including air strikes into North Vietnam), it was an unequivocal, unqualified support for the American role. On every point the Canadian statement was coterminous enough with the official American case that the whole speech may just as easily have been read by an American State Department spokesman. It was, therefore, entirely fitting that Martin should specifically accept the heart of the American objective. In the Vietnam problem, he said, Canada favored a settlement "that would set up an independent or neutral Viet Nam or, if the country cannot be unified, a neutral South Viet Nam and a neutral North Viet Nam." It bears repeating that Canada as a member of the ICSC was pledged to oversee implementation of the Geneva Agreements, the operative political part of which had called for reunification in 1956. In 1956, its foreign minister was officially declaring in Parliament that both Canada and the United States were equally aware of the danger points in Vietnam, but that "I only hope *that our combined efforts will see no violation of the rights of self-determination in the south*" (emphasis added). In other words, Canada fully subscribed, if by different means, to the American effort to create and preserve an independent South Vietnam. As Johnson declared five days later at Johns Hopkins University, "Our objective is the independence of South Viet-Nam and its freedom from attack."

On the same day that Martin gave total support to the American position, Pearson in his Temple University speech introduced at least some distance between himself and President Johnson. This is a useful indicator of the Pearson-Martin differences within the Canadian government. As a general rule, Martin was more enthusiastic in his support of American policy while Pearson was more qualified in his assessments.

Paul Martin went over essentially the same points as late as April 1967, in an appearance before the Committee on External Affairs. There was one fresh development on that date, however. When Martin mentioned that the American intervention was consistent with the right to individual and collective self-defense under Article 51 of the United Nations Charter, Andrew Brewin queried whether the applicability of the Charter was not controversial. Martin replied that "I do not believe it is, no." [77] As the introductory argument above shows, the applicability was controversial, whatever the final verdict.

Conclusion

Assessing Canada's relationship to the American military effort in Vietnam, Charles Taylor observes that the only ingredient missing was Canadian troops. He quotes an official as saying that "membership on the ICC was our chastity belt against LBJ."[78] In the minds of critics, there was a factual alliance between the Americans and Canadians, to paraphrase the 1962 special report. Canadian policies in Vietnam were subsumed under and subordinated to the dictates of larger foreign policy considerations. The argument is applicable to the Canadian strategy of quiet diplomacy. Membership in the Commission in particular enabled Ottawa to claim that neutrality demanded silence rather than condemnation, quiet as opposed to public diplomacy. In fact, Vietnam is of crucial importance in understanding the lengths to which quiet diplomacy was practiced by the Canadian government, and the resulting disillusionment with the technique.

In May 1967, Pearson claimed, in reference to his Temple University call for a bombing pause, that he had spoken publicly when he thought that was of value. "But this does not mean and will not mean . . . that we shall join that chorus which has denounced the United States for being in Viet Nam at all."[79] Paul Martin defended quiet diplomacy during the course of his review of Taylor's *Snow Job*: "Diplomacy, unlike war, is a quiet art devoted to the reconciliation of conflicting interests." Throughout the Vietnam war, a quiet accommodation between the parties was sought by many, not just Canada: England, France, Poland, Italy, and the United Nations Secretary-General. (His omission of India is interesting, especially as Poland is mentioned.) Public statements could conceivably limit the conduct of negotiation and harden positions. Even North Vietnam, he added, adhered to the tenets of quiet diplomacy.[80]

Paul Martin's belief in quiet diplomacy was strong enough that he had threatened to resign in 1965 in an attempt to dissuade Pearson from the bombing-pause speech. His argument was that the speech would destroy Canadian credibility in *Hanoi* by leading the North Vietnamese to believe that Ottawa had sacrificed its influence in Washington. Pearson's answer was that he was a political leader who had to reflect the fact that many Canadians were upset by the American bombings.[81]

Two years later, Martin demanded Walter Gordon's resignation because of Gordon's powerful public indictment, on 13 May 1967, of the American role in Vietnam. Gordon's speech more closely approximated the positions of the NDP and American dissenters than those of the Canadian cabinet. In June, he was taken by Martin to a

NATO Council meeting in Luxembourg, for a practical demonstration of quiet diplomacy. At a private session on Vietnam, Martin was impressively critical of American policy. Equally impressive was the fact that he did not receive the backing of any other foreign minister, while Dean Rusk dismissed his arguments. Martin confessed years later to Charles Taylor that his public demand at the United Nations for an end to American bombing was prompted by the realization that private diplomacy had been totally unsuccessful.[82] As has been shown, however, quiet diplomacy was not abandoned, not even by his successor in office.

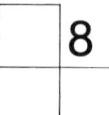 # 8 National Foreign Policies

Developments "in the field" in Vietnam have been covered; however, the Vietnamese policies of Canada, India, and Poland must be set in the context of their broader foreign policies. It is helpful to go briefly over policies decided in foreign ministries rather than in the International Commission in Vietnam. This has been done in respect of the French Indochina war of 1946–54. It has also been shown that there was indeed a coincidence of views between foreign offices and corresponding ICSC delegations on the vital issues at stake in Vietnam. Two substantive areas remain: relations with the rival Vietnamese regimes, and stands on the myriad peace formulas proposed to bring the war to a close. The discussion of Polish foreign policy will take a slightly different approach.

Canada

Canada's relations with the two Vietnams were subordinated to the communist-noncommunist dichotomy, and to dictates of prudence in relations with the United States. Thus Paul Martin tended to echo American sentiments toward Diem,[1] and Canada was among the Western countries that had recognized the new Republic of Vietnam by the end of 1955. Pearson informed Parliament on 8 March 1962 of his conviction that Chinese communism was "the force mainly responsible for the civil war" in Vietnam. On 2 April 1964, opposition leader Diefenbaker referred to the situation in South Vietnam as "one of the gravest challenges to the Western world and to freedom itself." He wondered whether Western forces were preventing "the spread of communism." Martin, in a statement to the House on 28 May 1965, assessed Vietnam in terms of the falling dominoes.

In the same debate, T. C. Douglas of the NDP outlined a position virtually identical to that of India. He described Ho Chi Minh's Vietminh as nationalists and anticolonialists, and reminded the House that the 17th parallel was a provisional boundary, that the elections stipulated for 1956 had been sabotaged by Saigon and Washington, and that a Commission report bearing Canada's signature had branded American intervention as illegal. Military support from Hanoi, he said, did not disguise the fact that the guerrillas were largely indigenous to South Vietnam, and enjoyed wide support in the populace. Dulles' domino theory had been proved false by the schism in the communist movement; nor did the Vietnamese want Chinese troops back on their soil. Douglas concluded, "we must not allow, under the guise of preventing acts of aggression, any great power to repress the legitimate aspirations of the people of any country for self-government and the right of self-determination."

Paul Martin's detailed reply came in committee on 10 June. In an incredible[2] sketch of Vietnamese history, he declared that the Vietminh were not to be credited for having driven the Japanese out. During the war, they "aided the allies by providing some intelligence information, distributing propaganda, and organizing the odd attack against the Japanese." In 1945, when the Japanese administration collapsed, the Vietminh took advantage of the resultant power vacuum to drive out other nationalists while refraining from any attacks on the Japanese. Martin argued that "the division of Viet Nam is not something created by the West in its own interests, but is something which represents the polarization of Vietnamese political forces into Communist and non-Communist sectors." Moreover, since South Vietnam had rejected the terms of the Geneva Agreements even before they were signed, "it cannot . . . be convincingly accused of violating international obligations."[3]

Insofar as the American war in Vietnam is concerned, Canada seemed for a while to be doing everything short of sending troops in support of that effort. Speaking in the House on 25 January 1966, Martin explained that contribution of a Canadian military contingent to Vietnam would not be compatible with its Commission responsibilities. This was not a "frivolous argument," he added. If Canada did not send troops, it was still involved in the war through economic dealings and later even through medical and hospital contributions. Additionally, Canadian spokesmen had begun to refer to two Vietnams, in contravention of the Geneva Agreements. Martin declared in Parliament on 25 January 1966 that "whatever the circumstances in which these dividing lines were drawn they have come to reflect political realities which it will take time to alter."

Such selective insensitivity to the Agreements also characterized the Canadian position on peace feelers. The points of contention between the two protagonists were: whether American bombing should cease unilaterally, unconditionally, and permanently as a first step to negotiations, or whether it should be reciprocal to de-escalation by Hanoi; the question of Hanoi's complicity or direction in the NLF war effort in the southern zone; the status of the NLF and the Saigon government during peace talks; and the status of South Vietnam after a cease fire.

Negotiations to end the war in Vietnam had to surmount four obstacles. The first was the tendency of the DRVN and American leaders to operate on the "inherent bad faith" model of the enemy,[4] which provides little prospect for reducing tensions. In such a situation,

> perceptions of low hostility are self-liquidating and perceptions of high hostility are self-fulfilling. The former, being associated with weakness and frustration, do not invite reciprocation; the latter, assumed to derive from strength and success, are likely to result in reactions which will increase rather than decrease tensions.[5]

The history of the Vietnam peace negotiations bears ample testimony to this unfortunate tendency.[6]

The second difficulty stemmed from the different assumptions underlying United States and DRVN negotiating strategies. Washington approached peace talks as a bargaining process through which it could extricate itself, leaving a reasonably secure and independent South Vietnam. Since the latter aim clashed with the basic DRVN objective, Hanoi treated negotiations as an extension of warfare. It engaged in the tactic of "protracted negotiation," in which talks served to frustrate the United States government, sap its will, and alienate its public and allies, while providing diplomatic and military advantages to Hanoi. Washington in turn countered with a graduated escalation that raised the cost of fighting for Hanoi, but also prolonged the war and undercut efforts to end it.[7] In part, the escalated war resulted from the fact that the causes of the war were not negotiable.

The third obstacle to negotiations was the government of South Vietnam. Saigon presented two barriers to peace. First, it was forever unwilling to concede the reality of the military battlefield. Saigon insisted on achieving through negotiations the objective that had eluded it through years of warfare: a South Vietnam free of communist presence. This unwillingness became significant only because of a second problem: allied insistence upon the sovereignty of South Vietnam *vis-à-vis* the DRVN. If the RVN was sovereign, and if its sovereign refusal to withhold consent from the 1954 Geneva Agreements was justifiable, then clearly it could not be compelled to sign another agreement against its will. Hence the ability of the Thieu regime to repeatedly sink or stall negotiations: the tail was wagging the dog with a vengeance.[8]

The final obstacle was the simple fact that American peacemakers had to engage in three different kinds of negotiations simultaneously: with the United States government and public, with authorities in Hanoi, and with authorities in Saigon.

In this context, friends and allies of the United States had to tread cautiously on the delicate subject of approaches to peace in Vietnam. Because Canada held Hanoi responsible for the war both in origins and continuance, its peace efforts were at first directed at securing North Vietnamese capitulation to American objectives. The restraints Ottawa urged on Washington stemmed not from a questioning of American objectives or means, but from the wish "to avoid the inevitable consequences of escalation."[9] American bombing, for example, was long treated with sympathetic understanding. Pearson's celebrated Temple University speech of 2 April 1965 is remarkable chiefly for the gingerness of its approach in advocating a measured pause in the air strikes against North Vietnam, at the right time and for a limited duration.

Ottawa's ideological blinders were most evident in its failure to see the two important conditions Washington included in successive offers, beginning with Johnson's Johns Hopkins speech of 7 April 1965, to negotiate for peace without posing any preconditions. Pearson gushingly described the Baltimore speech as "magnificent" and deserving of "wholehearted Canadian support; particularly for your declaration of willingness to engage in unconditional discussions looking towards an honourable settlement."[10] As T. C. Douglas emphasized, however, Johnson's speech did contain two major qualifications: the United States, although prepared to negotiate with the DRVN government, was not prepared to sit down with the NLF; and, in insisting upon the right to self-determination for *South* Vietnam, the United States was refusing to accept the basic tenet of the Geneva accords, that the 17th parallel was a provisional demarcation line.[11]

Canada supported the United States not simply because of the shared broad objective of preserving an independent and secure South Vietnam, but also because it feared the consequences to the Western world of an American defeat. A statement by Paul Martin to the House on 28 May 1965 shows that he was more apprehensive of a possible American retreat into isolationism, or a weakening of united Western resistance to communist aggression, than of possible American excesses in Vietnam. Noninvolvement, not intervention, was the greater threat, and had to be met by a show of support. The United States had to be helped to withdraw from Vietnam in a semblance of peace with honor.

However, in 1967, the concern over Atlantic unity propelled Canada in a different direction. When the Pearson-Martin government finally retreated from unqualified support for the United States, it was on the question of American bombing of North Vietnam. This took the form of a call for its unconditional cessation, first uttered publicly by Paul Martin in the United Nations General Assembly on 27 September 1967. The call resulted less from a change in Canadian or questioning of American objectives than from apprehensions of the consequences for the West of continued American involvement. The Pearson-Martin leadership never attacked the aims of the air strikes; it queried their efficacy in weakening Hanoi's resistance, and whether negotiation could begin without a permanent bombing halt.[12] There were other motives behind the call to cease the strikes, but all were currents in one stream: disagreement with official American policy—in Canada, the United States, the West, and elsewhere. The general guidelines of Canadian policy were aptly summed up by Martin in Parliament on 1 February 1966, as being "a peace directed policy based upon an understanding of the problems facing the United States." Canada's actions would be based upon considerations of American, rather than North Vietnamese, objectives.[13]

One peace initiative deserves special mention. When the December 1965-January 1966 bombing pause ended on 31 January, Canada decided to break the deadlock. Its emissary this time was Chester Ronning, a retired diplomat, born in China, at one time High Commissioner to India, and generally with a considerable stature in Asia. More importantly, on this occasion the initiative was Canada's (in consultation with Washington). Martin's proposals may have been motivated by the domestic political scene and the desire to have the record show that Canada had been more than a mere satellite. More germane here is the Canadian fear that the bombing of the north was moving dangerously close to the Chinese border. Canada was apprehensive that China might decide that its security was threatened and intervene, as in 1950 when General Douglas MacArthur had led United Nations troops up to the Yalu River. While the Americans formally welcomed Martin's proposals, they were somewhat alarmed at the choice of Ronning as the Special Representative, for they believed him to be an opponent for their Asian policies. Dean Rusk informed Ambassador Henry Cabot Lodge in Saigon that "Quite frankly, I attach no importance to his trip and expect nothing out of it."[14] Ronning himself understood Lodge's position to be, "Nothing can stop us. We are chewing them up."[15]

Ronning arrived in Hanoi on 7 March 1966. North Vietnam indicated its willingness to return to the Geneva Agreements, on the basis of its four points. Ronning responded that guaranteeing Vietnamese neutrality, sovereignty, and territorial integrity would not be a problem, but that Hanoi might be wise to compromise on the first two points, concerning the withdrawal of all American troops and a recognition of the NLF as the sole representative of the South Vietnamese people. In this, Ronning was able to achieve a major breakthrough when he met Pham Van Dong towards the end of his four-day visit. Pham described Pearson and Ronning as men of goodwill who should not support the American colonial war. In an interesting affirmation of quiet diplomacy, Pham stated that "our Canadian friends should persuade their American friends" into the right course of action. Ronning pointed out that Canada was not acting as a mediator, but if the DRVN made specific proposals, Canada could then seek to persuade the United States to move toward an acceptable arrangement. At this point Pham made his concession: the only precondition for starting talks was that "the

United States unconditionally stop all air raids against North Vietnam." Ronning was satisfied that Pham was demanding an unconditional cessation of the bombing against North Vietnam only, and had abandoned the total withdrawal of American forces from Vietnam as a prior condition. He replied, "We shall be glad to carry to the United States the proposal you make and your position."[16]

Unfortunately, while both Martin and Pearson were intrigued and hopeful, Washington was not interested. The American response towards the end of the month was that the North Vietnamese "ploy" was clever: the bombing question had always been linked before with the NLF's four points, and to accept Hanoi's present offer would be to implicitly accept the four points. The United States would halt the bombing raids only if North Vietnam stopped assisting the guerrillas in the south. Martin, in desperation, telephoned William Bundy at the State Department on 22 April, insisting that Canada had to go back to North Vietnam with something, even if contrived. Four days later the Americans suggested that Ronning tell Hanoi that they would not stop bombing "as a unilateral and non-reciprocated pre-condition to the holding of discussion." The Pentagon Papers have since revealed that Washington was at the time engaged in secret preparations to extend the air war to embrace petroleum, oil, and lubricants (POL) targets. When the bad "public relations" connotations finally dawned on Rusk, he urgently cabled Robert McNamara from Europe that the POL strikes not be initiated on 9–10 June. If Ronning "has a negative report, as we expect, that provides a firmer base for the action we contemplate and would make a difference to people like Wilson and Pearson." In any event, even without knowledge of these preparations, Martin began to doubt the American desire for negotiations when the United States refused to treat Pham's offer seriously.[17] The Pentagon Papers make clear that the State Department ultimately responded more for the sake of American relations with Ottawa than from a desire for peace.

Ronning returned to Hanoi "with a heavy heart" (14–17 June). In the meantime, the press in Hong Kong reported the American offer to stop bombing North Vietnam if Hanoi stopped assisting the NLF. This after the North Vietnamese had insisted, and Ottawa had strongly endorsed, that Ronning's missions be kept secret. Being a shrewd observer, Ronning realized that the only purpose . . . for this publicity was to prepare the people of the United States for an escalation of the bombing of North Vietnam by depicting the North Vietnamese as unreasonable. Only the President and the State Department knew that Hanoi was willing to negotiate peace if the United States would stop the bombing.

In the second visit, Ronning met Foreign Minister Nguyen Duy Trinh. Nguyen rejected the American offer as calling for abject surrender, but confirmed the March position that the cessation of bombing was not linked to the four points. He also accused the Canadians of being party to another American "peace offensive" and questioned the sincerity of Ronning's presence in Hanoi while the war was being escalated. The Americans for their part remained unimpressed, and continued to insist that acceptance of the offer would lead to the four points in the negotiations. Ronning concluded that the Americans had indeed publicized their own "fair offer" chiefly to justify to domestic and world opinion the bombing extension that followed. He suffered pangs of conscience as to whether his report had encouraged Washington to believe that Hanoi's concessions had flowed from hurts sustained by the bombing. He found his suspicions confirmed with the publication of the Pentagon Papers.[18] Bundy met Ronning and Martin in Ottawa on 21 June; the next day, Washington authorized air raids on POL targets in the Hanoi-Haiphong perimeter. They were delayed by bad weather until 29 June.

Canada served on the second supervisory commission in Vietnam for six months as well. A discussion of the second involvement is beyond the scope of this book, but a quote from Taylor will suffice: "Trudeau and Sharp decided to accept a new Vietnam role for one reason and one reason only: to help the Americans get out."[19] Soon after the Paris accords, on 7 February 1973, Canada announced its decision to recognize the DRVN while retaining all ties with Saigon. Ironically, the decision was put into force the day Canada withdrew from the ICCS (31 July).

On 8 April 1975, foreign minister Allan MacEachen declared in Parliament that Canada deplored the major offensive North Vietnam had launched against South Vietnam. The latter finally surrendered on 30 April. MacEachen stated the same day that recognition of the new regime was not possible because "it is really not yet clear exactly who the new regime is." Finally, on 15 May, MacEachen announced in the House that Canada had decided to extend diplomatic recognition to the new government in South Vietnam as of 14 May. The reason for the recognition, he said, was that "it was an appropriate time to recognize the reality of the situation."

Such resigned concessions to reality were a fitting climax to the Canadian involvement. For the surrender by Minh on 30 April 1975 was a symbolic defeat not only of the long and costly American effort, but of the long and arduous Canadian effort to preserve South Vietnam as an independent, noncommunist entity.

India

From 1954 to 1959, India's nonalignment and its relations with the great powers tilted it, in the ICSC, toward the communists. The difference in India's relations with the two Vietnamese regimes was evident outside the Commission as well. Nehru toured Indochina and China in the autumn of 1954, including the DRVN on 17–18 October. As the first foreign dignitary to visit the DRVN, he lent incalculable prestige to the government freshly emerged from the jungles. Little wonder that the journey was made as triumphal as possible. Of his meeting with Ho, Nehru noted in his diary on 17 October: "He came forward — almost leapt forward — and embraced and kissed me. Obvious that this was not a showpiece. He felt it and meant it."[20] The North Vietnamese also played to their guest's sentiments by repeatedly reminding them of contacts in the days of another era. They took care to to reaffirm *Panchsheel* at every opportunity, as in the Ho-Nehru communiqué of 17 October 1954 in Haiphong.[21]

When Nehru landed at Saigon on 30 October on the return journey from China, the contrast in reception was too sharp to be missed. Official hospitality was not remiss, but there was no shortage of people demonstrating against India's policy of coexistence with communism. A sign outside Diem's residence proclaimed: "Welcome to India's Prime Minister — Down with Coexistence." The South Vietnamese coolness is not difficult to understand. India was supervising the implementation of agreements to which the South Vietnamese were implacably opposed. Flags had flown at half mast in South Vietnam for three days after the agreements. At the preparatory conference in New Delhi, the South Vietnamese delegate repeated the complaint that his country was "the victim of the arrangements made against our will and interests to which we do not subscribe"[22]—arrangements to which India was fully committed. India was also less than enthusiastic about the southern regime's pretensions to government.

Pham Van Dong paid a visit to India in April 1955 to discuss "matters of common concern, more particularly the problem relating to Indochina and the work of the International Commission." Both sides advocated *Panchsheel* as the means of peaceful relations, and reaffirmed support for the Geneva Agreements "in their terms and spirit. They were agreed on the importance of free elections and the achievement of the unity of Viet-Nam."[23] After his departure, Pham was joined by Nehru in Rangoon. From there they journeyed to the Bandung Conference, the nonaligned response to SEATO as the American model of world order and stability. China's presence at the conference had a dual significance: it countered America's containment policy, by offering a ring of bases with the alternative of fraternity; and it encircled China with pledges of noninterference and public reiterations of *Panchsheel*. At Bandung, Nehru also drew the Indochinese countries into this system of pledged friendships. The conference was a triumph of nonalignment in the larger scheme of things, and of Indian policy in Indochina in the narrower perspective.

When Pham on 7 June 1955 proposed a consultative conference to discuss general elections, he received enthusiastic Indian support. Diem, on the other hand, launched a campaign against the communists, the Geneva Agreements, and the Poles and Indians on the ICSC. Diem's campaign culminated in a demonstration that resulted in a series of mob attacks on Commission personnel on 20 July 1955, the anniversary of the Agreements. A day earlier, sponsors of the demonstration, including members of the Diem cabinet, had called for the "elimination of Polish and Indian pro-Communist elements from the International Commission."[24] Crowds attacked Commission members and looted their property in Saigon, Qui Nhon, and Nha Trang, as well as other places. Their targets were Indians and Poles; the Canadians, said Lester Pearson, were "singularly fortunate in escaping the attention of the mob."[25]

Diem saw the riots as "clear proof of the determination of the Vietnamese people to fight communism."[26] The ICSC unanimously condemned the Saigon government for the incidents and the failure to protect Commission personnel and property; Desai in particular stressed the objectionable resolution of 19 July. South Vietnamese Foreign Minister Vu Van Mau met Desai on the afternoon of the 20th and offered an official apology and damages. The next day, Desai met Diem, who tried to blame the riots on students from North Vietnam, but did express regret and promised an official apology. The ICSC also resolved that adequate security should be provided to all its personnel and operations, and sent the resolution to New Delhi to be transmitted to the cochairmen. On 23 July, the government of South Vietnam stated that it "warmly regretted the incidents" and declared that "the necessary precautions to prevent a recurrence" had been taken. No apology was forthcoming; not only that, Diem had made his point: he, not the French High Command, was the effective authority in South Vietnam. It was time the ICSC recognized this if it wished to continue to operate. The riots caused outrage in India, with Nehru declaring in Parliament on 27 July that the South Vietnamese were as responsible for the protection of ICSC personnel as the French. The South Vietnamese security police, "who were present throughout, did not intervene to stop the looting and arson."

India was compelled to accept the realities of authority in mid-1955. A year later, when the cochairmen of the Geneva Conference failed to address themselves to the issue of general elections, India was also forced to recognize the *de facto* partition of Vietnam. India had hesitated to recognize either claimant to Vietnam before the conclusion of the Geneva Agreements. British Indian consulates-general accredited to the French authorities were continued in Hanoi and Saigon after 1947. The DRVN was given *de facto* recognition on 15 December 1954. The Agreements provided for the political reunification of Vietnam in July 1956, so there would be no point to recognizing the temporary administrative authorities in the southern zone. By that time, conditions had altered. Diem's regime was demonstrably stable and in effective control of the southern zone; reunifying elections had been jettisoned; and the dissolution of the French High Command in 1956 rendered India's accreditation to Saigon inoperative at the same time as it freed Diem of the puppet image. In October 1956, the Government of India chose to accord *de facto* recognition to the Republic of Vietnam.

The recognition was one among several acts indicating improved relations between New Delhi and Saigon. In August 1956, a South Vietnamese trade delegation visited India upon invitation, and was received by Nehru himself. Nehru also received Ngo Dinh Nhu, Diem's brother, in April 1957. On 4 November 1957, Diem arrived in New Delhi to a reception committee that included state dignitaries; at a state banquet the following day, President Prasad welcomed Diem as "the Head of a State, which like us has emerged as a free nation only recently after a long spell of foreign domination." Diem's visit was "a welcome reminder of the cordial relations subsisting between our two peoples." The visit helped dispel illusions of Diem as a puppet, and established him as a nationalist.

Diem paid generous tribute to India's role in Asia and to its past cultural influence in his own country. But he also welcomed the "purely defensive" protection extended to his country by SEATO. The joint communiqué issued on 9 November was notable chiefly for its lack of allusion to elections or unification. The only reference to the ICSC was a compliment to its contribution in maintaining peace in Vietnam.

A notable feature of Diem's visit was that he was accompanied by thirty experts and technicians. During the five-day visit, the party toured industrial and agricultural projects, and met Planning Commission experts. The joint communiqué stated that the two sides "have decided to continue and increase the co-operation between their two countries in the pursuit of their common goal of economic and social advancement."[27]

Although India made the attempt to establish working relations with Diem's government, its sympathy for the north remained undiminished.[28] Diem's visit was followed by a journey to India by Ho Chi Minh (5–13 February 1958). He was better known than Diem, and his revolutionary mystique-cum-Gandhian austerity appealed to Indians.[29] The official welcome accorded him was of the same level as Diem's, but was undoubtedly warmer. Nehru received Ho as "a great revolutionary and an almost legendary hero." Ho repeatedly mentioned items dear to India, such as *Panchsheel* and condemnation of military pacts. On 6 February, he struck a responsive chord in declaring that "we firmly believe that the Indian people are as eager to see the Viet-Namese reunified as the Viet-Namese are eager to see a speedy return of Goa to the Indian Union."

The difference in New Delhi–Hanoi and New Delhi–Saigon relations can be gleaned from a comparison of the communiqués issued at the conclusion of the respective visits of Diem and Ho. The Nehru-Ho statement of 13 February 1958 reaffirmed faith in *Panchsheel*, expressed a common approach to the problem of disarmament, argued against military blocs and colonialism, argued for independence struggles, and appreciated the efforts of the ICSC in attempting to implement the Geneva Agreements. The two leaders added the hope that the Commission would persevere in its efforts to reunify the country on the basis of the Agreements.

That Indian political sympathy for North Vietnam continued despite the equation of Hanoi and Saigon in correct dealings is quite clear in Nehru's Rajya Sabha statement of 11 December 1961. He described the Vietminh as having been "essentially . . . a nationalist force fighting for freedom, but with a considerable mixture of Communist element." Ho Chi Minh, he added, "is very popular not only among the Communists, but among others also as a national leader."

India's voting patterns in the ICSC for the 1952–62 period were earlier shown to have been strongly tilted towards Saigon. It remains briefly to discuss Hanoi's and Saigon's reactions to the 1962 special report. South Vietnam hailed it as a "tribute to the remarkable efforts of the ICC," while its rival castigated it as of "no value, is illegal and must be rejected." According to Hanoi, Canada and India by relying upon tendentious statements had falsified truth and were guilty of violating the agreements they were entrusted to implement. They were branded as being in collusion with American imperialists, on the logic that it could not be a "a matter of chance" that the report had been issued simultaneously with the United States "actively intensifying its armed intervention."[30]

Chairman Parthasarathi was personally attacked in a *Nhan Dan* editorial, the official organ of the Lao Dong party. In New Delhi, the North Vietnamese consulate-general breached etiquette by circulating a bulletin on 3 June 1962 that attacked the Indian delegation. The chronological coincidence with the China-India conflict ought not, however, to be carried too far. The unhappy 1954 trade agreement with China was not renegotiated; it lapsed on 2 June 1962 (the day the special report was signed). However, the trade agreement with North Vietnam was renewed on 22 September 1962 for an additional three-year period; and India also signed a three-year trading pact with South Vietnam on 25 April 1964. It was India's first agreement with South Vietnam, and contemplated not only increasing the volume of trade but also industrial and technical collaboration.

India's attempt to balance relations with the two regimes in Vietnam was not wholehearted, and lasted only briefly. The identification with Hanoi may on occasions have been dormant, but it was omnipresent. On 7 September 1969, for example, India was represented at the funeral of Ho Chi Minh by foreign minister Dinesh Singh. On 18–23 July 1970, Madame Nguyen Thi Binh paid a visit to New Delhi in her capacity as Minister of Foreign Affairs of the Provisional Revolutionary Government (PRG) of South Vietnam. She said that the PRG wished to establish more formal relations with India. The South Vietnamese Consul-General in New Delhi protested against her visit, describing it as "an infraction of international law." He decided to cool off in Katmandu for the period of her visit. In his absence, the acting Consul-General demanded, apparently without authorization from Saigon, that Madame Binh be arrested as a "rebel" and extradited to South Vietnam. On 27 July, demonstrators attacked the Indian consulate in Saigon. Swaran Singh, the new foreign minister, declared in the Lok Sabha on 29 July that India would not tolerate the use of Indians as "hostages" by the Saigon government. This particular saga came to a close on 3 August, when Saigon announced that its Consul-General in New Delhi had been retired as a "disciplinary measure." The news was interpreted in the Indian press as a censure of his conduct during the Binh visit, and as a gesture intended to improve South Vietnam's relations with India. On the last point at least, the move was a signal failure.

The formal statement of the final shift by New Delhi to Hanoi's position was in the manner of altering the *status quo* of parity in diplomatic representation between Hanoi and Saigon. On 7 January 1972 India and the DRVN raised the level of their representatives from consular to ambassador; relations between New Delhi and Saigon remained at the consular level. Swaran Singh explained in the Rajya Sabha on 16 March that "India's decision to raise the level of its mission in Hanoi . . . was a recognition of the realities of the situation and in exercise of our sovereign rights."

The reaction in South Vietnam to India's upward gradation of its relations with Hanoi was literally violent. Saigon witnessed a number of hostile demonstrations in front of the Indian consulate-general and ICSC headquarters between January and March. The demonstrators were protesting against India's chairmanship of and presence on the ICSC. The government of South Vietnam also reacted sharply to India's elevated representation in the north. It publicly expressed opposition to India's membership on and chairmanship of the Commission, and it refused to extend the visas of the Indian component of the Commission beyond 30 September 1972. On 28 September the Commission by a unanimous resolution decided to shift the Indian delegation, and thus the Chairman and Secretary-General, from Saigon to Hanoi. In a curious illustration of the fact that while Polish partiality to North Vietnam was acceptable, Indian partiality was not, the Canadian and Polish delegations continued in Saigon. The episode also revealed a Commission sadly divided. India and Poland unilaterally published their version, and Canada responded in kind. "Particularly as between Canada and India, it was a far cry from the day when each country, out of a common experience, had welcomed the other as a colleague in the commission."[31]

India and Poland in their joint statement of 28 September condemned the attitude and measures of the Saigon government. They held the government of South Vietnam to be in violation of Articles 27 and 35 of the cease-fire agreement, and brought the matter to the notice of the Geneva powers through the cochairmen under the provisions of Article 43 of the agreement. In their opinion,

> the unilateral denial of facilities clearly stipulated in the Geneva Agreement to Indian members of the ICSC, constitutes a clear violation of and disrespect for the Geneva Agreement. The Indian and Polish delegations to the ICSC, therefore, condemn the attitude adopted by the South Vietnamese Government and record their firm protest against it as it violates the competence and normal functioning of the Commission.[32]

Canada from the outset held the dispute to be a purely bilateral matter between the governments of India and South Vietnam. The Canadian statement of 29 September[33] expressed "surprise" that India had made the Commission resolution and the Indo-Polish statement public during the Commission's meeting. Canada also felt that the omission of the Canadian statement distorted "both the context and the content of the Commission's agreed communication to the co-Chairmen." In the Canadian statement of 28 September, R. D. Jackson argued that the difficulties facing the Commission were "a reflection of the long-standing paralysis of its apparatus, rather than a consequence of recent developments." Further, since the Commission had been dormant for many years, Canada failed to see how its substantive functioning was suddenly threatened. The Canadian statement also drew attention to the fact that South Vietnam's provisions of facilities to the Commission in the past had been entirely voluntary, in that it had not signed but protested against the Geneva Agreements. South Vietnam was within its sovereign competence, therefore, to deny facilities to the ICSC.

Indian attitudes to ending the Vietnam war were discussed in the previous chapter. In general, India's policies too were prudent and practical. Replying to parliamentary criticism that India should do more to decrease world tensions, Nehru said on 22 May 1957 that it was pointless to indulge in talk of courses beyond the country's capacity. In a statement strongly reminiscent of Pearsonian quiet diplomacy, he said:

> If we were in a measure effective, say, in the Korean affair or in the Indo-China affair—I think we were in a measure effective in helping to bring about peace—it was not through a conference, it was not through powerful speeches; it was through quiet, long continued hard work, conducted in all modesty, without any shouting, without any publicity.[34]

Beyond this, India's approach to solving the American phase of the Vietnam war was stated by Swaran Singh in the Rajya Sabha on 22 December 1964. India, he said, favored a "Geneva type" conference, because the basic principles of the Geneva Agreements had not been contradicted by any party. The final solution had to be political, and eradicate American and Chinese influences: "the solution lies in eliminating these outside influences, these extraneous influences and neutralizing these various countries." Two observations are in order. First, the term "Geneva type," which was a recurring theme in India's pronouncements, permitted the inclusion of parties that had not been full participants at Geneva in 1954, notably the United States, South Vietnam, the NLF, and the Commission countries, including India itself. Second, the concept of neutralization, which continued to attract India, would by eliminating external influences contribute significantly to India's nonalignment goals, and increase India's influence in the region.

In the immediate aftermath of the American bombing, India had appealed to all powers on 8 February 1965 for peace. Its position then took the middle ground. There had been interference from many quarters, and one thing had led to another. As a first step, in order to create the necessary atmosphere for the urgent convening of a "Geneva type" conference, "there should be an immediate suspension of all provocative action in South Vietnam as well as in North Vietnam by all sides involved in the Vietnam situation."[35] The seventeen-nation nonaligned appeal of 15 March 1965 was similarly balanced in its "urgent appeal to the parties concerned to start . . . negotiations as soon as possible without . . . preconditions." The American response was equivocal. While it officially welcomed the appeal, it changed the "parties" to the "governments concerned," in effect eliminating the NLF by definition. It also diluted the "negotiations without preconditions" to "unconditional discussions." India first openly supported a NLF inclusion in the Tito-Shastri Belgrade communiqué of 31 July 1965; Indira Gandhi reiterated it in the Lok Sabha on 4 August 1966.

At a reception for Tanzania's High Commissioner on 24 April 1965, President S. Radhakrishnan observed that the nonaligned countries deplored the loss of life in Vietnam, and were concerned that the conflict might drift into a nuclear war. He proposed a "cessation of hostilities in both parts of Viet-Nam, policing of boundaries by an Afro-Asian force and maintenance of the present boundaries so long as people desire it." The Chinese reaction was hostile; they failed to see a difference between the Indian and American stands. The Americans were publicly interested. Even the Afro-Asians showed unexpected interest. India then hurriedly pointed out that Radhakrishnan's proposals were not a statement of India's policy. On 9 August the foreign ministry "clarified" the proposals beyond recognition:

> The proposal envisaged the termination of aerial bombing of North Vietnam and cessation of fighting in South Vietnam. The purpose of an Afro-Asian force would be to police the cease-fire not only along the border and sea coast of South Vietnam but also at suitable points in the interior. It was also intended that

the present division of Vietnam would be maintained only so long as the people of the areas desired it. In that regard the proposal, it was hoped, would expedite and facilitate the unification of Vietnam.[36]

The three operative clauses of Radhakrishnan's proposal had been turned around completely.

In its annual report for 1965–66, the Ministry of External Affairs offered the first comprehensive statement of India's official policy on Vietnam. It included references to the impossibility of a military solution, the urgency of a "Geneva type" conference, the need to halt the bombing, the ending of fighting throughout Vietnam, the withdrawal of Americans from the south, and the peaceful reunification of Vietnam, free of foreign troops and military alliances. When the Americans requested clarification of the point about their withdrawal of troops, Gandhi sought to soften the report by declaring at a press conference on 15 June that "it is easy to say 'withdraw' but it is not so easy to do it in practice." In Parliament, Singh and Gandhi denied charges that the softening of India's stand on withdrawal of the Americans had been affected by food shortages in India, and declared that the Ministry of External Affairs report did have official endorsement.

In October 1966, the tripartite Tito-Nasser-Gandhi communiqué called for an unconditional end to the bombing of North Vietnam, the implementation of the Geneva Agreements, and the withdrawal of *all* foreign forces. When Chester Cooper and Averell Harriman visited New Delhi in October-November, India reiterated its position that the United States must immediately and unconditionally stop bombing North Vietnam. Indian sources in Hanoi and Moscow (in contrast with the Korean case, where Indian sources in Peking were operative), had indicated that after the bombing stopped, North Vietnam would encourage the NLF to move toward direct talks with Washington. To Harriman's query as to whether direct talks between Hanoi and Washington might not be preferable and more productive, India replied that talks with the NLF would circumvent Hanoi's unwillingness to admit a presence in the southern zone. Cooper and Harriman, in their two-week tour of eleven countries, heard variations on the theme from virtually every neutralist leader. Nevertheless, "it was hard to take the Indians seriously, not because they were deliberately dissembling or misleading us, but rather because it was so difficult to pin them down on details and documentation."[37]

In an address to the United Nations General Assembly on 6 October 1967, Swaran Singh declared that the first step to peace in Vietnam was an unconditional halt to the bombing, followed by a "Geneva type" meeting which would include the NLF. On 11 October, at the conclusion of Gandhi's visit to Poland, the Indo-Polish communiqué declared that a solution in Vietnam should be based on the 1954 Agreements, and that an unconditional cessation of the bombing was a necessary preliminary step. The call for a halt to the bombing of North Vietnam and for a political settlement, but not for a withdrawal of American forces, continued in 1968: on 31 January, at the conclusion of Kosygin's visit to India; on 2 February, in the President's address to Parliament; on 18 July, at the conclusion of President Zakir Hussain's visit to the USSR; and on 14 October, in Gandhi's address to the General Assembly.

This relatively mild stance continued into 1969. On 8 April Foreign Minister Dinesh Singh said in the Lok Sabha that he was pleased with the start of the Paris talks on Vietnam. He reported to the House on 13 August that discussions during Nixon's India tour had been limited to expressing hopes of success for the negotiations. The Indo-Soviet joint statement in Moscow on 17 September merely reaffirmed that a recognition of the Geneva Agreements was essential to a solution in Vietnam; the people were to decide their own destiny "without foreign interference." The even-handedness continued for most of 1970. On 8 April Dinesh Singh said in the Lok Sabha that the Vietnam problem had been caused by constant interference by foreign powers. The way to peace, he said, lay in the withdrawal of all foreign forces from Indochina. At the same time, he gave a hint of India's shifting position. Strengthening Indo-DRVN relations, he said, was in the best interests of India, North Vietnam, and peace, because it broke down isolation. Just a little earlier, an India-Yugoslavia note had contained only a mild reference to Vietnam, in the form of a declaration that a military solution was not possible, and that a return to the broad framework of the Geneva Agreements was necessary.

As the year progressed, however, India's position began to change rapidly, especially with the return of Swaran Singh to the foreign ministry. On 26 August, he remarked in the Rajya Sabha that the two parties to the dispute in South Vietnam were the official government and the PRG: "We are the only Asian country who are in touch with . . . all the relevant parties, to the dispute in Indo-China." India must be mindful of the fact that Asian blood was being spilled there; nevertheless, while strong statements would satisfy Indian sentiments, they would not help the situation. The Indian view was to urge a withdrawal of troops from Vietnam, *beginning with the American troops*, to be followed by a "broadbased government" in South Vietnam. (NLF participation in a coalition government in Saigon was a constant theme of the communist parties.)

In her speech on 9 September to the ideologically receptive setting of the third nonaligned summit at Lusaka, Gandhi repeated Singh's conclusions, stressing that those conditions were necessary to the success of the Paris talks. India's assessment, she said, was "based on talks with the various *parties* concerned" (emphasis added). She also expressed concern that chemical and biological methods of warfare were being used in Vietnam. In essence, the United States was specified as a foreign force, the DRVN was not; the United States was to lead the way in withdrawal, and unconditionally halt the bombing; and the NLF was to be included as a component of the government of South Vietnam.

Swaran Singh went a step farther in the General Assembly on 2 October. He called for a withdrawal of all foreign forces from Vietnam and a broad-based government in Saigon. In addition, he demanded a firm timetable for the withdrawal of American forces, including a date for the final withdrawal. India had "an abiding interest in peace and stability" in Indochina and would be prepared to join with others in working out arrangements through an international conference.

On 16 July 1971, commenting in the Lok Sabha on Kissinger's secret visit to China, Swaran Singh said that if the visit heralded a normalization of Sino-American relations, it was to be welcomed. He hoped that one consequence might be a satisfactory solution in Indochina, in particular in Vietnam, since the conflicts in Laos and Cambodia were extensions of the Vietnam war. India also felt that Madame Binh's seven-point proposal at Paris was the best Vietnam peace proposal to date. "We feel that these proposals can be the basis of a satisfactory negotiated settlement." The Indo-Soviet joint communiqué on 12 August, at the conclusion of Andrei Gromyko's visit and immediately after the Friendship Treaty, stated that India was grateful to the USSR for its understanding of the Bangladesh problem.

It then declared that outside interference in Indochina should cease, and that the seven-point proposal by the PRG was a welcome development in the search for peace. On 28 September, in a similar juxtaposition of Bangladesh and Vietnam, Gandhi declared at a speech in Moscow that "I will support the inalienable rights of all peoples, especially those of the Vietnamese people, to national independence and freedom."[38]

The juxtaposition was made most forcefully by Swaran Singh in the Lok Sabha on 26 April 1972. "The liberation of Bangladesh was a great heroic event. The liberation of Vietnam will be an equally heroic and great event." His lengthy statement on Vietnam on that occasion was in fact an extremely strong support for the forces opposed to the United States. There was virtual unanimity in the House, he said, in expressing solidarity "with the valiant freedom fighters of Vietnam; and there was also unanimous expression of our feeling of deploring the aggressive actions taken by the United States." The ability of the Vietnamese to have stood up to the might of a great military power, Singh said, was a tribute to their courage and heroism. He also expressed horror at the heavy, indiscriminate, and inhuman bombing of North Vietnam over the past few weeks which "far from cowing down the people of Vietnam, has only strengthened their determination to resist with even greater valour and success than before." A solution was to be found in the withdrawal of all foreign forces, "and particularly that of the United States," and in the negotiation of a broad-based agreement within the framework of the Geneva accords of 1954. Later in the year, in the Rajya Sabha on 30 November, Singh accused Thieu's government of sabotaging the peace effort.

At the conclusion of the peace accords in 1973, Gandhi sent a message of congratulations to Pham Van Dong, expressing great relief at the news of the peace: "I should like to convey our heartiest congratulations to you and the Vietnamese people who have shown undaunted courage and perseverance in defending the freedom of their country."[39] It was a fitting epitaph to the history of Indian involvement; it was also an indication of the difference in perspectives that had troubled Indo-Canadian relations during the ICSC years. The PRG was admitted to full membership of the nonaligned movement in September 1973. The subject of New Delhi-Saigon-Hanoi relations came to a close in 1975. On 30 April, the

South Vietnamese regime under President Duong Van Minh surrendered to the victorious NLF forces (Thieu had fled). India recognized the PRG within hours of the surrender; news of the NLF victory was greeted with "thunderous cheers and thumping of desks" in both the Lok and the Rajya Sabha.[40] In 1970, the Indian foreign secretary had been advised at Vientiane to return home rather than continue to Hanoi for an official visit. In 1975, a special delegation led by Parthasarathi was welcomed to the celebrations marking the thirtieth anniversary of the founding of the DRVN. (Parthasarathi had in 1962 chaired the ICSC that convicted North Vietnam of aggression and subversion.) During the visit, Pham accepted an invitation to visit India later in the year.

Poland and Intra-Communist Relations

Hanoi-Moscow-Peking
It will be clear by now that the Polish delegation to the ICSC functioned within the framework of Poland's place in the communist world. The difficulty for Poland lay in the fact that from the start, differences existed between Hanoi, Moscow, and Peking as to the proper course of action to be followed in Vietnam. They were generally suppressed during the war against the common enemy, the United States; but they never disappeared. China and the USSR did not always agree on Vietnam; the differences intensified during their schism in the 1960s. It has been argued that Ho could have been the Tito of the East, if only the Americans had played their cards right.[41] The corollary to this is the view that the DRVN feared a rupture in the communist world which would throw it under Chinese control. The Hanoi regime was not considered strong enough to play the dispute to its own purposes on the Rumanian model.[42]

Hanoi tilted cautiously toward Peking in 1963, when it condemned Moscow over the nuclear test limitation treaty; but the Vietnamese diplomatic environment was fundamentally transformed by the Tonkin Gulf incidents and the massive entry of American combat troops in 1964. In January 1965 Mao informed Edgar Snow that China would not go to war against the United States unless directly attacked.[43] However, when bombing raids were made into North Vietnam the next month, Peking became concerned on two counts. First, increasing American pressure might impel Hanoi towards Moscow. The DRVN leaders did in fact become more circumspect in their pronouncements on the Peking-Moscow dispute, and Kosygin paid a visit to Hanoi. DRVN polemical attacks on "modern revisionism" ceased, and the USSR promised economic and military aid.

The more important anxiety was over the question of American objectives, particularly in light of the continued buildup of American troops in Vietnam in 1966–67. The Chinese, not being privy to the information of limited American objectives that had reassured Pearson, could not partake of his comfort. They had to consider the possibility of a Vietnam-based American attack on China, and devise strategies to meet that contingency. The issue of an appropriate strategy for Vietnam, however, impinged on choices in internal leadership, social directions, and relations with the USSR. The higher echelons of the Peking leadership fiercely debated the proper strategy for supporting Hanoi without either provoking Washington or becoming dependent on Moscow. A more active participation in the DRVN's defense would strengthen the position of the professional army and require an accommodation with the USSR. These considerations help explain Peking's rejection of Moscow's tempting offer in 1965 for united action in Vietnam.[44]

The Chinese attacked Kosygin for having "stressed the need to help the United States find a way out of Vietnam,"[45] and asked why the USSR would not open a second front in Europe to alleviate American pressure in Indochina. (Moscow countered by accusing China of wanting a United States–USSR military conflict, "so that they may, as they say themselves, sit on the mountain and watch the fight of the tigers.")[46] At the same time, Peking was careful to signal its determination to save Hanoi should the need arise, by dispatching to the DRVN a large number of Chinese military personnel in the form of engineering and construction units. The point nevertheless remains that as early as 1965, rivalry with the USSR was substantially influencing key Chinese decisions in respect of Vietnam.[47]

The impact of the Sino-Soviet rivalry upon Sino-Vietnamese relations grew during the Cultural Revolution. Red Guard elements influenced events in Vietnam through such means as stopping trains that carried munitions from the citadel of revisionism. At the time, needing support of both communist powers, the Vietnamese held their peace. Today, the China-Vietnam polemical struggle makes it expedient for each to reveal the other's past politickings. Hoang Tung, editor of the Party daily *Nhan Dan,* points to 1966 as the beginning of the decay of socialism in China. Ever since, China is alleged to have favored a nonsocialist foreign policy. The Chinese had to aid and support Vietnam from 1966 to 1973 because their own security would have been directly threatened if the United States had seized control of all Vietnam. Interested in establishing an Asian communist bloc, the Chinese, it is alleged, tried to tie their aid to closer alliance between the two countries. The Sino-American *rapprochement* initiated in 1971–72 eliminated the most decisive factor in Chinese aid to Vietnam. Hanoi's leaders interpreted the Shanghai communiqué to mean that a Mao-Nixon deal on Taiwan would be in exchange for an Indochina *pax Americana*.

Although levels of support for Hanoi varied in both Moscow and Peking over the years, both did provide constant verbal and material assistance throughout the war against the United States. The USSR concentrated on heavy and sophisticated equipment; the Chinese complement was food and light arms. Accordingly, the monetary value of Soviet aid was greater; when the Americans had withdrawn, the USSR claimed a 70 percent share in all foreign aid to North Vietnam.

The constancy of support notwithstanding, there were ambiguities in the Soviet and Chinese positions. Moscow's reservations stemmed from the fact that it could not be assured of full control over Hanoi. In 1971, for example, Soviet military supplies to the DRVN were increased significantly, presumably in anticipation of a push. Perhaps the USSR hoped that Hanoi's leaders would launch an offensive in time to embarrass the hosts in the February 1972 meeting between Nixon and Chinese leaders in Peking. Instead, the offensive came on 30 March 1972, just a few weeks before Nixon's visit to Moscow—the first visit to the USSR by an American President. Michel Tatu, long-time Moscow correspondent of *Le Monde,* writes of having "overwhelming evidence to confirm the claim that the Soviet leaders were not informed, let alone consulted, prior to North Vietnam's massive offensive."[48] Nor did the USSR emerge with enhanced prestige when forced into a policy of studious indifference in response to Nixon's violent reaction to the DRVN offensive. (A show of force by the Soviet navy in the South China Sea failed to impress.)[49]

A second Soviet reservation must have stemmed from a closely related point: Hanoi's goal of reunification was not worth a central war. The socialist community had to be defended, by force if necessary, but war was to avoided in the cause of extending communist territorial jurisdiction; peaceful coexistence was safer. The temptation for the USSR lay in scoring propaganda points against its communist challenger while seriously weakening its global adversary.

Support for North Vietnam came more naturally to China; the war was on its doorstep and had intimate historical associations. Chinese reservations must have stemmed from the knowledge that a unified Vietnam, allied with the USSR and dominant in Indochina, could well become a thorn in China's side. With a Sino-American *rapprochement*, a residual American presence in Asia was to be preferred to fresh opportunities for extension of Soviet influence and presence. A divided Vietnam, with the southern half retaining ties with the United States, may have seemed a more attractive prospect than a unified Vietnam with strong links to the USSR.

The complexity of the communists' interests in Indochina was apparent in many forms in the 1970s. While providing massive aid to the DRVN, the USSR refrained from recognizing the government-in-exile of Cambodia's Prince Sihanouk, who was allied with Peking and Hanoi. Similarly, the USSR recognized the legitimate Souvanna Phouma government of Laos, while Hanoi actively fought for the insurgent Pathet Lao.

In 1972 Moscow and Peking were both open to suggestions that Hanoi should be made to conclude a peace. Henry Kissinger, in addition to being a master of negotiation, was also aware of the vulnerability of the North Vietnamese to a delicate confluence of diplomatic forces. While still at Harvard he wrote that "Hanoi is extraordinarily dependent on the international environment. . . . Its bargaining position depends on a fine assessment of international factors—especially of the jungle of intra-communist relations."[50] It is ironic that while American presence in Indochina was justified on grounds of containing international communist aggression, the Nixon-Kissinger strategy for peace successfully used Moscow and Peking to pressure Hanoi into negotiations.

Warsaw

One would expect Warsaw to align with Moscow against Peking in respect of Vietnam. Such was indeed the case. In the 1950s, before the Sino-Soviet split, Poland extended uncomplicated warm greetings to North Vietnamese comrades. Thus in a 1957 interview with *New Times*, Rapacki explained that Poland and the DRVN had "ties of friendship and cooperation stemming from our common social system and ideology." (Relations with India, by contrast, rested on *Panchsheel*.)[51] By 1965, increasing Soviet bloc influence after the American air war was evident in the series of bilateral aid agreements North Vietnam signed with Bulgaria, East Germany, Hungary, Poland, and the USSR, between June and December 1965. Formation of the PRG of South Vietnam was announced on 10 June 1969; it received prompt recognition on 13 June by the DRVN, Cambodia, Czechoslovakia, East Germany, Hungary, Poland, the USSR, and Yugoslavia; China followed suit the next day.

Rapacki was apparently an admirer of Ho's independence of both China and the USSR. In 1962, he directed Maneli (for his second tour of duty in the ICSC in Vietnam) that "you should try to understand what is really going on between the socialist superpowers and what our decisions should be, in light of the differences between them."[52] Concerning the United States, Rapacki argued that the question was when, not if, the Americans would retreat. He believed that the objective could be more speedily realized through a combination of military and diplomatic means than through protracted guerrilla warfare.[53]

Rapacki contended that because the DRVN and the NLF could not win the war militarily, they should be encouraged to explore negotiation with the United States. After clearance with a skeptical Gromyko in Moscow, Rapacki's deputy Jerzy Michalowski, who had once served on the ICSC, was dispatched to Hanoi in January 1966. To preserve appearances, he travelled via Peking, where the leadership at the time frowned upon peace efforts as a betrayal of the Vietnamese cause. His subsequent feelers in Hanoi were fruitless because of Peking's influence over the DRVN leadership, and because a high-ranking Soviet delegation in Hanoi at the time offered substantial new military aid to Ho and Giap.[54]

Rapacki returned to the initiative in the summer in the so-called "Marigold Affair."[55] On 27 June, shortly after Ronning's departure from Hanoi, the Polish ICSC representative, Janusz Lewandowski, was instructed to contact an Italian diplomat and dean of the diplomatic corps in Saigon, Giovanni D'Orlandi, about a specific peace offer. Hanoi was prepared to discuss negotiations if NLF representatives were allowed to participate and if the United States suspended its bombing raids. All other preconditions could be shelved. The proposal produced no immediate result, but it was revived in the fall. Several talks were held between Lewandowski and United States Ambassador Lodge, using D'Orlandi as an intermediary, during September-November.

Lewandowski summarized the American position in ten broad points and presented them to the DRVN leaders on 30 November. The DRVN was interested, and asked that the points be confirmed with the DRVN Ambassador in Warsaw. On 3 December, Lewandowski was informed that the United States Ambassador in Warsaw would contact his DRVN counterpart on 6 December or shortly thereafter. At the same time, Rapacki protested against an intensification of air raids on Hanoi (on 3-4 December) while the negotiations were in progress, and warned that this could destroy the talks.[56] On 13 December, American planes struck at new targets in Hanoi's residential areas and suburbs, including the Chinese and Rumanian embassies. The DRVN protested formally to the ICSC; several governments around the world expressed regret; the Poles terminated their mediation efforts; and the story was leaked to the *Washington Post,* which reported the affair with reasonable accuracy on 4 February 1967. Thus the Polish initiative too sank under assault from the air.[57]

Conclusion

The political objectives of the two regimes in Vietnam were mutually exclusive; therein lay the seeds of conflict. The latent dispute assumed global significance when, with rival international backing for the two regimes, the 17th parallel was transformed into a cold-war axis. When that happened, the terms of Canada's involvement changed. It was no longer true to say that Canada had no national interest. Once a conflict took on communist-noncommunist coloration, Canada by self-definition supported the cause of meeting, containing, and ultimately defeating communism. Canada felt that communism was, by definition, aggressive. As Pearson expressed it in 1955, "the only aggressive force that threatens us today, or that could commit a major aggression, is communist imperialism."[58] Consequently, where there was a war, and communists were involved; if the facts were difficult to ascertain, communists were under a strong presumption of guilt. It would then become the Canadian objective to contribute to the fight against communist aggression. Another important element in the Canadian world view was stated by Pearson in 1955: no communist question could be considered exclusively or even primarily in local terms. He added in two-value language that the Vietminh in North Vietnam were communist, while South Vietnam had a noncommunist government.[59]

The internationalization of the Vietnam war had important consequences for Canada's foreign policy. Pearson declared in Parliament on 24 March 1955 that "our right to be neutral has been limited by our desire to strengthen the security of our country." From 1964 until September 1967, Canada's foreign policy was identical to that of the United States. When the Pearson-Martin government finally retreated from unqualified support for the United States in September 1967, it was on the question of the bombing of North Vietnam, and took the form of a call for an unconditional cessation. Beyond that, Canadians were not prepared to go.

The St. Laurent, Diefenbaker, and Pearson governments supported American policy in Vietnam because they identified the political objectives underlying United States policy, *viz.*, the defeat of communism, as direct Canadian objectives. The Trudeau government, on the other hand, seemed to refrain from attacks on United States policy, despite possible disagreement because critical pronouncements on the distant war were deemed secondary to the web of relations between Canada and the United States.

During the course of J. Blair Seaborn's missions to Hanoi, Pham Van Dong told him that it was impossible for westerners to understand the strength of his people's will to resist, to continue, to struggle. "It has astonished us too."[60] India, as an Asian nation, sympathized with the political objectives of North Vietnam — reunification and elimination of Western influence. These objectives overlapped with India's policy of nonalignment. It was an occasion of pride for Indians that a small Asian state had humbled the mighty and arrogant Americans, particularly after the display of gunboat diplomacy in the Bay of Bengal during the Bangladesh war. There was also genuine satisfaction in the obliteration of the last vestiges of Western, white imperialism in Indochina.

India's relations with Vietnam were determined by the belief that the Hanoi regime was more representative of popular opinion, and the calculation that Hanoi was more likely to prevail in the long run.[61] If nonalignment demanded unqualified Indian support for North Vietnam, restraint prevailed in Indo-American relations. The American intervention accelerated less than two years after the Himalayan blunder in India's relations with China. The bombing of North Vietnam crossed a clear threshold, and invited a wider conflagration. It therefore had to be condemned, for it was always Indian policy in Indochina to keep the United States and China as distant as possible, preferably in their own countries. The Soviet role at Tashkent after the 1965 India-Pakistan war briefly de-emphasized the Washington connection. However, massive food shortages in India in 1966–67, and the fleeting Soviet flirtation with Pakistan in 1969–70, again brought in a measure of restraint so far as Indian pronouncements on American policy were concerned. The Sino-American *rapprochement*, finally, radically altered the entire environment. The development was as unsettling as the India-China war had been, and led to a clear Indian move towards the USSR. Abroad, the era after mid-1971 marks as aberrant a period for India's policy in Vietnam as the period of the 1959–62 Sino-Indian conflict.

Finally, Poland's task was the simplest of the three countries represented on the ICSC. It merely had to follow the Soviet example. The maze of USSR-China-DRVN relations, on the other hand, was exceedingly complex, and the Poles had always to be alert to its nuances. There is little evidence to suggest that they were unequal to the task.

9 Conclusions

National Foreign Policies

The experience of the International Commission for Supervision and Control in Vietnam was not a particularly happy one for any of its three delegations. It spanned almost two decades of difficult, onerous, and frustrating efforts to keep the peace. In this final chapter, before examining the lessons of the Vietnam experiences for international peacekeeping, it is useful to review briefly the national foreign policies of the three ICSC countries toward Vietnam.

Canada

Canadian perceptions of, involvement in, and policies toward events in Indochina have paralleled shifts in the local and international dynamics of the conflicts. No single thesis can sufficiently describe Canada's policy in respect of Vietnam since the Second World War. It is more fruitful to discuss Canadian foreign policy in terms of four distinct periods. In the French Indochina war years (1946–54), Canada perceived the conflict as a member of the Atlantic community, and spoke only in areas where there was agreement within that community. In the ICSC years prior to American fighting (1954–64), Canada attempted to promote principles of peacekeeping even while assuming guardianship of the interests of one side. In the American war years (1964–73), the Commission for practical purposes was lifeless, and Canada subordinated ICSC obligations to considerations of discretion in its relations with the United States, whose political objectives it supported. In the years since the American withdrawal from Indochina, the underlying principles guiding Canadian policy towards Vietnam seem to have reverted to those that informed Canadian statements on the French war in the first period.

Membership in the supervisory commissions marked the first real Canadian presence, other than a missionary one, in Indochina. Canadian diplomatic representation in Southeast Asia even five years after the Geneva Conference extended only to Burma, Malaya, and Indonesia.[1] Contacts increased somewhat in the 1960s, commercial trade in particular registering modest expansion. Thus, while in 1960 Canada's total trade with the five countries that make up the Association of South-East Asian Nations (ASEAN) was worth $55.7 million, the amount had increased to $355.2 million in 1975.[2] To put the last figure in perspective, however, Canadian-American trade in 1975 was worth $45,212 million.[3]

Missionary activity in Indochina was in the cause of spreading Christian values and brotherhood. Since 1975 (and especially in 1979), Indochinese refugees have exerted a claim on such universal values as compassion and global brotherhood. When the war between the two Vietnams finally ended, Canada received a modest legacy of some 3,000 refugees from the region in 1975. This had grown to 9,000 by the end of 1978. When the "boat people" rode the tides of misery in 1979, quotas were increased, and Canada welcomed some 60,000 refugees from Indochina during 1979 and 1980.

The Vietnam wars have left other legacies to Canada as well. By 1969, in Mitchell Sharp's phrase, "an astonishing 34 per cent of the officer strength" of the DEA had served in one or more of the three commissions in Indochina.[4] John Holmes has remarked upon the irony that in consequence of Canada's experiences in Indochina, its relations with friends and allies may have suffered more than its relations with antagonists.[5] A friend with whom relations suffered was India. In recognition of the troika membership of the ICSC, the Canadian delegation initially operated under the general directive from Ottawa that it should seek to enlist Indian support against the anticipated Polish intransigence. The directive became obsolescent as Indian policy changed over time, and as the Indo-Canadian entente became a casualty of the shared experience in the commissions: familiarity bred irritation.

The ally with whom relations were called sharply into question is the United States; five factors were involved. First, the displacement of the notion that in any major war involving the United States, Canada would be inevitably and directly involved. In Vietnam, the United States fought a major war for a decade, a war that Canada never considered joining. Second, the Vietnam war was instrumental in challenging quiet diplomacy, by bringing into question the two premises Peyton Lyon postulated as essential for the policy: responsible and beneficial American internationalism.[6] The Vietnam war dispelled the illusion that the United States would automatically be on the side of the angels. Third, the manner in which the Defense Production Sharing Agreements compromised Canada in Vietnam led to the realization that in addition to providing Canadians with a share in the profitable armaments industry, the agreements were the institutional mechanism for the Americans to harness Canadian resources to their war machine. The disconcerting realization that Canada and America could differ in the identification of enemies and in the choice of means to meet the threats led to re-evaluation of the logic of joint defense. Fourth, the scarring Vietnam experience strengthened the Canadian desire to seek nonmilitary solutions to the problems besetting the world. "Vietnam may have witnessed — and promoted — the rise and fall of Canada's affair with the middle power as a role, but it has also encouraged a sense of thanksgiving at not being a great power."[7] Fifth, the Vietnam experience helped destroy the concept of international peacekeeping as a sacred calling for Canadians.

In general, Canadian policy in Vietnam as elsewhere was informed by three considerations. The first was an interest in peace *per se,* practically expressed in support for the United Nations as a world peace body. The second was Canada's special concern with American policy, the consequences of which it could not escape. The third was a close concern with anything that weakened that coalition which, under the leadership of the United States, was believed by Canada to be the strongest deterrent against communist aggression and war.[8]

Canada's statements by 1979 had turned full circle to once again merge into common Western pronouncements. Ottawa's utterances in mid-1979 on Vietnam's responsibility for the exodus of refugees could just as easily have emanated from London or Washington. Canada can once more afford to take a distant and detached view of the region's problems. Thus in his address to the United Nations General Assembly on 21 September 1981, foreign minister Mark MacGuigan contented himself with expressing support for the proposals made at the international conference on Kampuchea. Earlier, at the ASEAN foreign ministers' meeting in Manila in June, MacGuigan recalled Canada's cosponsorship of the ASEAN resolution on Kampuchea at the 1980 General Assembly session. He reiterated Canadian support for the ASEAN initiative, involving a withdrawal of Vietnamese troops and supervised elections in Kampuchea.

India
India's policy in Vietnam is to be explained by a mix of four factors: the principle of nonalignment in general; an attempt to extend nonalignment to the Indochinese region and to the Geneva Agreements; the dynamics of the evolving local situation in Indochina; and the vagaries of India's own relations with the great powers. A unifying strand in these factors has been the desire to preclude great-power involvement in Indochina. Nehru remarked in the Lok Sabha on 25 March 1957 that "the Geneva Agreement was essentially based on the fact that the great power groups should not push in aggressively in the Indo-China States but leave them to function for themselves. In effect it meant that the Indo-China States should follow an independent and unaligned policy." In general, thus, India interpreted the Geneva Agreements in terms of its own foreign policy of nonalignment, and during the American war pressed consistently for a return to them. The Geneva framework had the corollary advantage of maximizing India's influence in the region by a decrease in great-power involvement.

At a five-day conference in New Delhi in April 1972, Indian envoys from twenty-eight countries in South, Southeast, and East Asia discussed India's interests regarding the possible future international relations of the region. They concluded that domination by any one power or group of powers would be unacceptable. India's preference instead was for a security system that would guarantee the national sovereignty, political independence, and territorial integrity of the countries in the region as part of an international convention or agreement. Again, and perhaps quite incidentally, such a configuration would allow India the greatest flexibility and opportunity in its own diplomatic maneuvers in the area. India's policy in Vietnam may thus be seen as logically consistent not only with its broader foreign policy, but also with its regional policy. In fact, it is more accurate to describe its regional policy as deriving from its general policy.

Another striking feature of Indian policy in Vietnam was the dictum of accepting things as they are. Initially, New Delhi believed tha colonialism was a contracting force, that Ho Chi Minh was the only realistic possibility in Vietnam, and that South Vietnam had little prospect of surviving the July 1956 elections. After 1956, India acknowledged a functionally independent South Vietnam as a *fait accompli*. During the American war, New Delhi acted on the assumption that South Vietnam would collapse without American support, that American withdrawal was a matter of time, and that it was therefore prudent and sensible to cultivate relations with North rather than South Vietnam.

The pragmatic approach was also a feature of Indian policy in the ICSC. Thus at the 431st meeting of the Commission on 20 September 1957, chairman T. N. Kaul (who subsequently became India's foreign secretary) observed:

> Our powers are limited. The implementation of the Geneva Agreement is a duty of the parties. We have merely to supervise such implementation. We have made every effort possible to secure that implementation. This is an admission of failure. I admit that but I think we should be realistic and objective and not create false hopes in the minds of people or ourselves that by taking any further action we will achieve any better results.

But what of the future? If relations with major powers are to guide India in its policy towards Indochina, then the situation would appear to be very fluid. The Chinese incursion into Vietnam while Foreign Minister Vajpayee was on Chinese soil was only a "setback" to improving India-China relations. Now that India's emotional identification with Vietnam has lessened, dialogue with China is resuming. On the one hand, Indo-Vietnamese relations may take second place to Sino-Indian relations. On the other hand, since Vietnam is closely allied to the USSR and will probably remain so, the pace of India's relations with China is not likely to be allowed to threaten the mutually profitable New Delhi-Moscow bonds.

India also comes into the picture in Soviet efforts at a diplomatic containment of China. New Delhi was among the first to distinguish between Chinese and Soviet foreign policies. In a flush of bitterness when his China policy began to crumble into ruins along the Himalayas, Nehru said: "I do not think there is any country in the world which is more anxious for peace than the Soviet Union. . . . But I doubt if there is any country in the world which cares less for peace than China today."[9] Nevertheless, India has consistently refused to be drawn into anti-China diplomatic groupings. Equally, friendship with the USSR does not preclude attempts to thaw Sino-Indian relations. Gandhi in opposition had attacked the Janata for failing to take a firmer line against the Chinese invasion of Vietnam; Gandhi back in power was seen to be conversing with Chairman Hua Kuo-feng at Josip Tito's funeral in Belgrade. The dialogue was continued in the visit to India by Foreign Minister Huang Hua in June 1981. Huang's visit, the first by a Chinese leader since the 1962 war, paved the way for a reopening of negotiations on the border dispute. Improving Sino-Indian relations, could, however, find themselves hostage to Chinese support for Pakistan. So could Indo-American relations.

Direct relations between India and Vietnam should continue to be cordial. The annual report of the Ministry of External Affairs for 1978 noted a new beginning in establishing bilateral economic relations with Vietnam, as well as a sympathetic Indian response to Vietnam's drive for economic reconstruction. During his visit in February 1978, Prime Minister Pham Van Dong both endorsed India's nuclear policy and secured Indian agreement to supply a wheat loan of 300,000 tonnes to help tide over his country's food shortages. When Pham toured India in April 1980, Mrs. Gandhi spoke of the "double standards" of those who expressed horror at events in Afghanistan but had remained conspicuously silent when Vietnam was invaded the previous year. Pham for his part accepted Kashmir as an integral part of India, visited Srinagar, and while there remarked that Pakistan and China "will have to vacate the Indian territory which they have been occupying."[10] When India's Foreign Minister P. V. Narasimha Rao visited Vietnam in February 1982, he announced a loan of Rs 100 million to Vietnam for 1982–83, to help explore its mineral deposits, conduct geological surveys, and provide wider facilities for training and technical expertise in the fields of agriculture, industry, and railways. He also assured the Vietnamese that a settlement of India's border question with China would not be at the expense of its friendly relations with other countries.

The Soviet connection in Indo-Vietnamese relations was also evident in Vietnam's Party Secretary Le Duan's visit to the USSR in 1981. At a meeting with Brezhnev on 7 September, discussions turned to an examination of the international situation. "The USSR and SRV are convinced that the consolidation of security in Asia should be the overall goal of Asian states. In this connection, they attach great importance to expanding cooperation with India."[11]

In a longer historical perspective, nevertheless, India could find itself with divided loyalties in the event of a clash between a more sinicized northern Vietnam and a resisting rest of Indochina. Asked to comment on the subject of Indo-Vietnamese relations, Pham said at a press conference in New Delhi on 25 February 1978, "Our feelings for you are as a cloudless sky." A cloudless sky is not the friendliest prospect in the heat and dust of an Indian summer.

Poland

Of the three ICSC delegations, the Poles had probably the least complicated task. They simply had to be good communists and, failing that, good allies of the USSR. When Hanoi, Peking, and Moscow were in agreement, the Poles had no difficulty in advocating the same line in the Commission. When assessments and policies diverged within the socialist community, Poland delicately adopted a pro-Soviet stance. In a logical continuation of this policy, Poland joined other East European countries (with the exception of Rumania and Yugoslavia) in strongly condemning the Chinese invasion of Vietnam in 1979.

Poland's relations with Vietnam in the foreseeable future will probably be similarly influenced. The Sino-Vietnamese war of 1979 was a culmination of the shifting nuances of great-power relations since the Second World War.[12] During the Sino-Soviet schism and then the Sino-American *rapprochement,* Chinese enthusiasm for the Hanoi leadership waned; when the United States withdrew from Indochina, differences in Sino-Soviet relations with the countries in the region came to prominence. Vietnam looked to the USSR to counter Chinese influence. Continuing American treatment of Vietnam as an outcast forced Vietnam into near-complete dependence on the USSR, which in turn inflamed Chinese passions even further. When Vietnamese surrogates ousted the Peking-backed Pol Pot government in Kampuchea, China struck back hard at Vietnam. Conscious of the menacing bear to the north, however, China went only so far in its punitive expedition.

If the military result of the war was a stalemate, what of political prospects? Here again we could expect the long-term destiny of a socialist Vietnam to be determined more by the interplay between Hanoi, Moscow, and Peking than by the hostility or benevolence of Washington. (This is not to imply that the last is without significance.) The United States presence in Vietnam was an itinerant one, an intrusion of the cold-war axis which hid but did not extinguish the rivalries within the socialist camp. It may be significant in this connection that in the 1979 war, while Vietnam, China, and the USSR played out their complicated moves, the American role was reduced to one of shuffling on the sidelines. The American military intervention in Vietnam had ensured an accommodating coexistence among the three socialist regimes; American withdrawal assured that long-smoldering conflicts would come to a flash.

At one time, China and Vietnam proclaimed themselves to be as close as lips and teeth. But their relations grew steadily more distant when the United States extricated itself from Indochina in 1973, and Vietnam reunified through force of arms in 1975-76. Today, curled lips hurl invective while the teeth have drawn blood. It is not accurate to describe the Kampuchea-Vietnam conflict as a proxy war between China and the Soviet Union; local dynamics of the war were as important as the international dynamics. However, conflicts in Indochina cannot be resolved until such time as China and the USSR have worked out a *modus vivendi* in respect of the region, including tacitly recognized protective spheres of influence.

Indo-Canadian Relations

Chester Ronning has written that he became actively involved in Indochina affairs as soon as he arrived in *New Delhi* as High Commissioner in 1957. Since "New Delhi kept a tight rein on each Commission Chairman, and Ottawa kept in very close touch with each Canadian Commissioner," that Ronning should have found himself in the thick of Indochinese affairs is not surprising. In fact, the file on Indochina was the largest single file in the Canadian office in New Delhi.[13] The official in charge of India's section on Indochina at the time was none other than M. J. Desai, the first chairman of the Vietnam Commission.

The joint Indo-Canadian venture was not immediately unlucky; in the early years leaders praised each other's role in the commission. In a private letter to Australian foreign minister R. G. Casey, Pearson wrote on 1 November 1954 that while on occasions there may have been departures, "on the whole we understand that most of the Indians endeavour to be truly impartial and objective" in the Indochina commissions. In May 1955, Pearson repeated the praise for India at the North Atlantic Council meeting which included the American Secretary of State. The Indians, he said, "have tried to play their role of the real neutral and have succeeded to a considerable extent."[14] At a speech to the Indian Council of World Affairs in November 1955, Pearson commented that India and Canada had worked together "amicably and well" for a year in the commissions in Indochina. "Through the friendships established in this joint endeavour, another strong link has been forged between our two countries." The two were not always in agreement in the ICSC, but not for lack of trying. Pearson concluded by praising the devotion, ability, and sincerity of the Indians, military and civilian: "They have earned the respect and friendship of their Canadian colleagues."[15] Even as late as 9 July 1959, Howard Green was paying parliamentary tribute "to the way in which India has fulfilled the difficult role of chairman of the three international commissions."

The early amicability between the Canadian and Indian delegations is not surprising. This was the heyday of the love affair between the two. It was also the time when the Commonwealth counted. In Indochina, Canadian and Indian officers would be natural social allies—by language, political tradition, Commonwealth affinity, and, in the case of defense officers, an almost identical military tradition. In fact, the natural social affinities between Canadians and Indians were so strong that the Canadian and Indian Commissioners decided, independently of each other, to see one another privately as infrequently as possible. They did not wish to give the Polish Commissioner cause to think that he was the victim of a "ganging up."[16] This study should also serve to debunk the myth of unceasing animosity between the Canadian and Indian delegations. No one will deny that the ICSC experience in the late 1960s soured Indo-Canadian relations, but few realize that the two countries began service on the ICSC with a strong similarity of outlooks and "world views." Indeed, if one admits that by the late 1960s no one seriously expected anything further of the ICSC, then one should base comparisons on the period in which it was active. And one of the surprising results of this study is that in the first decade of the ICSC's operations, Indo-Canadian similarities overshadowed differences.

As the years passed with no solution to the Vietnam problem, however, frustrations were inevitable. In the early years, the Canadians tried to settle on policies that were both satisfactory to their American allies and acceptable to their Indian friends. Once the Americans were directly and massively involved, however, differences in the Canadian and Indian perspectives came to the fore. Nor did it help that by that time the Indo-Canadian affair was coming to an end. Their special postwar relationship was as exceptional as the inflated status in which they had found themselves. Ottawa and New Delhi may also have exaggerated each other's importance and freedom of action in international affairs.[17] But because these perceptions had been cause for pride in Canada and India, their loss was lamented by people who had taken them to be the norm.

In Vietnam—and Indochina generally—the considerable Canadian exasperation with the Indians contributed to the demise of the special relationship. According to the *Globe and Mail* journalist David van Praagh, "a whole generation of Canadian External Affairs officers was turned off India by the non-cooperation they encountered over the years on the three-member truce commissions." Again, "it was largely because of Indochina" that India as the focus of Canadian aid changed, "that Canadian goodwill and encouragement toward India were transformed into bitterness and distrust."[18] Similarly, Barrie M. Morrison has written that few in the DEA appreciated India's interpretation of the origins and probable development of the conflict in Vietnam, and the proper role of the ICSC. Many Canadian officers remained bitter over the Indians' behavior in the Commission: "As far as many people in External Affairs and National Defence were concerned the special relations with India were finished by the mid-1960s."[19] Escott Reid has written of his impression that from the early sixties until the commissions came to an end in 1973 almost all the Canadian political officers who served on one of the three commissions came back to Canada firm supporters of United States policy in Indo-China and with profound distaste and contempt for Indian policy in Indo-China and for the Indians they had served with.[20]

Indian reactions to the Canadian record in Vietnam do not seem to have been as rancorous. In part this may be attributable to the appreciation among Indian officials that, in the last analysis, Canada could not be expected to dissociate itself from American policy in Vietnam.[21] The question of any bitterness over betrayal would not, therefore, arise for Indians in evaluating their Canadian colleagues' conduct. There is also a surprising degree of friendly feeling for Canada among the Indian public, as Table 13 shows. (The survey was limited to the literate population of Bombay, Calcutta, Madras, and New Delhi.) A negative image of Canada is almost nonexistent. In an August 1971 poll 45 percent of the respondents

TABLE 13
Indian Images of Canada, 1971–76

(Q. On the whole, what is your opinion of the following countries?)

	Very good	Good	Neither good nor bad	Bad	Very bad	Don't know
August 1971*	12	41	21	1	0	25
(For Australia* August 1971)	5	34	31	3	0	27
August 1972	7	42	17	7	1	26
October 1973	3	38	25	1	0	33
April 1975	2	31	29	2	0	36
April 1976	7	34	15	1	0	43
September 1976	11	40	22	1	0	26

Each row totals 100.

*Australia and Canada were included in the poll to measure international images for the first time in this poll.

Source: IIPO, *Monthly Public Opinion Surveys,* Relevant issues, 1971–76.

TABLE 14
Canadian Images of Selected Countries, 1975

	Dislike Very Much									Like Very Much	
	-5	-4	-3	-2	-1	1	2	3	4	5
Great Britain	2.0	0.4	1.0	1.4	4.0	9.2	11.4	24.1	17.8	28.7
United States	3.7	1.7	2.7	2.3	5.3	11.5	12.1	20.8	18.5	21.3
Russia	18.3	5.9	7.4	7.4	12.0	18.3	11.4	9.5	4.9	4.9
Mainland China	15.6	8.3	9.0	9.0	14.3	16.8	9.7	8.3	5.2	3.9
Japan	6.2	4.5	4.1	6.1	11.0	19.6	17.0	15.7	8.9	7.0
India	13.0	7.0	7.6	8.9	16.5	17.6	13.3	8.8	4.4	2.9

Source: CIPO 377, June 1975.

answered that Canada and India had mutual interests; 18 percent thought that their interests were rather different (13 percent) to very different (5 percent).[22] A comparison with Australia on this question is instructive: 33 percent expressed mutuality of interest between India and Australia; 27 percent believed the interests to be different. The goodwill toward Canada is thus "real," not simply a matter of inertia. In September 1976, 51 percent of respondents thought favorably of Canada; only 1 percent thought unfavorably!

Interestingly enough, the asymmetrical Canadian-Indian evaluations of each other's role in the Indochina commissions would appear to be paralleled by an imbalance in public perceptions. Favorable images of Canada among Indians are not reciprocated. The Canadian public was not as upset as the government over India's nuclear explosion in 1974. Only 51 percent had even heard of it. Of these, 41 percent were "quite concerned" to "very concerned"; 55 percent, on the other hand, were "not too concerned" or "not at all concerned" that this would increase the possibility of an atomic war.[23] More generally, a Gallup poll in June 1975 attempted to map the Canadian public's images of the world (Table 14). Although comparisons of dissimilar tables are hazardous, Tables 13 and 14 do establish an imbalance in how Canadians and Indians see each other. While it would undoubtedly be interesting to inquire into the causes of such asymmetrical perceptions, the task is beyond the scope of this book.

The adverse impact of ICSC membership on relations between Canada and India provides its own bitter lessons. In 1954, each had been pleased that the other was to be a colleague, and took that into consideration in deciding to accept the supervisory role. In future, countries having good relations with each other might well consider whether it is worth risking a ruptured relationship in order to serve together on peace bodies. At the very least, they might be well advised to take the ICSC lesson to heart, scrutinize the agreements minutely, and insist upon at least two conditions: responsibility for military functions only, the disputants being responsible for political settlement; and the setting of a specified time limit, beyond which the presumption would be strongly against a renewal of tenure. In any case, they should refuse to agree to a second extension, *whatever* the circumstances.

States taking such tough stands, although unlikely to endear themselves initially, might better serve the cause of "permanent" peace by leading to the realization that when it comes to peacekeeping, they do not serve who stand and wait. At least they will be able to extricate themselves gracefully from an otherwise impossible situation. Similarly, judging from the second round of Canadian experience in Vietnam, it may be wise to prepare for eventual withdrawal by initially stating tough conditions. (Would it have been preferable for Canada to have been a member of the supervisory commission in the spring of 1975?)

Why did Canada and India, despite mounting frustrations, persevere in their thankless membership in the ICSC? Four reasons become apparent. First, bureaucratic and political inertia. Once membership had been accepted, a withdrawal would necessarily be a conscious and major decision requiring compelling arguments in justification. Thus John Holmes wrote that the prevailing sentiment in Ottawa on the question of withdrawal was "to avoid rocking the boat in Indo-China."[24]

Second, the Commission's existence, which would have been imperilled by withdrawals, was a symbol of continuing concern by the international community. A collapse of a Commission would be an unacceptable admission of failure.

Third, both Canada and India seemed to agree that while the Commission did not ultimately prevent a new war, it performed valuable services in its early years, and helped contain the conflict for a few more years. On 25 May 1957, Nehru conceded that events in Indochina had not turned out entirely satisfactorily. At the same time, however, the Geneva Agreements "not only stopped the terrible war, but . . . helped in keeping peace and in improving the situation," even while great difficulties remained.[25] He admitted, in the Rajya Sabha on 27 August 1958, that Vietnam posed its own problems: "Laos and Cambodia offered difficulties, offered problems. True—but not that type of more intractable problems which North and South Viet-Nam offered." The Commission did not solve the problem in Vietnam, but the mere fact of its presence prevented it from getting out of hand. At a speech in New Delhi on 28 April 1961, Nehru said that the three Indochinese commissions functioned "in a way which at least prevented the situation from getting worse. They did not solve problems, perhaps always, but they did manage to keep things going more or less."[26] He repeated the argument in September 1962. Responding to demands for a withdrawal from the Vietnam Commission, he declared that "the presence of the Commission has done a great deal of good. It has prevented the situation from worsening, and definitely improved it occasionally. Therefore, we propose to carry on our work there."[27]

Pearson argued a similar position as early as 1955. (Ottawa was seriously debating the withdrawal option at this time.) Discussing the issue of freedom of movement for refugees wishing to flee to South Vietnam, Pearson pointed to the difficulties inherent in the Geneva Agreements in the need to gather evidence and reach agreed interpretations. Nevertheless, the Commission's existence and activity represented a steady pressure on the parties which made nonimplementation difficult.[28] Despite the less-than-satisfactory situation, Canada would not withdraw from the Commission; that would merely prejudice implementation of the main military provisions without materially benefitting those who wished to leave North Vietnam.[29] Howard Green expressed the same sentiment in Parliament on 8 March 1962. The commissions had been "a restraining influence" in Indochina, and their presence "prevented a big war breaking out." In effect, the argument boiled down to a "peace and containment" thesis: the existence of the Commission helped to preserve the peace and contain direct communist expansion.[30]

Fourth, India and Canada hoped that the Commission could help achieve peace, or at least be reactivated with the achievement of peace. Both Canada and India believed that the Commission could well prove to be the instrument to bring the warring parties together. As Martin put it on 8 July 1966, "Being the only body that has a continuing link with Hanoi and Saigon we thought that, quite apart from any authority given to that commission under the Geneva agreement, it might undertake the effort to try and bring about a narrowing in the position taken by various parties."[31] He was in fact responding to a suggestion made by Gandhi the day before. She had proposed a cessation of ground and air hostilities, to be followed by a reconvention of the Geneva Conference. The Commission would safeguard the *status quo* in the interim and while the Conference was in progress.[32] Furthermore, the possibility that the peacekeeping force might be useful in the future could not be entirely discounted. Reviving a dormant machine would be easier than establishing a new one.

International Peacekeeping

ICSC and Geneva Defects

The international commissions in Indochina were creatures of the 1954 Geneva Conference and integral parts of the Geneva accords. The authors of the accords had clearly expected that in two years' time, Cambodia, Laos, and Vietnam would be free, independent, united, and in no further need of international commissions. As it turned out, they were mistaken by nineteen years. The promise of the Geneva Agreements was not fulfilled. The question is to determine why the Geneva hopes were not realized for Vietnam, despite the fact that the ICSC did work reasonably satisfactorily in its first two years.

It is useful to recapitulate some of the more important difficulties of the Commission's operations. First, its mandate was limited in scope, in that it was required only to *supervise* the execution of the Agreements, with actual implementation being the direct responsibility of the disputants. The mandate was also limited in time, at least implicitly, to two years. After July 1956, the Commission subsisted with a progressively reduced staff and activity, on sufferance. In another sense, while the Commission was limited to a supervisory role, the extent of its supervision was unlimited—its mandate was both too narrow and too broad. Nor did it help that the Commission ended by assuming political obligations as well.

In the field, the most serious obstacle was the lack of effective cooperation from the parties. Another weakness was self-inflicted. The Commission very early acquiesced in a reactive rather than initiatory role. In a telling comment on the consequences of this, Bernard Fall witnessed

> U.S. warplanes being landed on an aircraft carrier in sight of Saigon's main thoroughfare while a handsomely turbaned Indian ICSC officer said: "Yes—but *officially* we have not been informed of the presence of the aircraft carrier."[33]

The weakness in the field in turn pointed up another inadequacy, *viz.*, the lack of a continuing political authority to which the Commission could be responsible and from which it could seek guidance and help. Neither the cochairmen nor the other members of the Geneva Conference displayed interest in the welfare of the

Commission after the Conference adjourned in July 1954. A comparison with the Indonesian experience is instructive in this regard. The original Good Offices Committee of 1947 had been limited to acting on the unanimity rule and upon invitation by the disputants. When the second round of hostilities broke out in December 1948, however, the Security Council reconstituted the GOC into a full-fledged subsidiary organ, the United Nations Commission for Indonesia. UNCI was charged with a dual function: it was a machinery at the disposal of the parties, but retained a broad freedom of action under Security Council sanction. It was thus given the power to *initiate* far-reaching measures in the search for a political settlement, including a call for the transfer of areas from one party to the other.

The above weaknesses notwithstanding, "in the last analysis it was the realities in Vietnam which defeated all the commissions."[34] At its most fundamental, the "reality" was the American refusal to countenance the loss of the southern half of Vietnam to the communists and the North Vietnamese refusal to allow a permanent partition of their country. As the struggle developed, the ICSC became more removed from the events in Vietnam.

The three delegations initially reflected the three chief strands of world politics in 1954: the West, the communist, and the nonaligned. This function was openly recognized by Krishna Menon at the time of the Geneva Conference on Laos in May 1961.[35] But eventually the Commission ceased to be representative of international politics. The significance of this for the operation of the Commission may be demonstrated in symbols. Figure 4 depicts the geometrically similar relationship between the Commission's structure and the international political system. Since the Commission was structured to reflect international politics in its organizational framework, it is not surprising, and neither was it a disability, that the Commission's processes mirrored international activities. At its simplest, this meant that the three delegations displayed attitudes and propensities in the Commission that paralleled the political preferences of their respective home governments. Nor is this surprising, given that in the absence of an effective "international" executive body, the Commission's delegations were continuously reporting to, and under the direction of, their individual foreign policy systems. At a more complex level, the two systems were also similar in the direction and outcomes of pressures. Thus, internationally,

FIGURE 4
Relationship between ICSC and International
Political Structures, 1954

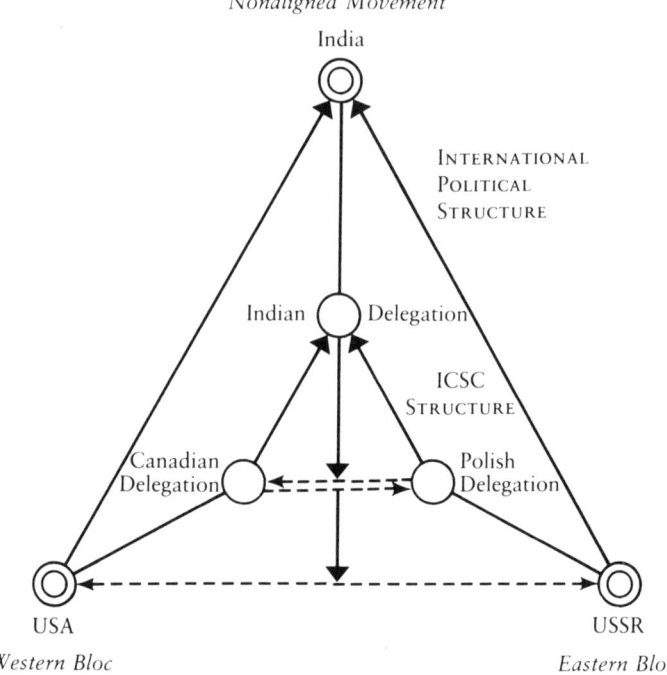

the military stalemate between the superpowers resulted in the fierce competition between them being transferred to the political plane—winning the allegiance of the nonaligned, India being the most coveted prize. Direct contacts or efforts at persuasion between the blocs were comparatively sporadic. (Hence the firm and broken arrows in Figure 4.) But India continued its policy of nonalignment, equidistant from the blocs on international, particularly cold war, issues. In the Vietnam Commission, similarly, the Canadians and the Poles may have made the odd ritualistic gesture to each other, but the point was to get to the Indians first. The Indian delegation was the effective arbiter, and in the Commission it ended up taking a position mid-way between the Canadian and Polish delegations.

In the 1960s, the ICSC and international political structures became discontinuous. Internationally, the United States—USSR military bipolarity formed the base of a political-cum-economic pentagonal configuration, with China, Japan, and Western Europe as the other three loci. The nonaligned group continued in membership and nomenclature, but as a force in international politics it had largely receded. Its activities became steadily more declamatory and less substantive. Within the group, India was no longer at the forefront, *primus inter pares;* it was only one of the several important leaders in the by-now *Afro*-Asian movement. Its policy after the 1962 India-China war shifted from equidistance to equiproximity *vis-à-vis* the superpowers. It may not be entirely a coincidence that the loosening of the international structure occurred simultaneously with the increasing futility of the Commission. The ICSC still engaged in sporadic bursts of activity, to be sure. But, by and large, it was content to be idle and its activities decreased, as it became a helpless spectator to events rather than the center stage for developments in Vietnam. The Polish and Canadian delegations had become quite unbending in support of North and South Vietnam, and did not really try to get past each other's armor. India still tried to maintain a middle position when the occasion arose, but it arose less and less often.

It may be objected, with justice, that the pentagonal configuration was as irrelevant to the Vietnamese situation as was the International Commission, if not more so. What was important in Indochina was the triangular relationship between the USSR, China, and the United States. The impact on the Commission of the shifting nature of this relationship is demonstrated in Figures 5 and 6. In 1962, China had begun to break away from the USSR, but had not yet broken through its isolation from the United States. However, by 1972, in the wake of the Mao-Nixon meeting, Peking stood closer to Washington than to Moscow.

As for India, 1962 was critical because it climaxed three years of border conflicts with China with a short but intense and shattering war. During the war, the USSR remained neutral between the parties, while the West came promptly to India's rescue. Consequently, even while India tried to discriminate between Moscow and Peking, a definite tilt towards the West was briefly perceptible in India's international relations. In the Commission, India's voting favored Saigon over Hanoi in crucial respects from 1959 to 1962; the change in India's position was even more dramatic in its pattern of voting.

FIGURE 5
ICSC and China-India-USA-USSR Structures, 1962

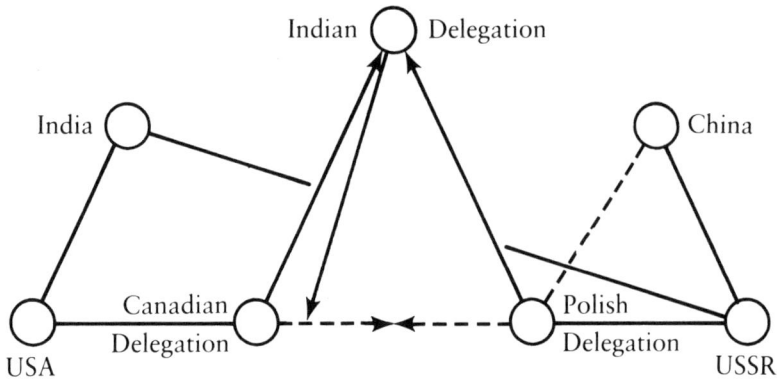

FIGURE 6
ICSC and China-India-USA-USSR Structures, 1972

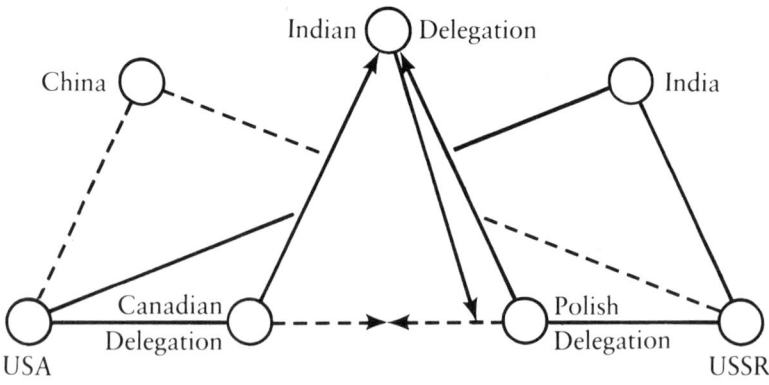

In 1972, India emerged victorious from the Bangladesh war of December 1971, first having signed a friendship treaty with the USSR in August 1971. The treaty was a swift reaction to the surprise China-United States *rapprochement*, especially in the context of the Pakistani civil war in the subcontinent. During the war, in a fitting image of the new world, China and America found themselves allies in the Security Council against the USSR, defender and champion of India. In Vietnam, India abandoned all pretense of equality as between the two halves directly after the Bangladesh war. The establishment of full diplomatic relations between India and the DRVN led to the expulsion of the Commission headquarters from Saigon, and its relocation in Hanoi.

With respect to either the pentagonal or the triangular international system of relationships, thus, the international and Commission structures were discrepant. It may be inherently impossible to establish causal linkages between the international structure and the performance of the Commission. But it is possible to demonstrate the chronological linkages between the effectiveness of the Commission and a congruence of the ICSC and international structures. It is also possible to relate the failure of the Commission to its increasingly nonrepresentative character in respect of world political forces. Perhaps the linkages could be explored through the authoritative aspect of the Commission. At any rate, by 1972, the ICSC was no longer representative of the main international strands. Nor did it have the mandate to regulate a conflict in which the internal parameters had changed. As Swaran Singh expressed it in the Lok Sabha on 26 April 1972:

> Instead of being able to supervise the implementation of a peace accord, the Commission is a helpless witness to a violent war. In the circumstances, there is little the Commission can do, because it is meant to supervise peace not war. . . . I would like to express my appreciation of the dignified, calm and patient manner in which the representatives of the three supervising powers have conducted themselves in the face of serious difficulties in South Vietnam.

Before the year was out, even dignity, calm, and patience had fallen prey to further difficulties in South Vietnam.[36]

According to John Holmes, "Of all the important peace-making documents of our time none was so badly drafted and curiously drawn as the so-called 'Geneva Settlement' of 1954."[37] In a general discussion of the failure of peace settlements, Robert Randle distinguishes broadly between failures caused by inadequacies intrinsic to a peace settlement, and failures arising from other causes.[38] He lists twelve intrinsic inadequacies, of which the first three are not relevant to the Geneva Agreements: failure of peace negotiations (which is not really a failure of a settlement, Randle notes, since no settlement has been reached), reaching an agreement limited to an armistice, and a technically defective cease-fire.

276 □ Peacekeeping in Vietnam

Before listing the inadequacies of the settlement, two points should be made. First, negotiators work under conditions of imperfect information and urgency of time. The pressing objective is always to stop the fighting by any agreement, and not to miss the chance in a futile quest for perfection. Second, the Commission did in fact perform valuable service. That its successes were not sufficiently exploited through political initiative should not diminish its performance. The ICSC's loss in credibility resulted from a misapprehension of its role as a peacekeeping force and from the clearly defined limits of its capability.

In *Geneva 1954*, Randle identified the following weaknesses in the 1954 Agreements.[39] First, there were no provisions to restrict the buildup of local forces by the disputants, even though they were not permitted to import men and arms. Second, the Commission lacked both the competence and the means even to observe adequately, let alone control or supervise, the introduction of arms and material into Vietnam. Third, the Geneva settlement failed to eliminate South Vietnamese insecurity. "Because Tran Van Do expressed his government's fears that the terms of the cease-fire agreement would reduce the SVN's ability to resist Communist expansion, it could be expected that the Diem government would do what it could to improve its defensive capabilities."[40] In addition, "the French made little effort to assuage the feelings of the South Vietnamese and set up a bitterness and an alienation from the whole Geneva settlement on the part of the Saigon Government which was to have unhappy results."[41] Fourth, confusion existed as to who was the final authority in interpreting the Agreements: the parties, the Commission, the cochairmen, or a reconvened Geneva Conference? This assumed practical importance in the many differing interpretations between the parties and the Commission. Fifth, the Commission lacked effective sanction: it could suggest and recommend, but not compel. The sixth defect was rather serious: the factor of nonobligated parties, in this case the United States and South Vietnam. A related and equally serious weakness was the vagueness and ambiguity of many of the provisions. Who, for example, were France's functional successors? Were elections mandatory? What was the effect of the French unilateral declaration to respect the sovereignty and independence of "Vietnam"? Ambiguity is a serious inadequacy in that it can—as it did—lead to further disputes over the original intent of the peacemakers. In this sense, the political terms of the Geneva accords were procedurally defective. At best, they laid the basis for a future political settlement.

Was the fact that none of the supervisory states had been a member of the Geneva Conference a source of weakness? Not according to Holmes. "There was . . . a sound argument for placing supervision in the hands of countries which were not themselves responsible for the terms of the Agreement. Their's not to reason why; their's but to see that the terms were respected."[42]

Regarding failures due to sources external to a peace settlement, the most serious and relevant is that of third-party intervention. Although it is not true to say that the Geneva Agreements would have produced peace if only the Americans had been sympathetic, American hostility did contribute significantly to wrecking the Agreements. To quote Holmes again, "the American alternative of trying to build up SEATO achieved little, but tore Asia apart." It also enabled the communists to claim, rightly, that the United States was altering the terms of coexistence that had been negotiated at Geneva.[43]

The defects of Geneva notwithstanding, it bears repeating that the conference brought peace to a war-torn region, enabled the belligerents to disengage, allowed France to withdraw from Indochina, and provided a framework within which a political settlement could and should have been worked out. The difficulty with peacekeeping forces is that when a conflict is peacefully resolved, credit is claimed by the parties or mediators; but when the conflict again erupts, the fault is laid on the peacekeeping machinery—its forces failed to keep the peace.

Implications

Three major implications can be derived from the present study for future peacekeeping operations. First, the tripolar structure-cum-troika composition should be avoided if an impossible strain is not to be placed on the neutral arbiter. There is little doubt that India's chairmanship in the Vietnam Commission ultimately became an intolerable burden. Paul Martin addressed himself to this issue in his 1967 speech at Columbia University. He declared that Canadian experience since 1954 showed that the troika system was ill-suited to international peacekeeping:

If the assumption is made that two of the three members of the *troika* will automatically assume the role of advocate for their respective "sides", it is obvious that an intolerable burden will be placed on the third member, which is cast in the role of an arbiter. In effect, the third member is expected to assume the full responsibility for every decision which is taken by the peacekeeping agency and to accept, as a result, the foreign policy implications of such decisions as they apply to the arbiter itself.[44]

Second, a rotating chairmanship ensures shared responsibility. The 1973 International Commission reverted to the four-member system of the Korean Neutral Nations Supervisory Commission and, of the three delegations from the original Commission, India's was the only one not accepted for service on the second. The 1973 ICCS also adopted a rotating chairmanship.

Third, the strain on all delegations can be reduced by placing a commission under the direction of a continuing political authority, as with the GOC/UNCI in Indonesia. Although foreign policy considerations are not eliminated, they are modified and screened. The GOC in Indonesia was itself tripartite, but neither tripolar nor troika in the sense used here. It had two members representing the interests of the protagonists, and the United States as the neutral middle. It did work, as did its successor the UNCI, but undoubtedly due to the dominant position of the superpower in the triangle.[45]

As Rikhye *et al.* remark in assessing Indonesia's relevance to the ICSC, in Indonesia there was an interrelationship maintained between the ground observation operation and the political mediatory body. Consequently, the military observer teams were placed under the direction of a higher civilian parent charged with assisting the two disputants to arrive at a peaceful settlement. Finally, the mandate given to the observer teams was adjusted and extended by the GOC, operating under formal United Nations auspices, to meet the changing circumstances of the conflict. Rikhye *et al.* observe that it is this lesson in coordination, communication, and control that the International Commission in Vietnam might well have followed.[46]

Individual representatives on the GOC/UNCI saw no inherent contradiction between acting in an individual capacity, as representatives of their respective governments, and as agents of the Security Council. In fact, they based their decisions *de jure* in terms of the Security Council but *de facto* in terms of their own governments: "they were concerned with interpreting their mandate from the Security Council (i.e., its resolutions) on the basis of directives received from their respective capitals."[47] Two observations are in order. First, in the absence of a formal attachment to a continuing body, the Commission delegations in Vietnam could afford to abandon the task of credibly interpreting their actions in terms of an international mandate. Second, it is at least plausible that the Security Council by the mere fact of its existence prevented the GOC/UNCI representatives from diverging too markedly from the requirements of the world body on the one hand, and their individual governments on the other. The Commission in Vietnam lacked an equivalent constraint.

As for implications that are not *sui generis*, the applicability of the lessons of the Vietnamese peacekeeping experience to international peacekeeping in general is necessarily qualified. International peacekeeping has usually been under United Nations auspices; under those conditions, considerations such as the need for a continuing political authority become irrelevant. The International Commission in Vietnam was unique in some other respects as well. It did not serve as a thin international force separating two belligerents divided by a cease-fire line. Nor, and again in contrast to the UNEF model, did it have its own troops; it had only control teams. United Nations forces have been restrained from fighting except in unquestionable self-defense; the ICSC teams and personnel were specifically dependent upon the local parties for even minimal security—which was not always provided. Finally, there were certain unique attributes of the Vietnam problem: the juridical status of the Agreements (especially the Final Declaration), and the manner of their relationship to South Vietnam.

The qualifications notwithstanding, the Vietnam experience does have some general application. To ascribe homogeneity to United Nations peacekeeping operations would be mistaken. Thus, the first chapter discussed some of the operational guidelines developed at the United Nations with respect to preventive diplomacy and peacekeeping. These were drawn mainly from the UNEF model, but have not always been followed. In the Congo (1960), for instance, the principle of no active combat was held in abeyance as Operation des Nations Unies au Congo (ONUC) troops took to the offensive. Similarly, United Nations troops there were not impartial as between the disputants, but instrumental in imposing a settlement on the secessionist faction by throwing their weight behind the central government. In the case of Cyprus (1964), the principle of having no great powers in peacekeeping troops was suspended to permit the inclusion of the British contingent, one of the largest in the United Nations Force in Cyprus (UNFICYP).

Finally, there are also some general similarities between the records of United Nations and ICSC peacekeeping operations. The most important is that no peacekeeping operation guarantees that a durable settlement of the underlying political dispute will be reached. The two defining attributes of peacekeeping operations are crisis insulation and conflict management. They may or may not provide a variety of other helpful functions; they do offer a visible symbol of the continuing link of crises to the international community; but they do not in themselves constitute the means to resolve disputes. Rikhye *et al.* observe about the ICSC, for example, that "the nature of the commissions meant that they could only provide a presence, and for a while achieve a de-escalation in the fighting, while serving primarily to allow the big powers to disengage."[48] The statement would be equally accurate if "the commissions" was replaced by "UNEF." In fact, one could argue the opposite: peacekeeping forces have been ultimately dysfunctional because they lull both the world at large and the disputants at hand into a false sense of security. In the absence of a crisis, the urge to negotiate a settlement is lost.

The scope for international peacekeeping in the future is impossible to predict. The potential for conflict has by no means diminished. But, just as middle-powermanship accumulated grudges as well as gratitude, so peacekeeping *per se* has thrown into relief drawbacks as well as advantages. This is particularly so from the point of view of the host governments; restoration of peace and order has inevitably involved an accompanying measure of loss of independence.[49]

The relevance of host-government suspicions of an international peacekeeping presence arises from the principle of introducing and maintaining forces by consent. Here again, the Vietnam experience offers confirmation of the basic soundness of the principle. In 1965, for example, the ICSC was forced to withdraw its teams from North Vietnam at Hanoi's insistence; and in 1972 it had to move its headquarters to Hanoi because of Saigon's displeasure at Indian presence in the south. But these were only symptoms. The problem arose from the fact that the International Commission was able to exercise only that authority which the two host governments permitted it. The Vietnam experience offers confirmation of a related principle as well: no international peacekeeping body can successfully oppose the self-defined vital interests of a superpower. A neutral presence can aid in the localization and insulation of a conflict, but cannot guarantee it; its success depends ultimately on a willingness of the superpowers to be excluded from the conflict.

Was the ICSC a neutral presence, however? In the words of Larry Fabian,

> Impartiality is difficult to find and hard to sustain for a long time under conditions of stress. But it is the sine qua non for whatever effectiveness, authority, and leverage peacekeepers have, and perhaps more than anything else it makes peacekeeping a distinctive kind of conflict control activity, one that has worked where partisan control methods would have failed.[50]

The membership criterion of the ICSC was not impartiality but representative character. Further, between 1954 and 1956 the Commission did perform valuable service. It could plausibly be argued that, contrary to Fabian's assertion, the "effectiveness, authority, and leverage" of the Commission as a peacekeeping body derived as much from its representative character as from the attempted impartiality (within the constraints that we have identified) in the first two years. That is, the ICSC arguably gained authority from its demonstrable reflection of all the major strands of international politics. As for the failure of the elections in 1956, which led directly to renewed fighting, it is difficult to see how a nonrepresentational body could have secured the elections, given the political realities. At the same time, however, once the Geneva system had effectively failed, a nonrepresentational commission would have avoided mirroring disagreements among the parties. And yet, in 1973, it was not impartiality that was in demand. The claim that, compared with India, Poland and Canada had been impartial in the first Commission would be untenable.

Perhaps the time has come for someone to study the "morphology" of international peacekeeping. Would it perhaps be appropriate to differentiate the structures of peacekeeping operations so as to make them more functionally specific? Are different skills required for the distinct roles of investigating alleged aggression or agreement violations; verifying and supervising cease-fires and disengagements; separating erstwhile and potential combatants by thin interpository lines; supervising and/or conducting plebiscites and elections, etc.? It is possible that the distinct roles call for correspondingly different organizational structures, logistical inventory, and standard operating procedures. For instance, the optimal civil-military relationship might well vary from role to role.

A final point worth noting here is that India's approach to international peacekeeping has differed from Canada's in two important respects. First, India has consistently opposed attempts to institutionalize United Nations peacekeeping forces, favoring *ad hoc* forces instead. Second, India has always insisted that the rights of host governments must be respected, whereas Canada has tended to view issues from the perspective of United Nations authority. In both respects, of course, a not inconsiderable factor in the Indian calculation is its own border problems.

To End It All

The difference between Canadian and Indian perceptions of the Vietnam war can be briefly explained by discussing Canada's and India's positions in terms of the individual, the state, and the world. Nehru was deeply apprehensive of devastation from a nuclear war, which impelled him into a policy of peaceful coexistence between the two blocs. Outside the bloc system, he was an "Asianist" dedicated to the proposition that it was time for the forgotten peoples of the world to surface into active participation in world affairs. In his parliamentary survey of the international situation on 31 March 1955, Nehru declared that "perhaps when the history of these times is written in the future, two things will stand out. One is the coming of the atomic energy and the other is the emergence of Asia." If independence movements had to rely on communist organizations for success, then so be it. And if they had to rely on violence in the face of obstinate relics of colonialism, then that too was acceptable and worthy of support. Finally, Nehru had a vision of the "Greater India" of times past, which stretched into Indochina.

For the St. Laurent–Pearson–Martin leadership, on the other hand, communism, under direction from Moscow, *was* the threat, and European powers in various outposts could be seen to be combating that threat. They also believed that nuclear war had to be avoided, but by a policy of deterrence, just as violence had to be renounced as a means of change. But they were aware, in a way that the Americans seemed not to be, of the danger of simply transposing the European situation to Asia. They realized that under some circumstances nationalism and communism could fuse, but did not believe this to be the case in Vietnam. Nevertheless, their stance was sufficiently mellow and flexible that in 1965, when the leadership of Harold Wilson became one of the liabilities for the abortive Commonwealth peace mission, some Afro-Asian members attempted to replace him with Lester Pearson.

Indian and Canadian perceptions of the Vietnam conflict always reflected these underlying possibilities of tension. To Nehru, the war was the result of nationalism struggling to emerge from the choking gasps of Western colonialism; to Pearson, the conflict stemmed fundamentally from communist expansionism and the Western decision, first French and then American, to resist. Their successors in both countries turned away from internationalism in efforts to pursue more pragmatic self-centered policies.

In a very closely related manner, at the second level, India was an Asian state, both geographically and racially, while Canada was geographically North American and racially European. They were on opposing sides in the Vietnam war insofar as "natural" sympathies were concerned. In an historical perspective, India had had contacts with Southeast Asia in the past, and would presumably have many in the future. Its involvement was, therefore, the greater of the two. There were mitigating factors, to be sure. For reasons of history, both countries could sympathize with aspirations for national independence, although Canada might be less prone to accept the necessity of violence. Their Commonwealth connection was helpful too, and a federal-parliamentary political system in both could be said to favor a compromise-oriented approach to politics in a world of scarcity. It is to this that Gandhi addressed herself in a speech in Ottawa on 18 June 1973 during a Canadian tour:

> Nations which consist of diverse elements are compelled to value the art of compromise and of accommodating different

viewpoints in a larger perspective. In the building of a Canadian nation you have discovered as have we in India through our long history that diversity not only enriches but can strengthen.[51]

At the third level, the most important feature is that the three delegations were representative of the three chief strands of international politics in 1954: the Western bloc, the Eastern bloc, and the nonaligned. Their respective approaches to the Vietnam conflict were inextricably tied to the international situation. Thus, while Canada's peacekeeping in the Commission was in approximate balance between the local parties, its peacemaking efforts basically reflected American premises and aims. India's peacekeeping, in contrast, was a balance between the delegations insofar as the Commission record is concerned, and varied with the twists and turns of its foreign policy outside the Commission. The most dramatic manifestations of this were the two strongly marked periods of recent Indian history: the 1959–62 conflict with China; and the time from 1971 when Washington and Peking seemed to move closer, and India veered sharply towards the USSR. In the first period, India voted for the South Vietnamese position on a number of critical issues. In the second, New Delhi effectively renounced the pretense to a "balanced" approach and moved decisively toward Hanoi.

On the basis of variables in all three levels of analysis, Canada could not be expected to accept the North Vietnamese statement of the war. India, on the other hand, for reasons extending over all three levels, could not be expected to accept the Western statement of the conflict. And there, insofar as Indo-Canadian relations are concerned, was the rub.

On 24 January 1966, in an earnest appeal to "all peace-loving governments and peoples the world over to resolutely stay the hand of U.S.A. war criminals," Ho Chi Minh wrote letters to President Radhakrishnan of India, Prime Minister Pearson of Canada, and the leaders of Poland and other socialist countries.[52] Ho called attention "to the war of aggression waged by U.S.A. imperialists in our country, Vietnam." He accused the United States of "seriously sabotaging the 1954 Geneva Agreement and preventing the peaceful reunification of Vietnam in an attempt to turn South Vietnam into a U.S.A. new-type colony and military base." Attention was also directed to the fact that the Americans had launched a "scorched earth" policy of air strikes against the independent country of North Vietnam. Peace, he wrote, could be achieved only if, upon unconditional and permanent cessation of its bombing raids, the United States entered into negotiations with the NLF, "the sole genuine representative of the people of South Vietnam." But because "real peace can by no means be dissociated from genuine independence," the Vietnamese would continue to fight as long as there were American troops in Vietnam. He concluded by pointing out that Canada was a member of the ICSC: "In face of the extremely serious situation brought about by the U.S.A. in Vietnam, I hope that your Government will fulfill its obligation under the Geneva Agreements."

Pearson replied by letter on 28 February. In a brief statement, he expressed concern over "the tragic toll in human suffering and the threat to international peace which the continuation of the conflict in Vietnam involves." He reiterated the Canadian stand that "the use of force is not an acceptable means of attaining political objectives," and hoped that unconditional discussions could be started in Vietnam. As a member of the ICSC, "Canada has at all times endeavoured to carry out its obligations in a spirit of objectivity and impartiality towards the facts as we know them." Pearson concluded by expressing a willingness "to explore all possibilities that may be open to the Commission in present circumstances to exert its efforts in the direction of peace."

An important feature of Pearson's letter is his admission that differences existed in Canadian and Vietnamese perceptions: "*You will not expect me to share the interpretation of the nature of the problem in Vietnam and the origins of the present conflict which is set forth in your letter.*"[53] The corresponding statement for India, were one to be made, would be almost exactly the opposite. Because of European colonialism in Asia, India could be expected to accept the nature of the Vietnamese problem and the 1966 conflict in the terms set forth in Ho Chi Minh's letter. India's approach to Western international behavior has been conditioned by its own experience of imperialism, colonialism, and racial discrimination. Consequently, India quite understandably profoundly distrusted the West. India also deeply resented its past exclusion from the conduct of international affairs. On the positive side, the experience-cum-resentment of the past were translated into the policy objectives of eradicating imperialism and colonialism, while securing for India and Asia a larger role in world affairs and a predominant voice in Asian affairs. As Ton Thien expressed it, India's twin objectives in Asia *vis-à-vis* the West were the termination of Western rule and the elimination of Western influence.[54]

The respective North American and Asian perspectives have been constant undercurrents in Canadian and Indian foreign policies. They have shaped their relations with the great powers, and determined their attitudes and guided their actions toward Vietnam. The Canadian lack of understanding of the basic difference in approach is surprising. When Pearson was in India in 1950, he sensed the "pathological" loathing and abhorrence among Asian countries of colonialism "in any form in any part of the world. There were a great many in Asia who would, in fact, have preferred communism to colonialism, if they had to make a choice."[55]

Similarly, at the start of the ICSC experience, Sherwood Lett's letter of instructions had clearly informed him that Indian foreign policy differed radically in many important respects from Canadian foreign policy. Ultimate objectives were similar, in that both wished to avoid a general war and to see former dependencies acquire free, as opposed to communist, self-government. Indo-Canadian differences lay largely in the choice of means to achieve these ends. On colonialism particularly, Lett was told, Indian opposition could be "irrational." External Affairs in Ottawa hoped that India's experience in dealing with the Poles and the Vietminh would make it more sympathetic to Canadian and allied policies.[56]

As it turned out, Indo-Canadian rather than Indo-Polish relations fell victim to the ICSC experience. If, however, to paraphrase Richard Nixon's 1972 statement in the Canadian Parliament,[57] the Indochina experience has contributed to a more mature relationship between India and Canada, based on a recognition of significant differences and separate identities, then it may have served yet another useful if unintended purpose.

Appendix I
Geneva Conference on Indo-China

A. Agreement on the Cessation of Hostilities in Viet Nam

July 20, 1954

Chapter I

Provisional Military Demarcation Line and Demilitarised Zone

Article 1

A provisional military demarcation line shall be fixed, on either side of which the forces of the two parties shall be regrouped after their withdrawal, the forces of the People's Army of Viet Nam to the north of the line and the forces of the French Union to the south.

The provisional military demarcation line is fixed as shown on the map attached (see Map No. 1).*

It is also agreed that a demilitarised zone shall be established on either side of the demarcation line, to a width of not more than 5 kms. from it, to act as a buffer zone and avoid any incidents which might result in the resumption of hostilities.

Article 2

The period within which the movement of all forces of either party into its regrouping zone on either side of the provisional military demarcation line shall be completed shall not exceed three hundred (300) days from the date of the present Agreement's entry into force.

---

*Map not printed—see Annex for details.

Article 3

When the provisional military demarcation line coincides with a waterway, the waters of such waterway shall be open to civil navigation by both parties wherever one bank is controlled by one party and the other bank by the other party. The Joint Commission shall establish rules of navigation for the stretch of waterway in question. The merchant shipping and other civilian craft of each party shall have unrestricted access to the land under its military control.

Article 4

The provisional military demarcation line between the two final regrouping zones is extended into the territorial waters by a line perpendicular to the general line of the coast.

All coastal islands north of this boundary shall be evacuated by the armed forces of the French Union, and all islands south of it shall be evacuated by the forces of the People's Army of Viet Nam.

Article 5

To avoid any incidents which might result in the resumption of hostilities, all military forces, supplies and equipment shall be withdrawn from the demilitarised zone within twenty-five (25) days of the present Agreement's entry into force.

Article 6

No person, military or civilian, shall be permitted to cross the provisional military demarcation line unless specifically authorised to do so by the Joint Commission.

Article 7

No person, military or civilian, shall be permitted to enter the demilitarised zone except persons concerned with the conduct of civil administration and relief and persons specifically authorised to enter by the Joint Commission.

Article 8

Civil administration and relief in the demilitarised zone on either side of the provisional military demarcation line shall be the responsibility of the Commanders-in-Chief of the two parties in their respective zones. The number of persons, military or civilian, from each side who are permitted to enter the demilitarised zone for the conduct of civil administration and relief shall be determined by the respective Commanders, but in no case shall the total number authorised by either side exceed at any one time a figure to be determined by the Trung Gia Military Commission or by the Joint Commission. The number of civil police and the arms to be carried by them shall be determined by the Joint Commission. No one else shall carry arms unless specifically authorised to do so by the Joint Commission.

Article 9

Nothing contained in this chapter shall be construed as limiting the complete freedom of movement, into, out of or within the demilitarised zone, of the Joint Commission, its joint groups, the International Commission to be set up as indicated below, its inspection teams and any other persons, supplies or equipment specifically authorised to enter the demilitarised zone by the Joint Commission. Freedom of movement shall be permitted across the territory under the military control of either side over any road or waterway which has to be taken between points within the demilitarised zone when such points are not connected by roads or waterways lying completely within the demilitarised zone.

CHAPTER II
Principles and procedure governing implementation of the present agreement

Article 10

The Commanders of the Forces on each side, on the one side the Commander-in-Chief of the French Union forces in Indo-China and on the other side the Commander-in-Chief of the People's Army of Viet Nam, shall order and enforce the complete cessation of all hostilities in Viet Nam by all armed forces under their control, including all units and personnel of the ground, naval and air forces.

Article 11

In accordance with the principle of a simultaneous cease-fire throughout Indo-China, the cessation of hostilities shall be simultaneous throughout all parts of Viet Nam, in all areas of hostilities and for all the forces of the two parties.

Taking into account the time effectively required to transmit the cease-fire order down to the lowest échelons of the combatant forces on both sides, the two parties are agreed that the cease-fire shall take effect completely and simultaneously for the different sectors of the country as follows: —

Northern Viet Nam at 8:00 a.m. (local time) on July 27, 1954.
Central Viet Nam at 8:00 a.m. (local time) on August 1, 1954.
Southern Viet Nam at 8:00 a.m. (local time) on August 11, 1954.

It is agreed that Peking mean time shall be taken as local time.

From such time as the cease-fire becomes effective in Northern Viet Nam, both parties undertake not to engage in any large-scale offensive action in any part of the Indo-Chinese theatre of operations and not to commit the air forces based on Northern Viet Nam outside that sector. The two parties also undertake to inform each other of their plans for movement from one regrouping zone to another within twenty-five (25) days of the present Agreement's entry into force.

Article 12

All the operations and movements entailed in the cessation of hostilities and regrouping must proceed in a safe and orderly fashion: —

(a) Within a certain number of days after the cease-fire Agreement shall have become effective, the number to be determined on the spot by the Trung Gia Military Commission, each party shall be responsible for removing and neutralising mines (including river- and sea-mines), booby traps, explosives and any other dangerous substances placed by it. In the event of its being impossible to complete the work of removal and neutralisation in time, the party concerned shall mark the spot by placing visible signs there. All demolitions, mine fields, wire entanglements and other hazards to the free movement of the personnel of the Joint Commission and its joint groups known to be present after the withdrawal of the military forces, shall be reported to the Joint Commission by the Commanders of the opposing forces;

(b) From the time of the cease-fire until regrouping is completed on either side of the demarcation line: —

(1) The forces of either party shall be provisionally withdrawn from the provisional assembly areas assigned to the other party.

(2) When one party's forces withdraw by a route (road, rail, waterway, sea route) which passes through the territory of the other party (see Article 24), the latter party's forces must provisionally withdraw three kilometres on each side of such route, but in such a manner as to avoid interfering with the movements of the civil population.

Article 13

From the time of the cease-fire until the completion of the movements from one regrouping zone into the other, civil and military transport aircraft shall follow air-corridors between the provisional assembly areas assigned to the French Union forces north of the demarcation line on the one hand and the Laotian frontier and the regrouping zone assigned to the French Union forces on the other hand.

The position of the air-corridors, their width, the safety route for single-engined military aircraft transferred to the south and the search and rescue procedure for aircraft in distress shall be determined on the spot by the Trung Gia Military Commission.

Article 14

Political and administrative measures in the two regrouping zones, on either side of the provisional military demarcation line: —

- (a) Pending the general elections which will bring about the unification of Viet Nam, the conduct of civil administration in each regrouping zone shall be in the hands of the party whose forces are to be regrouped there in virtue of the present Agreement.
- (b) Any territory controlled by one party which is transferred to the other party by the regrouping plan shall continue to be administered by the former party until such date as all the troops who are to be transferred have completely left that territory so as to free the zone assigned to the party in question. From then on, such territory shall be regarded as transferred to the other party, who shall assume responsibility for it.

  Steps shall be taken to ensure that there is no break in the transfer of responsibilities. For this purpose, adequate notice shall be given by the withdrawing party to the other party, which shall make the necessary arrangements, in particular by sending administrative and police detachments to prepare for the assumption of administrative responsibility. The length of such notice shall be determined by the Trung Gia Military Commission. The transfer shall be effected in successive stages for the various territorial sectors.

  The transfer of the civil administration of Hanoi and Haiphong to the authorities of the Democratic Republic of Viet Nam shall be completed within the respective time-limits laid down in Article 15 for military movements.
- (c) Each party undertakes to refrain from any reprisals or discrimination against persons or organisations on account of their activities during the hostilities and to guarantee their democratic liberties.
- (d) From the date of entry into force of the present Agreement until the movement of troops is completed, any civilians residing in a district controlled by one party who wish to go and live in the zone assigned to the other party shall be permitted and helped to do so by the authorities in that district.

Article 15

The disengagement of the combatants, and the withdrawals and transfers of military forces, equipment and supplies shall take place in accordance with the following principles: —

(a) The withdrawals and transfers of the military forces, equipment and supplies of the two parties shall be completed within three hundred (300) days, as laid down in Article 2 of the present Agreement;

(b) Within either territory successive withdrawals shall be made by sectors, portions of sectors or provinces. Transfers from one regrouping zone to another shall be made in successive monthly instalments proportionate to the number of troops to be transferred;

(c) The two parties shall undertake to carry out all troop withdrawals and transfers in accordance with the aims of the present Agreement, shall permit no hostile act and shall take no step whatsoever which might hamper such withdrawals and transfers. They shall assist one another as far as this is possible;

(d) The two parties shall permit no destruction or sabotage of any public property and no injury to the life and property of the civil population. They shall permit no interference in local civil administration;

(e) The Joint Commission and the International Commission shall ensure that steps are taken to safeguard the forces in the course of withdrawal and transfer;

(f) The Trung Gia Military Commission, and later the Joint Commission, shall determine by common agreement the exact procedure for the disengagement of the combatants and for troop withdrawals and transfers, on the basis of the principles mentioned above and within the framework laid down below: —

1. The disengagement of the combatants, including the concentration of the armed forces of all kinds and also each party's movements into the provisional assembly areas assigned to it and the other party's provisional withdrawal from it, shall be completed within a period not exceeding fifteen (15) days after the date when the cease-fire becomes effective.

The general delineation of the provisional assembly areas is set out in the maps* annexed to present Agreement.

In order to avoid any incidents, no troops shall be stationed less than 1,500 metres from the lines delimiting the provisional assembly areas.

During the period until the transfers are concluded, all the coastal islands west of the following lines shall be included in the Haiphong perimeter:

meridian of the southern point of Kebao Island,

---

*Maps not printed — see Annex for details.

northern coast of Ile Rousse (excluding the island), extended as far as the meridian of Campha-Mines,
meridian of Campha-Mines.

2. The withdrawals and transfers shall be effected in the following order and within the following periods (from the date of the entry into force of the present Agreement):—

Forces of the French Union

Hanoi perimeter	80 days
Haiduong perimeter	100 days
Haiphong perimeter	300 days

Forces of the People's Army of Viet Nam

Ham Tan and Xuyenmoc provisional assembly area	80 days
Central Viet Nam provisional assembly area—first instalment	80 days
Plaine des Joncs provisional assembly area	100 days
Central Viet Nam provisional assembly area—second instalment	100 days
Pointe Camau provisional assembly area	200 days
Central Viet Nam provisional assembly area—last instalment	300 days

CHAPTER III

Ban on the introduction of fresh troops, military personnel, arms and munitions. Military bases

Article 16

With effect from the date of entry into force of the present Agreement, the introduction into Viet Nam of any troop reinforcements and additional military personnel is prohibited.

It is understood, however, that the rotation of units and groups of personnel, the arrival in Viet Nam of individual personnel on a temporary duty basis and the return to Viet Nam of the individual personnel after short periods of leave or temporary duty outside Viet Nam shall be permitted under the conditions laid down below:—

(a) Rotation of units (defined in paragraph (c) of this Article) and groups of personnel shall not be permitted for French Union troops stationed north of the provisional military demarcation line laid down in Article 1 of the present Agreement during the withdrawal period provided for in Article 2.

However, under the heading of individual personnel not more than fifty (50) men, including officers, shall during any one month be permitted to enter that part of the country north of the provisional military demarcation line on a temporary duty basis or to return there after short periods of leave or temporary duty outside Viet Nam.

(b) "Rotation" is defined as the replacement of units or groups of personnel by other units of the same échelon or by personnel who are arriving in Viet Nam territory to do their overseas service there;

(c) The units rotated shall never be larger than a battalion—or the corresponding échelon for air and naval forces;

(d) Rotation shall be conducted on a man-for-man basis, provided, however, that in any one quarter neither party shall introduce more than fifteen thousand five hundred (15,500) members of its armed forces into Viet Nam under the rotation policy.

(e) Rotation units (defined in paragraph (c) of this Article) and groups of personnel, and the individual personnel mentioned in this article, shall enter and leave Viet Nam only through the entry points enumerated in Article 20 below;

(f) Each party shall notify the Joint Commission and the International Commission at least two days in advance of any arrivals or departures of units, groups of personnel and individual personnel in or from Viet Nam. Reports on the arrivals or departures of units, groups of personnel and individual personnel in or from Viet Nam shall be submitted daily to the Joint Commission and the International Commission.

All the above-mentioned notifications and reports shall indicate the places and dates of arrival or departure and the number of persons arriving or departing;

(g) The International Commission, through its Inspection Teams, shall supervise and inspect the rotation of units and groups of personnel and the arrival and departure of individual personnel as authorised above, at the points of entry enumerated in Article 20 below.

Article 17

(a) With effect from the date of entry into force of the present Agreement, the introduction into Viet Nam of any reinforcements in the form of all types of arms, munitions and other war material, such as combat aircraft, naval craft, pieces of ordnance, jet engines and jet weapons and armoured vehicles, is prohibited.

(b) It is understood, however, that war material, arms and munitions which have been destroyed, damaged, worn out or used up after the cessation of hostilities may be replaced on the basis of piece-for-piece of the same type and with similar characteristics. Such replacements of war material, arms and ammunitions shall not be permitted for French Union troops stationed north of the provisional military demarcation line laid down in Article 1 of the present Agreement, during the withdrawal period provided for in Article 2.

Naval craft may perform transport operations between the regrouping zones.

(c) The war material, arms and munitions for replacement purposes provided for in paragraph (b) of this Article, shall be introduced into Viet Nam only through the points of entry enumerated in Article 20 below. War material, arms and munitions to be replaced shall be shipped from Viet Nam only through the points of entry enumerated in Article 20 below.

(d) Apart from the replacements permitted within the limits laid down in paragraph (b) of this Article, the introduction of war material, arms and munitions of all types in the form of unassembled parts for subsequent assembly is prohibited.

(e) Each party shall notify the Joint Commission and the International Commission at least two days in advance of any arrivals or departures which may take place of war material, arms and munitions of all types.

In order to justify the requests for the introduction into Viet Nam of arms, munitions and other war material (as defined in paragraph (a) of this Article) for replacement purposes, a report concerning each incoming shipment shall be submitted to the Joint Commission and the International Commission. Such reports shall indicate the use made of the items so replaced.

(f) The International Commission, through its Inspection Teams, shall supervise and inspect the replacements permitted in the circumstances laid down in this Article, at the points of entry enumerated in Article 20 below.

Article 18

With effect from the date of entry into force of the present Agreement, the establishment of new military bases is prohibited throughout Viet Nam territory.

Article 19

With effect from the date of entry into force of the present Agreement, no military base under the control of a foreign State may be established in the re-grouping zone of either party; the two parties shall ensure that the zones assigned to them do not adhere to any military alliance and are not used for the resumption of hostilities or to further an aggressive policy.

Article 20

The points of entry into Viet Nam for rotation personnel and replacements of material are fixed as follows: —

- Zones to the north of the provisional military demarcation line: Lao-kay, Langson, Tien-Yen, Haiphong, Vinh, Dong-Hoi, Muong-Sen;
- Zone to the south of the provisional military demarcation line: Tourane, Quinhon, Nhatrang, Bangoi, Saigon, Cap St. Jacques, Tanchau.

CHAPTER IV

Prisoners of War and Civilian Internees

Article 21

The liberation and repatriation of all prisoners of war and civilian internees detained by each of the two parties at the coming into force of the present Agreement shall be carried out under the following conditions: —

(*a*) All prisoners of war and civilian internees of Viet Nam, French and other nationalities captured since the beginning of hostilities in Viet Nam during military operations or in any other circumstances of war and in any part of the territory of Viet Nam shall be liberated within a period of thirty (30) days after the date when the cease-fire becomes effective in each theatre.

(*b*) The term "civilian internees" is understood to mean all persons who, having in any way contributed to the political and armed struggle between the two parties, have been arrested for that reason and have been kept in detention by either party during the period of hostilities.

(*c*) All prisoners of war and civilian internees held by either party shall be surrendered to the appropriate authorities of the other party, who shall give them all possible assistance in proceeding to their country of origin, place of habitual residence or the zone of their choice.

CHAPTER V

Miscellaneous

Article 22

The Commanders of the Forces of the two parties shall ensure that persons under their respective commands who violate any of the provisions of the present Agreement are suitably punished.

Article 23

In cases in which the place of burial is known and the existence of graves has been established, the Commander of the Forces of either party shall, within a specific period after the entry into force of the Armistice Agreement, permit the graves service personnel of the other party to enter the part of Viet Nam territory under their military control for the purpose of finding and removing the bodies of deceased military personnel of that party, including the bodies of deceased prisoners of war. The Joint Commission shall determine the procedures and the time limit for the performance of this task. The Commanders of the Forces of the two parties shall communicate to each other all information in their possession as to the place of burial of military personnel of the other party.

Article 24

The present Agreement shall apply to all the armed forces of either party. The armed forces of each party shall respect the demilitarised zone and the territory under the military control of the other party, and shall commit no act and undertake no operation against the other party and shall not engage in blockade of any kind in Viet Nam.

For the purposes of the present Article, the word "territory" includes territorial waters and air space.

Article 25

The Commanders of the Forces of the two parties shall afford full protection and all possible assistance and co-operation to the Joint Commission and its joint groups and to the International Commission and its inspection teams in the performance of the functions and tasks assigned to them by the present Agreement.

Article 26

The costs involved in the operations of the Joint Commission and joint groups and of the International Commission and its Inspection Teams shall be shared equally between the two parties.

Article 27

The signatories of the present Agreement and their successors in their functions shall be responsible for ensuring the observance and enforcement of the terms and provisions thereof. The Commanders of the Forces of the two parties shall, within their respective commands, take all steps and make all arrangements necessary to ensure full compliance with all the provisions of the present Agreement by all elements and military personnel under their command.

The procedures laid down in the present Agreement shall, whenever necessary, be studied by the Commanders of the two parties and, if necessary, defined more specifically by the Joint Commission.

Chapter VI

Joint Commission and International Commission for for Supervision and Control in Viet Nam

Article 28

Responsibility for the execution of the agreement on the cessation of hostilities shall rest with the parties.

Article 29

An International Commission shall ensure the control and supervision of this execution.

Article 30

In order to facilitate, under the conditions shown below, the execution of provisions concerning joint actions by the two parties, a Joint Commission shall be set up in Viet Nam.

Article 31

The Joint Commission shall be composed of an equal number of representatives of the Commanders of the two parties.

Article 32

The Presidents of the delegations to the Joint Commission shall hold the rank of General.

The Joint Commission shall set up joint groups, the number of which shall be determined by mutual agreement between the parties. The joint groups shall be composed of an equal number of officers from both parties. Their location on the demarcation line between the re-grouping zones shall be determined by the parties whilst taking into account the powers of the Joint Commission.

Article 33

The Joint Commission shall ensure the execution of the following provisions of the Agreement on the cessation of hostilities: —

(*a*) A simultaneous and general cease-fire in Viet Nam for all regular and irregular armed forces of the two parties.
(*b*) A re-groupment of the armed forces of the two parties.
(*c*) Observance of the demarcation lines between the re-grouping zones and of the demilitarised sectors.

Within the limits of its competence it shall help the parties to execute the said provisions, shall ensure liaison between them for the purpose of preparing and carrying out plans for the application of these provisions, and shall endeavour to solve such disputed questions as may arise between the parties in the course of executing these provisions.

Article 34

An International Commission shall be set up for the control and supervision over the application of the provisions of the agreement on the cessation of hostilities in Viet Nam. It shall be composed of representatives of the following States: Canada, India and Poland.

It shall be presided over by the Representative of India.

Article 35

The International Commission shall set up fixed and mobile inspection teams, composed of an equal number of officers appointed by each of the above-mentioned States. The fixed teams shall be located at the following points: Laokay, Langson, Tien-Yen, Haiphong, Vinh, Dong-Hoi, Muong-Sen, Tourane, Quinhon, Nhatrang, Bangoi, Saigon, Cap St. Jacques, Tranchau. These points of location may, at a later date, be altered at the request of the Joint Commission, or of one of the parties, or of the International Commission itself, by agreement between the International Commission and the command of the party concerned. The zones of action of the mobile teams shall be the regions bordering the land and sea frontiers of Viet Nam, the demarcation lines between the re-grouping zones and the demilitarised zones. Within the limits of these zones they shall have the right to move freely and shall receive from the local civil and military authorities all facilities they may require for the fulfilment of their tasks (provision of personnel, placing at their disposal documents needed for supervision, summoning witnesses necessary for holding enquiries, ensuring the security and freedom of movement of the inspection teams, &c. . . .). They shall have at their disposal such modern means of transport, observation and communication as they may require. Beyond the zones of action as defined above, the mobile teams may, by agreement with the command of the party concerned, carry out other movements within the limits of the tasks given them by the present agreement.

Article 36

The International Commission shall be responsible for supervising the proper execution by the parties of the provisions of the agreement. For this purpose it shall fulfil the tasks of control, observation, inspection and investigation connected with the application of the provisions of the agreement on the cessation of hostilities, and it shall in particular: —

(a) Control the movement of the armed forces of the two parties, effected within the framework of the regroupment plan.
(b) Supervise the demarcation lines between the regrouping areas, and also the demilitarised zones.
(c) Control the operations of releasing prisoners of war and civilian internees.
(d) Supervise at ports and airfields as well as along all frontiers of Viet Nam the execution of the provisions of the agreement on the cessation of hostilities, regulating the introduction into the country of armed forces, military personnel and of all kinds of arms, munitions and war material.

Article 37

The International Commission shall, through the medium of the inspection teams mentioned above, and as soon as possible either on its own initiative, or at the request of the Joint Commission, or of one of the parties, undertake the necessary investigations both documentary and on the ground.

Article 38

The inspection teams shall submit to the International Commission the results of their supervision, their investigation and their observations, furthermore they shall draw up such special reports as they may consider necessary or as may be requested from them by the Commission. In the case of a disagreement within the teams, the conclusions of each member shall be submitted to the Commission.

Article 39

If any one inspection team is unable to settle an incident or considers that there is a violation or a threat of a serious violation, the International

Commission shall be informed; the latter shall study the reports and the conclusions of the inspection teams and shall inform the parties of the measures which should be taken for the settlement of the incident, ending of the violation or removal of the threat of violation.

Article 40

When the Joint Commission is unable to reach an agreement on the interpretation to be given to some provision or on the appraisal of a fact, the International Commission shall be informed of the disputed question. Its recommendations shall be sent directly to the parties and shall be notified to the Joint Commission.

Article 41

The recommendations of the International Commission shall be adopted by majority vote, subject to the provisions contained in Article 42. If the votes are divided, the chairman's vote shall be decisive.

The International Commission may formulate recommendations concerning amendments and additions which should be made to the provisions of the agreement on the cessation of hostilities in Viet Nam, in order to ensure a more effective execution of that agreement. These recommendations shall be adopted unanimously.

Article 42

When dealing with questions concerning violations, or threats of violations, which might lead to a resumption of hostilities, namely: —

(a) Refusal by the armed forces of one party to effect the movements provided for in the regroupment plan;
(b) Violation by the armed forces of one of the parties of the regrouping zones, territorial waters, or air space of the other party;

the decisions of the International Commission must be unanimous.

Article 43

If one of the parties refuses to put into effect a recommendation of the International Commission, the parties concerned or the Commission itself shall inform the members of the Geneva Conference.

If the International Commission does not reach unanimity in the cases provided for in Article 42, it shall submit a majority report and one or more minority reports to the members of the Conference.

The International Commission shall inform the members of the Conference in all cases where its activity is being hindered.

Article 44

The International Commission shall be set up at the time of the cessation of hostilities in Indo-China in order that it should be able to fulfil the tasks provided for in Article 36.

Article 45

The International Commission for Supervision and Control in Viet Nam shall act in close co-operation with the International Commissions for Supervision and Control in Cambodia and Laos.

The Secretaries-General of these three Commissions shall be responsible for co-ordinating their work and for relations between them.

Article 46

The International Commission for Supervision and Control in Viet Nam may, after consultation with the International Commissions for Supervision and Control in Cambodia and Laos, and having regard to the development of the situation in Cambodia and Laos, progressively reduce its activities. Such a decision must be adopted unanimously.

Article 47

All the provisions of the present Agreement, save the second sub-paragraph of Article 11, shall enter into force at 2400 hours (Geneva time) on July 22, 1954.

Done in Geneva at 2400 hours on the 20th of July, 1954, in French and in Vietnamese, both texts being equally authentic.

> For the Commander-in-Chief of the French Union Forces in Indo-China:
> DELTIEL,
> Brigadier-General.

> For the Commander-in-Chief of the People's Army of Viet Nam:
> TA-QUANG-BUU,
> Vice-Minister of National Defence
> of the Democratic Republic of Viet Nam.

Annex to the Agreement on the Cessation of Hostilities in Viet Nam

I. —*Delineation of the provisional military demarcation line and the demilitarised zone* (Article 1 of the Agreement; reference map: Indo-China 1/100,000)

(*a*) The provisional military demarcation line is fixed as follows, reading from east to west:—
The mouth of the Song Ben Hat (Cua Tung River) and the course of that river (known as the Rao Thanh in the mountains) to the village of Bo Ho Su, then the parallel of Bo Ho Su to the Laos-Viet Nam frontier.

(*b*) The demilitarised zone shall be delimited by Trung Gia Military Commission in accordance with the provisions of Article 1 of the Agreement on the cessation of hostilities in Viet Nam.

II.—*General delineation of the provisional assembly areas* (Article 15 of the Agreement; reference maps: Indo-China 1/400,000)

(a) North Viet Nam

Delineation of the Boundary of the Provisional Assembly Area of the French Union Forces

1. The perimeter of Hanoi is delimited by the arc of a circle with a radius of 15 kilometres, having as its centre the right bank abutment of Doumer Bridge and running westwards from the Red River to the Rapids Canal in the north-east.

   In this particular case no forces of the French Union shall be stationed less than 2 kilometres from this perimeter, on the inside thereof.

2. The perimeter of Haiphong shall be delimited by the Song-Van Uc as far as Kim Thanh and a line running from the Song-Van-Uc three kilometres north-east of Kim Thanh to cut Road No. 18 two kilometres east of Mao-Khé. Thence a line running three kilometres north of Road 18 to Cho-Troi and a straight line from Cho-Troi to the Mong-Duong ferry.

3. *A corridor contained between:*
   In the south, the Red River from Thanh-Tri to Bang-Nho, thence a line joining the latter point to Do-My (south-west of Kesat), Gia-Loc and Tien Kieu;
   In the north, a line running along the Rapids Canal at a distance 1,500 metres to the north of the Canal, passing three kilometres north of Pha-Lai and Seven Pagodas and thence parallel to Road No. 18 to its point of intersection with the perimeter of Haiphong.

Note. —Throughout the period of evacuation of the perimeter of Hanoi, the river forces of the French Union shall enjoy complete freedom of movement on the Song-Van-Uc. And the forces of the People's Army of Viet Nam shall withdraw three kilometres south of the south bank of the Song-Van-Uc.

Boundary between the perimeter of Hanoi and the perimeter of Haiduong
A straight line running from the Rapids Canal three kilometres west of Chi-ne and ending at Do-My (eight kilometres south-west of Kesat).

(b) Central Viet Nam

Delineation of the Boundary of the Provisional Assembly Area of the Forces of the Viet Nam People's Army South of the Col des Nuages Parallel

The perimeter of the Central Viet Nam area shall consist of the administrative boundaries of the provinces of Quang-Ngai and Binh-Dinh as they were defined before the hostilities.

(c) South Viet Nam

Three provisional assembly areas shall be provided for the forces of the People's Army of Viet Nam.

The boundaries of these areas are as follows: —

1. *Xuyen-Moc, Ham-Tan Area*—
    Western boundary: The course of the Song-Ray extended northwards as far as Road No. 1 to a point thereon eight kilometres east of the intersection of Road No. 1 and Road No. 3.
    Northern boundary: Road No. 1 from the above-mentioned intersection to the intersection with Route Communale No. 9 situated 27 kilometres west-south-west of Phanthiet and from that intersection a straight line to Kim Thanh on the coast.

2. *Plaine des Joncs Area*—
    Northern boundary: The Viet Nam-Cambodia frontier.
    Western boundary: A straight line from Tong-Binh to Binh-Thanh.
    Southern boundary: Course of the Fleuve Antérieur (Mekong) to ten kilometres south-east of Cao Lanh. From that point, a straight line as far as Ap-My-Dien, and from Ap-My-Dien a line parallel to and three kilometres east and then south of the Tong Doc-Loc Canal, this line reaches My-Hanh-Dong and thence Hung-Thanh-My.
    Eastern boundary: A straight line from Hung-Thanh-My running northwards to the Cambodian frontier south of Doi-Bao-Voi.

3. *Point Camau Area*—
    Northern boundary: The Song-Cai-lon from its mouth to its junction with the Rach-Nuoc-Trong, thence the Rach-Nuoc-Trong to the bend five kilometres north-east of Ap-Xeo-La. Thereafter a line to the Ngan-Dua Canal and following that Canal as far as Vinh-Hung. Finally, from Vinh-Hung a north-south line to the sea.

B. Final Declaration of the Geneva Conference on the problem of restoring peace in Indo-China, in which the representatives of Cambodia, the Democratic Republic of Viet Nam, France, Laos, the People's Republic of China, the State of Viet Nam, the Union of Soviet Socialist Republics, the United Kingdom and the United States of America took part

July 21, 1954

1. The Conference takes note of the agreements ending hostilities in Cambodia, Laos and Viet Nam and organising international control and the supervision of the execution of the provisions of these agreements.
2. The Conference expresses satisfaction at the ending of hostilities in Cambodia, Laos and Viet Nam; the Conference expresses its conviction that the execution of the provisions set out in the present declaration and in the agreements on the cessation of hostilities will permit Cambodia, Laos and Viet Nam henceforth to play their part, in full independence and sovereignty, in the peaceful community of nations.
3. The Conference takes note of the declarations made by the Governments of Cambodia and of Laos of their intention to adopt measures permitting all citizens to take their place in the national community, in particular by participating in the next general elections, which, in comformity with the constitution of each of these countries, shall take place in the course of the year 1955, by secret ballot and in conditions of respect for fundamental freedoms.
4. The Conference takes note of the clauses in the agreement on the cessation of hostilities in Viet Nam prohibiting the introduction into Viet Nam of foreign troops and military personnel as well as of all kinds of arms and munitions. The Conference also takes note of the declarations made by the Governments of Cambodia and Laos of their resolution not to request foreign aid, whether in war material, in personnel or in instructors except for the purpose of the effective defence of their territory and, in the case of Laos, to the extent defined by the agreements on the cessation of hostilities in Laos.
5. The Conference takes note of the clauses in the agreement on the cessation of hostilities in Viet Nam to the effect that no military base under the control of a foreign State may be established in the regrouping zones of the two parties, the latter having the obligation to see that the zones allotted to them shall not constitute part of any military alliance and shall not be utilised for the resumption of hostilities or in the service of an aggressive policy.

The Conference also takes note of the declarations of the Governments of Cambodia and Laos to the effect that they will not join in any agreement with other States if this agreement includes the obligation to participate in a military alliance not in conformity with the principles of the Charter of the United Nations or, in the case of Laos, with the principles of the agreement on the cessation of hostilities in Laos or, so long as their security is not threatened, the obligation to establish bases on Cambodian or Laotian territory for the military forces of foreign Powers.

6. The Conference recognises that the essential purpose of the agreement relating to Viet Nam is to settle military questions with a view to ending hostilities and that the military demarcation line is provisional and should not in any way be interpreted as constituting a political or territorial boundary. The Conference expresses its conviction that the execution of the provisions set out in the present declaration and in the agreement on the cessation of hostilities creates the necessary basis for the achievement in the near future of a political settlement in Viet Nam.

7. The Conference declares that, so far as Viet Nam is concerned, the settlement of political problems, effected on the basis of respect for the principles of independence, unity and territorial integrity, shall permit the Vietnamese people to enjoy the fundamental freedoms, guaranteed by democratic institutions established as a result of free general elections by secret ballot. In order to ensure that sufficient progress in the restoration of peace has been made, and that all the necessary conditions obtain for free expression of the national will, general elections shall be held in July 1956, under the supervision of an international commission composed of representatives of the Member States of the International Supervisory Commission, referred to in the agreement on the cessation of hostilities. Consultations will be held on this subject between the competent representative authorities of the two zones from July 20, 1955, onwards.

8. The provisions of the agreements on the cessation of hostilities intended to ensure the protection of individuals and of property must be most strictly applied and must, in particular, allow everyone in Viet Nam to decide freely in which zone he wishes to live.

9. The competent representative authorities of the Northern and Southern zones of Viet Nam, as well as the authorities of Laos and Cambodia, must not permit any individual or collective reprisals against persons who have collaborated in any way with one of the parties during the war, or against members of such persons' families.

10. The Conference takes note of the declaration of the Government

of the French Republic to the effect that it is ready to withdraw its troops from the territory of Cambodia, Laos and Viet Nam, at the request of the Governments concerned and within periods which shall be fixed by agreement between the parties except in the cases where, by agreement between the two parties, a certain number of French troops shall remain at specified points and for a specified time.

11. The Conference takes note of the declaration of the French Government to the effect that for the settlement of all the problems connected with the re-establishment and consolidation of peace in Cambodia, Laos and Viet Nam, the French Government will proceed from the principle of respect for the independence and sovereignty, unity and territorial integrity of Cambodia, Laos and Viet Nam.
12. In their relations with Cambodia, Laos and Viet Nam, each member of the Geneva Conference undertakes to respect the sovereignty, the independence, the unity and the territorial integrity of the above-mentioned States, and to refrain from any interference in their internal affairs.
13. The members of the Conference agree to consult one another on any question which may be referred to them by the International Supervisory Commission, in order to study such measures as may prove necessary to ensure that the agreements on the cessation of hostilities in Cambodia, Laos and Viet Nam are respected.

C. United States Declaration

July 21, 1954

The Government of the United States being resolved to devote its efforts to the strengthening of peace in accordance with the principles and purposes of the United Nations

Takes Note

of the Agreements concluded at Geneva on July 20 and 21, 1954, between (*a*) the Franco-Laotian Command and the Command of the People's Army of Viet Nam; (*b*) the Royal Khmer Army Command and the Command of the People's Army of Viet Nam; (*c*) Franco-Vietnamese Command and the Command of the People's Army of Viet Nam, and of paragraphs 1 to 12 of the Declaration presented to the Geneva Conference on July 21, 1954.

The Government of the United States of America

Declares with regard to the aforesaid Agreements and paragraphs that (i) it will refrain from the threat or the use of force to disturb them, in accordance with Article 2 (Section 4) of the Charter of the United Nations dealing with the obligation of Members to refrain in their international relations from the threat or use of force; and (ii) it would view any renewal of the aggression in violation of the aforesaid Agreements with grave concern and as seriously threatening international peace and security.

In connexion with the statement in the Declaration concerning free elections in Viet Nam, my Government wishes to make clear its position which it has expressed in a Declaration made in Washington on June 29, 1954, as follows: —

> "In the case of nations now divided against their will, we shall continue to seek to achieve unity through free elections, supervised by the United Nations to ensure that they are conducted fairly."

With respect to the statement made by the Representative of the State of Viet Nam, the United States reiterates its traditional position that peoples are entitled to determine their own future and that it will not join in an arrangement which would hinder this. Nothing in its declaration just made is intended to or does indicate any departure from this traditional position.

We share the hope that the agreement will permit Cambodia, Laos and Viet Nam to play their part in full independence and sovereignty, in the peaceful community of nations, and will enable the peoples of that area to determine their own future.

Thank you, Mr. Chairman.

D. Declaration by the Government of the French Republic

July 21, 1954

(Reference: Article 10 of the Final Declaration)

The Government of the French Republic declares that it is ready to withdraw its troops from the territory of Cambodia, Laos and Viet Nam, at the request of the Governments concerned and within a period which shall be fixed by agreement between the parties, except in the cases where, by agreement between the two parties, a certain number of French troops shall remain at specified points and for a specified time.

(Reference: Article 11 of the Final Declaration)

For the settlement of all the problems connected with the re-establishment and consolidation of peace in Cambodia, Laos and Viet Nam, the French Government will proceed from the principle of respect for the independence and sovereignty, the unity and territorial integrity of Cambodia, Laos and Viet Nam.

E. Declaration of Tran Van Do, Delegate of Vietnam

Statement not included in the Conference documents, which was noted by the Conference at its eighth and last session.

The delegation of the State of Vietnam presented a proposal whose aim was to obtain an armistice which did not even temporarily divide Vietnam, by means of disarming the belligerents after withdrawal to assembly areas, which were to be as circumscribed as possible, and through the establishment of a temporary UN authority over the whole country, until the return of peace and order would permit the Vietnamese people to decide its destiny through free elections. The Vietnamese delegation protests the summary rejection of this proposal which alone respects the aspirations of the Vietnamese people. It earnestly requests that the demilitarization and neutralization of at least the bishoprics of the Delta of North Vietnam be accepted by the conference. It solemnly protests the hasty conclusion of the armistice agreement by the French and Vietminh High Commands alone, because the French High-Command commanded the Vietnamese troops only by a delegation of the authority of the Vietnamese Chief of State, and above all because several clauses of the agreement are of a nature which would basically and seriously jeopardize the political future of the Vietnamese people.

It solemnly protests the fact that this armistice agreement abandons to the Vietminh some territories still occupied by Vietnamese troops, and which are at the same time essential to the defence of Vietnam against a greater Communist expansion, and the fact that in practice the end result of this armistice is to remove from the State of Vietnam its inalienable right to provide for its own defence by any other means than the stationing of a foreign army on its soil.

It solemnly protests the fact that the French High-Command has arrogated, without the preliminary agreement of the Delegation of the State of Vietnam, the right to fix the date of the future elections, even though this is a question of an obviously political nature.

As a result, the Government of the State of Vietnam requests that it be written into the record that it solemnly protests the manner in which the armistice was concluded and the conditions of this armistice which takes no cognizance of the deepest aspirations of the Vietnamese people, and that it reserves for itself complete liberty of action in order to safeguard the sacred right of the Vietnamese to territorial integrity, to national independence, and to freedom.

Appendix II
Chronology of ICSC Reports

Period	Covered by
11 August 1954–10 August 1955	First, Second, Third, Fourth Interim Reports
11 August 1955–31 July 1956	Fifth, Sixth Interim Reports
1 August 1956–30 April 1957	Seventh Interim Report
1 May 1957–30 April 1958	Eighth Interim Report
1 May 1958–31 January 1959	Ninth Interim Report
1 February 1959–31 January 1960	Tenth Interim Report
1 February 1960–28 February 1961	Eleventh Interim Report
2 June 1962	Special Report
13 February 1965	Special Report
27 February 1965	Special Report

Appendix III
Chronology of Events

1884	French complete conquest of Indochina. Vietnam divided into three parts: Tonkin, Annam, Cochin-China.
1930	Formation of Communist Party of Indochina.
1931	Communist Party of Indochina admitted into the Comintern.
1940	Japanese occupy Indochina, but allow continued French administration.
1941	"Vietnam Doc-Lap Dong Minh Hoi" ("League for the Independence of Vietnam," i.e., Viet Minh) formed.
1944	People's Liberation Army formed, under Vo Nguyen Giap.
1945	
March	Japanese terminate French rule in Indochina.
May	War in Europe ends.
July	UK, USA recognize Soviet-backed Polish coalition government. Potsdam Conference: divide Japanese surrender of Vietnam at 16th parallel, administered in north by China, south by UK. China leaves administration to Viet Minh. General Gracey refuses to recognize Viet Minh administration; helps French reestablish power.
August	Japan surrenders.
September	Viet Minh establish DRVN, provisional government for all Vietnam, capital at Hanoi. Emperor Bao Dai abdicates.
November	Communist Party of Indochina formally dissolved.
1946	
February	Franco-Chinese Treaty; China withdraws from North Vietnam, gains trade concessions in Indochina.

March		UK withdraws from Indochina. French-Viet Minh agreement: DRVN (Tonkin and Annam) recognized as free state in Indochinese Federation and French Union. French pledge referendum in Cochin-China re union with DRVN.
December		French and Viet Minh at war.

1947

March	Truman doctrine of containment.
August	India becomes a sovereign state.

1948

December	Communists take complete control of Polish government.

1949

March	French set up one "State of Vietnam" within French Union.
April	NATO established.
July	Bao Dai formally establishes State of Vietnam, recognized by France.
October	People's Republic of China proclaimed.
December	India recognizes PRC.

1950

January	DRVN recognized by China, USSR.
February	DRVN recognized by Poland. USSR-China Treaty. 25 Western states, including UK, USA, recognize SVN as Associate State of French Union, Bao Dai as Head. US Consulate-General in Saigon raised to Legation.
May	USA announces help to France in Indochina.
June	Korean War starts.
August	American Military Assistance Advisory Group (MAAG) established in Saigon.
December	USA and SVN, Cambodia, Laos: Mutual Defense Assistance Agreement: material for national armies, assistance for French Expeditionary Corps.

1951

September	USA to provide economic assistance direct to Vietnam.

1952

January	USA-SVN mutual security agreement.
July	USA and SVN establish embassies.
October	Bao Dai withdraws from Vietnamese politics.
December	Canada recognizes SVN, Laos, and Cambodia as Associated States in French Union.

1953

July	Korean armistice.
September	France-USA statement, aim of France: total defeat of communism in Indochina.
November	Ho Chi Minh offer of truce negotiations.

1954

January–February	Berlin Conference of "Big Four"; decision to convene Geneva Conference on Korea and Indochina.
February, May, September	Pakistan joins Western bloc: US military aid, US military agreement, SEATO.
February	Nehru's Indochina cease-fire appeal.
March	Dulles—united action in Indochina.
April	Nehru's 6-point solution for Indochina. France declares Vietnam independent. India-China trade agreement on Tibet formally incorporates *Panchsheel*.
May	Colombo Conference communiqué. French defeat at Dien Bien Phu. First plenary session at Geneva on Indochina.
June	Franco-Vietnamese treaty of independence. Diem appointed Premier of SVN.
July	Geneva Agreements on Indochina: cease-fire agreements and Final Declaration; Canada, India, and Poland to constitute ICSC; Vietnam divided along 17th parallel.
August	ICSC preliminary meeting, New Delhi; cease-fire in Vietnam, ICSC in place, HQ Hanoi. Dulles—important not to mourn past but prevent future loss; collective arrangements for Southeast Asian security under investigation.
September	SEATO; Protocol extends protection to "Free" Indochina.
October	Hanoi formally transferred to DRVN. Nehru visits North Vietnam, China, South Vietnam, Cambodia, Laos.
November	Eisenhower appoints General Lawton Collins his Special Representative to Saigon.
December	ICSC *First Interim Report*. Dulles—Geneva Agreements "setback" for USA offset by SEATO; India's formal recognition of Cambodia, Laos, *de facto* recognition of DRVN.

1955

January	US direct assistance to SVN.
February	US MAAG takes over training of SVN army. Eisenhower letter to Bao Dai: support for Diem.
March	ICSC *Second Interim Report*.

April	Pham of DRVN in India. Bandung Conference, with DRVN and SVN in attendance. ICSC *Third Interim Report*.
May	Warsaw Pact.
June	DRVN demands consultations for July 1956 reunifying elections.
July	Diem rules out SVN participation in elections. Geneva Agreements' anniversary; day of mourning in SVN; demonstrations against ICSC hotels.
October	ICSC *Fourth Interim Report*. SVN declared Republic of VN (RVN) after referendum; Bao Dai deposed; Diem self-proclaimed President.
December	US Consulate in Hanoi closed. India-USSR joint communiqué: full implementation of political provisions of Geneva accords.

1956

January	ICSC *Fifth Interim Report*.
June	French command withdraws from South Vietnam.
July	Nixon in RVN, hails Diem, declares "militant march of communism has been halted." Scheduled date of Vietnamese reunifying election passes; RVN refusal to hold elections.
September	ICSC *Sixth Interim Report*.
October	Indian *de facto* recognition of RVN.

1957

May	Diem in USA: Diem-Eisenhower communiqué, "peaceful unification" of Vietnam.
July	ICSC *Seventh Interim Report*.
November	Diem in India.

1958

February	Ho Chi Minh in India.
April	ICSC functioning in Saigon, sub-office in Hanoi.
May	PAVN liaison mission to ICSC withdrawn at request of Saigon.
June	ICSC *Eighth Interim Report*.
July	ICSC (Laos) disbanded *sine die* at request of Souvanna Phouma government.
August	Sihanouk in India.

1959

March	President Prasad in Indochina. ICSC *Ninth Interim Report*. Dalai Lama crosses into India from Tibet, granted asylum.
May	North Vietnam takes control of insurgency in South.
July	Terrorist raid on Bien Hoa base; 2 American military advisers killed: first US casualties.
August	First public disclosure of Chinese seizure of Indian territory. Nehru informs Parliament/India of Chinese highway across Aksai Chin plateau in Ladakh.
December	Eisenhower in India.

1960

April	ICSC *Tenth Interim Report*. Hanoi protests to UK-USSR against formidable increase in MAAG, accusing USA of turning country into "a military base for the preparation of a new war."
May	USA increases MAAG strength from 327 to 685.
November	Saigon accuses Hanoi of direct aggression: regular DRVN forces via Laos.
December	NLF formed. 900 US military personnel in Vietnam. Soviet airlift of military supplies to DRVN.

1961

February	NLF 10-point program (essentials—overthrow US colonialism and Diem; establish coalition government; implement agrarian reforms; neutralist foreign policy; relations with DRVN and eventual reunification).
March	SEATO Ministers' Council notes with concern efforts of externally supported armed minority to destroy South Vietnam.
May	Kennedy: use of US forces under consideration to help South Vietnam resist communism. ICSC (Laos) reconstituted in New Delhi. Johnson visits South Vietnam. Geneva Conference on Laos opens.
September	ICSC *Eleventh Interim Report*. Kennedy at UN: South Vietnam under attack.
October	SEATO military experts meet in Bangkok to discuss guerrilla war in South Vietnam. Diem: struggle is real war. US Joint Chiefs of Staff estimate 40,000 US troops required to "clean up the Vietcong threat." Rostow, General Taylor in South Vietnam. Kennedy renews pledge to help Saigon resist communism.

November	Kennedy, following Taylor recommendations and NSC approval, increases military advisers and equipment; no combat troops.
December	DRVN Special Envoy Thach meets Nehru in New Delhi.

1962

February	USA reorganizes military command in South Vietnam into MAC under General Harkins; strategic hamlet program begun in South Vietnam.
May	McNamara visits Vietnam.
June	ICSC *Special Report*: North Vietnam *prima facie* guilty of subversion and aggression in specific instances; South Vietnam/USA guilty of factual military alliance.
July	End of Laos Conference; declaration of neutrality.
October	India-China war. Cuban missile crisis.

1963

January	Admiral Felt: South Vietnam victory in 3 years.
January–February	Sihanouk in India.
June	Buddhist demonstrations against Diem. Buddhist monk, Thich Quang Duc, self-immolated; riots, troops.
August	Second Buddhist monk's self-immolation. Government troops raid Saigon's Xa Loi pagoda; monks arrested in hundreds; martial law. Cabot Lodge arrives in Saigon as Ambassador.
October	Seventh Buddhist monk's self-immolation.
November	Diem assassinated. Minh government recognized by USA. Australia-India-UK-USA air exercises. Kennedy assassinated; Johnson reaffirms support for South Vietnam.
November 1963– March 1965	Nine governments in 15 months in Saigon.

1964

January	de Gaulle: guaranteed neutrality of Indochina.
February	Dean Rusk rules out neutralization.
April	SEATO Ministers meet in Bangkok; communiqué: defeat of "Vietcong" essential to security of Southeast Asia. India-RVN 3-year trade pact.
May	US transport ship *Card* sunk in Saigon harbour. Nehru's death.

June	Seaborn's first trip to Hanoi. General Westmoreland replaces Harkins as Commander, MAC. General Taylor replaces Lodge as Ambassador.
July	de Gaulle/Sihanouk: reconvene Geneva Conference; U Thant supports, USSR accepts; Johnson: "we do not believe in conferences called to ratify terror"; UK supports call for Conference. General Khanh supports taking the war to the DRVN; SVN pilots in training for attacks on DRVN.
August	USS *Maddox*, USS *Turner Joy* attacked in Tonkin Gulf by three DRVN patrol boats. US aircraft destroy 25 boats in retaliatory attacks on three major coastal bases. Johnson submits Southeast Asian resolution to Congress; approved 416–0 in House and 88–2 in Senate. Johnson signs Resolution into law (PL 88-408). Thant fails to get USA and DRVN to meet in Rangoon. Seaborn's second trip to Hanoi.
November	Terrorist attack on Bien Hoa.
December	Seaborn's third message to Hanoi.

1965

February	Kosygin in Hanoi. NLF attacks on Pleiku, Camp Holloway killing 8 Americans. US bombing raids against North Vietnam. Indian appeal for necessary atmosphere in Vietnam for Geneva-type conference. NLF attacks US barracks at Qui Nhon, killing 23 Americans. ICSC *Special Report*, re bombing. Kosygin: new conference on Vietnam, without preconditions. USA begins bombing communist concentrations in South Vietnam. Thant urges informal negotiations; withdrawal of US troops. ICSC *Special Report*, re withdrawal of teams from North.
March	"Rolling Thunder" bombing of North Vietnam begins. Seaborn's fourth message to Hanoi. US marines land at Da Nang. Thant proposes preliminary conference, rejected by USA; nonaligned appeal for unconditional negotiations; NLF 5-point plan (repeating essentials of 1961 10 points). Bomb outside US Embassy in Saigon, 2 Americans killed.
April	Pearson's Temple University speech: call for measured pause in bombing of North Vietnam. Johnson approves offensive role for US marines in SVN. Johnson's Johns Hopkins speech: ready for unconditional discussions with governments to secure independent South Vietnam. DRVN 4-point plan: US to withdraw from South Vietnam,

military truce per 1954 agreements, South Vietnamese to determine own internal affairs per NLF plan, reunification settled by Vietnamese themselves. China rejects USSR offer of united action on Vietnam. Radhakrishan's proposals for truce in Vietnam.

April–May   Indo-Pakistan Rann of Kutch war.

May   Tran Van Do of South Vietnam in India. Bombing pause, resumption. Seaborn's fifth (final) message to Hanoi.

June   Commonwealth Peace Mission, rejected by Moscow, Peking, Hanoi. Thieu becomes President of South Vietnam. South Vietnam's 4-point peace plan: end to northern aggression and subversion, including dissolution of the NLF and withdrawal of DRVN cadres; freedom for South Vietnam to choose and shape its own destiny; upon the cessation of northern aggression, military measures against the DRVN would be terminated, and Saigon would ask for an allied troop withdrawal from South Vietnam; and effective guarantees for the independence and freedom of the South Vietnamese people. Johnson appeal for UN help to settle war. NLF attack Saigon floating restaurant. US troops take part in first major search-and-destroy operation.

July   Lodge returns to Saigon as Ambassador. McNamara visits Vietnam.

August   Indian "clarification" of Radhakrishnan proposals.

October–November   Anti-war demonstrations begin in USA. Pacifists burn to death in front of Pentagon, UN.

December   USA bombs thermal power plant in North—first raid on major industrial target. Christmas truce in Vietnam; USA resumes ground action, bombing halt continues.

1966

January   Johnson's peace offensive; 14-point plan: Geneva Agreements of 1954 "are an adequate basis for peace"; a conference on Southeast Asia was welcome; negotiations without preconditions were welcome; unconditional discussions were welcome; a cease-fire could be discussed either at a conference or in preliminary talks; Hanoi's four points could be discussed; the US did not seek bases in the area; it did not desire its troops in the area after peace had been secured; South Vietnam should have free elections to choose its own government; the question of reunification was a matter for Vietnamese determination; Southeast Asian countries could be nonaligned or neutral; US resources could be used for economic reconstruction, to a tune of one billion dollars; "Viet-Cong" representation was not an insurmountable problem; the USA could stop the bombing of North Vietnam as a step towards peace, but there had been no indication from Hanoi in public or in private as to its choice of action upon the cessation of bombing. Martin: Canada appreciates and supports purposes and objectives of US policy in Vietnam. Bombing resumes.

February Swaran Singh's statement in Lok Sabha re Ho Letter to President. Senator R. Kennedy suggests NLF be offered share in power.

March Ronning's first visit to Hanoi.

May Johnson orders POL strikes in North.

June Ronning's second visit to Hanoi. POL strikes on Hanoi, Haiphong outskirts.

July Indira Gandhi, on eve of Moscow visit, asks UK/USSR to reconvene Geneva Conference; in USSR, she demands halt to US bombing first. Thant's 3-point plan; Premier Ky proposes invasion of North.

September de Gaulle: USA must withdraw, state timetable prior to negotiations; Johnson: US timetable dependent upon communist. Hanoi rejects US point of mutual withdrawal. Ambassador Goldberg in UN proposes graduated, reciprocal de-escalation; rejected by China and North Vietnam.

October USSR announces new economic, military aid to Hanoi. Manila Conference: USA and allied reciprocal troop withdrawals; rejected by Peking, Hanoi.

December On basis of Lodge-Lewandowski talks, efforts to open Polish channel of communication in Warsaw. USA bombs targets in Hanoi, USSR charges of residential bombing denied. Peking alleges its embassy bombed; Polish officials say talks not possible after bombings. Harrison Salisbury of *New York Times* visits North Vietnam. US acknowledgment that civilian areas accidentally bombed. Thant urges unconditional bombing halt as first step to peace.

1967

January Mai Van Do in Paris states Hanoi will study peace proposals if USA halts bombing unconditionally and permanently: Lodge: "sensational military gains" in 1967, doubts peace

	talks will get started. DRVN Foreign Minister Trinh: talks only after bombing halt. State Department: Trinh's statement is no change.
February	Johnson: bombing to stop if Hanoi took "almost any step." Johnson's letter to Ho: bombing to stop if infiltration ceased. Kosygin arrives in London; urges USA to halt bombing in exchange for peace talks. Vietnamese New Year (Tet) truce begins; ends as Allies resume ground operations; bombing pause continues. Kosygin leaves London. Wilson asks Johnson for time to let Moscow persuade Hanoi to check its actions. Kosygin returns to Moscow. USA resumes air action on grounds of resupply efforts by Hanoi. Wilson: "peace was almost within our grasp . . . one simple act of trust could have achieved it." Mai Van Do repeats offer of talks after bombing halt.
March	USA begins to bomb North Vietnamese heavy industrial targets. Thant's modified 3-point plan. Bunker replaces Lodge in Saigon.
April	Canada, South Vietnam, USA proposals for reactivating DMZ. Martin's 4-point plan. 160,000 strong antiwar demonstrations in New York and San Francisco.
May	US/South Vietnamese forces move into DMZ, for first time in the war. Power plant 1 mile north of Hanoi city centre bombed.
June	USSR charges USA with bombing Soviet vessel in Campha; denied at first, but then Defense Department acknowledges Soviet vessel bombed. USA expresses regret in note to Soviet Embassy.
September	Johnson's San Antonio formula: bombing to stop if other side didn't take advantage of US restraint. Martin: bombing must stop as first step.
December	NLF announces cease-fire for Christmas, New Year, Tet.
1968	
January	Radio Hanoi broadcasts Trinh December statement of peace talks after bombing halt. Allies cancel Tet truce in I Corps due to massive NLF buildup near Khe Shanh. Tet offensive by NLF.
March	Johnson: bombing halt except around DMZ; no reelection.
April	Hanoi offers to meet US representatives.
May	USA/DRVN first formal negotiating session in Paris.

August	Thieu: Saigon will not talk to NLF.
October	Johnson: cease all bombing of North on 1 Nov. Thieu: US action unilateral.
November	Nixon wins election on platform of progressive de-Americanization of war, peace with honour. Saigon: will take part in Paris talks with Hanoi, NLF ("without implying recognition"), and USA.

1969

April	Dinesh Singh in Lok Sabha: India supports USSR in border dispute with China.
May	NLF 10-point proposal; main features: unconditional US withdrawal, free elections, coalition government, DMZ, POW exchange, eventual reunification. Nixon's 8-point plan: mutual withdrawals of major portions of forces over a year, then reciprocal.
June	Nixon: 25,000-troop withdrawal by end of August. Formation of PRG (NLF and National, Democratic, and Peace Forces), recognized by 16 communist governments, including China, USSR, and Poland; replaces NLF delegation at Paris.
July	Nixon Doctrine.
September	Ho Chi Minh funeral, Dinesh Singh in attendance. Second troop withdrawal by USA—35,000 by end of December.
November	Large crowds for moratorium on war, in Washington and other places.
December	Third troop reduction—50,000 by April 15.

1970

January	Nixon, in State of Union Message: end of Vietnam war a major goal in US foreign policy. USA bombs antiaircraft base 150 km inside DRVN.
March	Coup in Cambodia; Lon Nol replaces Sihanouk.
April	Troop withdrawal—150,000 during coming year. Nixon sends combat troops into Cambodia after enemy sanctuaries/supplies.
May	Sharp in Parliament: Canada not given advance information of American entry into Cambodia, "deeply regretted" action. Dinesh Singh regrets American entry in Cambodia. USA bombs supply dumps in North Vietnam.
June	Senate cuts off fund for future US operations in Cambodia; repeals Gulf of Tonkin resolution.

July	PRG Foreign Minister Madame Binh in New Delhi.
August	USSR-West Germany treaty.
September	PRG 8-point plan: US withdrawal by 30 June 1971, with talks on POW if withdrawal agreement.
October	Nixon 5-point plan: cease-fire in place; Indochina peace conference, timetable for US withdrawal negotiable, immediate POW release.
November	Unsuccessful US attempt to rescue POWs from Son Tay in North Vietnam.
December	Poland-West Germany treaty. Riots in Poland; Gierek replaces Gomulka.

1971

March	Free Bangla Radio announces Provisional Bangladesh Government.
April	100,000-troop reduction in US strength in Vietnam.
June	DRVN (secret) 9-point plan.
July	PRG 7-point plan: US withdrawal, POW release by end 1971, coalition government without Thieu, step-by-step reunification, peace and neutrality in foreign policy, US reconstruction aid, international guarantees for accords. Kissinger in Peking via Pakistan; announcement that Nixon to visit China.
August	India-USSR friendship treaty.
October	Canada recognizes People's Republic of China. DRVN-USSR arms assistance agreement.
November	45,000 US troop reduction announced.
December	India-Pakistan war.

1972

January	India upgrades representation in Hanoi to Embassy, retains consulate in Saigon. Nixon announces further 70,000-troop withdrawal by 1 May.
February	Nixon in Peking.
March	Paris peace talks broken; NLF offensive.
April	USA bombs targets near Hanoi and Haiphong, reversing 4-year de-escalation of air war against North Vietnam. Paris talks resume.
April–May	DRVN agricultural delegation in India.

May	US (Linebacker-I) retaliation against communist offensive, including mining of North Vietnamese ports. Paris talks stalled again.
July	Paris talks resume.
September	ICSC HQ moves back to Hanoi because of Saigon refusal to extend Indian visas. Indian-Polish and Canadian statements all made public.
October	Bombing halt north of 20th parallel. Kissinger: peace at hand.
December	Bombing resumed (Linebacker-II), then halt at 20th parallel.

1973

January	Canadian Parliament deplores US bombings over Christmas. Paris Peace Accords; Canada agrees to serve on ICCS for trial 60 days.
February	Canada establishes diplomatic relations with Hanoi; recognizes both North/South Vietnam; ambassador in Bangkok accredited to Saigon, in Peking to Hanoi (temporarily barred entry because of Canadian refusal to recognize PRG). Kissinger visits Hanoi.
March	Canadian parliamentary delegation in Vietnam, led by Sharp; Canada to stay in ICCS for another 60 days, then announce withdrawal with 30-day grace period for successor to be found. Last US troops leave Vietnam.
April	ICCS helicopter downed in NLF territory, killing one Canadian.
May	Sharp: Canada definitely withdrawing, but by end of July at US request. First withdrawal by Canada from peacekeeping group.
June	Congress cuts off funds for all US military activity in Indochina, effective 15 August.
July	Canada withdraws from ICCS.
November	War Powers Resolution formalizes Congressional oversight of use of US troops abroad by President.

1974

August	Nixon resigns from Presidency.

1975

April	Saigon regime surrenders; India recognizes PRG within hours.
May	Canada announces recognition of new PRG government.

1976
July — Vietnam reunified; Socialist Republic of Vietnam.

1977
March — Indira Gandhi voted out of office.

1978
February — Pham Van Dong visits India.
July — Vietnam joins Comecon; China terminates all aid to Vietnam.
August — China-Japan peace and friendship treaty.
October — Cardinal Archbishop of Cracow becomes Pope John Paul II.
November — USSR-Vietnam Treaty of Friendship and Cooperation.

1979
January — China-USA diplomatic relations begin. Phnom Penh falls to Vietnam-supported Kampuchean rebels.
February–March — China invades Vietnam.
December — USSR invades Afghanistan.

1980
January — Indira Gandhi returns to India's helm.
April — Pham Van Dong visits India.
September — Gierek replaced as Polish leader.

Appendix IV
Glossary

Bao Dai	Emperor of Viet Nam, 1932–55.
Desai, M. J.	First Chairman, ICSC(V); head of Indian delegation.
Diefenbaker, John G.	Prime Minister of Canada, 1957–63.
Diem, Ngo Dinh	Prime Minister and President of South Vietnam, 1955–63.
Do, Tran Van	Head of South Vietnam's delegation to the Geneva Conference in 1954; later Foreign Minister of South Vietnam.
Douglas, T. C.	Leader of the New Democratic Party of Canada, 1961–71.
Drew, George	Leader of the Progressive Conservative Party of Canada, 1948–56.
Dulles, John Foster	United States Secretary of State, 1952–59.
Eden, Anthony	Prime Minister of Britain, 1955–57; foreign minister 1951–55; cochairman, Geneva Conference, 1954.
Gandhi, Indira	Prime Minister of India, 1966–77, 1980–.
Giap, General Vo Nguyen	Commander-in-Chief of the People's Army of Viet-Nam since 1946; Deputy Premier and Defense Minister in the Socialist Republic of Vietnam, 1976.
Gierek, Edward	First Secretary of the Communist Party of Poland, 1970–80.
Gomulka, Wladyslaw	Polish communist leader; dismissed from office in 1948, kept in protective custody

	1951–55 in Stalinist purges; readmitted to party in August 1956; First Secretary, October 1956-December 1970.
Green, Howard	Canadian foreign minister, 1959–63.
Ho Chi Minh	Born Nguyen Tat Thanh; wrote articles under the name of Nguyen Ai Quoc (Nguyen the Patriot); assumed the alias Ho Chi Minh (Ho, the Seeker of Light) during WW II. Founder-member of the French Communist Party; founder-President of the Democratic Republic of Vietnam, 1945–69.
Lao Dong	Communist Party of North Vietnam.
Lett, Sherwood	First Canadian Commissioner, ICSC(V), 1954–55.
Lewis, David	Leader of the New Democratic Party of Canada, 1971–75.
Lodge, Henry Cabot	United States Ambassador to South Vietnam, 1963–64 and 1965–67.
Maneli, Mieczyslaw	Member (Legal Adviser), Polish delegation, ICSC(V), 1954–55; Chairman, Polish delegation, ICSC(V), 1963–64.
Martin, Paul	Canadian foreign minister, 1963–68.
Menon, Krishna	Nehru's "alter ego." Defense Minister of India 1957–62, "Ambassador at Large," unofficial delegate at 1954 Geneva Conference, High Commissioner to the United Kingdom, 1947–52.
Minh, General Duong Van	"Big Minh," head of the government of South Vietnam, 1963–64, and at time of final surrender in 1975.
Molotov, V. M.	Soviet foreign minister, 1953–56; cochairman, Geneva Conference, 1954.
Nehru, Jawaharlal	Prime Minister of India, 1947–64.
Panchsheel	The five principles of peaceful coexistence formulated by China and India in April 1954: (1) mutual respect for each other's territorial integrity and sovereignty; (2) mutual nonaggression; (3) mutual noninterference in each other's internal affairs; (4) equality and mutual benefit; (5) peaceful coexistence.

Pearson, Lester B.	Prime Minister of Canada, 1963–68; Canadian foreign minister, 1948–57.
Pham Van Dong	Leader of North Vietnam after death of Ho Chi Minh; head of DRVN delegation to Geneva Conference in 1954.
Rapacki, Adam	Polish foreign minister, 1956–58.
Ronning, Chester	Canadian High Commissioner to India; intermediary between Hanoi and Washington, 1966.
Rusk, Dean	United States Secretary of State, 1961–69.
Seaborn, J. Blair	Canadian Commissioner, ICSC(V); intermediary, 1964–65, between Hanoi and Washington.
Sharp, Mitchell	Canadian foreign minister, 1968–74.
Shastri, Lal Bahadur	Prime Minister of India, 1964–66.
Singh, Dinesh	Indian foreign minister under Mrs. Gandhi.
Singh, Swaran	Indian defense minister, foreign minister.
St. Laurent, Louis	Prime Minister of Canada, 1948–57; Canadian foreign minister, 1946–48.
Tet	Lunar New Year
Thieu, Nguyen Van	President of South Vietnam, 1967–75.
Trudeau, Pierre Elliot	Prime Minister of Canada, 1968–79, 1980–.

Appendix V
Abbreviations

AICC	All India Congress Committee
ASEAN	Association of South-East Asian Nations
CATO	Combat Arms Training Organization
CBC	Canadian Broadcasting Corporation
CCF	Co-operative Commonwealth Federation (Canada)
DEA	Department of External Affairs (Canada)
DMZ	Demilitarized Zone (Vietnam)
DRVN	Democratic Republic of Viet Nam (North Vietnam 1945–1976)
FUF	French Union Forces
GOC	Good Offices Committee (Indonesia)
ICC	International Control Commission (same as ICSC) (1954–1973)
ICCS	International Commission for Control and Supervision (1973–1975)
ICSC	International Commission for Supervision and Control (1954–1973)
MAAG	Military Assistance Advisory Group (American, in South Vietnam)
MAC	Military Assistance Command (American, in South Vietnam)
NATO	North Atlantic Treaty Organization
NDP	New Democratic Party (Canada)
NEFA	North East Frontier Agency (India)
NLF	National Liberation Front (South Vietnam)

NORAD	North American Air Defense Command
ONUC	Operation des Nations Unies au Congo
PAVN	People's Army of Viet Nam (North Vietnam)
PDL	Provisional Demarcation Line (17th parallel in Vietnam)
POL	Petroleum, Oil, Lubricants (American targets in North Vietnam)
PRG	Provisional Revolutionary Government (South Vietnam)
RVN	Republic of Viet Nam (South Vietnam, 1955–1975)
SEATO	Southeast Asia Treaty Organization (1954–1977)
SMM	Saigon Military Mission (American)
SRV	Socialist Republic of Vietnam (1976–present)
SVN	State of Viet Nam (under Bao Dai, 1949–1955)
TERM	Temporary Equipment Recovery Mission
TRIM	Training and Reorganization Inspection Organization
UNCI	United Nations Commission for Indonesia
UNEF	United Nations Emergency Force
UNFICYP	United Nations Force in Cyprus
USSR	Union of Soviet Socialist Republics
VNA	Vietnamese National Army (South Vietnam)

Notes

The following title abbreviations appear in these notes:

FAR   *Foreign Affairs Record* (India)
HCD   *House of Commons Debates* (Canada and Great Britain)
LSD   *Lok Sabha Debates* (India)
S & S *Statements and Speeches* (Canada)

References to most books and articles have been shortened; complete details of publication appear in the Bibliography.

Preface

1. Cohen and Harris, "Foreign Policy," 384.
2. East *et al., Why Nations Act,* 23.
3. Poland receives less than equal attention, both because of my lesser competence in Polish affairs and because of the relatively scarce sources.

1 Peacekeeping and Foreign Policies

1. Confidential source.
2. USA, DOD, *US-Vietnam Relations,* Book 3, IV.B.3:6. (The ICSC was commonly referred to as the ICC, or International Control Commission.) For a discussion of the Commission's handling of the issue, see pp. 88–93.
3. India, *Rajya Sabha Debates,* 24 August 1962, col. 3051-56.
4. Maneli, *War of the Vanquished,* 23-24. Maneli was legal adviser to the Polish delegation (1954-55), and later its chairman (1963-64).
5. Introduction to the *Annual Report of the Secretary-General on the Work of the Organization,* 16 June 1959-15 June 1960, A/4390/Add. l.
6. "Address at Harvard University, 13 June 1963," *United Nations Review* (July 1963).

7. Swift, "United Nations Military Training for Peace." See also *Peacekeeper's Handbook.* Some of the traits of peacekeeping operations are neatly captured in titles, e.g., Fabian, *Soldiers Without Enemies,* and Rikhye et al., *Thin Blue Line.*
8. Mitchell, "Peace-keeping: The Police Function."
9. The text of the speech is in Canada, DEA, *S & S* 47/2 (January 1947)
10. Pearson, *Words and Occasions,* 25, 31.
11. St. Laurent in Parliament. Canada, *HCD,* 29 April 1948, 3443.
12. Pearson, "Development of Canadian Foreign Policy," 26.
13. Pearson, *Mike II,* 35.
14. What follows is a summary of his "Quiet Diplomacy Revisited," in Clarkson, ed., *An Independent Foreign Policy for Canada?* 29–41.
15. *External Affairs Bulletin,* July 1948, 7.
16. Pearson, *Mike II,* 25.
17. Quoted in Gathorne-Hardy, *Short History of International Affairs,* 72.
18. *S & S,* 48/59.
19. Brecher, *India and World Politics,* 181, 201.
20. *Foreign Policy for Canadians;* "Canada-U.S. Relations: Options for the Future," *International Perspectives* (Autumn 1972).
21. Lyon, "The Trudeau Doctrine"; see also Thomson and Swanson, *Canadian Foreign Policy.*
22. Nehru, *India's Foreign Policy,* 2–3.
23. Brecher, *India and World Politics,* 3.
24. Nehru, *India's Foreign Policy,* 271.
25. *FAR* 3 (December 1957): 226.
26. Gandhi, *Aspects of our Foreign Policy,* 19.
27. For a concise and balanced summary of the two countries' positions on Kashmir, see Sayeed, *Political System of Pakistan,* 261–67. Detailed studies include Brecher, *Struggle for Kashmir,* and Gupta, *Indo-Pakistan Relations.*
28. See Nehru's statement in Parliament: *Debates, House of People,* 23 December 1953, vol. 10, pt. ii, col. 2976–77.
29. Rose, "The Superpowers in South Asia," 396.
30. Nehru, *Discovery of India,* 562–63.
31. Better accounts of the boundary technicalities of the dispute include Lamb, *China-India Border,* and Mehra, *McMahon Line and After.* Maxwell, *India's China War* is a must.
32. *LSD,* 28 August 1959, col. 4869.
33. *Notes, Memoranda and Letters Exchanged between the Governments of India and China* (White Paper) 6: 3–4, 10, 18.
34. Alain Jacob, "The Soviet Union is Forced to Review its World Strategy," *Survival* 12 (September 1971): 196–97.
35. Gandhi said as much in an interview with *The Washington Post* in 1980. Jonathan Power, "Indira Gandhi and the Facing of Reality," *Guardian Weekly,* 13 January 1980, 8.
36. See Ramesh Thakur, "Afghanistan: The Reasons for India's Distinctive Approach," *Round Table* 280 (October 1980): 422–33.
37. See David van Praagh, "Canada and Southeast Asia," and Barrie M. Morrison, "Canada and South Asia," in Lyon and Ismael, *Canada and the Third*

World, 307–08, 333, and 32–33; and Thomson and Swanson, *Canadian Foreign Policy,* 117. For the entente phase of Indo-Canadian relations, see Thomson, "India and Canada: A Decade of Co-operation, 1947–1957," and Rajan, "The Indo-Canadian Entente," *International Journal,* 17 (Autumn 1962): 358–84. The demise of the special relationship notwithstanding, relations between the two countries continue to be friendly, even if no longer warm. Canada has been a major participant in India's development, contributing more than $1.5 billion in grants and loans from 1951–81. In 1981, they signed a further three agreements providing for $125 million in development assistance to India. *Canada Weekly* 10 (13 January 1982): 6.
38. *Indian and Foreign Review,* 1 February 1981, 28. Indo-Polish trade was given a further boost with the imposition of American sanctions on Poland's military regime. *Statesman Weekly,* 20 February 1982.
39. For details, see Balawyder, *Maple Leaf and the White Eagle.*
40. Ibid., 273, 293.
41. Quoted in Ulam, *Expansion and Coexistence,* 210.
42. See Bromke, "Nationalism and Communism in Poland."
43. See Mieczyslaw Dalecki, "October 1956 and After," in Ostaszewski, *Modern Poland between East and West,* 90–92.
44. *New Times* 48 (November 1956): 37–40 (emphasis added).
45. For a documentary account of the ferment, see Zinner, ed., *National Communism and Popular Revolt in Eastern Europe.* See also Brzezinski, *The Soviet Bloc,* chaps. 12, 14; Dallin, *Soviet Foreign Policy After Stalin,* 358–64.
46. *New Times* 48 (November 1956): 39.
47. Kintner and Klaiber, *Eastern Europe and European Security,* 228, 323–27. Conformity was defined (221) as "the adoption, pursuit, or articulation of policy positions by East European countries in accordance with related Soviet policies or objectives."
48. *New York Times,* 15 January 1957.
49. Zagoria, *Sino-Soviet Conflict,* 66–74.
50. Cited in M. K. Dziewanowski, "Poland," in Bromke, *Communist States at the Crossroads,* 64.
51. See Adam Bromke, "Polish Foreign Policy in the 1970's," in Bromke and Strong, *Gierek's Poland,* 194; and Rachwald, "Poland Between the Superpowers."

2 The French Indochina War

1. *Foreign Policy for Canadians,* "Pacific," 10.
2. Thomson and Swanson, *Canadian Foreign Policy,* 107.
3. *Foreign Policy for Canadians,* "Pacific," 12.
4. Canada, DEA, *External Affairs,* 2 (October 1950): 375–76.
5. USA, DOS, *American Foreign Policy 1950–1955* 2:2368–69.
6. Canada, DEA, *Report, 1952,* 24.
7. Canada, HCD, 20 June 1952, 3502 (emphasis added).
8. "Don't Let Asia Split the West," *S & S* 53/50.
9. For Nehru's statement see below, pp. 37–38.

10. *External Affairs* 6 (May 1954): 162.
11. Nehru, *Discovery of India*, 193, 197.
12. Ibid., 423.
13. Karunakaran, *India in World Affairs, 1947–1950*, 106.
14. The exchange of correspondence between Bose and Nehru can be found in *The Statesman*, 23 March 1947.
15. Asian Relations Organization, *Asian Relations*, 62–78.
16. India, *Press Conferences, 1950*, 22. Interestingly, American diplomats in Vietnam in 1947 concurred in the assessment that Ho was the "symbol of nationalism and the struggle for freedom to the overwhelming majority of the poulation." Cited in Herring, *America's Longest War*, 8.
17. India, *Press Conferences, 1950*, 36.
18. S.I.P.R.I., *Arms Trade with the Third World*, 468.
19. Cited in SarDesai, *Indian Foreign Policy*, 18.
20. Reid, *Envoy to Nehru*, 69–70.
21. Nehru, *India's Foreign Policy*, 396–400. Nehru's speech was ill-received in the United States: *New York Times*, 25 April 1954. But in Britain, the Labour Party's national executive committee endorsed the peace proposal in an amended form: *Economist*, 1 May 1954, 360.
22. Burma, Ceylon, India, Indonesia and Pakistan.
23. See McLane, *Soviet Strategies in Southeast Asia*.
24. Cited in Hammer, *Struggle for Indochina*, 185.
25. Editorial in *New Times*, 6 February 1950, 1.
26. See Hinton, *China's Relations with Burma and Vietnam*, 18; and Kahin and Lewis, *United States in Vietnam*, 30.
27. McLane, *Soviet Strategies in Southeast Asia*, 442.
28. See, for instance, Dallin, *Soviet Foreign Policy After Stalin*, 153; and Ulam, *Expansion and Coexistence*, 553, 698.
29. USA, DOS, *American Foreign Policy* 2: 2376 (emphasis added).
30. Canada, *HCD*, 31 March 1954, 3542.
31. USA, DOS, *American Foreign Policy* 1: 1704–05.
32. Great Britain, Papers by Command, *Documents Relating to British Involvement in the Indo-China Conflict*, Cmnd. 2834 (1965), 67.
33. Eden, *Memoirs*, 94–99. According to C. M. Roberts, "Dulles felt that Eden had switched his position and suspects that Eden did so after strong words reached London from Prime Minister Nehru in New Delhi." "The Day We Didn't Go to War," in Gettleman, ed., *Vietnam*, 102.
34. Speaking about the Geneva Conference after the event, Eden informed his Parliament that "Canada knew everything about this at every stage of the proceedings. They were fully informed at every stage and expressed themselves in terms of warmest approval." Great Britain, *HCD*, 8 November 1954, col. 930.
35. Holmes, "Geneva: 1954," 462–63.
36. Ronning, *Memoir of China in Revolution*, 220–23.
37. Ibid., 231.
38. Eden, *Memoirs*, 113–14, 127.
39. Canada, *HCD*, 10 May 1954, 4547.

40. USA, DOS, *American Foreign Policy* 2: 2389.
41. Eden, *Memoirs,* 119–20, 128.
42. Holmes, "Geneva: 1954," 467.
43. USA, DOS, *Bulletin,* 21 June 1954; 28 June 1954.
44. USA, DOD, *US-Vietnam Relations*, Book 9:271–75.
45. Ibid., 349–50.
46. Ibid., 457–59.
47. Ibid., 625–30.
48. See Great Britian, Accounts and Papers, 1953–54, vol. 21, no. 12, *Further Documents Relating to the Discussion of Indo-China,* Cmd. 9239 (August 1954).
49. USA, DOS, *American Foreign Policy* 2: 2397–98.
50. USA, DOS, *Bulletin,* 2 August 1954.
51. USA, DOD, *US-Vietnam Relations,* Book 10: 692.
52. India, *Debates,* House of the People, 1 March 1954, vol. 1, pt. i, col. 963–72. Robertson was present at Geneva for most of the time as a member of the American delegation. Even John Holmes of Canada has described him as "the most fanatical member of the State Department." Holmes, "Geneva: 1954," 466.
53. Eden, *Memoirs,* 128, 109–10, 141.
54. India, *LSD,* vol. 5, pt. ii, 15 May 1954.
55. Brecher, *India and World Politics,* 44.
56. Randle, *Geneva 1954,* 195.
57. Cited in SarDesai, *Indian Foreign Policy,* 48.
58. Nehru, *India's Foreign Policy,* 403.
59. India, *LSD,* 29 September 1954, vol. 7, no. 30, pt. ii, col. 3676–77.
60. Holmes, "Geneva: 1954," 464.
61. Canada *HCD,* 28 May 1954, 5188–92.
62. *S & S,* 54/36.
63. Holmes, "Geneva: 1954," 472.
64. Krishna Menon has claimed that he had great difficulty in persuading China to accept Canada, because of its NATO connection. Brecher, *India and World Politics,* 49, 75. It is possible that Chou was merely being clever in playing up to Menon's ego. Nevertheless, John Holmes for one believes that Krishna Menon was instrumental in securing Chinese acceptance of Canada. Holmes, "Geneva: 1954," 470.
65. Canada, DEA, *Report, 1954,* 24.
66. Both letters are on DEA files. Cited in Bridle, *Canada and the International Commissions,* 10.
67. See Devillers and Lacouture, *End of a War,* 293, 308–09. The Vietminh too were anxious to avoid American intervention. Even before the Geneva Agreements were signed, the Lao Dong party changed its strategic line from concentrating on final victory over the French, to compromising with them in order to ward off direct American involvement in the war. Porter, ed., *Vietnam* 1:632.
68. United States Consulate General in Hong Kong, *Survey of the China Mainland Press,* no. 843, 8 July 1954, 1.
69. Cameron, *Viet-Nam Crisis,* doc. no. 134: 309–10. In 1954, the protests of the South Vietnamese could be ignored. Eleven years later, however,

Do's statement was appended to the minutes of the Canadian parliamentary committee on external affairs—the times they were a'changing. Canada, House of Commons, Standing Committee on External Affairs, *Statements and Proceedings,* 10 June 1965, no. 1.
70. USA, DOD, *US-Vietnam Relations,* Book 9: 662.
71. A comprehensive discussion of the Geneva Agreements with respect to their juridical foundations is in Randle, *Geneva 1954.*
72. Cited in Herring, *America's Longest War,* 41.
73. Quoted in Moraes, *Witness to an Era,* 220–21.

3 The Commission in Action: The Military Record

1. The transfer was apparently due to the DRVN desire that the ICSC be seen to be for the whole of Vietnam and not just for the North alone. Kaul, *India, China and Indochina,* 72–73.
2. After the Geneva Agreements, the United States intelligence assessment concluded that the Vietminh would "refrain from deliberately taking major military action . . . while seeking to gain every advantage in the implementation of the agreements." USA, DOD, *US-Vietnam Relations,* Book 10: 694.
3. ICSC, *Third Interim Report,* para. 18.
4. Confidential source.
5. The designation "F" before a number was used to indicate mobile element of a fixed team.
6. ICSC, *Fifth Interim Report,* paras. 37–40.
7. Ibid., para. 45.
8. Maneli, *War of the Vanquished,* 31–32.
9. ICSC, *Sixth Interim Report,* paras. 41–43.
10. Quoted in Ross, "In the Interests of Peace," 731.
11. ICSC, *Special Report to the co-Chairmen of the Geneva Conference on Indo-China* (1962), para. 21.
12. Protocol 23 of the Central Joint Commission, signed at Quynh Khe. The Protocol, without ICSC participation, committed it to many tasks that it was not equipped to perform, e.g., to determine whether a given item had been rendered inserviceable since the cease-fire, or verification of on-the-spot destruction. The Operations Committee of the International Commission did succeed in coming up with some sort of a scheme, which went into effect in April 1955—nine months after the cease-fire.
13. ICSC, *Ninth Interim Report,* para. 37.
14. ICSC, *Sixth Interim Report,* paras. 44–58.
15. See, for instance, ICSC, *Eleventh Interim Report,* para. 37.
16. ICSC, *Tenth Interim Report,* para. 58.
17. Maneli, *War of the Vanquished,* 29.
18. See Sheehan et al., *Pentagon Papers,* 19.
19. The discussion so far of the SEATO issue has been based on confidential sources.
20. McNaught, "Ottawa and Washington Look at the U.N., " 670.

21. Sarvepalli Gopal, *Jawaharlal Nehru* 2:240. Gopal had access to Nehru's private papers. Escott Reid, the Canadian High Commissioner in New Delhi at the time, informed Ottawa that the failure to establish a Locarno-type pact *with* India and China, rather than SEATO, was "one of the tragic lost opportunities of the middle fifties." Reid, *Envoy to Nehru*, 74.
22. Pakistan withdrew from SEATO on 8 November 1972.
23. See Eden, *Toward Peace in Indochina*, 4–6; Randle, *Geneva 1954*, 363; and SarDesai, *Indian Foreign Policy*, 62.
24. 27 August 1954. Quoted in SarDesai, *Indian Foreign Policy*, 65 (emphasis added). Nehru expressed similar sentiments to T. N. Kaul on the eve of the latter's departure as Chairman of the ICSC in 1956; Kaul, *India, China and Indochina*, 61.
25. 26 November 1954. Quoted in Ton That Thien, *India and South East Asia*, 319.
26. *FAR* 1 (1955): 53.
27. ICSC, *Seventh Interim Report*, para. 56.
28. The Canadian delegation was also at the time "under standing instructions not to embarrass Indians by voting or submitting statements in minority." Porter, ed., *Vietnam* 2, doc. 62: 127.
29. ICSC, *Eleventh Interim Report*, para. 50.
30. Porter, *Vietnam* 2, doc. 40: 93–94.
31. Ibid., 93.
32. Ibid., docs. 48, 49: 101–04.
33. Ibid., doc. 51: 105–06.
34. Ibid., doc. 53: 110–12. The document, a telegram from Ambassador Nolting to Secretary Rusk, was declassified by the State Department on 25 March 1975.
35. ICSC, *Sixth Interim Report*, para. 63.
36. ICSC, *Eighth Interim Report*, para. 32, *Ninth Interim Report*, paras. 31, 34.
37. ICSC, *Tenth Interim Report*, para. 47.
38. Ibid., para. 50.
39. USA, DOD, *US-Vietnam Relations*, Book 3, IV.B.3: i, 6.
40. Ross, "In the Interests of Peace," 760–62.
41. See above, p. 3.
42. Ross, "In the Interests of Peace," 761.
43. ICSC, *Special Report* (1962), paras. 11–20.
44. Hanoi had good reason to be worried about the visits—their purpose was to determine the feasibility and level of American commitment to Saigon, including combat troops. See Sheehan et al., *Pentagon Papers*, chap. 3.
45. ICSC, *First Interim Report*, 29.
46. See Associated Press story, filed 21 November 1954, quoting B. S. N. Murti, the Commission Press Officer. The Commission was also reported to have said on 20 November that there were no allegations from either side about the other having increased forces in violation of the Agreements. *Globe and Mail*, 22 November 1954.
47. Cited in SarDesai, *Indian Foreign Policy*, 84.
48. ICSC, *First Interim Report*, 33–35. The nonpublic section is based on confidential sources.
49. Canada, *HCD*, 24 March 1955, 2339.

50. "Holmes to Pearson, Memorandum for the Minister: Prospects in Indochina," (July 1955), cited in Ross, "In the Interests of Peace," 553.
51. ICSC, *Fifth Interim Report,* para. 29.
52. ICSC, *Tenth Interim Report,* Appendix A, 27.
53. Ross, "In the Interests of Peace," 711–13.
54. The two accounts of the legal committee positions, and Commission reactions to the reports, are taken from Ross, "In the Interests of Peace," 719–22, and SarDesai, *Indian Foreign Policy,* 196–97.
55. ICSC, *Eleventh Interim Report,* para. 61.
56. See Maneli, *War of the Vanquished,* 52–55.
57. Ross, "In the Interests of Peace," 842–44.
58. ICSC, *Special Report* (1962), paras. 7–10.
59. See, for example, "Canadian-Indian Report Distorts Truth: Peking," *Globe and Mail,* 8 June 1962.
60. Reports to this effect were carried in the Indian press on 16 November 1961.
61. *New York Times,* 13 November 1961.
62. ICSC, *Fourth Interim Report,* 3.
63. Canada, Committe on External Affairs, *Statements and Proceedings,* 24 May 1955, 539.
64. The account of the transfers that follows is based on confidential sources.
65. Sheehan et al., *Pentagon Papers,* doc. 15: 53–66.
66. The report confirms also the differential civilized behavior of PAVN personnel and the rapine Vietnamese National Army troops; the Mission was "working on this problem." Ibid., 63.
67. ICSC, *Special Report to the co-Chairmen of the Geneva Conference* (13 February 1965). For a brief sketch of the United States involvement, see below, chap. 7, "The American Intervention."
68. Ibid., "Statement of the Canadian Delegation" (emphasis added).
69. Ibid., "Indian Statement on the Canadian Statement."
70. Canada, HCD, 8 March 1965, 12065–66.
71. Maneli, *War of the Vanquished,* 55–57. I was unable to obtain any satisfactory clarification of this puzzling item in my own interviews with officials.
72. ICSC, *Special Report to the co-Chairmen of the Geneva Conference* (27 February 1965). The Commission message and the accompanying documents can be found in Canada, DEA, *Press Releases and Speeches,* 1965, Communiqué No. 19, 5 April 1965.
73. Canada, DEA, *Press Releases and Speeches,* 1965, Communiqué No. 19, 5 April 1965.

4 The Commission on the Descendant: Human Rights

1. Confidential source.
2. The following account of the Commission's activity with respect to these incidents is based on confidential sources. For the Commission's public account of the incidents in south and central Vietnam, see *First Interim Report,* paras. 108–16.

3. ICSC, *Sixth Interim Report*, para. 16.
4. Ibid., paras. 20-22.
5. ICSC, *Seventh Interim Report*, paras. 19-23.
6. See, for example, ICSC, *Ninth Interim Report*, para. 15, *Tenth Interim Report*, para. 18, and *Eleventh Interim Report*, para. 12.
7. Ross, "In the Interests of Peace," 802-03.
8. Kaul, *India, China and Indochina*, 74.
9. For full details of the affair, see Ross, "In the Interests of Peace," *819-30.*
10. The following account of the Commission's actions and decisions with respect to Law 10/59 is drawn from the *ICSC's Tenth* and *Eleventh Interim Report,* paras. 22 and 17 respectively.
11. No. IC/ADM/III-6/56/400 to the PAVN, No. IC/ADM/III-6/56/401 to the FUF.
12. Article 1 of Law 10/59, for example, decreed the death penalty *and* confiscation of property for murder, poisoning, kidnapping and destruction of property. For the text of the law, see Gettleman, *Vietnam,* 256-60.
13. Sheehan et al., *Pentagon Papers,* 62.
14. See Bridle, *Canada and the International Commissions,* 14. The Catholic population was in fact the important factor in the refugee movement to the south. Of the 600,000 Catholics in the north at the time of the cease-fire, more than 500,000 moved south.
15. ICSC, *Third Interim Report,* para. 17.
16. Maneli, *War of the Vanquished,* 38.
17. See above, p. 78.
18. ICSC, *Fourth Interim Report,* paras. 28, 31.
19. Confidential, to author. Appendix V of the *Fourth Interim Report* documents the charges of delaying and obstructionist tactics by both parties, including incidents of the type referred to in the Canadian amendment.
20. ICSC, *Fourth Interim Report,* Canadian amendment to paras. 24-34, para. 5.
21. ICSC, *Sixth Interim Report–Seventh Interim Report.*
22. ICSC, *Ninth Interim Report–Eleventh Interim Report.*
23. Sheehan et al., *Pentagon Papers,* doc. 15.
24. See also Devillers and Lacouture, *End of a War,* 333-37. The Pentagon Papers confirmed that in August 1954, the National Security Council recommended a policy of "covert operations on a large and effective scale" to maintain non-communist governments in Indochina and destabilize the DRVN. USA, DOD, *US-Vietnam Relations,* Book 10: 737.
25. Canada, *HCD,* 24 March 1955, 2339.
26. Ibid., 3 May 1955, 3388-89.
27. Canada, Committee on External Affairs, *Statements and Proceedings,* 26 May 1955, 578.
28. Ross, "In the Interests of Peace," 398-99.
29. Ibid., 472.
30. Maneli, *War of the Vanquished,* 41.
31. ICSC, *Sixth Interim Report,* paras. 36-37.
32. Ibid., para. 38.
33. ICSC, *Seventh Interim Report–Ninth Interim Report.*

5 The Commission in the Background: Vietnamese Reunification

1. ICSC, *Fifth Interim Report,* para. 7.
2. Great Britain, *Documents,* Cmnd. 2834 (1965), doc. 55.
3. Ibid., doc. 60.
4. Randle, *Geneva 1954,* 389–454. I have avoided the detailed doctrinal underpinnings contained in Randle.
5. See ibid., chap. 22.
6. John Norton Moore, "The Lawfulness of Military Assistance to the Republic of Viet-Nam," in Falk, *Vietnam War and International Law,* 260.
7. Daniel G. Partan, "Legal Aspects of the Vietnam Conflict," in Falk, *Vietnam War and International Law,* 210–12.
8. Canada, Committee on External Affairs, *Statements and Proceedings,* 26 May 1955, 580.
9. Ross, "In the Interests of Peace," 743–45.
10. Kaul, *India, China and Indochina,* 60.
11. Canada, Committee on External Affairs, *Statements and Proceedings,* 10 June 1965, 38–39.
12. Canada, *HCD,* 13 February 1967, 12990. Interestingly, the United States Defense Department's adviser on international law, George H. Aldrich, believed that South Vietnam was bound by the Agreements. USA, DOD, *US-Vietnam Relations,* Book 11: 330.
13. *FAR* 1 (1955): 149–50.
14. AICC, *The Background of India's Foreign Policy,* 33–34.
15. John Holmes said much the same thing in his report to Pearson at about the same time. Ross, "In the Interests of Peace," 557. See also Reid, *Envoy to Nehru,* 82.
16. Cited in SarDesai, *Indian Foreign Policy,* 101.
17. Great Britain, *Documents,* Cmnd. 2834 (1965), doc. 47.
18. Ibid., doc. 49.
19. "Res inter alios acta" is defined as "a matter which, in law, exclusively concerns others"; Sorensen, *Manual of Public International Law,* lix.
20. Great Britain, *Documents,* Cmnd. 2834 (1965), doc. 50.
21. ICSC, *Sixth Interim Report,* para. 89.
22. ICSC, *Seventh Interim Report,* Appendices A and C. For a look at the dilemma from the French point of view, see extracts from a debate in the Council of the French Republic on 23 February 1956, in Cameron, *Viet-Nam Crisis,* doc. 176.
23. USA, DOD, *US-Vietnam Relations,* Book 9: 616. The American intelligence community predicted in its first assessment of the post-Geneva outlook (3 August 1954) that the Vietminh would "almost certainly win" the scheduled elections; ibid., Book 10: 692.
24. Devillers and Lacouture, *End of a War,* 319–23, 362–63.
25. USA, DOS, *Aggression from the North.*
26. USA, DOS, *A Threat to the Peace.*
27. USA, DOS, *Bulletin,* 26 April 1965, 606–10.
28. *Survey of the China Mainland Press* 856 (27 July 1954): 7–9.
29. USA, DOD, *US-Vietnam Relations,* Book 2, IV.A.5 (Tab. 4): 5.

30. In 1967, the South Vietnamese consul-general in India wrote that the Final Declaration at Geneva "was only a statement of intent, not signed by any country. It therefore, did not have the legal value of a treaty." Moreover, "the Republic of Vietnam is . . . not bound by *any* document of the Geneva Conference." Nguryen Trieu Dan, "The Problem of Vietnam," *Foreign Affairs Reports* 16 (October 1967): 1. For an earlier but fuller account of the South Vietnamese position by his predecessor, see Do Vang Ly, "The Emergence of Vietnam," ibid. 7 (January 1958): 1–19.
31. Randle, *Geneva 1954*, 442. Randle terms the position of both the DRVN and the RVN in July 1956 "quasi-sovereign"; ibid., 445.
32. U.S. State Department, "The Legality of United States Participation in the Defense of Viet-Nam," in Falk, *Vietnam War and International Law*, 595–96.
33. John Norton Moore, "International Law and the United States Role in the Viet-Nam War: A Reply," in Falk, *Vietnam War and International Law*, 408–15.
34. Richard A. Falk, "International Law and the United States Role in the Viet Nam War: A Response to Professor Moore," in Falk, *Vietnam War and International Law*, 461–69. The ordering of arguments is mine.
35. Quincy Wright, "Legal Aspects of the Viet-Nam Situation," in Falk, *Vietnam War and International Law*, 280–87.
36. Eisenhower, *Mandate for Change*, 372.
37. USA, DOD, *US-Vietnam Relations*, Book 2, IV.A.5: 5. According to a document declassified in 1977, the National Security Council concluded in May 1955 that if elections were held in 1956, the advantage would lie with the communists. Nevertheless, Diem was to be encouraged to agree to preliminary consultations in order to avoid extreme unpopularity in South Vietnam. Such a position would also be consistent with United States policy in other parts of the world, and with British-french commitment to the elections. Porter, *Vietnam* 1:697–702. In the event, the Lao Dong party did *not* change its policy of "peaceful political struggle." The Eleventh Central Committee Plenum in December 1956 is believed to have accepted that a peaceful line was desirable because the people of South Vietnam ardently wished for peace, and feasible because agents in the South could escape detection. In addition, of course, the Hanoi regime was yet to fully consolidate its rule in the North. Ibid., 2:24–30. Yet another document captured in July 1959 indicated that despite mounting claims for action from its southern cadres, the Hanoi leadership was not ready even in 1958 to abandon the peaceful political struggle. The severity and success of Diem's repression had led to the deviationist tendency of individual assassinations. Ibid., 36–41. The military struggle was placed on a par with political struggle only in October 1961. Ibid., 119–23.
38. USA, DOD, *US-Vietnam Relations*, Book 2, IV.A.5: 6.
39. Confidential source. An alternative interpretation of Pearson's remark is that it indicates he had conceded the loss of southern Vietnam, but was drawing the defence line at Vietnam's borders with Laos and Cambodia. See Reid's comments in note 46 below.
40. *External Affairs* 19 (1967): 224.
41. Ross, "In the Interests of Peace," 509.
42. Ibid., 513–15.

43. Ibid., 536.
44. Kaul, *India, China and Indochina*, 72.
45. Ross, "In the Interests of Peace," 541–42.
46. Reid, *Envoy to Nehru*, 83. Reid adds in brackets the comment that "twenty years and millions of deaths later not only they but also the Laotians and Cambodians would be 'betrayed' into the hands of the communists."
47. Ross, "In the Interests of Peace," 608–11. Ross does better justice to the complex story of the Canadian position on the elections than is possible here, in his extensive chap. 5, "The Elections that Never Were," 506–664.
48. Great Britain, *Documents*, Cmnd. 2834 (1965), doc. 50.
49. Canada, Committee on External Affairs, *Statements and Proceedings*, 24 May 1955, 539–45 (emphasis added).
50. Canada, *HCD*, 31 January 1956, 710.
51. Ibid., 2 August 1956, 6879–80 (emphasis added).
52. Howard Green in Parliament on 8 March 1962. The remark was in the context of Commission jurisdiction, not elections. *External Affairs* 14 (1962): 151.
53. Canada, Committee on External Affairs, *Statements and Proceedings*, 10 June 1965, 18.
54. Compare this to Pearson's attitude in September 1954, that the same procedure could not be transposed from Europe to Asia, and that in any case the conditions that necessitated NATO in Europe did not exist in the Pacific. *External Affairs* 2 (1950): 375–76.
55. USA, DOS, *Aggression from the North*.
56. Canada, *HCD*, 23 May 1967, 484.
57. *Foreign Policy of India*, 169, 178, 186–87, 191, 215.
58. SarDesai, *Indian Foreign Policy*, 104–05.
59. *LSD*, III, i, 4 May 1956, col. 3333–34.
60. *FAR* 2 (1956): 200.
61. *Foreign Policy of India*, 282–283, 319.
62. Cited in Ton That Thien, *India and South East Asia*, 143.
63. *Foreign Policy of India*, 328.
64. Devillers and Lacouture, *End of a War*, 391–93.
65. DRVN, *Documents*, 37–40.
66. Great Britain, *Documents*, Cmnd. 2834 (1965), doc. 53.
67. Cameron, *Viet Nam Crisis*, doc. 166.
68. Great Britain, *Documents*, Cmnd. 2834 (1965), doc. 55.
69. Ibid., docs. 62–64.
70. Cameron, *Viet Nam Crisis*, docs. 184, 186.
71. Great Britain, *Documents*, Cmnd. 2834 (1965), docs. 58, 65–67.
72. Holmes, "Geneva: 1954," 476–79.
73. Gettleman, *Vietnam*, 162.
74. SarDesai, *Indian Foreign Policy*, 84–85.
75. India's general position can perhaps be better deduced from its expressions on some other issues. In December 1961, Krishna Menon refuted the charge that India's forcible "liberation" of Goa was an act of aggression. Rather, permanent aggression had collapsed. C.S. Jha offered a similar agument in the Security Council, declaring that because the original (forcible) occupation

by Portugal was itself illegal, there was "no legal frontier" between India and Portugal. Moreover, "there can be no question of aggression against your own people, whom you want to bring into freedom." *Security Council Official Records,* 18 December 1961, 10–17. In an interview with the author in 1975, Jha allowed that if the Vietnamese were held to be one people, and Vietnam one country, then the old Indian argument about there being no question of aggression against one's own people would indeed apply to North Vietnamese movement across the provisional demarcation line. If a 450-year frontier was of no consequence, then a three-year frontier would be of even less consequence. However, he was quick—and right—to point out that to his knowledge the argument had never been made as such by Hanoi. Nevertheless, it does add a second dimension to the claim that after elections had been frustrated, North Vietnam was relieved in Indian minds of the obligation to respect the cease-fire line, the country *de facto* became one, and Hanoi was free to continue the war for independence and reunification that had been held in abeyance. As the ICSC chairman, India could not state such a position, and in fact in the Commission continued to cite violations against North Vietnam. But the argument is pertinent to understanding the political sympathies of India.

76. ICSC, *Second Interim Report,* 6.
77. ICSC, *Fourth Interim Report,* paras. 42–43.
78. ICSC, *Sixth Interim Report,* paras. 39, 67, and 84.

6 The Commission Record: A Summing Up

1. "Decisions" comprise decisions and/or findings on investigations and complaints, including the question of whether to proceed with one or not, where this question is itself a matter for dispute. Possibilities of distortions in the set of tables include: behind-the-scenes Commission discussions may vary significantly from the published reports; where "n" instances are reported at once, the weight given is "n", but there may have been times when they were reported merely as one, in which case they would be weighted "1"; similarly, where investigation of "x" complaints is rejected by a party, there will be only one Commission decision, and correspondingly only "1" weight against the party. The apparent discrepancies between the figures in Tables 3 and 4 are to be explained by the fact that often, the delegations responded to a category of issues by attaching a minority note for all.
2. *External Affairs* 19 (1967): 225–28.
3. See above, pp. 2–3. The fact of Canada being forced into a reactive partisanship was then put to good use by "conservatives" in their internal DEA debates with the "liberal moderates." The latter dominated up to 1956–57, shared control until early 1960, and then lost policy control to the conservatives thereafter. Ross, "In the Interests of Peace," 795–802 and *passim.*
4. David Cox, "Peace-keeping in Canadian Foreign Policy," in Clarkson, *An Independent Foreign Policy for Canada?* 194.
5. ICSC, *Fourth Interim Report,* Appendix VI.

6. Kaul, *India, China and Indochina*, 73–74.
7. By tripolar I mean three members of roughly comparable status and prestige or influence internationally; by troika composition, on the other hand, I mean politically representational composition of the three major ideological streams.
8. Bridle, *Canada and the International Commissions*, 22.
9. Kaul, *India, China and Indochina*, 72.
10. David van Praagh, "Canada and Southeast Asia," in Lyon and Ismael, *Canada and the Third World*, 311. Contrast this with Kaul's remark that his 1956–58 chairmanship of the ICSC "was my most educative and rewarding experience in 30 years of India's diplomatic service." Kaul, *India, China and Indochina*, 72.
11. For a further comment on this, see Thakur, "Liberalism, Democracy and Development," 344–48.
12. 27 September 1954; cited in SarDesai, *Indian Foreign Policy*, 54.
13. Confidential source.
14. Lyon, *Canada in World Affairs*, 316.
15. Confidential source.
16. Thus while a few Canadians in Vietnam interpreted discoveries of arms caches in the South as weapons dumped by a retreating army, most were convinced that they represented menacing omens of malevolent acts to follow. Similarly, Canadian intelligence analysts *assumed* that the guerrilla operations were Peking-controlled and directed. Ross, "In the Interests of Peace," 712, 735–36.
17. Martin, *Canada and the Quest for Peace*, 30–31.
18. Holmes, "Canada and the Vietnam War," 188.
19. See above, pp. 120–24.
20. SarDesai, *Indian Foreign Policy*, 202.
21. To author, 1975.
22. SarDesai, *Indian Foreign Policy*, 202.
23. USA, DOD, *US-Vietnam Relations*, Book 2, IV.A.5:30; Porter, *Vietnam* 2:44–46, 53–56. The emphasis upon armed force only as an auxiliary to political struggle was reiterated in a letter from the Lao Dong party committee to its chapters in the south on 28 March 1960. On 20 April 1960, party secretary Le Duan stressed the DRVN desire to avoid at all costs a war in the south that could spread north. Porter, *Vietnam* 2:59–70.
24. Similarly, when Maneli met Chou En-lai in Peking in 1963, the latter, not normally emotional, "spoke about the Indians with anger, contempt, and disdain." Maneli, *War of the Vanquished*, 77–78.
25. Bridle, *Canada and the International Commissions*, 24–25.
26. Ibid., 26.
27. Ibid., 25.
28. Ibid., 12.

7 The American Intervention

1. Pearson, *Words and Occasions*, 32.

2. For a survey of the American war, see Herring, *America's Longest War*. Another recent study has argued that the disastrous *outcome* for the United States in Vietnam resulted from policy *outputs* produced by the American foreign-policy decision-making system functioning as intended. Gelb and Betts, *Irony of Vietnam*.
3. USA, DOD, *US-Vietnam Relations*, Book 1, II.A: 17.
4. Ibid., 2.
5. Lewy, *America in Vietnam*, 451–53.
6. Sheehan et al., *Pentagon Papers*, 119–25.
7. Kahin, "Political Polarization in South Vietnam." See also Porter, *Vietnam 2*: 182–219, and USA, DOD, *US-Vietnam Relations*, Book 3, IV.B.5.
8. Thus the Pentagon analyst concluded that "the air war against the North was launched in the hope that it would strengthen GVN confidence and cohesion. . . . " USA, DOD, *US-Vietnam Relations*, Book 4, IV.C.3:i. Even a sympathetic chronicler of the American involvement writes: "Frustrated over lack of progress in the war in the South and without searching for the deeper causes of South Vietnam's lagging military fortunes, the decision was taken to bomb North Vietnam." Lewy, *America in Vietnam*, 416.
9. USA, DOD, *US-Vietnam Relations*, Book 3, IV.C.1:46–55.
10. For a convincing argument that Congress approved the resolution in full awareness of its implications, see Lewy, *America in Vietnam*, 32–36.
11. John McNaughton, the Assistant Secretary of Defense; USA, DOD, *US-Vietnam Relations*, Book 6, IV.C.7 (a): 42.
12. Ibid., 21. Other objectives of the bombing campaign included: increasing South Vietnamese morale, demonstrating American credibility as an ally, and using it as a bargaining chip in future negotiations. See Schandler, *The Unmaking of a President*, 297–99; USA, DOD, *US-Vietnam Relations*, Book 4, IV.C.3:i–viii.
13. USA, DOD, *US-Vietnam Relations*, Book 6, IV.C.7(a): 27–28. A recent article has shown that the North Vietnamese will to resist despite severe fatalities was exceptionally high by historical standards of war and surrender. Mueller, "The Search for the 'Breaking Point' in Vietnam."
14. Kissinger, "The Vietnam Negotiations," 215–16; Schandler, *The Unmaking of a President*, chap. 4; and Brodie, "The Tet Offensive."
15. See Johnson, *Vantage Point*. Johnson had at least three motives in withdrawing from presidential politics. He wanted the sincerity of his bombing pause underscored by elevating it above personal political considerations; he wished to reunify his nation and heal the wounds of Vietnam; and he desired to give the remaining Democratic candidates sufficient time to organize their campaigns. Ibid., 427–31, and Schandler, *Unmaking of a President*, 301–19.
16. Canada, HCD, 8 March 1962, 1602 (emphasis added).
17. Canada, DEA, *Report, 1962*, 22.
18. Ibid., *1964*, 36–37.
19. Ibid., *1965*, 38 (emphasis added).
20. Canada, HCD, 25 January 1966, 234.
21. Canada, Committee on External Affairs, *Statements and Proceedings*, 9 July 1964, 1514.

22. James Steele, "Canada's Vietnam Policy: The Diplomacy of Escalation," in Clarkson, *An Independent Foreign Policy for Canada?* 77.
23. See "Dissent in the Senate," in Gettleman, *Vietnam*, 382-86.
24. Canada, *HCD*, 2 April 1965, 13106.
25. Canada, Committee on External Affairs, *Statements and Proceedings*, 10 June 1965, 14, 20.
26. Canada, *HCD*, 24 May 1967, 529.
27. USA, DOS, *Aggression from the North*.
28. In this claim, as in some others, the 1965 White Paper contradicted its 1961 forerunner: "The weapons of the VC are largely French—or U.S.—made, or handmade on primitive forges in the jungles." USA, DOS, *A Threat to the Peace*, 9.
29. The record, however, was far from conclusive. See, for instance, *I.F. Stone's Weekly*, 8 March 1965, 1-4.
30. USA, DOS, *Bulletin*, 26 April 1965. It is worth noting that while American military leaders stressed the interdictory role of the bombing and the damage it inflicted upon North Vietnam, civilian leaders preferred to emphasize its utility as a firm "signal" of American resolve.
31. Pearson, *Mike III*, 137.
32. Pearson quoted excerpts from the speech in Parliament; Canada, *HCD*, 6 April 1965, 35.
33. In 1969, Pearson explained that his speech had been the result partly of proddings by senior Americans loyal to their country, but in disagreement with its Vietnamese strategy. The reason for keeping the speech secret from External Affairs was to avoid leaks or pressures to rescind it. Bruce Hutchinson, "Mike," *Globe and Mail*, 24 September 1976.
34. Pearson, *Mike III*, 139-43. For corroboration of Johnson's desire not to provoke Chinese or Soviet intervention, see Johnson, *Vantage Point*, 119. See also USA, DOD, *US-Vietnam Relations*, Book 6, IV.C.7(a):36.
35. Canada, *HCD*, 24 May 1967, 528; 8 July 1966, 7420-23.
36. Pearson, *Mike III*, 145.
37. *External Affairs* 19 (1967): 465-67.
38. Ibid., 20 (1968): 442.
39. Warnock, *Partner to Behemoth*, 246-63, and Taylor, *Snow Job*, 120-25.
40. Canada, Committee on External Affairs, *Statements and Proceedings*, 13 April 1967, 341.
41. *S & S*, 67/8.
42. See Canada, *HCD*, 16 March 1970, 5099, and 19 May 1971, 5949.
43. Canada, Committee on External Affairs, *Statements and Proceedings*, 11 April 1967, 317-19.
44. Canada, *HCD*, 24 March 1971, 4561.
45. Ibid., 23 May 1967, 483.
46. Ibid., 1 May 1970, 6494-6502.
47. Taylor, *Snow Job*, 185.
48. Sheehan et al., *Pentagon Papers*, doc. 15, pp. 53-66.
49. Reid, *Envoy to Nehru*, 89, 93.
50. *FAR* 7 (1961):143. See also Holmes, "Geneva: 1954," 471.

51. See Lewy, *America in Vietnam,* 14.
52. Taylor, *Snow Job,* chap. 2. For the government statement on the Seaborn missions with the publication of the Pentagon Papers, see Canada, *HCD,* 17 June 1971, 6803–06. The relevant extracts from the Papers on the subject, not printed in 1971, were declassified by the Defense Department in March 1975. USA, DOD, *US-Vietnam Relations,* Book 12, VI.C.1.
53. Taylor, *Snow Job,* 84. There is little doubt that the Canadians were in fact used and abused. Thus in the wake of the Tonkin Gulf incidents in August 1964, Seaborn was asked to convey a message to Hanoi which held the DRVN attack on the *Maddox* to be the result of a premeditated "ambush." It was described as "deliberate and unprovoked," and any link with attacks against North Vietnamese islands was rejected. Yet this disclaimer flatly contradicted an earlier telegram from Rusk to Ambassador Taylor on 3 August which indicated a direct link between South Vietnamese attacks on the island, the *Maddox* patrol, and North Vietnamese reactions. Porter, *Vietnam* 2, doc. 163: 301–02. The point remains, nevertheless, that *Ottawa* was acting in good faith.
54. Quoted in Hohenberg, *Between Two Worlds,* 342–43.
55. Barrie M. Morrison, "Canada and South Asia," in Lyon and Ismael, *Canada and the Third World,* 23; Barnds, *India, Pakistan and the Great Powers,* 224.
56. Power, "India and Vietnam," 750.
57. *India News* (Ottawa) 40/71:9. For the PRG plan, see Appendix III.
58. *India News* (Ottawa) 20/72: 2–3.
59. *New Times* 30 (July 1962): 13.
60. Radvanyi, *Delusion and Reality,* 120–23.
61. *FAR* 18(1972): 207.
62. Canadian Institute of Public Opinion (CIPO), Poll 312, June 1965; Poll 318, April 1966; Poll 320, Aug. 1966; Poll 325, Sept. 1967; Poll 326, Nov. 1967; Poll 340, March 1970; and Poll 350, Nov. 1971.
63. Indian Institute of Public Opinion, *Monthly Public Opinion Surveys,* 14 (November-December 1968): 56–59.
64. Ibid., 14 (June – July 1969): 45–47.
65. Ibid., 15 (August 1970): 8–9.
66. Ibid., 10 (June – July 1965): 43. The opinion in Calcutta, India's only major left-wing city, would, of course, be the most extreme of the four major cities.
67. Ibid., 9 (October 1963): 18–19.
68. Ibid., 10 (June – July 1965): 40–41; 15 (August 1970): 28; 16 (August 1971):6.
69. Ibid., 7 (February – March 1962): 5.
70. See Van Hollen, "The Tilt Policy Revisited," and Kissinger, *White House Years,* chap. 21, "The Tilt," 842–918.
71. John Norton Moore, "Lawfulness of Military Assistance," 238.
72. Quincy Wright, "Legal Aspects of Viet-Nam Situation," 288, 290.
73. Wolfgang Friedmann, "Law and Politics in the Vietnamese War: A Comment," in Falk, *Vietnam War and International Law,* 301. A recent discussion of the legal issues is so highly selective as to confirm yet again the accuracy of Friedmann's comment; Lewy, *America in Vietnam,* chap. 1.

74. Canada, *HCD*, 30 March 1965, 12939. This was also Richard Falk's contention.
75. Ibid., 2 April 1965, 13106-110. Compare this with Dean Rusk's argument (23 April 1965) that if the insurgency in South Vietnam were truly indigenous, international law would not be involved. But in fact it receives "vital external support—in organization and direction, in training, in men, in weapons and other supplies"; in Gettleman, *Vietnam*, 333.
76. USA, DOD, *US-Vietnam Relations*, Book 10: 994-96.
77. Canada, Committee on External Affairs, *Statements and Proceedings*, 13 April 1967, 350.
78. Taylor, *Snow Job*, 84.
79. Canada, *HCD*, 24 May 1967, 529.
80. *Globe and Mail*, 14 September 1974, 33.
81. Taylor, *Snow Job*, 39. Note the possible contradiction between this and Bruce Hutchinson's report that Pearson kept the speech a secret from External Affairs; above, p. 346, n. 33.
82. Ibid., 125-27.

8 National Foreign Policies

1. See statement by Dulles, DOS, *Bulletin*, 21 March 1955. For a matching statement by Martin, see *HCD*, 25 July 1958, 2701. By 1962, however, Pearson at least questioned Diem's base of popular support and warned against uncritical American support for him. Ibid., 8 March 1962, 1606.
2. The word "incredible" is used advisedly. The Paul Martin version of the historical origins of the Vietminh during the Second World War is at variance with the consensus of scholarly work on the subject. The Vietminh formation came into existence at the Eighth Party Plenum of the Communist Party of Indochina in May 1941. The principal resolution adopted at the plenum affirmed that "at the present time, the watchword of the Party is first *to liberate the Indochinese people from the Japanese and French yoke . . . . to smash the French and Japanese invaders*." The Sixth Plenum of November 1939 had similarly called for "*opposing all foreign invaders, either white or yellow-skinned.*" Giap, *People's War, People's Army*, 74.
3. Canada, Committee on External Affairs, *Statements and Proceedings*, 10 June 1965, 15-17.
4. The phrase is Henry Kissinger's; Kissinger, *Necessity of Choice*, 201.
5. Ole R. Holsti, "The Belief System and National Images," 549.
6. See, in particular, Goodman, *The Lost Peace*, 2, 67, 70, 180.
7. Ibid., 1-12.
8. Ibid., 147-51.
9. Martin in Parliament; Canada, *HCD*, 8 March 1965, 12066-67.
10. Pearson, *Mike II*, 143.
11. Canada, *HCD*, 28 May 1965, 1793-96, and 29 June 1965, 2991. At the same time, it is only fair to recognize that Johnson was sincere in the quest for peace on the basis of his minimum condition of a secure South Vietnam. There were eight complete bombing halts and five partial cessations in all.

When peace on the minimum American terms was not forthcoming, the pauses could be used to justify a stiffened resumption of bombing. For a study of the rather complicated story of American peace feelers, see Goodman, *Lost Peace, passim.*
12. See Canada, HCD, 29 September 1967, 2646, and *External Affairs* 19 (1967):465–67.
13. For Canadian peace proposals that seemed to be based upon such an understanding of American objectives, see Martin's statement in Parliament: Canada, HCD, 13 February 1967, 12962–67; and in committee: Committee on External Affairs, *Statements and Proceedings,* 11 April 1967, 305–15. On the latter occasion, Martin suggested resurrecting the demilitarized zone. This aspect of "the Canadian proposal had a special appeal for the United States," which had suffered heavy casualties in the region. Cooper, *Lost Crusade,* 372.
14. Cable, State to American Embassy Saigon, 25 February 1966; USA, DOD, *US-Vietnam Relations,* Book 12, VI.C.1., "Ronning Missions," 8. The Americans suspected that Paul Martin had three ulterior motives for the Ronning trip: to test the wind for possible recognition of Communist China and its representation in the United Nations, and to demonstrate that Canada was not a United States "satellite." Ibid., 1.
15. Ronning, *Memoir of China in Revolution,* 258.
16. Ibid., 258–66.
17. USA, DOD, *US-Vietnam Relations,* Book 12, VI.C.1., "Ronning Missions," 16, 18, 24.
18. Ronning, *Memoir of China in Revolution,* 267–68. In fact, even Martin had expressed grave concern that American escalation in the wake of the Ronning visits "would jeopardize Canadian good faith with Hanoi and make it appear U.S. used Ronning as means of obtaining negative readout on negotiations which would justify escalation"; cable, Ottawa to Secretary of State, 20 June 1966; USA, DOD, *US-Vietnam Relations,* Book 12, VI.C.1., "Ronning Missions," 29.
19. Taylor, *Snow Job,* 156.
20. Quoted in Gopal, *Nehru,* 227.
21. India, *Foreign Policy of India: Documents,* 131.
22. Quoted in SarDesai, *Indian Foreign Policy,* 76–78.
23. India, *Foreign Policy of India: Documents,* 169–70.
24. Nehru in Parliament, *LSD,* 27 July 1955, 4, i, col. 3056.
25. Canada, HCD, 22 July 1955, 6572. Ottawa did, however, advise its representative to associate himself with the other members in protesting to the South Vietnamese authorities.
26. Quoted in SarDesai, *Indian Foreign Policy,* 91.
27. India, *Foreign Policy of India: Documents,* 319.
28. Ross misinterprets this policy to argue that from late 1956 onwards, India crossed a watershed in shifting away from a pro-DRVN stance for a period of about six years. He then goes on to suggest a link between the changed Indian policy and Canadian aid to India, in particular the nuclear reactor agreement of April 1956. "In the Interests of peace," 587–90. Ross concedes that

the linkage is purely speculative, in that Ottawa made no effort toward such an end. Unfortunately, as well as being fanciful, the suggestion is also highly implausible: (1) The superpowers are a more important point of reference for Indian policy-making than Canada is. In general, the years 1954–59 saw a steady improvement in Indo-Soviet relations, and frequent irritations in Indo-American relations. Nehru exchanged triumphal visits with Nikolai Bulganin and Nikita Khrushchev in 1955. The Soviets did not only court India verbally: they also supported its vital interests. On the Kashmir dispute, for instance, Bulganin and Khrushchev supported the Indian stand during their late 1955 visit, and a Soviet veto rescued India from a Cuba-United Kingdom-United States resolution in the Security Council on 18 February 1957 that would have introduced a temporary United Nations force for a plebiscite in Kashmir. Similarly, on the question of the Portuguese enclave of Goa, while the Soviets supported the Indian position in 1955, Dulles on 6 December 1955 acknowledged Goa as a "province" of Portugal (USA, DOS, *American Foreign Policy* 2:2294–95). In a letter to Vijaylakshmi Pandit on 15 December 1955, Nehru wrote of the "astounding stupidity" of Dulles in lining up thus with Portugal. Gopal, *Nehru*, 254. For an evaluation of the Bulganin-Krushchev visit to India in 1955, see Reid, *Envoy to Nehru*, chap. 10. (2) The volume of aid that India has received from Canada, while important, is less than that from the United States. Even the Americans have found it difficult to link aid to foreign policy changes by New Delhi. As for Canada, one foreign service officer complained in a letter to Escott Reid in October 1977 that "there is no evidence that during the period in which the special relationship was supposed to exist India ever modified its policies to suit the interests of Canada." Reid, *Envoy to Nehru*, 261. (3) India also expanded its ties with Poland in the period. Nehru toured Poland in June 1955 for three days. Prime Minister Jozef Cyrankiewicz was in India for ten days in March-April 1957, en route to the DRVN and China. In addition to expressing full support for India on the subjects of Goa and Kashmir, he signed an Indo-Polish cultural cooperation agreement. Another Indo-Polish agreement, signed on 6 May 1960, provided credit for purchases in Poland for India's third Five Year Plan; repayment was to be made through Indian raw materials and industrial goods. An agreement signed on 16 November 1962 provided for the development of seven deep coal mines in India; the list of Indo-Polish agreements can go on.

In other words, trying to assert linkages between Indo-Canadian aid and Indian policy in Vietnam is a risky proposition. It certainly should not be attempted in the absence of evidence (documentary or interview), especially where plausible alternatives can explain the phenomenon equally well. A policy of accepting things as they are, on the other hand, is a fairly consistent (but not universal) strand in India's foreign affairs.

29. At a press conference during the visit, Ho remarked: "I and others may be revolutionaries, but we are disciples of Mahatma Gandhi, directly or indirectly." SarDesai, *Indian Foreign Policy,* 286, n. 215. Kaul found in Ho "a man who combined Gandhi's simplicity and humility and Nehru's humanism and nationalism with his own Vietnamese pride and Marxism." *India, China and Indochina,* 75.

30. *Asian Recorder* (New Delhi), 23–29 July 1962, 4703–04.
31. Bridle, *Canada and the International Commissions*, 20.
32. *FAR* 18 (1972): 273–74.
33. Canada, DEA, *Communiqué No. 71,* 3 October 1972.
34. *FAR* 3 (1957): 104–05.
35. Government of India, *Press Release,* 8 February 1965.
36. Great Britain, *Recent Exchanges,* Cmnd. 2756 (1965), 68, 76–77.
37. Cooper, *Lost Crusade,* 321.
38. *FAR* 17 (September 1971).
39. Ibid., 19 (1973): 33.
40. *Statesman,* 1 May 1975. I was in New Delhi at the time and able to observe firsthand the affinity that Indian intellectuals and politicians felt for a fellow-Asian, "tiny Vietnam," that had humbled the might of the West.
41. See, for instance, USA, DOD, *US-Vietnam Relations,* Book 1, I.C., "Ho Chi Minh: Asian Tito?"
42. "Canada in the Pentagon Papers," *Canadian Forum* (September 1973): 14. See also USA, DOD, *US-Vietnam Relations*, Book 12, VI.C.1., "Seaborn Missions," for the Pentagon Papers account of Seaborn's trips to Hanoi.
43. Snow, *Red Star Over China,* 36.
44. See Radvanyi, *Delusion and Reality,* 54, 85–90, and Edgar Snow, "Aftermath of the Cultural Revolution: Mao Tse-tung and the Cost of Living," *New Republic,* 10 April 1971.
45. "Refutation of the New Leaders of the CPSU on 'United Action'," *Peking Review,* 12 November 1965. The article bluntly stated that on all fundamental issues of the day, the Sino-Soviet relation "is one of sharp opposition; there are things that divide us and nothing that unites us, things that are antagonistic and nothing that is common."
46. "Letter of the CPSU to other Communist Parties regarding the split with the Chinese Communist Party," *New York Times,* 24 March 1966.
47. Lach and Wehrle, *International Politics in East Asia,* 221–26; Whiting, *Chinese Calculus of Deterrence, 180–87;* "Nixon's Gamble: War with China?" *New Republic,* 20 May 1972, 12–13; and Zagoria, *Vietnam Triangle,* 76–91.
48. Michel Tatu, "Moscow, Peking and the Conflict in Vietnam," in Lake, *Vietnam Legacy,* 31.
49. Hanoi's sense of betrayal by its two major socialist allies is evident in the *Nhan Dan* editorial of 17 August 1972, which accused Moscow and Peking of pursuing "immediate and narrow interests while shirking . . . lofty internationalist duties." Porter, *Vietnam* 2, doc. 308, pp. 569–70.
50. Kissinger, "The Vietnam Negotiations," 219. See also Morton H. Halperin, "The Lessons Nixon Learned," in Lake, *Vietnam Legacy.*
51. *New Times* 12 (March 1957):4.
52. Maneli, *War of the Vanquished,* 48–49. It is interesting to recall in this connection reports that in 1968, Rapacki objected to the Soviet invasion of Czechoslovakia, and was in consequence forced to resign. Radvanyi, *Delusion and Reality,* 273, chap. 6, n. 3.
53. Radvanyi, *Delusion and Reality,* 120.

54. Ibid., 124–28, and Averell Harriman, *America and Russia*, 120.
55. USA, DOD, *US-Vietnam Relations*, Book 12, VI.C.2. This volume is devoted entirely to a chronology and discussion of the Marigold initiative.
56. Ibid., 39–41.
57. In a telegram to Ambassador John Gronouski on 15 December 1966 (declassified in July 1978), Acting Secretary of State Nicholas Katzenbach indicated that in the American view, Rapacki had merely been "opportunistic" in trying to get maximum concessions. The State Department was dubious of a serious involvement by Hanoi in Rapacki's communications with the United States. It also believed that the best chance of establishing a contact with Hanoi lay in maintaining and strongly defending the American position on bombing. Porter, *Vietnam* 2 doc. 244, pp. 444–46.
58. Canada, *HCD*, 24 March 1955, 2343.
59. Canada, Committee on External Affairs, *Statements and Proceedings*, 26 May 1955, 581.
60. USA, DOD, *US-Vietnam Relations*, Book 12, VI.C.1., "Seaborn Missions," 17.
61. Private interviews. See also the remarks of B. K. Nehru, India's ambassador to the United States, to a Hungarian diplomat; Radvanyi, *Delusion and Reality*, 44; and Bridle, *Canada and the International Commissions*, 26.

9 Conclusions

1. Canada, DEA, *Report, 1959*, 36.
2. *International Perspectives* (May/June 1976): 14.
3. *Canada Handbook*, 255–56.
4. *External Affairs* 21 (1969): 198.
5. Holmes, "Canada and the Vietnam War," 191.
6. Peyton Lyon, "Quiet Diplomacy Revisited," in Clarkson, ed., *An Independent Foreign Policy for Canada?* 31.
7. Holmes, "Canada and the Vietnam War," 193–94.
8. These points were made in Parliament by Pearson in respect of the Formosa crisis of 1955. *External Affairs* 7 (1955): 126.
9. In the Lok Sabha on 27 November 1959. Nehru, *India's Foreign Policy*, 370.
10. *Indian and Foreign Review* 17 (15–30 April 1980): 5.
11. *Current Digest of the Soviet Press* 33 (7 October 1981): 12
12. See Thakur, "Coexistence to Conflict."
13. Ronning, *Memoir of China in Revolution*, 245. The choice of emphases for New Delhi's and Ottawa's relative control over their delegations may or may not be significant.
14. Confidential source.
15. *S & S*, 55/43.
16. Confidential source.
17. Reid, *Envoy to Nehru*, 10, 23, 259–60.
18. David van Praagh, "Canada and Southeast Asia," in Lyon and Ismael, *Canada and the Third World*, 333; see also 307–08.

19. Barrie M. Morrison, "Canada and South Asia," in Lyon and Ismael, *Canada and the Third World*, 32–33. See also Thomson and Swanson, *Canadian Foreign Policy*, 117.
20. Reid, *Envoy to Nehru*, 260.
21. Thus in May 1956 Krishna Menon, then in charge of India's policy on Indochina, disparagingly commented to Escott Reid that he did not expect Canada to do anything but faithfully execute United States policy in the ICSC. Ibid., 85.
22. IIPO, *Public Opinion Surveys* 16 (August 1971): 30.
23. CIPO 366 (June 1974).
24. Quoted in Ross, "In the Interests of Peace," 827–28.
25. Nehru, *India's Foreign Policy*, 404.
26. *FAR* 7 (1961): 136.
27. Ibid., 8 (1962): 202.
28. Canada, Committee on External Affairs, *Statements and Proceedings*, 26 May 1955, 578.
29. *HCD*, 3 May 1955, 3389.
30. See letter from Acting Commissioner Saul Rae to John Holmes, 16 January 1956, quoted in Ross, "In the Interests of Peace," 606–07.
31. *HCD*, 8 July 1966, 7426. In July 1958, Martin argued that the ICSC should continue in existence as a guarantee of free elections whenever they were agreed to and held. Ibid., 25 July 1958, 2701.
32. *FAR* 12 (1966): 172–73.
33. Cited in Gettleman, *Vietnam*, 164.
34. Bridle, *Canada and the International Commissions*, 23.
35. See above, p. 208.
36. See also Holmes, "Geneva: 1954," 473.
37. Ibid., 459.
38. Randle, *Origins of Peace*, chap. 12.
39. Randle, *Geneva 1954*, 560–68.
40. Ibid., 432.
41. Holmes, "Geneva: 1954," 469.
42. Ibid., 461. "Theirs not to reason why; theirs but to do and die" might, in the circumstances, have been equally apt.
43. Ibid., 460. Dulles himself, at a news conference on 31 December 1954, said that the Geneva Agreements had been a "setback" for the United States, which had been offset by SEATO. USA, DOS, *Bulletin*, 10 January 1955.
44. *External Affairs* 19 (1967): 227–28.
45. The most comprehensive treatment of the United Nations role in Indonesia is Taylor, *Indonesian Independence*.
46. Rikye, Harbottle, and Egge, *Thin Blue Line*, 142–43.
47. Taylor, *Indonesian Independence*, 419–20.
48. Rikye, Harbottle, and Egge, *Thin Blue Line*, 206.
49. See Stegenga, "Peacekeeping: Post-Mortems or Previews?" 382–83.
50. Fabian, *Soldiers Without Enemies*, 21.
51. *FAR* 19 (1973): 224.
52. The text was published in *External Affairs* 18 (1966): 182–84.

53. Ibid., 184–85 (emphasis added).
54. Ton That Thien, *India and South East Asia,* 308.
55. Pearson, *Mike II,* 118.
56. Confidential source.
57. *HCD,* 14 April 1972, 1328.

Bibliography

Documents

i. Canada
Canada. Department of External Affairs. *Canada and the United Nations.*
———. *External Affairs.*
———. *Press Releases and Speeches.*
———. *Report.*
———. *Statements and Speeches.*
Canada Handbook. Ottawa: Statistics Canada, 1977.
Canada. House of Commons, Committee on External Affairs. *Statements and Proceedings.*
Canada. *House of Commons Debates.*
———. Ministry of Defence. *White Paper on Defence* (1964, 1969, 1971).
Foreign Policy for Canadians. 6 pamphlets. Ottawa: Information Canada, 1970.
Gray Report. *Foreign Direct Investment in Canada.* Ottawa: Information Canada, 1972.
Sharp, Mitchell. *Vietnam: Canada's Approach to Participation in the International Commission of Control and Supervision, October 25, 1972–March 27, 1973.* Ottawa: Information Canada, 1973.
Wahn Report, House of Commons. *Special Committee Respecting Canada–U.S. Relations.* Ottawa: Queen's Printer, 1970.

ii. India
All India Congress Committee. *The Background of India's Foreign Policy; Resolutions of the Indian National Congress on Foreign Policy, 1885–1952.* New Delhi: AICC, 1952.
———. *Resolutions on Foreign Policy, 1947–1957.* New Delhi, AICC, 1958.
Asian Relations Organization. *Asian Relations: The Report of the Proceedings and Documentation of the First Asian Relations Conference in New Delhi, March–April, 1947.* New Delhi, Asian Relations Organization, 1948.
Bangladesh Documents. New Delhi: Government of India, Ministry of External Affairs, 1971.

Foreign Affairs Record. New Delhi: Government of India, Ministry of External Affairs.
Foreign Policy of India: Texts of Documents, 1947–1959. 2d ed. New Delhi: Lok Sabha Secretariat, 1959.
India. *Lok Sabha Debates* (1954–1975).
_____. *Parliamentary Debates* (1950–1954).
_____. *Rajya Sabha Debates* (1954–1975).
Nehru, Jawaharlal. *India's Foreign Policy: Speeches on Foreign Policy from 1946 to 1961*. New Delhi: Publications Division, Government of India, Ministry of External Affairs, 1961.
_____. *Jawaharlal Nehru's Speeches*. 4 vols. New Delhi: Publications Division, Government of India, Ministry of Information and Broadcasting.
_____. "Report on the International Congress against Imperialism." Submitted to the AICC on the International Congress against Imperialism held at Brussels in February 1927. In *The Indian National Congress, 1927*. Madras: AICC, 1928.
Notes, Memoranda and Letters Exchanged and Agreements Signed Between the Governments of India and China: 1954–59, White Paper. New Delhi: Government of India, Ministry of External Affairs, 1960.
Prime Minister Chou En-lai's Visit to India. New Delhi: Government of India, Ministry of External Affairs, 1954.
Prime Minister's Press Conferences. New Delhi: Government of India, Ministry of External Affairs, 1950–54.
Report, Ministry of External Affairs. New Delhi: Government of India, Ministry of External Affairs.
Shastri, Lal Bahadur. *Speeches of Prime Minister Lal Bahadur Shastri*. New Delhi: Government of India, 1965.
The Tashkent Declaration. New Delhi: Government of India, Ministry of External Affairs, 1967.

iii. Indochina

Democratic Republic of Viet-Nam. Ministry of Foreign Affairs, Press and Information Department, *Documents Related to the Implementation of the Geneva Agreements Concerning Viet-Nam*. Hanoi, 1956.
Great Britain. Parliament. *Documents Relating to British Involvement in the Indo-China Conflict 1945–1965*. London: H. M. Stationery Office, Cmnd. 2834, 1965.
Great Britain. Foreign Office. *Documents Relating to the Discussion of Korea and Indochina at the Geneva Conference*. Misc. No. 16 (1954), Cmd. 9186. London, 1954.
_____. *Further Documents Relating to the Discussion of Indochina at the Geneva Conference*. Misc. No. 20 (1954), Cmd. 9239. London, 1954.
_____. *Recent Exchanges Concerning Attempts to Promote a Negotiated Settlement of the Conflict in Viet-Nam*. Viet-Nam No. 3 (1965). Cmnd. 2756. London, 1965.
_____. *Special Report to the co-Chairmen of the Geneva Conference on Indo-China*. Vietnam No. 1 (1965). Cmnd. 2609. London, 1965.

———. *Special Report to the co-Chairmen of the Geneva Conference on Indo-China.* Vietnam No. 2 (1965). Cmnd. 2634. London, 1965.
International Commission for Supervision and Control in Vietnam. *First Interim Report* (for the period 11 August to 10 December 1954). New Delhi: Government of India, Ministry of External Affairs, 1954.
———. *Second Interim Report* (for the period 11 December 1954 to 16 February 1955); 1955.
———. *Third Interim Report* (for the period 11 February 1955 to 10 April 1955); 1955.
———. *Fourth Interim Report* (for the period 11 April 1955 to 10 August 1955); 1955.
———. *Fifth Interim Report* (for the period 11 August 1955 to 10 December 1955); 1956.
———. *Sixth Interim Report* (for the period 11 December 1955 to 31 July 1956); 1956.
———. *Seventh Interim Report* (for the period 1 August 1956 to 30 April 1957); 1957.
———. *Eighth Interim Report* (for the period 1 May 1957 to 30 April 1958); 1958.
———. *Ninth Interim Report* (for the period 1 May 1958 to 31 January 1959); 1959.
———. *Tenth Interim Report* (for the period 1 February 1959 to 31 January 1960); 1960.
———. *Eleventh Interim Report* (for the period 1 February 1960 to 28 February 1961); 1961.
———. *Special Report to the co-Chairmen of the Geneva Conference on Indo-China,* June 2, 1962.

iv. *United States*
Senator Gravel, ed. *The Pentagon Papers.* 4 vols. Boston: Beacon Press, 1971.
Sheehan, Neil, Hedrick Smith, E.W. Kenworthy, and Fox Butterfield, eds. *The Pentagon Papers.* New York Times ed. New York: Bantam Books, 1971.
United States. Department of Defense. *United States-Vietnam Relations, 1945–1967.* 12 vols. Washington, D.C.: U.S. Government Printing Office, 1971. Vol. 6.C.1–4, the diplomatic sections, were declassified and released only in 1975.
United States. Department of State. *American Foreign Policy 1950–1955: Basic Documents.* 2 vols. Washington, D.C.: Government Printing Office, 1957.
———. *Bulletin.*
———. *Aggression from the North: The Record of North Vietnam's Campaign to Conquer South Vietnam.* DOS Pub. 7839; Far Eastern Series 130. Washington, D.C.: February 1965.
———. *A Threat to the Peace: North Vietnam's Effort to Conquer South Vietnam.* DOS Pub. 7308; Far Eastern Series 110. Washington, D.C.: December 1961.
———. "The Legality of United States Participation in the Defense of Viet-Nam." *American Journal of International Law* 60 (1966): 565–85.

———. Senate Committee on Foreign Relations. *Background Information Relating to Southeast Asia and Vietnam.* July 1967.

v. Other
The Conference of Heads of State or Government of Non-aligned Countries, Belgrade, September 1–6, 1961. Publicistico, Izdavacki Zavod, Yugoslavia.
Major Policy Speeches by President Ngo Dinh Diem. Saigon: Government of RVN, 1957.
Renmin Ribao Editorial Department. *The Truth About How the Leaders of the CPSU Have Aligned Themselves with India against China.* Peking: Foreign Languages Press, 1963.
Selected Documents of the Bandung Conference. New York: Institute of Pacific Relations, 1955.
The Sino-Indian Boundary Question. Peking: Foreign Languages Press, 1962; No. II, 1965.

Newspapers and Journals

Current Digest of the Soviet Press.
The Globe and Mail.
I.F. Stone's Weekly.
India News.
Indian and Foreign Review.
The New York Times.
The Statesman.
The Times of India.

Polls

Canadian Institute of Public Opinion.
Indian Institute of Public Opinion.

Books and Articles

Abraszewski, A. *Poland in the United Nations.* Warsaw: Interpress, 1977.
Appadorai, A. *Domestic Roots of India's Foreign Policy 1947–1972.* New Delhi: Oxford University Press, 1979.
Appadorai, A., and V. K. Arora. *India in World Affairs, 1957–58.* New Delhi: Sterling Publishers, 1975.
Armstrong, J. D. *Revolutionary Diplomacy: Chinese Foreign Policy and the United Front Doctrine.* Berkeley: University of California Press, 1977.
Axline, A., J. Hyndman, P. Lyon, and M. Molot, eds. *Continental Community?* Toronto: McClelland and Stewart, 1974.

Balawyder, A. *The Maple Leaf and the White Eagle: Canadian-Polish Relations, 1918–1978.* Boulder, Colo.: East European Monographs No. 66, 1980.
Barnds, William J. *India, Pakistan and the Great Powers.* New York: Praeger (for Council on Foreign Relations), 1972.
Bell, Coral. *The Asian Balance of Power: A Comparison with European Precedents.* London: IISS, Adelphi Paper No. 44, February 1968.
Berkes, Ross N., and Mohinder S. Bedi. *The Diplomacy of India: Indian Foreign Policy in the United Nations.* Stanford: Stanford University Press, 1958.
Boyd, James M. *United Nations Peace-Keeping Operations: A Military and Political Appraisal.* New York: Praeger, 1971.
Brecher, Michael. *India and World Politics: Krishna Menon's View of the World.* London: Oxford University Press, 1968.
——. *Nehru: A Political Biography.* London: Oxford University Press, 1959.
——. "Non-Alignment Under Stress: The West and the India-China Border War." *Pacific Affairs* 52 (Winter 1979–80): 612–30.
——. *The Struggle for Kashmir.* Toronto: Ryerson, 1953.
——. "The Subordinate State System of Southern Asia." *World Politics* 15: (January 1963): 213–35.
Bridle, Paul. *Canada and the International Commissions in Indochina, 1954–1972.* Toronto: CIIA, 1973.
Brodie, B. "The Tet Offensive." In *Decisive Battles of the Twentieth Century,* edited by N. Frankland and C. Dowling. London: Sidgwick & Jackson, 1976.
Bromke, Adam. "Nationalism and Communism in Poland." *Foreign Affairs* 40 (July 1962): 635–43.
——, ed. *The Communist States at the Crossroads.* New York: Praeger, 1965.
——, and John W. Strong, eds. *Gierek's Poland.* New York: Praeger, 1973.
Brown, W. A. *Prelude to Disaster: The American Role in Vietnam, 1940–1963.* New York: Kennikat, 1975.
Brzezinski, Zbigniew K. *The Soviet Bloc: Unity and Conflict.* Rev. ed. New York: Praeger, 1961.
Cameron, Allan W., ed. *Viet-Nam Crisis: A Documentary History.* Vol. 1, *1940–1956.* Ithaca, N.Y.: Cornell University Press, 1971.
"Canada in the Pentagon Papers." *Canadian Forum* (September 1973): 8–19.
Chakravarti, P. C. *India's China Policy.* Bloomington: Indiana University Press, 1962.
Chawla, Sudershan, M. Gurtov, and A.G. Marsot, eds. *Southeast Asia Under the New Balance of Power.* New York: Praeger, 1974.
——, and D. R. SarDesai, eds. *Changing Patterns of Security and Stability in Asia.* New York: Praeger, 1980.
Chen, K. C. *Vietnam and China, 1938–1954.* Princeton: Princeton University Press, 1969.
——. "Hanoi and Peking." *Asian Survey* 12 (September 1972): 806–17.
Choudhury, G. W. *India, Pakistan, Bangladesh, and the Major Powers.* New York: Free Press, 1975.
Clarkson, Stephen, ed. *An Independent Foreign Policy for Canada?* Toronto: McClelland and Stewart, 1968.
Claude, Inis L. *Swords into Plowshares.* 4th ed. New York: Random House, 1971.

Cohen, B. C., and S. A. Harris, "Foreign Policy." In *Handbook of Political Science,* edited by Fred I. Greenstein and Nelson W. Polsby, vol. 6, pp. 381-437. Reading, Mass.: Addison-Wesley, 1975.
Cooper, Chester L. *The Lost Crusade.* New York: Dodd, Mead and Co., 1970.
Culhane, Claire. *Why is Canada in Vietnam?* Toronto: NC Press, 1972.
Dallin, David J. *Soviet Foreign Policy After Stalin.* London: Methuen, 1962.
Das, Parimal Kumar. *India and the Vietnam War.* New Delhi: Young Asia Publications, 1972.
Davidson, J. *Indo-China: Signposts in the Storm.* Singapore: Longman, 1979.
Devillers, Philippe, and Jean Lacouture. *End of a War: Indochina, 1954.* New York: Praeger, 1969. Original French edition 1960.
Do Vang Ly. "The Emergence of Vietnam." *Foreign Affairs Reports* 7 (1958): 1-19.
Dobell, Peter C. *Canada's Search for New Roles: Foreign Policy in the Trudeau Era.* Toronto: Oxford University Press, 1972.
Documents on International Affairs. London: Oxford University Press, yearly.
Donaldson, Robert H. *Soviet Policy Toward India: Ideology and Strategy.* Cambridge, Mass.: Harvard University Press, 1974.
_____. *The Soviet Union in the Third World.* Boulder, Colo.: Westview, 1981.
Duiker, William J. *The Communist Road to Power in Vietnam.* Boulder, Colo.: Westview, 1981.
Dutt, V. P. and Vishal Singh. *Indian Policy and Attitudes Towards Indochina and SEATO.* New Delhi: Indian Council of World Affairs, 1954.
East, Maurice A., Stephen A. Salmore, and Charles F. Hermann, eds. *Why Nations Act: Theoretical Perspectives for Comparative Foreign Policy Studies.* Beverly Hills: Sage, 1978.
Eayrs, James. *Canada in World Affairs, 1955-1957.* Toronto: CIIA, 1959.
_____. *In Defence of Canada: Peacemaking and Deterrence.* Toronto: University of Toronto Press, 1972.
Eden, Anthony. *Memoirs - Full Circle.* London: Cassell, 1960.
_____. *Toward Peace in Indochina.* Boston: Houghton Mifflin, 1966.
Eisenhower, Dwight D. *Mandate for Change, 1953-1956.* New York: Doubleday, 1963.
Elliot, David W. P., ed. *The Third Indochina Conflict.* Boulder, Colo.: Westview, 1980.
Etinger, Y., and O. Melikayan. *The Policy of Non-Alignment.* Moscow: Progress Publishers, 1966.
Fabian, L. *Soldiers Without Enemies.* Washington: Brookings, 1971.
Falk, Richard A., ed. *The Vietnam War and International Law.* Princeton: Princeton University Press, 1968.
Fitzgerald, Frances. *Fire in the Lake: The Vietnamese and the Americans in Vietnam.* Boston: Little, Brown and Co., 1972.
Foote, Wilder, ed. *Dag Hammarskjöld: Servant of the Peace.* New York: Harper, n.d.
Fox, Annette Baker, Alfred O. Hero, and Joseph S. Nye, eds. *Canada and the United States: Transnational and Transgovernmental Relations. International Organization* 28 (Autumn 1974) (Special Issue).
Gafurov, Bobojan. *Neutralism and the National Liberation Movement.* Moscow: Novosti Press, 1966.

Gandhi, Indira. *Aspects of our Foreign Policy; Speeches and Writings.* New Delhi: AICC, 1973.
Gathorne-Hardy, G. M. *A Short History of International Affairs, 1920–1939.* London: Oxford University Press, 1950.
Gelb, Leslie H. "The Essential Domino: American Politics and Vietnam." *Foreign Affairs* 50 (April 1972): 459–75.
_____, and Richard K. Betts. *The Irony of Vietnam: The System Worked.* Washington, D.C.: Brookings Institution, 1979.
Gettleman, Marvin E., ed. *Vietnam: History, Documents and Opinions on a Major World Crisis.* New York: Fawcett, 1965.
Giap, Vo Nguyen. *People's War, People's Army.* Hanoi: Foreign Languages Publishing House, 1961.
Girard, Charlotte S. M. *Canada in World Affairs 1963–1965.* Toronto: CIIA, n.d.
Goodman, Allan E. *The Lost Peace: America's Search for a Negotiated Settlement of the Vietnam War.* Stanford: Hoover Institution Press, 1978.
Gopal, Sarvepalli. *Jawaharlal Nehru: A Biography; Volume Two, 1947–1956.* London: Jonathan Cape, 1979.
Gordon, J. King, ed. *Canada's Role as a Middle Power.* Toronto: CIIA, 1966.
Granatstein, J. L. *Canadian Foreign Policy Since 1945: Middle Power or Satellite?* Toronto: Copp Clark, 1969.
Gregg, Robert W., and Charles W. Kegley, eds. *After Vietnam: The Future of American Foreign Policy.* New York: Doubleday, 1971.
Gupta, Bhabani Sen. *The Fulcrum of Asia: Relations among China, India, Pakistan and the USSR.* New York: Pegasus, 1970.
_____. *Soviet-Asian Relations in the 1970s and Beyond.* New York: Praeger, 1976.
Gupta, J. B. Das. *Indo-Pakistan Relations (1947–1955).* Amsterdam: Djambatan, 1958.
Gupta, Sisir. *India and Regional Integration in Asia.* Bombay: Asia Publishing, 1964.
Halberstram, David. *The Best and the Brightest.* New York: Fawcett, 1973.
Hamilton, W. B., K. Robinson, and C. D. W. Goodwin, eds. *A Decade of the Commonwealth, 1955–1964.* Durham, N.C.: Duke University Press, 1966.
Hammer, E. J. *The Struggle for Indochina, 1940–1955.* Stanford: Stanford University Press, 1955.
Harriman, Averell. *America and Russia in a Changing World.* Garden City: Doubleday, 1971.
Head, Ivan L. "The Foreign Policy of the New Canada." *Foreign Affairs* 50 (January 1972): 237–52.
Heimsath, Charles H., and Surjit Mansingh. *A Diplomatic History of Modern India.* New Delhi: Allied Publishers, 1971.
Herring, George C. *America's Longest War: The United States and Vietnam, 1950–1975.* New York: Wiley, 1979.
Higgins, H. *Vietnam.* London: Heinemann, 1975.
Hinton, Harold C. *China's Relations with Burma and Vietnam: A Brief Survey.* New York: Institute of Pacific Relations, 1958.
Hohenberg, John. *Between Two Worlds: Policy, Press and Public Opinion in Asian-American Relations.* New York: Praeger, 1967.

Holmes, John W. *The Better Part of Valour: Essays on Canadian Diplomacy.* Toronto: McClelland and Stewart, 1970.
———. *Canada: A Middle-Aged Power.* Toronto: McClelland and Stewart, 1976.
———. "Canada and the Vietnam War." In *War and Society in North America,* edited by J. L. Granatstein and R. D. Cuff. Toronto: Nelson, 1971.
———. "Geneva: 1954." *International Journal* 22 (Summer 1967): 457–83.
Holsti, Ole R. "The Belief System and National Images: A Case Study." In *International Politics and Foreign Policy: A Reader in Research and Theory,* 2d ed. edited by James N. Rosenau, 543–50. New York: Free Press, 1969.
Innis, Hugh, ed. *International Involvement.* Toronto: McGraw-Hill Ryerson, 1972.
Jacobsen, C. G. *Sino-Soviet Relations Since Mao.* New York: Praeger, 1981.
Jain, Girilal. *Panch Sheel and After: A Reappraisal of Sino-Indian Relations in the Context of the Tibetan Insurrection.* London: Asia Publishing House, 1960.
James, Alan. *The Politics of Peace-Keeping.* New York: Praeger, 1969.
———. "Recent Developments in United Nations Peace-Keeping." *Year Book of World Affairs* 31 (1977): 75–97.
Jansen, G. H. *Afro-Asia and Non-Alignment.* London: Faber and Faber, 1966.
Jetly, Nancy. *India-China Relations 1947–77.* New Delhi: Radiant Publishers, 1978.
Johnson, Lyndon B. *The Vantage Point: Perspectives of the Presidency, 1963–1969.* New York: Holt, Rinehart and Winston, 1971.
Kahin, George McTurman. "Political Polarization in South Vietnam: U.S. Policy in the Post-Diem Period." *Pacific Affairs* 52 (Winter 1979–80): 647–73.
———, and John Wilson Lewis. *The United States in Vietnam.* Rev. ed. New York: Dial, 1969.
Kaplan, Morton A., et al. *Vietnam Settlement: Why 1973, Not 1969?* Washington, D.C.: American Enterprise Institute, 1973.
Karunakaran, K. P. *India in World Affairs, 1947–1950.* London: Oxford University Press, 1952.
———. *India in World Affairs, 1950–53.* Calcutta: Oxford University Press, 1958.
Kaul, T. N. *India, China and Indochina: Reflections of a "Liberated" Diplomat.* New Delhi: Allied, 1980.
———. *The Kissinger Years: Indo-American Relations.* New Delhi: Arnold-Heinemann, 1980.
Kavic, Lorne J. *India's Quest for Security: Defense Policies, 1947–67.* Berkeley: University of California Press, 1967.
Keirstead, Burton. *Canada in World Affairs, 1951–1953.* Toronto: CIIA 1956.
Kintner, William R., and Wolfgang Klaiber. *Eastern Europe and European Security.* New York: Dunellen, 1971.
Kirsch, Marian P. "Soviet Security Objectives in Asia." *International Organization* 24 (Summer 1970): 451–78.
Kissinger, Henry. *The Necessity of Choice.* Garden City, N.Y.: Doubleday, 1962.
———. "The Vietnam Negotiations." *Foreign Affairs* 47 (January 1969): 211–34.
———. *White House Years.* Boston: Little, Brown & Co., 1979.
Kremnyev, Mikhail. "The Nonaligned Countries and World Politics." *World Marxist Review* 6 (April 1963).
Kripalani, Acharya J. B. "For Principled Neutrality." *Foreign Affairs* 38 (October 1959): 46–60.

Kun, Joseph C. *Communist Indochina: Problems, Policies, and Superpower Involvement*. Washington, D.C.: Center for Strategic and International Studies, Georgetown University, 1976.
Kundra, J. C. *Indian Foreign Policy, 1947–54*. Groningen: J.B. Wolters, 1955.
Lach, Donald F., and Edmund S. Wehrle. *International Politics in East Asia Since World War II*. New York: Praeger, 1975.
Lake, Anthony, ed. *The Vietnam Legacy*. New York: New York University Press, 1976.
Lamb, Alastair. *The China-India Border: The Origins of the Disputed Boundaries*. London: Oxford University Press, 1964.
_____. *The Sino-Indian Border in Ladakh*. Canberra: ANU, 1973.
Lancaster, Donald. *The Emancipation of French Indochina*. London: Oxford University Press, 1961.
Lewy, Guenter. *America in Vietnam*. New York: Oxford University Press, 1978.
Lloyd, Trevor. *Canada in World Affairs, 1957–1959*. Toronto: CIIA, 1968.
Lyon, Peyton V. *Canada in World Affairs, 1961–1963*. Toronto: CIIA, 1968.
_____. *The Policy Question*. Toronto: McClelland and Stewart, 1963.
_____. "The Trudeau Doctrine." *International Journal* 26 (Winter 1970–71): 19–43.
_____, and Tareq Y. Ismael, eds. *Canada and the Third World*. Toronto: Macmillan, 1976.
Mackay, R. A., ed. *Canadian Foreign Policy 1945–1954: Selected Speeches and Documents*. Toronto: McClelland and Stewart, 1970.
Maneli, Mieczyslaw. *War of the Vanquished*. Translated by Maria de Gorgey. New York: Harper and Row, 1971.
Martin, Paul. *Canada and the Quest for Peace*. Toronto: Copp Clark, 1967.
Masters, Donald C. *Canada in World Affairs, 1953–1955*. Toronto: CIIA, 1959.
Mates, Leo. "Nonalignment and the Great Powers." *Foreign Affairs* 48 (April 1970): 524–36.
Maxwell, Neville. *India's China War*. New York: Pantheon, 1970.
McLane, Charles B. *Soviet Strategies in Southeast Asia*. Princeton: Princeton University Press, 1966.
McNaught, Kenneth. "Ottawa and Washington Look at the U.N." *Foreign Affairs* 33 (July 1955): 663–78.
McVey, Ruth T. *The Calcutta Conference and the Communist Uprisings in South East Asia*. Ithaca, N.Y.: Cornell University Press, 1958.
Mehra, Parshotam. *The McMahon Line and After: A Study of the Triangular Contest of India's North-Eastern Frontier between Britain, China and Tibet, 1904–47*. Columbia, Mo.: South Asia Books, 1976.
Merchant, Livingston, and A. D. P. Heeney. "Canada and the United States: Principles for Partnership." U.S. Dept. of State, *Bulletin*, 2 August 1962.
Minifie, James M. *Peacemaker or Powder-Monkey: Canada's Role in a Revolutionary World*. Toronto: McClelland and Stewart, 1960.
Mitchell, C. R. "Peace-keeping: The Police Function." *Year Book of World Affairs* 30 (1976): 150–73.
Moraes, Frank. *Witness to an Era*. London: Weidenfeld and Nicolson, 1973.
Mueller, John E. "The Search for the 'Breaking Point' in Vietnam: The Statistics of a

Deadly Quarrel." *International Studies Quarterly* 24 (December 1980): 497-519.

Murti, B. S. N. *Vietnam: The Cycle of Peace:* New Delhi: Indian Society of International Law, 1968.

Naik, J. A. *Soviet Policy Towards India: From Stalin to Brezhnev.* Delhi: Vikas, 1970.

Nehru, Jawaharlal. "Changing India." *Foreign Affairs* 41 (April 1963): 453-65.

―――. "The Defence of India." *Young India*, 25 September and 1 October 1931.

―――. *The Discovery of India.* London: Meridian, 1960.

―――. *Recent Essays and Writings on the Future of India, Communism and Other Subjects.* Allahabad: Kitabistan, 1934.

―――. *Soviet Russia: Some Random Sketches and Impressions.* Bombay: Chetana, 1949 (first published 1929).

―――. *Towards Freedom: The Autobiography of Jawaharlal Nehru.* New York: John Day, 1941 (first published 1936).

Nguryen Trieu Dan. "The Problem of Vietnam." *Foreign Affairs Reports* 16 (1967): 1-5.

Nixon, Richard M. "Asia After Vietnam." *Foreign Affairs* 46 (October 1967): 111-25.

Nutt, Anita Lauve. *Troika on Trial: Control or Compromise?* Washington, D.C.: Department of Defense, 1967.

Ostaszewski, Jan, ed. *Modern Poland between East and West.* London: Polish School of Political and Social Science, 1971.

Pandit, Vijaya Lakshmi. "India's Foreign Policy." *Foreign Affairs* 34 (April 1956): 432-40.

Pannikar, K. M. *In Two Chinas: Memoirs of a Diplomat.* London: Allen & Unwin, 1955.

Papp, Daniel. *Vietnam: The View from Moscow, Peking, and Washington.* Jefferson, N.C.: McFarland, 1981.

Patti, Archimedes L. *Why Vietnam?* Berkeley: University of California Press, 1980.

Paul Martin Speaks for Canada: A Selection of Speeches on Foreign Policy, 1964-67. Toronto: McClelland and Stewart, 1967.

Pavlov, V. I., ed. *A Soviet View of United States Policy in Southern Asia.* Moscow: Progress Publishers, 1961.

The Peacekeeper's Handbook. New York: International Peace Academy, 1978.

Pearson, Lester B. "The Development of Canadian Foreign Policy." *Foreign Affairs* 30 (October 1951): 17-31.

―――. *Diplomacy in the Nuclear Age.* Cambridge, Mass.: Harvard University Press, 1959.

―――. "Force for UN." *Foreign Affairs* 35 (April 1957): 395-404.

―――. "Forty Years On: Reflections on our Foreign Policy." *International Journal* 22 (Summer 1967): 357-63.

―――. *Mike: Memoirs of the Right Honourable Lester B. Pearson. Vol. II, 1948-1957; Vol. III, 1957-1968.* Edited by John A. Munro and Alex I. Inglis. Toronto: University of Toronto Press, II -1973; III - 1975.

―――. *Words and Occasions.* Toronto: University of Toronto Press, 1970.

Porter, Gareth. *A Peace Denied: The United States, Vietnam, and the Paris Agreements.* Bloomington: Indiana University Press, 1975.
_____, ed. *Vietnam: The Definitive Documentation of Human Decisions.* 2 vols. Stanfordville, N.Y.: Earl M. Coleman Enterprises, 1979.
Power, Paul F. "India and Vietnam." *Asian Survey* 7 (October 1967): 740–51.
Prasad, Bimla. *The Origins of Indian Foreign Policy: The Indian National Congress and World Affairs, 1885–1947.* Patna: Bookland Private Ltd., 1960.
Prazsky, Jan. "The Lessons of South Asia." *World Marxist Review* 15 (May 1972): 97–101.
Preston, Richard A. *Canada in World Affairs, 1959–1961.* Toronto: CIIA, 1965.
Race, Jeffrey. *War Comes to Long An.* Berkeley: University of California Press, 1972.
Rachwald, A.R. "Poland between the Superpowers: Three Decades of Foreign Policy." *Orbis* 20 (Winter 1977): 1055–83.
Radvanyi, Janos. *Delusion and Reality.* South Bend, Ind.: Gateway, 1978.
Rajan, M. S. *India in World Affairs, 1954–1956.* New York: Asia Publishing House (for Indian Council of World Affairs), 1964.
_____. "Indo-Canadian Entente." *International Journal* 17 (Autumn 1962): 358–84.
Rana, Swadesh. "The Changing Indian Diplomacy at the United Nations." *International Organization* 24 (Winter 1970): 48–73.
Randle, Robert F. *Geneva 1954: The Settlement of the Indochinese War.* Princeton: Princeton University Press, 1969.
_____. *The Origins of Peace: A Study of Peacemaking and the Structure of Peace Settlements.* New York: Free Press, 1973.
Raskin, Marcus G., and Bernard B. Fall, eds. *The Viet-Nam Reader.* New York: Random House, 1967.
Reid, Escott. *Envoy to Nehru.* Delhi: Oxford University Press, 1981.
Renmin Ribao and *Hongqi* Editorial Departments. *Refutation of the New Leaders of the CPSU on "United Action."* Peking: Foreign Languages Press, 1965.
Rikhye, Indar Jit, Michael Harbottle, and Bjorn Egge. *The Thin Blue Line: International Peacekeeping and its Future.* New Haven, Conn.: Yale University Press, 1974.
Ronning, Chester. *A Memoir of China in Revolution: From the Boxer Rebellion to the People's Republic.* New York: Pantheon, 1974.
Roos, Hans. *A History of Modern Poland.* Translated by J. R. Foster. London: Eyre and Spottiswoode, 1966.
Rose, Leo E. "The Superpowers in South Asia: A Geostrategic Analysis." *Orbis* 22 (Summer 1978): 395–414.
Ross, Douglas Alan. "In the Interests of Peace: Canadian Foreign Policy and the Vietnam Truce Supervisory Commission." Ph.D. thesis, University of Toronto, 1979.
_____. "Middlepowers as Extra-Regional Balancer Powers: Canada, India, and Indochina, 1954–62." *Pacific Affairs* 55 (Summer 1982): 185–209.
SarDesai, D. R. *Indian Foreign Policy in Cambodia, Laos and Vietnam, 1947–1964.* Berkeley: University of California Press, 1968.
Sayeed, K. B. *The Political System of Pakistan.* Karachi: Oxford University Press, 1967.
Sayegh, Fayez A., ed. *The Dynamics of Neutralism in the Arab World: A*

Symposium. San Francisco: Chandler Publishing Co., 1964.
Schandler, Herbert Y. *The Unmaking of a President: Lyndon Johnson and Vietnam.* Princeton, N.J.: Princeton University Press, 1977.
Schou, August, and Arne Olav Brundtland, eds. *Small States in International Relations.* Stockholm: Almqvist & Wiksell, 1971.
Segal, Gerald. *The Great Power Triangle: Moscow, Peking, Washington.* London: Macmillan, 1982.
Shah, A. B., ed. *India's Defence and Foreign Policies.* Bombay: Manaktalas, 1966.
Shakhnazarov, G. "'Great-Power' Approach to International Politics." *World Marxist Review* 15 (May 1972): 110–18.
Shariddin, S. "From National to Social Revolution." *World Marxist Review* 15 (March 1972): 144–52.
Siegel, R. L. *Evaluating the Results of Foreign Policy: Soviet and American Efforts in India.* Denver: University of Denver Press, 1969.
Singh, Vishal. "The End of the Conflict in Vietnam and the Prospects for Southeast Asia." *International Studies* 12 (October-December 1973): 541–58.
S.I.P.R.I. *The Arms Trade with the Third World.* Harmondsworth: Penguin, 1975.
Smith, R. B. *The International Relations of the Vietnam War.* London: Macmillan, 1979.
Snow, Edgar. *Red Star Over China.* Harmondsworth: Pelican, 1972.
Solomon, Richard H., ed. *Asian Security in the 1980s: Problems and Policies for a Time of Transition.* Cambridge, Mass.: Oelgeschlager, Gunn & Hain, 1980.
Sørensen, Max, ed. *Manual of Public International Law.* London: Macmillan, 1968.
Spencer, R. A. *Canada in World Affairs, 1946–1949.* Toronto: CIIA, 1959.
Stairs, Denis. *The Diplomacy of Constraint: Canada, The Korean War and the United States.* Toronto: University of Toronto Press, 1974.
Staron, Stanislaw. "State-Church Relations in Poland." *World Politics* 21 (July 1969): 575–601.
Stegenga, J. A. "Peacekeeping: Post Mortems or Previews?" *International Organization* 27 (Summer 1973): 373–85.
Stein, Arthur. *India and the Soviet Union.* Chicago: University of Chicago Press, 1969.
Subrahmanyam, K. *The Asian Balance of Power in the Seventies: An Indian View.* New Delhi: Institute for Defence Studies and Analyses, 1968.
Sullivan, Marianna P. *France's Vietnam Policy: A Study in French-American Relations.* Westport, Conn.: Greenwood, 1978.
Swift, R. N. "United Nations Military Training for Peace." *International Organization* 28 (Spring 1974): 267–80.
Taylor, A. M. *Indonesian Independence and the United Nations.* London: Stevens, 1960.
——, D. Cox, and J. Granatstein. *Peacekeeping: International Challenge and Canadian Response.* Toronto: CIIA, 1968.
Taylor, Charles. *Snow Job: Canada, the United States and Vietnam (1954 to 1973).* Toronto: Anansi, 1974.
Taylor, Jay. *China and Southeast Asia: Peking's Relations with Revolutionary Movements.* New York: Praeger, 1974.

Thakur, Ramesh. "Change and Continuity in Canadian Foreign Policy." *India Quarterly* 33 (October-December 1977): 401-18.

―――. "Coexistence to Conflict: Hanoi-Moscow-Peking Relations and the China-Vietnam War." *Australian Outlook* 34 (April 1980): 64-74.

―――. "India's Vietnam Policy, 1946-1979." *Asian Survey* 19 (October 1979): 957-76.

―――. "Liberalism, Democracy and Development: Philosophical Dilemmas in Third World Politics." *Political Studies* 30 (September 1982): 333-49.

―――. "Peacekeeping and Foreign Policy: Canada, India and the International Commission in Vietnam, 1954-1965." *British Journal of International Studies* 6 (July 1980): 125-53.

―――. "Tacit Deception Reexamined: The Geneva Conference of 1954." *International Studies Quarterly* 26 (March 1982): 127-39.

Thayer, Carlyle A. "Viet Nam's External Relations: An Overview." *Pacific Community* 9 (January 1978): 212-31.

Thies, Wallace J. *When Governments Collide: Coercion and Diplomacy in the Vietnam Conflict, 1964-1968.* Berkeley: University of California Press, 1980.

Thomson, Dale C. "India and Canada: A Decade of Co-operation, 1947-1957." *International Studies* 9 (April 1968): 404-30.

―――, and Roger F. Swanson. *Canadian Foreign Policy: Options and Perspectives.* Toronto: McGraw-Hill Ryerson, 1971.

Thornton, R. C. "Soviet Strategy and the Vietnam War." *Asian Affairs* 1 (March 1974): 204-28.

Ton That Thien. *India and South East Asia, 1947-1960.* Geneva: Librairie Droz, 1963.

Ulam, Adam B. *Expansion and Coexistence: Soviet Foreign Policy 1917-73.* 2d ed. New York: Praeger, 1974.

Van Eekelen, W. F. *Indian Foreign Policy and the Border Dispute With China.* The Hague: Martinus Nijhoff, 1964.

Van Hollen, Christopher. "The Tilt Policy Revisited: Nixon-Kissinger Geopolitics and South Asia." *Asian Survey* 20 (April 1980): 339-61.

Verrier, Anthony. *International Peacekeeping: United Nations Forces in a Troubled World.* Harmondsworth: Penguin, 1981.

Viet-Nam: What Kind of Peace?: Documents and Analysis of the 1973 Paris Agreement on Viet-Nam. Washington, D.C.: Indochina Resource Center, 1973.

Wainhouse, David W. *International Peacekeeping at the Crossroads.* Baltimore: Johns Hopkins University Press, 1974.

Warnock, John W. *Partner to Behemoth: The Military Policy of a Satellite Canada.* Toronto: New Press, 1970.

Weiner, Myron. "India: Two Political Cultures." In *Political Culture and Political Development,* edited by Lucian W. Pye and Sidney Verba, 199-244. Princeton: Princeton University Press, 1965.

―――. "Neutralism and Nonalignment." In vol. 2 of *International Encyclopedia of the Social Sciences,* edited by David L. Sills, 166-72. New York: Macmillan and Free Press, 1968.

Whiting, Allen S. *The Chinese Calculus of Deterrence: India and Indochina.* Ann Arbor: University of Michigan Press, 1975.

Wich, Richard. *Sino-Soviet Crisis Politics.* Cambridge, Mass.: Harvard University Press, 1980.

Willetts, Peter. *The Non-Aligned Movement: The Origins of a Third World Alliance.* London: Frances Pinter, 1978.

Zagoria, Donald S. *The Sino-Soviet Conflict, 1956–1961.* Princeton: Princeton University Press, 1962.

———. *Vietnam Triangle: Moscow, Peking, Hanoi.* New York: Pegasus, 1967.

Zasloff, Joseph J., and MacAlister Brown. *Communist Indochina and U.S. Foreign Policy.* Boulder, Colo.: Westview, 1978.

Zhukhov, Y. *The Third World: Problems and Prospects.* Moscow: Progress Publishers, 1970.

Zinner, Paul E., ed. *National Communism and Popular Revolt in Eastern Europe: A Selection of Documents on Events in Poland and Hungary, February-November, 1956.* New York: Columbia University Press, 1956.

Index

Afghanistan, 22, 260
Aldrich, G. H., 340 n. 12
Ansari, S. S., 86
ASEAN, 256, 258
Asian Relations Conference, 35–36
Australia, 31, 44, 49, 192, 215, 265, 267

Ball, G., 191
Bandung Conference, 17, 235
Bangladesh, 22, 212, 219, 245–46, 253, 274
Bao Dai, 31, 36, 41, 43, 54, 144, 158, 167–68
Berlin Conference, 37
Binh, Nguyen Thi. *See* Nguyen Thi Binh
Blum, L., 41
Bombings, 108–14, 184, 191, 193, 195, 198–204, 208–14, 220–25, 229–33, 242–47, 251–54, 285
Bose, S. C., 35
Brandt, W., 29
Brecher, M., 12
Brewin, A., 223
Brezhnev, L., 26, 261
Bridle, P., 182, 187–88
Bulganin, N., 350 n. 28
Bulgaria, 27, 251
Bundy, W., 232–33
Burma, 256

Cadieux, M., 132
Cambodia, 32, 35, 45, 47, 52, 54, 75, 79, 84, 96, 114, 160, 184, 206, 211, 217, 245, 250–51, 268, 270. *See also* Kampuchea
Carter, T. Le M., 92
Casey, R. G., 263
CCF Party (Canada), 32
Chagla, M. C., 211
Chauvel, J., 152
China, 5, 31, 39–43, 48, 102, 168, 189, 196, 202, 210, 211, 231, 235, 241, 266
  and Geneva Conference, 45, 50–51, 54–55
  and India, 16, 19–22, 33, 44, 57, 177, 186–88, 209, 217–18, 234, 238, 242, 254, 259–61, 273–74, 284
  and Pakistan, 21, 260, 274
  and Poland, 3–4, 27–28, 247–54, 261–62
  and North Vietnam, 54, 71–72, 74, 78, 93–98, 103, 165, 167, 193
  and USA, 193, 245, 249, 254, 261–62, 273–74, 284
  and USSR, 42, 273–74
  and Vietnam, 247–54, 259–62
  and Vietnam, 1, 40–42, 75, 222, 227, 247–54, 259–62
Chou En-lai, 27, 50, 54, 168, 344 n. 24
Churchill, W., 44, 49, 50
Coldwell, J. M., 32
Collins, J. L., 79–81
Colombo Powers, 39, 49–51

Comintern, 39, 40
Commonwealth, 8, 12, 18, 44–45, 49, 56–57, 159, 263, 283
Communist Party of Indochina, 39, 40
Congo, 279
Congress Party (India), 34, 35, 148, 213
Cooper, C., 243
Cuba, 350 n. 28
Cyprus, 280
Cyrankiewicz, J., 27, 350 n. 28
Czechoslovakia, 22, 26, 27, 50, 213, 251, 351 n. 52

Dalai Lama, 20
Dandurand, R., 11
de Beaufort, G., 81, 93
Demilitarized Zone (DMZ), 59–61, 65, 70, 103–04, 113, 117, 173, 204, 210–11, 349 n. 13
Desai, M., 22
Desai, M. J., 68, 80–81, 93–97, 106, 122, 132, 183, 236, 263
Devillers, P., 152
Diefenbaker, J., 14, 162, 203, 226–27, 253
Diem, Ngo Dinh. *See* Ngo Dinh Diem
Dien Bien Phu, 46, 108
Dier, O. W., 204
Do, Tran Van. *See* Tran Van Do
Do Vang Ly, 341 n. 30
Dominican Republic, 215
Dong Dang Fixed Team, 73, 96
Dong, Pham Van. *See* Pham Van Dong
D'Orlandi, G., 251–52
Douglas, T. C., 146–147, 195, 206, 227, 230
Drew, G., 46
Duder, R., 184
Dulles, J. F., 19, 43–48, 56, 152, 207, 227, 348 n. 1, 353 n. 43
Duong Van Minh, 234, 247

Eden, A., 43–46, 49–50, 53, 54, 93

Eisenhower, D., 46, 48, 50, 56, 79, 80, 83, 153, 158, 168
Elections (1956), 98, 135, 140–43, 151–75, 177, 185, 220, 222, 227, 235–37, 259, 276, 281
Ely, P., 153
Erichsen-Brown, J. P., 86, 127–28
European Defense Community, 42

Fabian, L., 281
Falk, R. A., 156–57
Fall, B., 270
Felt, H. D., 92
France, 8, 12, 37, 41, 44, 51, 53, 66, 79, 82–83, 93–95, 106, 139, 145–48, 150, 153–59, 164, 166–67, 181, 215, 224
 and Geneva Conference, 45–48, 54–57, 82, 116, 276–77
French Communist Party, 39
French Indochina War, 3, 30–57, 176, 181, 189, 206, 226, 255–56
French Union Forces, 58–60, 68, 70, 77, 86–87, 104–06, 117, 125–26, 142, 150, 151
Friedmann, W., 220

Gandhi, I., 18, 22, 210–12, 242–46, 260, 269, 283–84
Gandhi, M. K., 350 n. 29
Geneva Conference, 3, 5, 15, 32, 33, 37, 42–58, 66, 67, 72, 75, 83, 110, 116, 124, 134, 140–46, 149–53, 156, 168–69, 189, 208, 236, 256, 269–77
 and nonalignment, 84–85
Geneva Protocol, 11
"Geneva type" Conference, 241–44
Germany, 24–25
Germany, East, 27, 29, 251
Germany, West, 26, 29, 42, 214, 215
Gettleman, M. E., 170
Giap, Vo Nguyen. *See* Vo Nguyen Giap
Gierek, E., 28

Goa, 19, 84, 166, 237
  342–43, 350 n. 28
Gomulka, W., 23, 25–29, 213–14
Gordon, W., 224–25
Great Britain, 8, 12, 31, 32, 34, 36,
  37, 39, 146, 150, 156, 164,
  168–69, 210, 215, 224,
  266, 350 n. 28
  and French Indochina War, 32,
    42–45
  and Geneva Conference, 42–46,
    49–50, 52, 55–57, 143, 149
Green, H., 194, 263, 269, 342 n. 52
Gromyko, A., 245, 251
Gronouski, J., 352 n. 57

Ha Van Lau, 132
Hammarskjöld, D., 6–7
Harkins, P. D., 92
Harkness, D., 14, 203
Harriman, W. A., 214, 243
Herridge, H. W., 197
Hitler, A., 24, 35
Ho Chi Minh, 31, 227, 247
  and China-USSR, 251
  and Chou En-lai, 54
  and elections, 135, 152, 154,
    157–58, 167–68
  and France, 41
  and India, 35–36, 166, 237–39,
    259, 285
  and Martin, 222
  and Nehru, 34, 181, 234, 238
  and Pearson, 284–85
  and USA, 43, 189, 284–85
Hoang Thuy Nam, 101
Hoang Tung, 249
Holmes, J., 46, 73, 97, 170, 185,
  256, 268, 275, 277, 340 n.
  15, 353 n. 30
Hooton, F. G., 93, 100
Hua Kuo-feng, 260
Huang Hua, 260
Hussain, Z., 244
Hungary, 22, 25–27, 212, 251

ICCS, 233, 278
Indonesia, 34, 36, 256
  United Nations Commission for,
    271, 278–79
Italy, 224

Jackson, R. D., 241
Janata Party (India), 22, 260
Japan, 31, 34, 38, 40, 266, 273
Jha, C. S., 342–43
Johnson, D., 73
Johnson, L. B., 147, 153–54, 191,
  193, 200–04, 209–10,
  223–24, 229–30
Joint Commission, 59–61, 76, 77,
  103, 105, 106, 113,
  117–20, 132, 173, 210

Kampuchea, 258, 262. *See also*
  Cambodia
Karunakaran, K. P., 34
Kashmir, 19, 260, 350 n. 28
Katzenbach, N., 352 n. 57
Kaul, T. N., 91, 146, 159,
  259, 337 n. 24, 344 n. 6, n.
  9, n. 10, 350 n. 29
Kennedy, J. F., 102, 190
Khrushchev, N., 25, 28, 350 n. 28
Kissinger, H., 193, 245, 250
Korea, 15–16, 32, 33–34, 41, 42,
  45, 51, 75, 143, 189, 192,
  210, 241, 243
Korean Neutral Nations Supervisory Commission, 278
Kosygin, A., 210, 244, 248
Kripalani, J. B., 35
Ky, Nguyen C. *See* Nguyen C. Ky

Lacouture, J., 152
Lansdale, E. G., 135
Lang Son Fixed Team, 67, 71, 96
Lao Dong Party (Vietnam), 186,
  238, 335 n. 67, 341 n. 37,
  344 n. 23
Laos, 32, 35, 45, 47, 52, 54, 75,
  79, 84, 99, 114, 160, 193,
  196, 206, 245, 250–51,
  268, 270–71
League of Nations, 11
Le Duan, 261, 344 n. 23
Lemnitzer, L. P., 92
Lett, S., 2–3, 81, 96, 98, 132,
  158–60, 176, 183, 286
Lewandowski, J., 251–52
Liberal Party (Canada), 14

Lodge, H. C., 231, 252
Lok Dal Party (India), 22
Lyon, P., 10–11, 257

MacArthur, D., 231
Macdonnell, R. M., 158
MacEachen, A., 233–34
MacGuigan, M., 258
McNamara, R., 191, 192, 232
MAAG, 79, 81, 85–93, 108
MAC, 92–93
Mai The Chou, 35
Malaya, 256
Maneli, M., 72, 112, 137, 187, 251, 331 n. 4
Mao Tse-tung, 41, 247, 249, 273
Marigold, 251–52
Martin, P., 185, 283
  and Diem, 226
  and Ho, 222
  and ICSC, 176, 269, 277–78
    and 1962 report, 111–12 147, 195
  and Poland, 214;
  and quiet diplomacy, 206, 224–25;
  and Ronning mission, 231–33
  and South Vietnam and Geneva Agreements, 146–48
  and USA, 196–98, 205, 221–23, 227–28, 230
    and bombings, 202–04, 216, 221, 225, 253
  and Vietminh, 227
  and Vietnamese elections, 159, 162–63, 222
Mendes-France, P., 47, 152
Menon, G., 100
Menon, K., 12, 17, 45, 50, 51, 136, 159, 165, 208, 271, 342–43, 353 n. 21
Michalowski, J., 251
Michener, R., 32–33
Minh, Duong Van. *See* Duong Van Minh
Mitchell, C. R., 7
Molotov, V., 24, 54, 169
Moore, J. N., 145, 155–56, 220
Morrison, B. M., 264
Morse, W., 191, 198
Murti, B. S. N., 337 n. 46

Nagy, I., 26
Nasser, G. A., 243
National Liberation Front (South Vietnam), 190, 192, 199, 210, 213, 228–32, 241–47, 251, 285
NATO, 9, 11–12, 26, 32, 33, 84, 162, 225
Nehru, B. K., 352 n. 61
Nehru, J. L., 282, 350 n. 29
  and Bandung Conference, 235
  and China, 20–21, 57, 260
  and Chou En-lai, 50
  and Diem, 165, 234, 237
  and French Indochina war, 32, 35–39, 283
  and Geneva Agreements, 48, 50–51, 84–85, 149, 258, 268
  and Geneva Conference, 37
  and Ho, 34, 181, 234, 237–38
  and ICSC, 149, 268–69
  and Indian foreign policy, 17–18, 34
  and Pearson, 53
  and quiet diplomacy, 241
  and SEATO, 83–85
  and South Vietnam, 148, 236
  and Southeast Asia, 16, 33, 57
  and USA, 19, 43, 49, 102–103, 350 n. 28
  and USSR, 19, 212, 260, 350 n. 28
  and Vietnamese elections, 164–65, 235
New Delhi Preparatory Meeting of ICSC, 58–59, 63, 65, 103, 118, 235
New Democratic Party (Canada), 14, 198, 203, 224, 227
New Zealand, 31, 44, 45, 49, 192
Ngo Dinh Diem, 54, 106, 130, 168, 190, 208, 226, 276, 341 n. 37
  and Eisenhower, 79, 83
  and elections, 136, 153–54, 158, 160, 162, 164, 167, 170, 222
  and Geneva Agreements, 142, 147, 149, 155–56, 159
  and ICSC, 149, 235–36
  and India, 165–66, 235–38

Ngo Dinh Diem (*continued*)
  and Nehru, 165, 234
  and USA, 88, 92, 146, 159, 190
Ngo Dinh Nhu, 237
Nguryen Trieu Dan, 341 n. 30
Nguyen C. Ky, 197
Nguyen Duy Trinh, 211, 233
Nguyen Thi Binh, 239, 245
Nguyen Truong Sinh, 139
Nguyen Van Thieu, 229, 246–47
Nhu, Ngo Dinh. *See* Ngo Dinh Nhu
Nixon, R., 21, 193, 204, 212, 214, 244, 249–50, 273, 286
Nolting, F. E., 88, 92, 337 n. 34
Nonalignment, 16–18, 22, 50, 57, 83, 187, 234–35, 242, 253–54, 258, 272–73, 284
  and Geneva Agreements, 84–85, 258
NORAD, 12
Norodom Sihanouk, 250

Ogrodzinski, P., 132
ONUC, 279

Pacific Defense Pact, 31
Pakistan, 12, 50, 274
  and China, 21, 260
  and India, 18–19, 21, 209, 212, 254
  and USA, 19, 219
  and SEATO, 84
  and USSR, 210–11, 218–19, 254
Panscheel, 20, 39, 48, 50, 84, 177, 187, 234–35, 237–38, 251
Pandit, V. L., 85, 350 n. 28
Paris Accords, 58, 193, 213, 233, 246
Partan, D. G., 145–46
Parthasarathi, G., 100, 102, 238, 247
Patel, V. B., 36
Pathet Lao, 250
Peace Negotiations, 193, 214, 224, 228–33, 241–46, 250–53, 283
Pearson, L. B., 43, 158, 183, 195, 226, 232, 235, 241, 248, 286, 342 n. 54, 348 n. 1
  and Canada-US relations, 8–9, 189, 205, 207
  and French Indochina war, 31–32, 181
  and Geneva Conference, 33, 51–53
  and Ho Chi Minh, 284–85
  and ICSC, 97, 105
  and India's role in, 263
  and Nehru, 53
  and quiet diplomacy, 10
  and refugees, 135, 269
  and South Vietnam and Geneva Agreements, 146
  and Vietnamese elections, 160–63
  and UN peacekeeping, 14
  and US Intervention, 197–209, 221, 230
  and call for bombing halt, 200–02, 223–24, 229
  and Canadian military sales, 205
  and USSR/communism, 11, 252–53, 283
Pentagon Papers, 3, 47, 107, 154, 158, 207, 232–33
Pham Van Dong, 54, 75, 87, 166–69, 171, 186, 231–32, 235, 246–47, 253, 260–61
Philippines, 192
Phuc Hoa Mobile Team, 70–73, 97, 173
Pol Pot, 262
Prasad, R., 36, 237
Progressive Conservative Party (Canada), 14, 32–33, 161–62, 203
Provisional Demarcation Line, 59, 65, 103–05, 151, 163, 230, 343 n. 75
Provisional Revolutionary Government, 212, 217, 239, 245–47, 251

Quiet Diplomacy, 9–11, 13, 16, 36, 206, 224–25, 231, 241, 257

Radhakrishnan, S., 242–43, 284
Rae, S., 353 n. 30
Rahman, M. A., 110–11
Randle, R. F., 143–45, 275–76

Rao, P. V. N., 260
Rapacki, A., 28, 214, 251–52
Refugees, 104, 108, 118, 130–37, 162, 184, 256–57, 269
Reid, E., 160, 207, 264–65, 337 n. 21, 350 n. 28, 353 n. 21
Rikhye, I. J., 278, 280
Robertson, W. S., 49, 158
Ronning, C., 51, 231–33, 251, 262
Rose, L., 19
Ross, D. A., 342 n. 47, 349–50 n. 28
Rumania, 247, 252, 261
Rusk, D., 196, 225, 231–32, 337 n. 34, 347 n. 53, 348 n. 75

Saigon Military Mission, 107, 130
St. Laurent, L., 8, 11, 37, 253, 283
SarDesai, D. R., 164, 171
Seaborn, J. B., 208–09, 253
SEATO, 12, 78–85, 146, 184, 191, 235, 237, 277, 353 n. 43
Sharp, M., 204, 206, 233, 256
Shastri, L. B., 209–10, 242
Sihanouk, Prince Norodom. See Norodom Sihanouk
Singh, D., 211, 239, 244
Singh, S., 209, 212–14, 239, 241, 243–46, 275
Smith, B., 46, 152
Snow, E., 247
Southeast Asian Collective Defense Organization, 42–45, 48, 50, 153
Souvanna Phouma, 250
Soviet Union. See USSR
Spain, 192
Stalin, J., 24, 25
Steele, J., 197
Stevenson, A., 103
Subversion, 97–103, 184–86, 194, 196, 198–200, 247
Suez Crisis, 56
Swift, R. N., 7

Taiwan, 192
Tanzania, 242
Tatu, M., 249
Taylor, C., 206–09, 223–25, 233

Taylor, M., 92, 347 n. 53
TERM, 3, 88–92
Tet Offensive, 193
Thailand, 192
Thant, U, 6, 211
Thieu, Nguyen Van. See Nguyen Van Thieu
Tibet, 20, 21
Tito, J. B., 242–43, 247, 260
Ton That Thien, 286
Tonkin Gulf, 191, 197, 209, 247, 347 n. 53
Tran Quy Minh, 139
Tran Van Do, 54–55, 276
Trudeau, P., 9, 13, 31, 204–06, 233, 253
Tyabji, B., 102

UNEF, 6, 13, 14, 182, 279–80
UNFICYP, 280
United Nations, 1, 5–7, 11, 13, 15, 19, 23, 33, 35, 36, 39, 45, 52, 56, 145, 154–55, 156, 176, 185, 198, 203, 212, 220–25, 230–31, 244–45, 257–58, 278–80, 282, 350 n. 28
USA, 8, 32, 39–49, 55, 78–79, 172, 189–225, 238, 241, 247–50, 258–59, 262, 272, 278
and Canada, 4, 9–13, 31, 52, 83, 87–88, 91–92, 182, 184–85, 226–34, 253–57, 264–66
and China, 193, 245, 249, 254, 261–62, 273–74, 284
and Geneva Agreements, 56, 107, 151, 207, 276–77, 284, 353 n. 43
and India, 19–20, 49, 88, 102, 212, 217–19, 242–46, 254, 260, 350 n. 28
and North Vietnam, 107–08, 168, 190–91, 197. See also Bombings
and Pakistan, 19, 219, 274
and South Vietnam, 79–80, 145–47, 168, 217, 284–85
military missions in 85–93, 102–03, 170, 186. See also

USA, (continued)
 MAAG, MAC, TERM
 and Vietnamese elections, 151–58,
  164–65, 170, 185
USSR, 39–43, 156, 164, 168, 202,
  212–13, 272
 and Canada, 11, 266
 and China, 42, 273–74
 and Vietnam, 4, 247–54,
  259–62
 and Geneva Conference, 45,
  54–55, 67, 143
 and India, 19–22, 78, 137,
  210–12, 217–19, 244–46,
  254, 259–61, 273–74, 284,
  350 n. 28
 and North Vietnam, 54, 71–72,
  78, 98, 103, 137, 167,
  186, 193
 and Pakistan, 210–11, 218–19,
  254
 and Poland, 3–4, 24–29, 72,
  137, 187, 193, 211, 214,
  247–54, 261–62
 and Vietnam, 39–42, 247–54,
  259–62

Vajpayee, A. B., 22, 259

Van Praagh, D., 264
Versailles, Treaty of, 24, 25
Vietminh, 1, 3, 38, 40–42, 54, 57,
  58, 59, 66, 75, 93, 104–08,
  119–23, 130, 146, 154,
  156, 158, 170, 176–77,
  208, 227, 238, 253,
  340 n. 23
Vo Nguyen Giap, 80–81, 87,
  96, 251
Vu Van Mau, 86, 168, 236

Warsaw Pact, 27
Westmoreland, W. C., 191, 193
Williams, B., 86
Wilson, H., 232, 283
Wilson, W., 24
Wisniewski, T., 86
Woodsworth, C. J., 88
Wright, Q., 157, 162

Yugoslavia, 244, 251, 261

Zagur, M. B., 138
Zinkin, T., 165–66